Flesh of My Flesh

SUNY SERIES IN CONTEMPORARY JEWISH LITERATURE AND CULTURE

EZRA CAPPELL, EDITOR

Dan Shiffman, *College Bound:*
The Pursuit of Education in Jewish American Literature, 1896–1944

Eric J. Sundquist, editor, *Writing in Witness:*
A Holocaust Reader

Noam Pines, *The Infrahuman: Animality in Modern Jewish Literature*

Oded Nir, *Signatures of Struggle:*
The Figuration of Collectivity in Israeli Fiction

Zohar Weiman-Kelman, *Queer Expectations:*
A Genealogy of Jewish Women's Poetry

Richard J. Fein, translator, *The Full Pomegranate:*
Poems of Avrom Sutzkever

Victoria Aarons and Holli Levitsky, editors,
New Directions in Jewish American and
Holocaust Literatures: Reading and Teaching

Jennifer Cazenave, *An Archive of the Catastrophe:*
The Unused Footage of Claude Lanzmann's Shoah

Ruthie Abeliovich, *Possessed Voices:*
Aural Remains from Modernist Hebrew Theater

Victoria Nesfield and Philip Smith, editors,
The Struggle for Understanding: Elie Wiesel's Literary Works

Ezra Cappell and Jessica Lang, editors,
Off the Derech: Leaving Orthodox Judaism

Nancy E. Berg and Naomi B. Sokoloff, editors,
Since 1948: Israeli Literature in the Making

Patrick Chura, *Michael Gold: The People's Writer*

Nahma Sandrow, *Yiddish Plays for Reading and Performance*

Alisha Kaplan and Tobi Aaron Kahn, *Qorbanot*

Sara R. Horowitz, Amira Bojadzija-Dan, and Julia Creet, editors
Shadows in the City of Light: Images of Paris in
Postwar French Jewish Writing

Flesh of My Flesh

Sexual Violence in Modern Hebrew Literature

Ilana Szobel

SUNY PRESS

Cover image: *Step 2*, by Hilla Ben Ari, 2006. © Hilla Ben Ari.

Published by State University of New York Press, Albany

For information, contact State University of New York Press, Albany, NY
www.sunypress.edu

Library of Congress Cataloging-in-Publication Data

Names: Szobel, Ilana, author.
Title: Flesh of my flesh : sexual violence in modern Hebrew literature / Ilana Szobel.
Description: Albany : State University of New York Press, [2021] | Series: SUNY series in contemporary Jewish literature and culture | Includes bibliographical references and index.
Identifiers: LCCN 2020043046 | ISBN 9781438484556 (hardcover : alk. paper) | ISBN 9781438484563 (pbk. : alk. paper) | ISBN 9781438484570 (ebook)
Subjects: LCSH: Hebrew literature, Modern—20th century—History and criticism. | Sex crimes in literature. | Violence in literature.
Classification: LCC PJ5012.S49 S96 2021 | DDC 892.409/3556—dc23
LC record available at https://lccn.loc.gov/2020043046

10 9 8 7 6 5 4 3 2 1

you left me with / *enough of self-destructiveness* / *as the sole form of* *violence* / *permitted to women* / with *a dream of a common language* / with Audre's: *Poetry is not only dream* / *where that language does* *not yet exist* / *it is our poetry which helps to fashion it* / *for women* / *poetry is not luxury* / as if all I had to do was turn my pen into a sword / turn that sword toward out / not in / practice / the opposite of sword swallowing

—Marva Zohar, *"from marginalized notes* *on silence/suicide/violence"*

Contents

ACKNOWLEDGMENTS   ix

INTRODUCTION
"A Great, Oppressive, Suffocating Blasphemy":
Sexualized Violence as an Insidious Trauma   1

CHAPTER ONE
"Lights in the Darkness": Prostitution, Power, and Vulnerability
in Early Twentieth-Century Hebrew Literature   15

CHAPTER TWO
Sepharadi Jewry in Pre-State Israel: Ethnicity, Gender, and
Sexual Violence in the Work of Shoshana Shababo   41

CHAPTER THREE
"Do Not Bandage the Wounded": Wounded Soldiers and
Nonconsensual Relations in Israeli War Literature   69

CHAPTER FOUR
"Subduing the Terrible Sound of Silence": Memoirs of
Incest Survivors   99

CHAPTER FIVE
"The Girl with the Billy-Goat's Hoof": Parental Abuse,
Metamorphosis, and Poetics in the Poetry of Tsvia Litevsky   129

CONCLUSION
"Silence Cries Out"   159

NOTES   175

BIBLIOGRAPHY   229

INDEX   253

Acknowledgments

I would like to start by thanking my eight and ten year-old daughters, who one evening, probably after hearing me complaining about something related to this book, suggested that instead of writing this book I should write a mystery book with lots of secrets and challenging mysteries. While it was a funny suggestion, I think that to some extent I actually did accept their recommendation, and in fact wrote a kind of a mystery book. Thus, I want to also thank my readers in advance for accompanying me in this at times ambiguous journey, and for allowing me to raise questions while not really solving the mystery of sexualized gender-based violence.

I am fortunate not to have gone through this writing adventure alone. I am part of a welcoming and intellectually stimulating environment at Brandeis University. I am grateful to my brilliant colleagues in the Department of Near Eastern and Judaic Studies, ChaeRan Freeze, Jonathan Decter, Eugene Sheppard, and Bernadette J. Brooten, who in various conversations provided expertise and much-needed support. I would also like to thank Gannit Ankori for countless fascinating conversations about art, trauma, gender, and resilience. Our conversations, as well as your wisdom and warmth, are interwoven throughout the book. I take great pleasure in extending my deepest gratitude to Sylvia Fuks Fried, who followed the development of the manuscript patiently, and who no matter when I arrived at her office, always listened to me calmly and gave me valuable advice in a delightful mixture of English, Hebrew, and Yiddish.

I am thankful to my Hebrew literature circle in the US, England, and Israel: Yael Feldman, Hannan Hever, Ofra Yeglin, Nitsa Kann, Mikhal Dekel, Karen Grumberg, Maya Barzilai, Orian Zakai, Adriana X. Jacobs,

Tamar Hess, and Andrea Siegel. Who else but you would talk with me about unknown and forgotten Hebrew writers as if there was nothing more important in the world? A precious interlocutor was Nili Scharf Gold, who carefully read the manuscript and contributed her generous, sensitive, and unfailing literary attention and insight. I am fortunate to have had such an engaged reader.

This book was written from a feminist position and as such it could not have been written without the sympathetic ear of my smart and creative friends Michal Ben-Josef Hirsh, Kimberly Stewart, Talya Meltzer, Merav Opher, Shirly Bahar, Dana Bar-el Shwartz, Ahuva Ashman, Einat Grunfeld, and Miriam and Avi Hoffman. With each of you I laughed and cursed the world, and each and every time your wisdom and generosity enabled me to return to writing with fresh zeal and renewed vigor.

Parts of the book were written during my sabbatical leave. I want to express my gratitude to the Department of Near Eastern Studies and to the Berkeley Institute for Jewish Law and Israel Studies at UC Berkeley for hosting me during that year. I thank Ron Hassner, and especially Rebecca Golbert, for being so friendly, accommodating, and generous. This year turned out to be enchanting especially thanks to Chana Kronfeld's hospitality. Not only did she share her peaceful office with me, but she also read excerpts of the manuscript and had an inspiring and fruitful dialogue with me about it. Many thanks also to the brilliant graduate students at the "Writing Gender in Modern Hebrew Literature" seminar we co-taught, for their comments and insights on parts of the manuscript.

The book was also deepened and developed as a result of the time I spent at the Center for Jewish Studies at Harvard University during my research leave. I am grateful to David Stern, and especially to Irit Aharoni for her thoughtful and generous soul. Your love of Hebrew literature makes this world a better place.

I gratefully acknowledge the support of several fellowships from Brandeis University, including the Graduate Student and Faculty Research Fund, The Department of Near Eastern and Judaic Studies; Creativity, Art, and Social Transformation (CAST) Grant; Senior Faculty Research Leave, The School of Arts and Sciences; The Provost Innovation in Research Award; and The Theodore and Jane Norman Award for Faculty Scholarship. Two chapters have been previously published elsewhere: Chapter 5, " 'The Girl with the Billy-Goat Hoof': Parental Abuse, Metamorphosis, and Poetics in the Poetry of Tsvia Litevsky" was originally published in *Jerusalem Studies in Hebrew Literature* 28 (2016): 199–227. I thank Deborah Greniman

for translating it from the Hebrew. Chapter 1, " 'Lights in the Darkness':
Prostitution, Power, and Vulnerability in Early Twentieth-Century Hebrew
Literature" was originally published in *Prooftexts* 34: 2 (2015): 170–206.
I thank each of these publishers for their generous permission to include
the pieces in this book. I am also grateful to Stephen Gulley for his expert
and careful feedback on the chapter about disability, and to Mikayla Zag-
oria-Moffet for her thorough and wise editing of the book.

This book could not have been written without the ongoing encouragement and critical feedback from Hannah Naveh, who will always remain
my beloved teacher and friend. I guess it is not so common to thank her
for the advices she gave me in various conversations I had with her in
my mind. But it is certainly a great privilege to express gratitude to her
not only for following the evolution of the manuscript chapter-by-chapter
and contributing her sharp and accurate comments, but especially for her
relentless trust in me. How shall I thank you for your gaze that turned
me from an invisible person into a writing woman?

And finally, I happily acknowledge the affirming security I have
been giving by my siblings and their partners, as well as by my dearly
loved parents, who taught me to always strive for a meaningful life. I am
also deeply indebted to my encouraging and unique husband, and to my
daughters, who I hope will never know what this book is all about.

Introduction

"A Great, Oppressive, Suffocating Blasphemy"[1]

Sexualized Violence as an Insidious Trauma

~~~✦~~~

> And none of these [gestures] hurt her terribly, but at the end it's the cumulative amount that threatens to kill her.
>
> —Nano Shabtai[2]

In honor of International Women's Day in 2016, Nechama Rivlin, wife of Israeli president Reuven Rivlin, hosted survivors of sexual violence at Beit HaNassi, the official residence of the president of Israel. The event received wide media coverage, and was of great importance in relation to the Israeli public discourse on sexual violence. Because of the dominance of the military ethos in Israeli culture, Israeli media gives precedence mainly to men's traumas, especially those related to war. In rare cases where public visibility is given to the sexual abuse of women and girls, their trauma is not perceived as a national trauma but is structured as a private (and usually secretive) matter. To use Judith Lewis Herman's words, "The most common trauma of women remains confined to the sphere of private life, without formal recognition or restitution from the community. There is no public monument for rape survivors."[3] In light of this, the significance of the 2016 presidential event becomes clear. Beit HaNassi is a public space, a civic symbol of statehood and nationalism, and the fact that survivors of sexual abuse were invited there shows that sexual violence is a national matter.

1

Moreover, Rivlin's presidency shared the same administration as that chaired by President Moshe Katsav, who in 2010 was convicted of rape, committing an indecent act, and sexually harassing women who were subordinate to him. In this context, Nechama Rivlin's hosting the 2016 event may be seen as a kind of *tikkun*, or repair. The national space that had been headed by a rapist was now occupied by women telling their stories of enduring sexual violence. In the concluding chapter of the book, I will return to that state of "repair," and will examine it in light of the spectrum of voices presented throughout this book, but for now I will focus on the act at hand, namely on the message the president's wife conveyed on this special occasion.

In the speech Nechama Rivlin delivered at the event, she alluded to an excerpt from Nano Shabtai's novel *The Book of Men* (Sefer hagvarim, 2015), which refers to Pina Bausch's dance piece *1980*. Addressing the novel's description, Nechama Rivlin portrays Bausch's dance as follows: "A female dancer stands in a simple and childish dress, surrounded by men in suits. Each of them touches her in a series of repetitive small gestures. One repeatedly pinches her nose, one caress her head, a third touches her belly, her foot, her hand. No one blatantly harms her with unequivocal and jarring harm, but the repetition of these small, dubiously legitimate touches, in the face of her submissive and confused passivity, makes this dance an unbearably difficult artistic moment. A cumulative load of small injuries that has become a great, oppressive, suffocating blasphemy."[4]

When Nechama Rivlin sought a way to talk with the survivors and the public about sexual violence, she turned to a literary text. Moreover, she did not quote, for example, Shaul Tchernichovsky's prominent 1936 poem "Parashat Dinah" (The Dinah Affair or The Dinah Portion), which deals with the biblical narrative of the rape of Dinah; nor did she quote the well-known scene in which Hannah, the heroine of Amos Oz's 1968 novel *My Michael* (*Michael Sheli*), fantasizes about being raped by Arab twins. Rivlin did not cite isolated rape scenes but rather dealt with the "cumulative load of small injuries."

She referred her audience to Nano Shabtai's novel, which features the main protagonist's long sequence of emotional and sexual encounters with different men in her life. The book, which one critic called "an injuring erotic journey,"[5] presents a wide range of men—some kind and sensitive, others pathetic or miserable—who all end up not just being aggressive in one way or another but also taking advantage of social privileges related to their own gender, race, and professional position. Despite its title, *The Book of Men* is told from the perspective of the female character, and is more about women than about men. It describes women's experiences, and presents women and girls as constantly exposed to a wide spectrum of harassment and gender-based violence. Thus, Nechama Rivlin did not refer to sexual abuse as an incident "outside the range of human experience" but rather she addressed a lurking, quotidian, and continuing trauma that women and girls experience as part of an ongoing wounding social reality.

In effect, Nechama Rivlin thus used her position within the presidential institution to make a three-part statement: first, by inviting survivors of sexual violence to the presidential hall she called on Israeli society to listen to them seriously; second, by quoting a novel, she reminded the nation of the political and social influence of literature; and third, by referring specifically to *The Book of Men* she exposed the repetitive and insidious nature of sexualized trauma.

In those statements, Nechama Rivlin actually touched on all of the main modes of representing sexual violence in Modern Hebrew literature. Modern Hebrew literature is saturated with various forms of sexual violence, such as male and female prostitution, incest, the rape of girls and women, and verbal assault. It locates sexual aggression in various historical contexts (such as the Holocaust, Israel's wars, and religious rituals), as well as in different social and institutional contexts (such as sexual harassment in the army). At times, sexual violence stands at the center of the literary representation, and at others, it dwells in the margins of the narrative; sometimes it is explicit, and sometimes it is implicit. Although it is difficult to organize such an abundance of representation within historical or ideological coordinates, *Flesh of My Flesh* argues that the key position that characterizes most of the representations of sexual violence in Hebrew literature is that sexual violence is not perceived as a *personal* trauma but rather as an *insidious* trauma.

In its initial formulation in the third edition of the *Diagnostic and Statistical Manual of Mental Disorders*, a traumatic event was conceptualized as a catastrophic stressor that was outside the range of usual human experience,[6] and the trauma was situated "as an essential category of human existence, rooted in individual rather than social dynamics."[7] This dehistoricizing universalism created and perpetuated a context in which victims of trauma were approached not as historical actors but rather as "victims in general: universal man, universal woman, universal child."[8] The term "insidious trauma," on the other hand, reflects current approaches to trauma that locate specific traumatic events in a larger context of societal oppression. "Insidious trauma" thus refers to daily incidents of marginalization, objectification, discrimination, intimidation, et cetera, that are experienced by members of groups targeted by heterosexism, racism, ableism, and other forms of oppression. Insidious trauma, explains Maria P. P. Root, "is characterized by repetitive and cumulative experiences. It is perpetrated by persons who have power over one's access to resources and one's destiny, and directed towards persons who have a lower status on some important social variable. The types of experiences that form insidious traumas are repeated oppression, violence, genocide, or femicide—both historical and contemporary."[9] In other words, in contrast to "personal" or "extreme" trauma—that is, trauma as an experience that is outside the typical range of human experience or that occurred in the past and then ended—the term "insidious trauma" refers to trauma as an experience that takes place as a result of ongoing conditions of oppression (such as chauvinism, homophobia, racism, and ableism) that occur within normative reality. Unlike the definition of "posttrauma," which is based on the fact that the event that has engendered such pain is over, the stubbornness of insidious trauma exists as the product of an ongoing and cumulative traumatic social reality.[10]

Flesh of My Flesh claims that Modern Hebrew literature, from its early stages until recently, refuses to adhere to the decontextualization in regard to sexual trauma.[11] It disaffirms the universalization and depoliticization of sexual trauma, and—without ever using the term—refers to it as an "insidious trauma." Hebrew literature emphasizes the social context of sexual trauma, often referring to the victims as members of various oppressed groups (women, girls, Palestinians, Mizrahi, poor). It thus highlights the importance of examining the overlap between individual and cultural oppression, and therefore exposes the social norms and mechanisms that enable (and at times encourage) sexual violence. Though each story of gender-based violence is singular and unique, Hebrew literature insists on framing and understanding sexualized violence as collectively emblematic. Hebrew literature, then, not only provides a platform for the articulation of sexual violence but, since it takes into account the cultural, social, and poetic matrix of trauma, also becomes a political act by exposing the social roots of gender-based trauma.

The Trope of Sexual Violence

Hosting the survivors in the president's house, as mentioned, was a public statement of enormous importance. However, while the media covered

Nechama Rivlin's speech, it did not broadcast the victims' voices. Their stories were mediated through Nechama Rivlin's speech, which, while addressed to them, was at the same time also a public (and as such, official) speech delivered to the nation. In other words, their stories of sexual violence were presented in order to serve a cause, in this case, a feminist-national one. Without getting into the various motivations embodied in this presidential event, what is important to me is the fact that the story of sexual violence was mediated—and articulated—in order to serve a purpose.

Flesh of My Flesh explores a variety of social interests embodied not in the act of sexual violence itself but in its cultural mediation, namely, in its articulation. Even though sexual violence is, first and foremost, a severe act of violence, especially (but not only) against women and girls, the representations of sexual violence that are discussed in this book are literary ones; they are a construct that articulates social reality while taking part in shaping its social power relations. The book thus examines the trope of sexual violence in Hebrew literature, and then asks how it participates in, encourages, or resists concurrent ideologies in Hebrew and Israeli culture.

Representations of sexual violence in Hebrew literature serve a variety of social interests, at times incompatible with actual victims' experiences or interests. While survivors' stories are central to the discussion of sexual violence, they are not the main narratives that appear in literature. In fact, in Hebrew literature the introduction of sexual violence into poetic and narrative settings is more often than not a literary device, meant not only to move the plot forward in particular ways but more importantly to cultivate ideological positions related to gender, ethnicity, national identity, and disability in Israeli society. This book thus presents various roles of sexual violence tropes, some of which destabilize hegemonic notions while others reinforce norms or modes of conduct.

Accordingly, through discussions about Hebrew representations of prostitution, as well as examinations of sexual relations between wounded soldiers and their caregivers, the book shows how sexual violence is used as a rhetorical tool to construct Jewish and Israeli heterosexual masculinity. By attending to Hebrew Sepharadi literature, it explores the relationship between sexual violence and the establishment of Mizrahi femininity. And while reading memoirs of incest survivors, this book examines the therapeutic effects of writing, and shows the interests of survivors in a social dialogue, and while reading contemporary poetry it explores the poetic processing of sexual trauma.

Engaging with various sociopolitical intersections in the representation of sexual violence will thus allow us to observe the numerous
ways in which sexual aggression intersects with social circumstances and
with the literary act. In turn, these moments of intersection inform the
discourse(s) on sexual violence in the Israeli culture of the last century,
and they are accompanied by nuanced negotiations between the various
participants in the construction of literature.

Sexual Violence:
Affirming the Status Quo and Challenging It

Feminist scholars and activists have rightly called for a social and legal
change in regard to sexual violence. Numerous studies have been dedicated
to unveiling social mechanisms of suppression in the domestic, educational,
legal, and therapeutic systems, detailing the lack of proper enforcement to
protect the victims. These calls are justified, but they stem from a basic
assumption that refers to the legal and ethical prohibition of sexual violence as actually opposed to the very real existence of sexual violence. In
other words, according to these calls, sexual violence disrupts the social
and legal order rather than dwelling within these structures intrinsically.

In contrast to this assumption, Judith Lewis Herman shows that
sexual violence does not interfere with patriarchal power dynamics but
rather actually conforms to and even authorizes patriarchal norms.[12] Other
feminist scholars have also argued that the existence of sexual violence
is but a means to train women and children "to regard themselves as
inferior objects to be used by men."[13] Accordingly, *Flesh of My Flesh* reads
the centrality of sexual violence in Hebrew literature (and Israeli society)
within this complex framework of cultural doings that are simultaneously
permitted and forbidden. The book thus addresses sexual violence in
Hebrew literature not only as insidious trauma characterized by repetitive
and cumulative experiences but also as a typical function of heteropatriarchy
rather than a breach or breakdown of social order. In other words, this
book examines the ways in which the literary-social organization not only
challenges but also enables (and perhaps even encourages) sexual violence.

Thus, although sexual violence is—at least in some cases—prohibited
and legally punishable, I examine its literary depictions in two ways: as
an exception to the social order and as a built-in element of patriarchal
interest within that same order. Since representations of sexual violence

are at least as much about affirming the status quo as about challenging it, this book shows, on the one hand, how sexual violence stands at the heart of the sociocultural mainstream—in that sexual violence is not just a personal tendency, cultural pathology, or historical oddity[14]—and yet, on the other, how writers position themselves in relation to those patriarchal power relations. Hebrew literature manages to represent the varied political contexts of sexual violence and reveal the different interests it serves, while pointing to the various mechanisms that enable it. Hence, this book presents readings about sexual violence that move between adopting or assimilating the patriarchal power relations, and expressions of women's writings of critical voices that undermine the patriarchal framework and enable what Shira Stav calls the "possibilities of action within a cohesive structure."[15]

"Your Own Private Bed"[16]

The unpublished and undated story "Mistake" (Shgaga),[17] written by Rivka Alper, may be the first story in Hebrew literature that addresses rape from the perspective of the raped woman.[18] Alper was born in 1902 in the town of Avitzi in the Vilna Governorate, and she immigrated to Palestine in 1926. With extraordinary sensitivity, the story tells about Dina, a young pioneer from a *kvutza* (a communal settlement in Palestine during prestate Israel), who was raped by a young Jewish Zionist man. The story not only describes the rape itself and the mechanisms of dissociation she experienced during the assault but also the aftermath: her sense of guilt and shame, her social exclusion, and her inability to process or overcome her traumatic experience.

Alper's story addresses rape as a personal experience while simultaneously locating it within the wider context of the Zionist movement, without attempting to disrupt or undermine it. At the same time, "Mistake" reveals the hidden violent aspects of the Zionist project, which aspired to establish a safe home for the Jewish people but failed to provide emotional or physical safety to its female (and at times, also male) members.

The story depicts the rape as a difficult and unexpected experience that does not actually deviate from the sexual harassment and violence to which Dina and her female pioneer companions are exposed on a regular basis. To use Orian Zakai's words, "Sexual violence is reproduced rather than repudiated in the Zionist space. The boundaries of the victimized body are not protected, as hoped, by the constitution of a distinct national identity. Rather, sexual violence is transposed to the national setting and becomes part and parcel of the making of Zionist masculinity."[19] Perhaps this is why the story ends with what we might understand as a call for a fundamental change in the Jewish Zionist world. In the Balfour Declaration (1917), the Zionist request was for the establishment of a "national home for the Jewish people" in Palestine, and Virginia Woolf in her writings calls for "A Room of One's Own" (1929); Rivka Alper seems to balance these demands by speaking of the desperate desire for "your own private bed": "Onward mountains again: valleys, communal settlement. [. . .] *Nimas* [I am fed up with it]. Fatigue. . . . There is a desire to have a corner, your own private bed. Homeward, to her collective settlement, she has returned. Again the same life. There was nothing new, nothing was added, kitchen, laundry, yard again . . . and the worm was sucking, sucking over there . . . under the heart."[20] The story does not end with the abandonment of the Zionist dream or with Dina's departure from the *kvutza*. Rather, it ends with a call for women's own ownership of their bodies and life. It is a call to protect the female body; it is a desperate plea, deeply aware of its own powerlessness, to create a private and safe space for women.

In a way, this short story is an embodied articulation of that plea: it not only carries a feminist manifesto but becomes, in itself, "a corner," a literary space to preserve, process, and communicate the traumatic experience. Tsvia Litevsky writes in one of her poems, "Pain is not emotion. Pain is a place,"[21] which helps to describe the creation of the literary space that manifests as a result of shared pain and violence. It is this space—the location of the poetics of the embodied effects of sexual violence—that stands at the heart of this book. Therefore, *Flesh of My Flesh* explores the poetic possibilities of writing within a patriarchal framework, looking not only at the political dimension of writing itself but also at the way in which the poetics of writing relates to, transmits, and processes sexual violence.

The Illusion of Progress

Rivka Alper's story "Mistake" (Shgaga) was written almost a century before Nechama Rivlin invited the survivors of gender-based sexual violence to Beit HaNassi. Even though Alper's story is indeed exceptional for her time, it does not stand alone. Despite various mechanisms of silencing, some stories about the rape and sexual harassment of both Jewish and Palestinian women at the early stages of the Zionist movement found their way into Hebrew writings. One of the central examples is the memoir of the Jewish pioneer Henya Pekelman, *The Life of a Woman Worker in the Homeland* (Hayey po'elet ba-aretz),[22] which she self-published in Hebrew in 1935. Pekelman was born in 1903 in Bessarabia and emigrated to the British Mandate of Palestine in 1922. Unlike her fellow pioneers, who praised the act of pioneering and glorified their daily woes, Henya Pekelman provided firsthand testimony of her rape at the hands of her former business partner, Yeruham Mirkin, in the fall of 1924 while on a visit to Tel Aviv.[23]

While describing the rape itself, Pekelman does not use words but rather attempts to denote this violence with punctuation, using two lines of hyphens: "I wanted to leave the room, but Yeruham held me tightly. A war broke out between us until I hit my head hard and fell to the floor. --- ----------------------------------- I do not remember anything more."[24] The huge gap between Pekelman's two lines of hyphens that (do not) describe the rape and the flow of words in Nano Shabtai's *The Book of Men* quoted in Nechama Rivlin's speech raises questions about the changes that have taken place in Hebrew literature and Israeli culture in relation to sexual violence. Does this difference signify progress, and if so, what is the nature of that progress? Would the reception of Pekelman's autobiography be different if she were to publish it today?

It is difficult to predict how Pekelman's autobiography would be received if were published today, but we do know that it was largely ignored by Hebrew readers until it was reprinted in Israel in 2007.[25] We might understand the initial neglect as a typical case of silencing a testimony about sexual violence, and the reprint of the memoir as an example of the recent increase in awareness about sexual assault and rape. However, this narrative of silence about sexual violence in Mandatory Palestine versus openness toward the issue in the State of Israel oversimplifies things. To begin with, the very existence of Pekelman's autobiography, which was self-published in 1935, undermines the claim about silence. Moreover, not only does Pekelman name the rapist but her autobiography also contains her varied attempts to tell her story, and depicts internal and external mechanisms of silencing. Thus it is not only a testimony of her rape but also a poetic and political act of emotionally coping and socially confronting sexual violence. Therefore, Pekelman's memoir challenges the contemporary popular assumption that until the development of the feminist discourse, victims of sexual violence were silence and silenced. The very existence of Pekelman's memoir raises the question of whether—despite events like Nechama Rivlin's—there is indeed more openness to the subject today, and if there is, what the nature of this openness is.

I argue that despite the immense importance of the feminist movement, and without undermining its enormous contribution to the visibility of gender-based sexual violence and to the creation of support systems for victims of sexualized violence, Hebrew literature does not follow a simple arc of progressive improvement. The contemporary narrative—noticeable in literature, film, social media (including the #GamAni [#MeToo] movement), and public accusations of sexual misconduct—emphasizes progress (attributed mainly to extensive feminist efforts) in changing societal attitudes toward sexual violence. This discourse argues that even though much work remains to be done, significant accomplishments—such as greater awareness and social sensitivity to sexual violence—have been made and additional positive changes are underway. It is a discourse that talks about empowering victims, and that believes that survivors have more and more of a voice in the public discourse.

When I started this project, I was highly influenced by this approach and assumed that I would find nothing but conservatism in Hebrew literature of the beginning of the twentieth century, and nothing but feminist radicalism in the writing of the nineties and beyond. This was quickly complicated by the stories of prostitution written by Gershon Shofman, from the first decade of the twentieth century, which revealed not only compassion and sensitivity to women engaged in the sex industry but also a surprisingly forward-thinking awareness around questions of agency and choice. When I was exposed to the work of Shoshana Shababo—to her direct and decisive descriptions of gender-based violence and her evaluations of the complexity of female sexuality in the thirties and forties—I felt awash in a sea of confusion; these texts blatantly contradicted my presumed knowledge of the early years of Modern Hebrew literature. Similarly, as I ventured into work on memoirs of incest survivors of the last two decades, I expected to find texts rooted in revolutionary feminism and psychoanalysis but instead discovered, to my surprise, that it was a genre torn between expressive, poetic innovation and often clichéd narratives of overcoming trauma. The more I ventured into reading these representations of sexual violence in Modern Hebrew literature, the less

was I able to map them out onto concrete ideological or historical trajectories of change and social awareness.

In view of that, by looking at representations of sexual violence in
Hebrew literature from the turn of the century to the present, *Flesh of
My Flesh* challenges the narrative of progress, and argues that the very
idea of "progress" in regard to sexual violence in Hebrew literature—from
lack of concern about sexual violence to thoughtfulness, for instance, or
from a sexist approach to a feminist one—is not only an illusion but has
become a form of oppression in the current Israeli discourses around sexual
violence. In other words, while the narrative of progress may be true in
certain cases, I would argue that first, this narrative overshadows various
experiences that do not conform to this model, and second, it is a partial
narrative that does not represent Hebrew literature as a whole. What can
actually be found in Hebrew literature is a complex and productive chaos
of a variety of attitudes toward sexual violence that still tells us something
coherent and important when seen this way.

While there may be fewer representations of sexual violence in
the prestate period and the first decades of the new Jewish state that
was established in 1948, this topic blossomed within women's writing in
Israel in the 1990s and 2000s, gaining both presence and visibility. Issues
of voice, agency, the female body, wounded subjectivities and bodies,
victimhood, and vulnerabilities characterize many of the current Israeli
representations of sexual violence. This body of work is of enormous
importance, and the study of it has long-reaching implications for the
representation of sexual exploitation and abuse, but it is crucial to realize
that the supposedly silent period is of no less consequence. These texts—as
in the case of Rivka Alper's "Mistake" and Henya Pekelman's autobiography, for instance—bring out particular intersections where a few forms
of oppression come together and capture the way experiences of sexual
violence at the beginning of the twentieth century in Jewish Europe and
Palestine were hidden and marginalized.

Whereas current representations are, to some extent, informed by
academic discourses such as trauma studies, psychoanalysis, and especially
women, gender, and sexuality studies, *Flesh of My Flesh* also explores the
seemingly prediscursive stage of sexual violence in Hebrew culture. By
examining the underlying ideologies that spawned these representations
and addressing their sociopoetic conditions, the book offers a depiction
of some of the "raw" poetic moments in which Hebrew literature and

culture encounters its own prohibitions and violence. By identifying the ways in which violence—usually, though not always, against women and girls—becomes a trope representative of power relations, this study highlights "unrefined" representations of sexual assault as a major component of the social construction of gender, ethnicity, and national Jewish-Hebrew identity.

Book Structure

Since the notion of a universally experienced rape culture flattens out the very different hierarchies of power that contribute to sexual violence, I present two (not necessarily binary) movements in the book. While some chapters focus on literature written by marginalized or disempowered groups affected by insidious trauma, other chapters center on texts written from a more privileged position. In other words, on the one hand, I look at how women and survivors write about sexual violence and how they relate to the gendered and ethnic oppression they experience, and on the other I also explore representations of sexual violence written from a gendered and racialized privileged position, and I ask what kind of interests they serve.

Although the book is organized chronologically, in view of the fact that sexualized violence is always rooted in the intersection of various types of oppression, the book's structure is also starlike: the key concept is sexualized violence, and each of the five chapters indicates a different branch related to it. Each chapter thus examines a different aspect of the intersectionality that is inherent to sexual trauma, and addresses a different kind of cultural utilization.

The book opens with a fin de siècle European space that uses the experience of sexual violence and female prostitution as a means to negotiate questions of strength and weakness in the masculine Jewish world. The first chapter explores the juxtaposition of prostitution, masculinity, and nationalism in the works of the Hebrew writers David Vogel (1891–1944), Gershon Shofman (1889–1971), and Hayim Nahman Bialik (1873–1934) at the beginning of the twentieth century. The second chapter, while close chronologically, addresses an altogether differently gendered and geographical space. It focuses on the literary work of the oft-overlooked Sepharadi Hebrew writer Shoshana Shababo (1910–1992) during the Yishuv period (the prestate Jewish community in the Land of Israel/

Palestine). This chapter reveals the way Shababo's literary depictions of gender-based violence challenge ethnicity itself, as well as Zionist perceptions and utilizations of sexual violence. The third chapter focuses the discussion about Zionist masculinity on issues related to sexual violence and disability. More specifically, it explores the role of sexual harassment in the construction of heterosexual, able-bodied Israeliness in the late sixties and early seventies. By focusing on writers such as Yoram Kaniuk (1930–2013), Dan Ben-Amotz (1923–1989), Yaacov Haelyon (b. 1937), and Shalom Babayoff (year of birth unknown), this chapter explores the national ableist motivation of linking representations of disability with sexual aggression.

Moving from a focus on writing about sexual violence by authors who do not indicate any autobiographical experience of such in their works, to the survivor's perspective, the fourth chapter centers on memoirs of incest victims published in Israel over the last two decades. It focuses on the emotional and social needs of the writers, as well as on the challenges and barriers of the readers, and explores the ways the memoirs generate creative spaces that enable the survivors to communicate their reality and to have a lasting social impact. The fifth chapter addresses the writings of Tsvia Litevsky (b. 1949), an Israeli incest survivor and poet. It centers on Litevsky's poetic and expository writing on parental abuse, while exploring the complex relationship between creative writing and emotional distress.

The chapters as a whole thus embody the intersectionality that the book examines.[26] In other words, while the book looks at poetic and social possibilities of action in relation to sexual violence, it also exposes the Gordian knot of gender-based violence and the interests of patriarchy, heteronormativity, nationalism, ableism, and the like. Such critical analysis of both canonical and lesser-known texts uncovers the complex power dynamics, ideologies, and anxieties entwined in the constructions of the Hebrew cultural imagination.

Chapter One

"Lights in the Darkness"

*Prostitution, Power, and Vulnerability in
Early Twentieth-Century Hebrew Literature*

~~~꧁꧂~~~

"A Woman like That"

On one of his nocturnal wanderings, Gurdweil, the protagonist of David
Vogel's novel *Married Life* (Ḥayei nisu'im, 1929), is solicited by a prostitute.
Rejecting her proposition,

> [he] hurried away with a disagreeable feeling of oppression. He
> could not overcome this disgust, and was angry with himself
> because of it. They were poor, miserable creatures, and there
> was no reason to be disgusted by them, he said to himself. But
> it did not help. This was the first time he had ever spoken to
> a woman of the streets. Whenever one of them accosted him
> he would mumble something unintelligible even to him and
> hurry past. Or he would make a wide detour when he saw
> them in the distance. His boyhood fear had never left him,
> and needless to say, they never gave rise in him to the faintest
> stirring of desire. As far as he was concerned, they scarcely
> belonged to the female sex. And although he had made up his
> mind on a number of occasions in the past to go with one
> of them—both because his attitude seemed to him unmanly,

morbid, and childish, and because he believed it his duty as
a writer to penetrate every corner of life—as soon as he was
about to take the plunge he found some excuse to put it off.[1]

A plethora of feelings and insights emerges from this single paragraph:
encountering the prostitute arouses fear and revulsion in the protagonist,
to the point that he negates her womanhood ("they scarcely belonged to
the female sex") and, no less important, his own manhood ("his attitude
seemed to him unmanly, morbid, and childish"). At the same time, he con-
siders going to prostitutes as part of his duty as a writer, but what exactly
is that duty? Is he being loyal to a European conception of prostitution
as a life experience that a writer must undergo, or is he perhaps expressing an attitude more characteristic of Hebrew writers of his generation,
of compassion for prostitutes ("they were poor, miserable creatures")? I
would ask, too, why our alienated protagonist begins to stammer when
he encounters a streetwalker. What is it about a prostitute that gives rise
to such stammering? Whence this stammer of the turn-of-the-century
writer? What disjuncture—linguistic, poetic, or cultural—is expressed in
the representation of a prostitute? In other words, what associations are
conjured by Vogel and other contemporaneous Hebrew writers between
prostitution and manhood, poetics and nationality?

Although prostitution was not a frequent subject in modern Hebrew
literature of the early twentieth century, a not inconsequential number of
female figures who plied the prostitute's trade are found in the works of
some major writers, among them Gershon Shofman (1880–1972), Yosef
Haim Brenner (1881–1921), Aharon Reuveni (1886–1971), Levi Arieh
Arieli (1886–1943), and David Vogel (1891–1944). These writers' attitudes
toward female prostitution were not all of a piece but ranged from scorn,
revulsion, and disgust to pity and even identification with them. Yet,
despite their differences in style and poetics, these early twentieth-century
writers share a basic empathy for the marginal status of the prostitute.
Their representations of prostitutes construct a narrative of otherness,
aberration, and exploitation.[2]

This attitude contrasts with the stance found in European and
particularly Russian, French, and German literature of the same period,
which tended toward the idealization and romanticization of the prostitute.[3] European literature frequently employs the image of the prostitute
as a means of challenging the complacent bourgeoisie. Charles Baudelaire
and Thomas de Quincey, the latter the author of *Confessions of an English*

Opium Eater (1821), celebrate the prostitute's impropriety and deploy her image to glorify what Walter Benjamin calls "the asocial."[4] The prostitute's world also embodies perceptions of urbanization at the turn of the century and the excitement, as well as the terror, aroused by the great city.[5] Deborah Nord, in discussing the ambivalent attitudes expressed in Victorian literature toward cities and urbanization, describes a dialectic between senses of isolation and overcrowding, of liberation and entrapment, of the masses around one as remote and alienated or as stifling and threatening. At the center of this dialectic is the image of the prostitute, the fallen woman, the woman of the streets, who plays a major role in molding the nineteenth- and twentieth-century urban milieu. Her representations in European literature, too, are not monolithic: she is a symbol of social distress and debasement but also of empowerment, pleasure, and liberation. Even as a writer uses her to expose society's decadence, she reflects the solitary roamer's own lonesome, tormented soul.[6]

How are we to understand the distinctive, nontrivial stance of the Hebrew writers, who, though active in the European milieu and nurtured on its literature, frequently display striking sensitivity toward the women of the streets? Did that sensitivity stem from poetic-emotional identification, such that these Jewish writers perhaps saw in the prostitute an embodiment of the diaspora's corrupted, perverted life? And if so, what was the nature of this identification? Beyond that, did the writers of the revival generation tend to relate to prostitution as a mark, symbol, or metonymy of a moral, social, and national crisis within Jewish society? Or did they perhaps, antithetically to the European tradition within which they had grown up, refuse to assign symbolic value to prostitution and refrain from exploiting it for other purposes?

I will examine several of these issues in Vogel's and Shofman's representations of prostitution, focusing on the cultural and national underpinnings of their constructions. By discussing the psychopoetical elements that underlie Vogel's depiction of prostitution and the ideological elements in Shofman's, and by exposing their poetic dialogue with Nahman Bialik, I will investigate issues of power, gender, nationalism, and, primarily, victimhood and vulnerability in the Hebrew literature of the first half of the twentieth century.

The Hebrew writers' sensitivity to women engaged in prostitution, and their attitude toward prostitution as a distress situation, is perhaps attributable to the minority status of Jews in Europe, which may have made these authors more sensitive to the vulnerability inherent to prostitution.

This is surely true of the *telushim*, the members of the "uprooted" generation, who were cast off from their familial surroundings and were often
bereft of economic, emotional, and intellectual support.[7]

The Hebrew writers' sensitivity may also have to do with their textu-
al-cultural background: while they were well versed in European literature
(and sometimes were also its translators[8]) and were greatly influenced by
the Western culture within which they lived, they were, of course, also
well versed in the Jewish sources that were an integral part of the Jewish
education they had received. According to Tali Artman-Partock, who has
compared conceptions of prostitution in Christian and Jewish texts, early
Christianity considered prostitution to be a "natural" occupation of women,
as women were considered to be temptresses by nature; therefore, the only
possible path of rehabilitation for a prostitute was for her to forswear her
sexuality altogether and become a nun. Rabbinic literature, by contrast,
saw prostitution more as a situation in which a woman might be caught
up against her will, an abject plight that could be ended by a change of
circumstance, allowing her to return to her own social and familial surroundings without being permanently marked. Thus, while Christianity
essentially linked prostitution to femininity, rabbinic literature regarded it
not as an identity but rather as an occupation or profession. In the Mishnah and the Talmud, prostitution is understood as a temporary distress
situation, a lapse.[9] Moreover, unlike in Christianity, the Rabbis ascribe
concupiscence not to the prostitute but to the man, her client. In stories
from rabbinic literature, it is the man who is lustful and fulfills his desires
by seeking the services of a prostitute.[10] Studying the representations of
prostitution in the writings of Shofman, Vogel, Brenner, and others discloses
an affinity between them and rabbinic conceptions of prostitution: in the
literature of the revival period, prostitution is not seen as an embodiment
of female seduction; indeed, dominance (or the drive to dominate) in the
prostitute-client relationship is always the role of the client.[11]

Notwithstanding these writers' sensitivity to the prostitutes of whom
they write, the story isn't the women's story but that of the males who
gaze at them. Thomas Heise has remarked that representations of the
underworld enable sociologists and criminologists to give us a glimpse
of the milieu of others who share our world, but those representations
are also what enable us to misrecognize such others and not have to deal
with their subjectivity.[12] Similarly, representations of prostitution in the
literature of the revival period clearly tell us less about prostitutes than
about the desires and terrors of those who write (and read) about them.

Even the moments when these deracinated young men identify with the prostitute do not yield expressions of the women's own voices. Thus, I wish to examine the specific way in which the relative sensitivity of these early twentieth-century writers to the image of the prostitute is channeled toward them to meet their own emotional and ideological needs.

Gershon Shofman:
Prostitution and Social Determinism

For Vogel, Brenner, and Reuveni, the theme of prostitution is mostly at the margins of their prose, functioning as a kind of symbolic backdrop to the plot. Shofman, however, sets this world (with its panoply of characters: prostitutes, madams, pimps, and johns) at the center of his writing and even devotes whole stories to it, such as "Trifles" (Katnut, 1904), "Henia" (1908), "The City's Edge" (Bekitsvei hakerakh, 1914), "Between Night and Day" (Bein laylah leyom, 1918), and "Lights in the Darkness" (Orot ba'ofel, 1922).[13] Joseph Klausner saw in Shofman's representations of prostitution a means of conveying unvarnished reality, which "in all its plainness and ordinariness could drive one from his senses."[14] By contrast, Shalom Kraemer, noting that Shofman's whores are not Jewish, concludes that his aim in describing the degenerate non-Jewish world was to glorify the life of Jewish communities, illustrating a "humble, downtrodden Jewry, holding fast to its innocence even within the cold gentile environment."[15] Yeshurun Keshet argues that Shofman's representations of prostitutes do not focus on the women themselves; rather, they are a means for describing "the man who goes to a harlot," that same "man wandering lost in the life of the city," "the ravenous bachelor, giddy with stimulation, in the thrall of a tainted physicality."[16] These interpretations see in Shofman's representations of prostitutes a symbol or image by which he expressed his views on loftier matters: the brutality of existence, relations between Jews and non-Jews, and the difficulties faced by the deracinated male. Rivka Gorfein is the only scholar to relate to the compassion Shofman shows for these half-grown women and to his revulsion for their pimps.[17]

To Shofman, prostitution is not a matter of unfortunate happenstance but a product of broad-ranging social collusion. In a contemporary theoretical context, we might say that his position rejects the notion of prostitution as a choice and sees prostituted women as victims.[18] Although Shofman does not, of course, take direct part in the theoretical discussion of whether prostitution can ensue from free choice, his stories reflect an unequivocal view of the prostitute as a victim. For Shofman, prostitution is never conceived as a chosen trade; it is, rather, a symptom of weakness and oppression. Psychological trauma and distress, violence, and economic and gender inferiority are inherent to prostitution, which is represented as a predicament from which there is no escape. Women and girls who engage in prostitution, in Shofman's view, are victims by definition—and not only because they may have been entrapped into "white slavery" or experienced direct physical violence. The social-gender determinism worked by Shofman into his prostitution stories is expressive of an ethical-ideological conception according to which prostitution is not a consequence of choice, mainly because the concept of choice itself is irrelevant to the lives of the women and girls who have been caught up in it. In these stories, Shofman shapes the image of the prostitute as a product of social determinism, and she is therefore always, necessarily, a victim.[19]

"Henia," perhaps the best-known of Shofman's prostitution stories, sketches the brief life of such a woman: her childhood in a country village, her adolescence and move to the big city, her slide into prostitution, and her premature death in the brothel where she "worked."[20] At first sight, this story would seem to belong to the widespread European literary genre of tales of innocent country girls whose move to the great city leads to their moral and physical demise.[21] But a closer look at Shofman's story shows that this genre, for him, was mainly a vehicle for dealing with the phenomenon of prostitution itself—the women enmeshed in it, its causes and its significance—from the point of view of the victimized position embodied by the image of the prostitute, and, of no less importance, also with the issues of power and weakness with which the Jewish world was preoccupied at the turn of the twentieth century.

"And Ye Shall Suck One from the Other":[22]
Gershon Shofman and Hayim Nahman Bialik

Shofman's breed of social determinism might seem to make "Henia" and his other stories "universal," expressing a kind of generalized critique of violence and of the exploitation of adolescent girls in a society that lacks the wisdom to channel its life potential and appetites in worthy directions, and so has become corrupt, aggressive, and exploitative. However, the closing statement in "Henia," which links human apathy to an indifferent cosmos—"Water splashed out, burbling and gushing, and the cricket chirped"[23]—alludes to a well-known couplet in Hayim Nahman Bialik's famous poem "In the City of Slaughter" (Be'ir haharegah): "For God has called forth Spring and Slaughter at once: / The sun has risen, the acacias have bloomed, the slayer has slain."[24] Shofman thus set his "universal" discussion into a nationalist-Zionist context as well.

"In the City of Slaughter," written in the aftermath of the 1903 Kishinev pogrom and first printed, due to Russian censorship, under the title "Masa Nemirov" (The Vision of Nemirov), has been read by scholars as a call to arms that led to a fundamental change in the agenda of Jewish national life. It is seen as one of the most influential texts in that it brought about a change in the way the Jewish world at the turn of the twentieth century understood power.[25] The poem sharply censures the Jewish mindset, which its speaker presents as one of condemnable weakness and cowering. In their book *Revisiting "In the City of Slaughter"* (Be'ir haharegah: Bikur me'uhar), Michael Gluzman, Hannan Hever, and Dan Miron take on the difficulties raised by this conception, particularly in relation to the speaker's dispassionate attitude toward the victims of the pogrom. Miron is appalled by the poem's dehumanization of the victims and by Bialik's ability to distance himself from their separate individuality; Hever investigates the structure of the Zionist discourse that allowed, and perhaps even demanded, the blaming of the victims, and asks how the paradox of Bialik's simultaneous recognition of the suffering and condemnation of the sufferers might be resolved; while Gluzman offers a nationalist-gendered-biographical explanation for Bialik's rejection of identification with the victims and the transformation of that rejection into rage.[26]

As Miron remarks, the cruelty and indifference found in Bialik's poem evoked discomfort even at the time of its publication, as can be seen, for example, in the sharp response it evoked from S. Y. Abramovich (Mendele Moykher-Sforim).[27] In this context, Shofman's "Henia" might be regarded as an additional response to Bialik's poem—an indirect, poetic response addressing not only the issue of rage as opposed to identification with and empathy for the victims, but also addressing the very significance of victimhood.

The composition of "Henia," like that of Shofman's other prostitution stories, took place in a Jewish ideological milieu of nationalist stirrings and new ways of thinking about issues of power, weakness, and responsibility. To bring the discussion back within the concrete intertextual limits that constructed Shofman's world, these stories were players in the nation-alist-cultural-poetic struggle embodied in the two almost contradictory responses penned by Bialik to the Kishinev pogrom. The first, "On the Slaughter" (Al hashehitah), written in Odessa when word of the pogrom first reached there, is a cry of empathetic identification with the victims ("Heavens, beg mercy for me!"). The second, "In the City of Slaughter" (Be'ir haharegah), published some two years after Bialik's visit to Kishinev, castigates Jews for their passivity and channels the narrator's feelings of identification into rage against the victims:[28]

> And your tears you will have stored up, tears not spilled,
> And you will build on them a fortress of iron and copper wall
> of deadly wrath, hell-like hatred, and pent-up enmity,
> Caught in your heart and nurtured there like a viper in its nest,
> And you will suckle from each other and you will find no rest.[29]

> וְדִמְעָתְךָ אַתָּה תֶּאֱצָר דִּמְעָה בְלִי-שְׁפוּכָה,
> וּבָנִיתָ עָלֶיהָ מִבְצַר בַּרְזֶל וְחוֹמַת נְחוּשָׁה
> שֶׁל-חֲמַת מָוֶת, שִׂנְאַת שְׁאוֹל וּמַשְׂטֵמָה כְבוּשָׁה,
> וְנֶאֱחָזָה בִלְבָבְךָ וְגָדְלָה שָׁם כְּפֶתֶן בִּמְאוּרָתוֹ,
> וִינַקְתֶּם זֶה מִזֶּה וְלֹא-תִמְצְאוּ מְנוּחָה;

To be sure, Shofman and Bialik are dealing with different traumas, but they share a similar posture in relation to them: both observe the trauma rather than experience it personally or directly.[30] However, their emotional (and, necessarily, poetic) responses are utterly different: Bialik rages; Shofman empathizes.

Bialik, in Gluzman's words, "gendered the massacre."[31] Raging, he reads the scenes of the pogrom as expressions of womanlike passivity, embodied not only in images of the violated women but also and primarily in the responses of the men, who do nothing to defend them:

> Lay husbands, bridegrooms, brothers, peeping from the holes
> While holy bodies quivered beneath asses' flesh,
> Being strangled in their impurity and swallowing in the blood
> of their throats,
> And like a man dividing his delicacies so the abominable goi
> divides their flesh—
> Lying down in their shame and seeing—neither stirring nor
> moving.[32]

שָׁכְבוּ בְעָלִים, חֲתָנִים, אַחִים, הֵצִיצוּ מִן-הַחוֹרִים
בְּפַרְפֵּר גְּוִיּוֹת קְדוֹשׁוֹת תַּחַת בְּשַׂר חֲמוֹרִים,
נֶחֱנָקוֹת בְּטֻמְאָתָן וּמְעַלְּעוֹת דַּם צַוָּארָן,
וּכְחַלֵּק אִישׁ פַּת-בָּגוֹ חִלֵּק מְתֹעָב גּוֹי בְּשָׂרָן –
שָׁכְבוּ בְּבָשְׁתָּן וַיִּרְאוּ – וְלֹא נָעוּ וְלֹא זָעוּ,

Exposing this weakness was meant to address both the survivors and the readers of the poem with a call for a reordering of national and gender priorities. The rage thus provoked was meant to arouse their own masculine activism, their male instinct to respond physically and defend themselves:[33]

> Let them raise their fists at me and demand their shaming's
>   recompense,
> The shaming of all the generations, first to last,
> Let them batter heaven and my very throne with their fists.

יָרִימוּ-נָא אֶגְרוֹף כְּנֶגְדִּי וְיִתְבְּעוּ אֶת עֶלְבּוֹנָם,
אֶת-עֶלְבּוֹן כָּל-הַדּוֹרוֹת מֵרֹאשָׁם וְעַד-סוֹפָם,
וִיפוֹצְצוּ הַשָּׁמַיִם וְכִסְאִי בְּאֶגְרוֹפָם.

If the speaker's rage in "In the City of Slaughter" preserves and reinforces gender stereotypes associated with the victims and with responses to victimhood,[34] Shofman's empathy for them enables him to mold a differ- ent kind of gendered conception of victimhood, unlike either the total identification of "On the Slaughter" ("Hangman! Here's a neck—to the slaughter! Break my neck like a dog's; yours is the mighty arm with the axe") or the victim-blaming of "In the City of Slaughter."

Just as Shofman's "Henia" can be seen as a response to Bialik's poem, so Vogel, too, responds indirectly to "In the City of Slaughter" in the suppressed poem "I've Butchered My Wife" (Tavaḥti ishti, 1923):

> I've butchered my wife
> and burnt my home—
> Now let me drink
> and my dead bemoan.
>
> The rain has pierced me with its needles;
> The world has shed its splendor.
> It's time for me to heave off my days,
> to have done with this futile endeavor!

I've allotted my eyes to the night—
may the lights thrive on ever more,
to shine upon all of the burdened with grief
for what's been and is gone, never more.[35]

טָבַחְתִּי אִשְׁתִּי
וָאֶשְׂרֹף אֶת בֵּיתִי -
תְּנוּנִי לִשְׁתּוֹת
וְלִבְכּוֹת אֶת מֵתִי.

מָטָר בִּי נוֹעֵץ מְחָטָיו;
תֵּבֵל הִתְפָּרְקָה אֶת הוֹדָהּ.
עֵת לִי לִזְרֹק כָּל יָמַי,
לִגְמֹר זוֹ שָׁוְא-עֲבוֹדָה!

עֵינַי הִנְחַלְתִּי לַלֵּיל -
תִּפְרַחְנָה לָעַד מְאוֹרוֹת,
לְאִיר לַעֲמוּסֵי הַיָּגוֹן
עַל עֶבְרֵי הַדּוֹרוֹת.

The prophecy of doom referenced by Vogel at the end of the poem (together with the prophecy of doom in Jeremiah 19:6: "Assuredly a time is coming—declares the Lord—when this place shall no longer be called Topheth or Valley of Ben-Hinnom, but Valley of Slaughter [gei haharegah]") is the scriptural source of Bialik's coinage "Be'ir haharegah." Vogel's poem issues, as it were, from the throats of the men accused by Bialik of impotence and feminization. Vogel's speaker blames himself for the slaughter and the conflagration, and internalizes the feminization imposed on him by Bialik's attitude ("The rain has pierced me with its needles; / The world has shed its splendor"). Yet he simultaneously adopts the attitude of a leader and visionary; he is the pillar of smoke lighting the way for those burdened with grief in the dark world in which they are imprisoned. The "womanish,"[36] deflowered leadership, so familiar with grief, rejects the attitude adopted by the poet Bialik, that of a wrathful prophet hammering accusations at the victims. The biblical God demands of his prophet, "As for you, do not pray for this people, do not raise a cry of prayer on their behalf" (Jeremiah 7:16). Bialik, seen by many interpreters as a modern prophet,[37] takes that divine imperative on himself and does not pray for the victims. Sara R. Horowitz argues that "In the City of Slaughter" is an antinarrative, antiliturgical poem, refusing for the most part to tell a story or to turn that story into a prayer.[38] Vogel, by contrast, refuses the divine imperative, the law of the Father, the disciplining power; he sounds the wail of those burdened with existential grief, making no move to suppress or disregard their suffering. Rather than ignoring Jewish history or the emergent Zionism of his time, as Glenda Abramson has argued,[39] Vogel suggests an alternative way of relating to the same events by refusing to collaborate with the discourse that appropriates the victims' distress for the purpose of national revival.[40]

In a brilliant analysis of "In the City of Slaughter," Hamutal Tsamir shows how the speaker in Bialik's poem presents two different uses to which the distress and pain he experiences in confronting the people's suffering might be put—the one shameful and the other constructive. The first possibility, identification and pity, is viewed as whining, while the second, hoarding the pain and tears to turn them on the people in fury, is seen as a process that will enable the people to make a genuine move toward rectifying their situation. Bialik identifies with this latter position, which, according to Tsamir, embodies Zionist ideology.[41] Shofman's poetic response, and in many senses Vogel's as well, reveals the negotiation that played out over the character of that Zionist ideology, or ideologies. But reading the Zionist ideology as utterly rejecting of a victimized, feminized way of being is, I believe, marred by anachronism—by a reading of Zionist currents of thought at the time in light of what was to become the dominant position, namely, the type of nationalism advocated by Bialik and the (imagined) "sabra" attitudes of the Palmach generation.

A Mise-en-Scène of Desire: The Trope of Prostitution

Preserving the dichotomy between weakness, passivity, and victimhood, on the one hand, and power and activism, on the other, Bialik seeks to exchange the position of weakness for one of strength. Shofman, by contrast, calls for blurring this distinction and recognizing an identity that at once embraces both weakness and strength. Writing about prostitution allows Shofman to move through a range of options, including strength, weakness, and victimhood, and to experience them simultaneously, without any one cancelling out another. Very much as in the theory of fantasy put forward by psychoanalysts Jean Laplanch and Jean-Bertrand Pontalis, Shofman's representations of prostitution—that is, the ways he fantasizes the prostitute into his writings—allow him to oscillate among a variety of identities without tying himself down to any one of them in particular.

According to Laplanch and Pontalis, fantasy is not a direct, one-dimensional, metonymic expression of the desires of the fantasizing subject, for fantasy "is not the object of desire, but its setting."[42] Fantasy does not mark a specific object of identification; rather, it presents an array of images within which the fantasizer is entangled. The fantasizer, then, is not posing the object of his desire but is participating actively in a scene—or more precisely, a mise-en-scène—of desire.[43] The fantasy is a kind of Rashomon, "a scenario with multiple entries" in which the subject can wander among various identities and perspectives.[44] The fantasy does not necessarily attest to the subject's specific location or to identification with a particular object within the fantasy; it is, rather, an arena of multiple possibilities. Laplanch and Pontalis give the example of a fantasy of a father seducing his daughter, in which the fantasizer may position himself as the daughter, the father, or the seduction itself.[45] In other words, the subject's identifications are not necessarily fixed in one dimension of the fantasy; they may rove among different images, attitudes (authority/weakness, activity/passivity, maturity/childhood), and gender patterns. To be sure, emphasizes Teresa de Lauretis, this location is not entirely random; it is conditioned by gender, society, race, sexuality, and personal history.[46]

The mise-en-scène shaped by Shofman in his prostitution stories enables him to formulate a multidimensional notion of victimhood, one that combines gender and national sensitivities.[47] As a man, he is able to retain the dominant position while writing about the image of the prostitute, for the "man with the money" is ever the man in charge; the client is in a position of physical, economic, gender, and social power. At the same time, the prostitute, by definition, enables the fulfillment of desires (not only sexual ones) and therefore allows the client to fantasize about loss of control; she allows him, as it were, to lose his position of power. More precisely, the image of the prostitute allows him to play with the option of losing control and to test the limits of his power. Like in the Freudian game of *fort-da*, in which the baby on the one hand relives the painful situation of abandonment and on the other hand controls it, so the prostitute offers a convenient poetic image for thinking about issues of power, control, and victimhood without risking loss of the position of power, but also without denying the position of weakness.

Moreover, the image of the prostitute allows Shofman, along with other male Jewish writers, such as Brenner and Reuveni, to identify from a gender point of view with the client (the man, the victimizer) and from an ethnic/national point of view with the prostitute (the weak woman, the victim). In other words, the image of the prostitute allows both the writers and their fictional characters to move in a not necessarily dichotomous way between the positions of strength and weakness, victimizer and victim. This type of identification with both the client's position of strength and the prostitute's position of weakness can be seen, for example, in L. A. Arieli's story "Adventures in Love" (Herpatka'ot shel ahavah), which tells of sexual encounters between a Jewish youth and three Russian women.[48] Varia, one of the women the youth sleeps with, filches the money in his wallet; when he finds out about it, he steals all her money, but after a while feels ashamed and regretful.[49] Varia is not overtly a prostitute, but the story is a variation on the theme of prostitution: at the beginning, the woman steals the young man's money, thus demanding cash in consequence of their relations (making her the prostitute and him the client), and afterward the tables are turned. The power relations between them are thus ambiguous: the protagonist has the advantage over Varia from a gendered and economic point of view, but from an ethnic/national point of view, as a Russian living under her uncle's roof, the woman is better protected than the Jew.

Shofman's story "Trifles" (Katnut) describes the visit of Hillel, an uprooted Jewish youth, to a brothel.[50] As part of the "seduction" game, Hillel and the prostitute tussle with each other light-heartedly, and she compliments him on the strength of his hands.[51] This bit of flattery seems ludicrous to the reader, to whom Hillel's frailty and alienation have been obvious throughout the story. Nevertheless, considering the power relations that underpin their situation, this flattering declaration is quite precise: Hillel's hands, despite his physical frailty, will always be stronger than the prostitute's. Moreover, her ingratiating words expose the recurrent role-play between man and woman, client and prostitute. Thus, by highlighting the gendered-performative dimension of the behavior of prostitute and client (with the prostitute's flattering words to the client echoing gender stereotypes and male sexual fantasies), Shofman exposes us to the cultural, emotional, and poetic arena in which gender, sexuality, power, and national identity come together.[52] Moreover, he molds a performative scene that simultaneously embraces the victimhood of the prostitute, the powerful position of the client, the client's fantasy of power, and his weakness.[53]

Bialik and Shofman, then, both deal with the nexus of gender, identity, and victimhood, but they set different coordinates for mapping

and comprehending this subject. The plane on which Bialik moves is
that of victimhood and reaction (that is, victimhood, weakness, and
femininity as against reaction, power, and masculinity), while Shofman
organizes his concept of victimhood around a dynamic subjectivity that
may ponder different positions on the axis of the power relations between
victim and victimizer. Accordingly, while Bialik sees a feminine element
in weakness, in and of itself, and a masculine (and therefore desirable)
element in autonomy, Shofman reads femininity as reflecting a vulnerable social situation and masculinity as a position of social power that
exerts violence against women and tramples feminine desires.[54] Shofman
thus refrains from creating a dichotomous, one-dimensional relationship
between femininity and victimhood, on the one hand, and masculinity
and power, on the other. This allows him to shape a conception of identity
that can fluctuate between ethnic inferiority and gender superiority while
recognizing a diffuseness between the two positions.

Accordingly, the image of the axe serves these two writers in different
ways. The axe in "On the Slaughter" is divested of its phallic overtones,
returned as it is to the primal image of the hand grasping the hatchet:
"Hangman! Here's a neck—to the slaughter! Break my neck like a dog's;
yours is the mighty arm with the axe." In "In the City of Slaughter," by
contrast, the axe boils and drips blood, serving as a visual, metonymic
image embodying the horror of the rampage of rape and murder:

> Grope with your own hand the befouled coverlet and crimsoned
>   pillow
> wallow of boars and roost of human stallions
> with an axe dripping blood boiling in their hands.

וּבְיָדְךָ תְמַשֵּׁשׁ אֶת-הַכֶּסֶת הַמְטֻנֶּפֶת וְאֶת-הַכָּר הַמְאָדָּם,

מִרְבַּץ חֲזִירֵי יַעַר וּמִרְבַּעַת סוּסֵי אָדָם

עִם-קַרְדֹּם מְטַפְטֵף דָּם רוֹתֵחַ בְּיָדָם.

Though the blood of the victims is clearly intended, the image alludes
to the ritual of circumcision. The rapes, for Bialik, return the victims
(again, the husbands of the raped women rather than the raped women
themselves) to the constitutive moment of the nexus between individual,
people, and masculinity. The violent phallic image embodies the people's
feeble masculinity, for the rape of the women is a mark of injury and
blemish to its potency and virility. In Shofman's story "Henia," by contrast,

"a well-worn, honed axe was stuck" in the garden of Henia's childhood home—well-worn, perhaps, from frequent use, and stuck in a perpetual pose of striking. The phallic quality of the axe and the violence inherent in it represent not a one-time event but a recurrent reality; Shofman's axe thus highlights the recurrent and insidious nature of the injury and, most importantly, returns the focus of the discussion to women's victimization.[55]

Exposure to trauma thus evokes opposing responses in these two writers: Bialik calls for a rearousal of masculine violence, while Shofman critiques that violence and calls for its restraint. To be sure, this wouldn't seem to be the same violence: Shofman is dealing with men's violence against women, while Bialik is dealing with ethnic/national violence and calling for self-defense, not violence for its own sake. Moreover, the two have different motivations for writing: where Shofman is concerned with the victims of prostitution, Bialik is writing about the victims of a pogrom and the state of the Jewish people; and where Shofman sets sexual violence at the center of his discussion, Bialik uses it to concretize the horrors, since the direct motivation for his writing is to raise issues of national import. Nevertheless, despite the differences, both writers treat victimhood, violence, sexualized aggressiveness, and identity, and their juxtaposition also exposes the unbreakable bond not only between ethnicity and gender but also between ethnicity and gender-based violence.

"My Sister . . ."

When Rost and his friend Enker from Vogel's *Viennese Romance* (Roman Vina'i, 2012 [original date unknown]) encounter prostitutes roaming the streets of the city like themselves, Enker muses, "There's nothing between me and them . . . , just like them, I'm alone at the end of everything, alone and bled dry."[56] Why does Enker declare himself to be "just like them," and whence springs the contradiction between the identification embodied in that declaration and his equally forceful declaration that he has nothing in common with them?

Abramson, the protagonist of Brenner's novel *Around the Point* (Misaviv lanekudah, 1904), despairs of involvement in the Hebrew literary revival and tries his hand at writing a review essay in Russian, on Russian literature. In the process, he sinks into a deep depression that is expressed in thoughts of suicide and the loss of his sanity. For his sustenance, Abramson works in the Jewish library, a well-known center of Zionist activity. After receiving his first paycheck, wandering the streets dejected and full of self-loathing, he runs into "a woman well on in years, selling her withered body for scraps of bread and a few sips from the bottle." He stops her and gives her all his money, thinking to himself, "She is my sister."[57] The whore, for him, represents a marginal figure at the bottom of the socioeconomic ladder, a kind of archetype devoid of any gendered or sexual dimension, as well as a projection of his own feelings of being alone, forlorn, and bereft. And yet, Abramson calls her "my sister." She is a female embodiment of his own uprootedness. At his lowest point, as he ponders self-destruction, with his masculine agency as it were in tatters, he meets a prostitute and sees in her the uprooted soul in himself.[58]

Abramson gives the whore his wages, a material embodiment of the Zionist enterprise and of the new Jewish masculinity, without even using her "services," as though she were a beggar. This is less an act of pity than an expression of self-loathing, in which he creates a kind of mirror image of himself. On the one hand, he gives her the money, which, at this stage, he detests for what it symbolizes; on the other hand, in recreating the scene of receiving his own wages, he in effect turns the whore into himself and himself into a whore. In other words, by way of his identification with the prostitute, he not only maintains his own lowly self-image but, primarily, also maintains the ambivalence of being both the client (the man with the money and the power) and the prostitute (the powerless woman).[59]

The writers of the revival generation, for the most part, do not deny the gender, social, and economic chasm between themselves and the prostitutes they encounter, but at the same time they challenge the dichotomy between masculinity and power and femininity and weakness. In *Viennese Romance*, Enker, one of the characters, converses with the prostitute, but when she mocks him for not wanting to sleep with her, he gives her a slap on the cheek. Afterward, he feels ashamed and remorseful for what he has done.[60] The slap he gave the whore had turned his weakness into strength, but the shame that came with it turns his strength back into weakness. Although he understands the slap as an appropriate, impulsive outburst that has likely saved him from "a lengthy route of hesitation, doubt, and self-probing,"[61] this manifestation of a covert violence within himself stirs within him a sense of connection with the whore, "a kind of psychological kinship, or more precisely, a familiar resemblance between those living on the edges of society; the element of defiance, by will or by force, was common to them both; both were unchecked and at liberty. She, just like him, was living unchained from society."[62] Hitting the whore manifests Enker's superiority and masculinity but at the same time perpetuates his (sexual and emotional) impotence and "effeminacy" and exposes his weakness and dereliction. Vogel, like Brenner, Shofman, and Arieli, was riveted by this oscillation between the positions of femininity and masculinity, power and weakness, victimhood and victimizer.[63]

David Vogel: "A Suspect Hatred"

Upon the first meeting between Gurdweil, the protagonist of Vogel's *Married Life* (hayei nisu'im), and Thea, who will become his wife, they stroll around the streets of Vienna and run into prostitutes who, like themselves, are "saunter[ing] to and fro."[64] Thea proclaims that she hates them. On the face of it, she might be expressing nothing more than the hatred of a respectable woman for her disreputable counterpart. The prostitute holds up a mirror not only to social respectability and propriety but also to the enormous dependence of women on men. Downtrodden, defiled, wretched, and alone, she represents the situation of the derelict woman—that is, the woman bereft of male protection.[65] Thea, who herself will later turn out to be a woman uninterested in her husband's protection, loathes this reflection of the dangers bound up with the lifestyle she so desires. Gurdweil's sensitivities warn him that this is "a suspect hatred."[66] He is unable, at this stage in the novel, to understand that Thea's hatred for the streetwalkers and the violence they arouse in her ("I hate them! I could kill them!") attests to his future wife's repressed fear of sharing a similar fate. He also cannot imagine that the tables will be turned three hundred pages later: overcome with hatred for his wife who has played the whore, he will murder her.

Why does Gurdweil suspect his wife's hatred for the streetwalkers? How does he intuit that it goes beyond the commonplace? It would appear that what Gurdweil intuits is a defect in himself. As the relations between him and his wife develop in a sadomasochistic direction, he grows increasingly afraid of her. On one of the few evenings that they sit together at home, with him resting on her breast, Thea jokingly asks her husband whether he doesn't worry that she may one day strangle him.[67] "A sharp fear [runs] through his body like an electric current," stirring up in him "his old fear as a child when, at night, he had to pass the only brothel in the little town."[68] Gurdweil goes back to being a fourteen-year-old boy frightened of the raucous laughter emerging from the brothel, while Thea becomes the very source of that fear, of the place "where people were swallowed up and regurgitated."[69] In Gurdweil's unconscious, the home they share becomes a brothel, a place of unbridled sexuality, fearful and threatening. But that which can exist in Gurdweil's emotional world cannot be maintained in their shared world. When Thea fulfills Gurdweil's worst fears by turning their home into a kind of brothel, in which she whores with a stranger before her husband's eyes, the violence latent in him erupts, and he stabs her to death. Gurdweil murders his wife not because she has abused and betrayed him, but because she has actualized his fears, forcing him to confront that place "where people are swallowed up and regurgitated."

What is the nature of this threatening, dangerous place—the place that casts such fear into the heart of Vogel's protagonist? I believe that we may use Gurdweil's suspicion as a reader's guide to the novel, offered by the protagonist himself. Just as Gurdweil understands that Thea's hatred is suspect, so, too, do I see Gurdweil's fear as suspect. An element of gynophobia—of men's fear of women, or, in a more colorful variation, of the Freudian "vagina dentata," representing the imagined threat posed by femininity and female sexuality, of castration and impotence—is, of course, part of the picture.[70] While prostitution, in itself, may have nothing to do with female sexuality,[71] from a patriarchal perspective it constitutes an exaggeration of that female sexuality to the extreme, and as such, it menaces.

To be more specific, not much is told to us of Gurdweil's background, but we learn in an entirely roundabout way of one of the most humiliating and formative experiences in his early life:

> Often I would wander aimlessly about in byways and alleys where I had never been before, straying and searching for something undefinable, until it grew dark and I had to go home. At that time I was once attacked by a gang of Christian boys. I fought desperately, as if I was fighting for my life. But I was alone and I was defeated. When I came home battered and beaten, I felt a curious satisfaction, a kind of contentment and peace of mind. Once I was hit by a stone—here, you see?— Gurdweil pointed to his left temple, next to the ear—there's still a little scar. You can feel it with your fingers.[72]

The violence experienced by Gurdweil gives him a sense of satisfaction; it is a repeated source of pleasure, preserved and embodied in the scar

that cannot be seen but can still be felt. This remembrance of a gratifying violence is connected, for Gurdweil, to his attraction to the churches
of his native town: "By then I already knew about the Inquisition, the
Crusades, the persecution of the Jews, and I was constantly afraid that
they would suddenly seize me and drag me inside and force me to do
something terrible. . . . You might say that in the depths of my soul I was
even eager for the thing to happen."[73]

Gurdweil's weakness as a Jewish boy is replicated in his adult relationship with his abusive Christian wife. But between his boyhood beatings by
Christian youths and his marriage to an abusive woman, he had another
traumatic experience in his youth: at the age of fifteen, he was raped by
the twenty-five-year-old maid working in his parents' home, who had
"glittering eyes, and sharp, shining, little teeth like an animal's."[74] The event
was repeated, "and in the course of time," he recalls, "I grew accustomed
to it and I no longer saw anything wrong in it."[75] As the householders'
son, Gurdweil was in a position of power in relation to the maid, but as
a minor coerced into a sexual encounter, he was, of course, in a position
of weakness. This traumatic experience underpinned the blurring, in
Gurdweil's adult life, of issues surrounding power, weakness, and sexuality.

It could be this experience that enables Gurdweil to visualize the
scene of Lotte, another character in the book, being sexually assaulted by
her uncle in her childhood.[76] Although Gurdweil might seem to display
a great deal of sensitivity on hearing of Lotte's traumatic experience, it
is not clear with whom he actually identifies. Is it with the weakness of
Lotte the child, both as someone who had a similar experience in childhood and because his wife Thea often relates to him as a baby? Or does
he identify, rather, with the "failure" of the attacker, whose "cane [falls]
to the ground"[77]—that is, with the crumpling of the phallus? Or, on the
contrary, considering the use Gurdweil makes of his "open penknife" at
the end of the novel to murder his adulterous wife,[78] does he perhaps
identify with the attacker's aggression?[79]

These pendulum swings between strength and weakness, violence
and victimhood, are evident as well in Gurdweil's relations with his wife,
which are ambivalent from the outset. At the end of his first nighttime
tryst with Thea, he roams the streets of the city and sees streetwalkers
waiting for the tram: "With lusterless eyes he looked at the two prostitutes
waiting there, and the picture of the hotel room in which he had spent
the night rose up before him. The memory gave him such a disagreeable
feeling that he was forced to avert his eyes. But at the same time he was

filled with a great longing for Thea."[80] Gurdweil's whole relationship with
Thea will be that of a man with a woman who has played the whore
on him, an unfaithful wife. Their intimacy, from the very beginning of
the novel, is unconsciously bound up with prostitution. But Gurdweil's
position is ambivalent: the prostitutes may remind him of that first night
with Thea, but can we conclude from this that Thea looks to him like a
prostitute? Or, considering his passivity, is it, rather, that he understands
that Thea is "using" him, "consuming" his body as though the whore were
none other than himself?

The trauma of Gurdweil's childhood rape is scripted by way of his
transformation from a powerless victim (a boy who was raped) into someone who, as it were, gets pleasure from illicit intimacy (a classic scene of
the master of the house having sex with the maid). Similarly, throughout
the entire novel we witness the complex, violent relations between Gurdweil
and Thea, who abuses, cuckolds, humiliates, and even beats him, while
Gurdweil responds to it all with abjection and acceptance of the punishment meted out to him. Gurdweil is described throughout the novel as
an effeminate man—weak, lovelorn, lost, and nurturing the baby, while
his wife is depicted as mannish, violent, aggressive, and adulterous. But
this overturning of the genders is "solved" when Gurdweil's restrained,
repressed anger, which grows ever more powerful toward the end of the
novel, bursts out with the thrust of his open penknife into his wife's body.

The murder, then, is an act of revenge not only on his wife but also,
or perhaps especially, on the maid who raped him in childhood, and on
his own weakness and effeminacy. Gurdweil redirects and internalizes the
strength and rage that he cannot hurl against his oppressors. What he
internalizes is not the force that the Christian youths, the maid, and Thea
used against him but his rage at his own impotence in these humiliating
situations. Gurdweil's repressed violence and thirst for revenge erupt in
the murder of his wife, but they have been present all the time in his
complex attitude of simultaneous identification with and fear of prostitutes.

Gurdweil's aggressiveness toward the whore—and mainly toward
his "whoring" wife—should, to my mind, be understood as terror of his
own weakness, or, to use the term coined by Melanie Klein, as *paranoid
anxiety*—the fear of annihilation, of being utterly effaced, of being invaded
by evil.[81] The evil experienced as coming from without in fact emanates
from the infantile death instinct. According to Klein, the infant, in the
earliest stages of its life, must split his external world (both the objects
in it and himself) into two dichotomous categories: good (gratification,

satiety, love) and bad (frustration, hate, mistreatment). This splitting protects the infant in his early stages and enables him, later on when his ego is more developed, to internalize the good, create a hierarchy of good and evil, and incorporate ambivalent positions, as well as to deal with conflictual situations.

As we have seen, for Gurdweil as for many of his "uprooted" contemporaries, an encounter with a prostitute stirs up his paranoid anxiety—his fear of his own vulnerability.[82] The archetypically "uprooted" prostitute makes it impossible for the uprooted young writer to deny his own weakness. This weakness is grasped both as an external threat to the nascent Zionist enterprise and as the internal threat posed to these European Jewish youths by their inherent debility. Thus, in a milieu in which abandonment of the old world stirred them to a sense of strength and power (along with their terror and confusion), coming together with the many voices within the Zionist world calling on the Jewish man to shed his weakness and gird himself with a mantle of national power and a muscular body, weakness is turned into an inhibiting element, a kind of evil that threatens to do away with the emergent Zionist enterprise.

Another type of anxiety associated with aggression, according to Klein, is *depressive anxiety*, in which fear of being destroyed by others is replaced by fear of destroying the other. In the next stage of infantile development, the infant develops the ability to internalize whole objects (as opposed to the previous stage, which was characterized by splitting). Consequently, he understands that his mother is the source of both the "good" and the "bad." Klein applies the term *depressive anxiety* to the infant's terror of the object he has destroyed. While paranoid anxiety is bound up with fear of the destruction of the self from without, depressive anxiety is bound up with fear for the fate of others, within and without, as a consequence of the fantasized destruction born of the child's own aggression.[83] In a variation of the integration of the "good" breast and the "bad" breast, the encounter with the prostitute expresses Gurdweil's acceptance, and that of his contemporaries, of the duality of weakness and strength. Moreover, if, in the paranoid anxiety stage, the fear was of weakness itself, in this stage of depressive anxiety the fear is of *violating the weakness*, of losing it. Gurdweil's aggression, then, is not only an internalization of strength and a marker of self-hatred but also an expression of his fear of the destruction of the weakness within himself.

In other words, contrary to the accepted scholarly understanding of the revival generation, according to which its members' expressed wish was to shake off their exilic past as effeminate "old-time" Jews and turn into "new," masculine Jews,[84] a different process may be discerned in Vogel's writings, one of fear of losing his vulnerability. Vogel's protagonist, then, is not indifferent to the nationalist voices surrounding him; he is terrified of them.[85] The shedding of weakness demanded by Bialik—who came to symbolize the call for empowerment—may be taken as a rejection of what he saw as his own shameful weakness and effeminacy, as suggested by Michael Gluzman,[86] or as a call for the reworking, redirection, and transformation of weakness into strength, as suggested by Hamutal Tsamir.[87] Either way, it was not only Vogel who did not identify with this call by Bialik and others of the same persuasion for the establishment of a new Jewish masculinity, but Vogel also refuses to undergo the transformation that is demanded of him.[88] Like the child trying to resolve his depressive anxiety and the powerful guilt feelings that accompany it by rebuilding his image of his mother on the basis of restorative fantasies and behaviors, so, too, does Vogel refuse to join in the celebration of his own strength. He tries, instead, to recreate the other that he has destroyed, the subjectivity that can simultaneously contain both strength and weakness. This embrace of weakness, concern for its future, and fear of its loss constitute not an inverted response to his own destructiveness but rather sincere expressions of the love and regret that, according to Klein, develop together with the infant's gratitude for the good that he has received from his mother.[89]

"From Nowhere to Nowhere / Without Me":[90] Conclusion

Jessica Benjamin understands penis envy as the yearning of the young child—boy or girl—to identify with the father, who represents the outside world. The father is "the ideal in which the child wants to recognize himself," because he possesses subjectivity and agency, unlike the mother, who is devoid of desire.[91] I wonder why Benjamin—like most psychoanalytic theorists before her, including feminist ones—assumes that the child's "natural" desire, its obvious choice, is to identify with activism, strength, and masculinity. The world's literature, including that of the Hebrew "uprooted" generation, is filled with examples of characters who identify with weakness and impotence. Nor does this necessarily express an abjection opposed to dominance; it may express acceptance or establishment of a subjectivity stripped of agency, or perhaps "agentically challenged."

According to Benjamin, "the child wants recognition of her will, of her desire, of her act";[92] in other words, *will, desire,* and *act* are almost overlapping terms. There is no such thing as will to do nothing, or desire for a lack of will. Accordingly, the literature produced by the revival generation can be read as having failed at this developmental stage; or it can be read, very differently, as challenging the basic assumptions of Benjamin and her predecessors. Following Daniel Boyarin and others, Hamutal Tsamir rightly argues that the poetry of the revival generation must be understood as poetry that strives to establish the new Jewish man as an individual-universal-national subject, and the concepts of awakening, renewal, and empowerment imbuing that subjectivity must be understood not only as national sentiments but also as having a gendered and libidinous element.[93] What I wish to accentuate in relation to this charged meeting of masculinity, nationalism, and gender is that within the process of establishing the "new man," efforts were made to test the range of alternatives for masculinity. Even as Bialik's choice of a sovereign masculinity became the dominant one within Zionist discourse, the voices represented by Shofman and Vogel expressed different notions of gender and power.[94]

In other words, to understand the force of the dilemmas and of the poetic, national, and gendered struggles characterizing the literature of the revival generation, one must be attuned not only to the notions of awakening, renewal, and empowerment expressed in it but also to the expressions of weakness, frustration, loss, rage, and aggression that construct that generation's literary world. In writing about their prostitutes—and fundamentally about themselves and the members of their generation— Vogel and Shofman express pendulum swings between empathy and repulsion, acceptance of weakness and its disdain, embracing vulnerability, and clinging to strength. Their representations of prostitution are a prism refracting their poetic-ideological negotiation of issues of strength and weakness within the Jewish world at the turn of the century and in the aftermath of World War I. Hence, their works formulate a subjectivity that cannot easily be delimited or organized into distinct categories of strength, weakness, masculinity, and femininity.

In Bialik's evocation of it, the situation of victimhood may be extremely traumatic, but it is in many senses a one-time event, or one whose repetition can be prevented. To Bialik's way of thinking, at least, it implies the possibility of rehabilitation and establishes a linear narrative that advances from problem to solution, from trauma to healing. Once the people overcome its weakness and "effeminacy," they will be able to circumscribe the trauma within the bounds of past memory. Bialik's conception is constructed on the time lag built into the experience of trauma, the gap separating the traumatic event from its psychological impact, given that a Freudian *Nachträglichkeit*—"afterwardness," retroaction, deferred action—is the primary condition for remembering and bearing witness.

Shofman uses prostitution to deal with victimhood, strength, and weakness. The prostitute's trauma is not a one-time experience but a continuous one, a trauma constantly repeated (not in flashbacks of deferred or repressed memory but as constantly repeated violence). As such, she is denied any Freudian *Nachträglichkeit*. In other words, this is a trauma that cannot be circumscribed within the bounds of the past or of memory. This absence of the time lag built into the experience of trauma may obviate any place for poetic expression as a vehicle of remembrance and witness bearing. It also threatens to destabilize any coherent narrative set within a certain time and following the rules of cause and effect. To borrow an expression coined by Raya Morag, this kind of repetitive trauma establishes an antimemory.[95] It is a chronic trauma that is not-yet-memory, a trauma caught between what-has-already-happened and what-is-about-to-happen. Thus, Bialik in effect calls for overcoming a traumatic memory that, according to Shofman, intrinsically cannot be relegated to the bounds of memory.

This distinction is not rhetorical but essential, and it is connected to the spaces in which subjectivity meets gender. As a cultural symbol, masculinity overcomes its past (as it overcomes pitfalls and other obstacles), while femininity is obliged to oblivion, forgetting, and repression. As Julia Kristeva has shown, femininity is simultaneously repression and its refusal, that which is suppressed and the power that will not be held back, that undermines, bursts out, breaks through, and causes tumult.[96] And if to forget is really to cast off, as we were taught by the nineteenth-century French psychologist Théodule-Armand Ribot (1839–1916),[97] then being trapped in the depths of oblivion is not a mark of failure of the effort to overcome the traumatic past but is depressive anxiety in the sense defined by Klein, of fear of violating the weakness itself, of the loss of vulnerability. Shofman and Vogel, like Brenner in such works as *Nerves* (Atsabim) and *Breakdown and Bereavement* (Shekhol vekhishalon) and Agnon in *Only Yesterday* (Tmol shilshom), not only struggle with their failure to live up to the expectations of the Zionist enterprise and with their "doubts, dismissiveness, sarcasm and lack of faith regarding that vision";[98] they also set out a different conception of identity and gender (for men, not for women); and they mold a masculinity in which strength and weakness are different facets of identity, without the one necessarily cancelling out the existence of the other. Vulnerability, for Vogel and Shofman, is not "the shadow side of the worthy nationalist male";[99] their notion of identity is incapable of relinquishing the feminine and the vulnerable within themselves, and also sees no reason to do so.

Despite Vogel's and Shofman's centrality in Hebrew literature of the time, their multidimensional attitudes toward victimhood, masculinity, and nationalism remained at the margins of Zionist thinking. As Dan Pagis remarked, it seems that "under the blazing sun [of Eretz Israel], the 'dark gate' looks rather distant and hazy."[100] Indeed, after Shofman immigrated to pre-State Israel in 1938, he himself desisted from his poetic exploration of the meeting points between gender, victimhood, and national identity, and he published no additional stories about prostitution. The characters of Henia, Sutra, Stefka, and Olga were all fated to be left behind in Europe, the repressed land of Jewish exile. Trapped as they are in the space of Shofman's stories, they perhaps bear within them not only the key to understanding a multileveled and multifaceted conception of victimhood but also the potential for a different kind of thinking about traumatic subjectivity, time, memory, and history.

Chapter Two

Sepharadi Jewry in Pre-State Israel

*Ethnicity, Gender, and Sexual Violence
in the Work of Shoshana Shababo*

‿◠◡◠◜◠◞◠‿

Arachne's Legacy

At the center of Nitza Keren's *Like a Sheet in the Hand of the Embroideress:
Women Writers and the Hegemonic Text* (Kayeria beyad harokemet, 2010)
lies the mythological figure of Arachne. In Keren's book, this weaving spider
spins her story from her own bodily materials, and in so doing functions
as a fundamental icon for women's creativity in Modern Hebrew literature.[1]
The figure of Arachne, adapted to Jewish culture, represents a unique
feminine poetic stance, suggesting that creativity is an existential need for
Israeli women writers, and driven by a desire for *tikkun olam* (repairing
the world). Keren's book presents the work of literary weaving, while
discussing poetic and epistemological questions related to women's poetic
subjectivity. Keren is fascinated by the figure of Arachne, and especially
by the inherent bond between her physical body and the story she tells.

However, what Keren does not integrate in this somatic-poetic
space—that which is omitted from her representation of a feminine *tikkun
olam*—is the content of the story Arachne actually spins. In her competi-
tion with Athena, Arachne wove the story of the rape of Europa by Zeus.
Whereas Athena wove images of the Gods' glory and emphasized their
magnificent power, Arachne's work depicted the violence of the Gods

against women, which undermined the dominant narrative regarding the production of culture and civilization. According to Arachne's woven tale, human culture is based on male rape, physical domination, and brutality against women, and women's bodies are at the core and the basis of civilization. However, the discussion in Keren's book—as well as in much of the scholarly work about (women's) Hebrew literature, Israeli identity, and Zionist hegemony—ignores, obliterates, and perhaps even represses the story of violence and rape. In the words of Lynn Higgins and Brenda Silver, "Rape exists as an absence or gap that is both product and source of textual anxiety, contradiction, or censorship."[2] In fact, among the hundreds of pages of Keren's book, in the vastness of her fascinating discussions on major Israeli female writers, there is not a single discussion of the representation of sexual violence, the relationship between sexual trauma and writing, or the poetics of sexual abuse and objectification.

This chapter seeks to return indirectly and symbolically to the story Arachne spins and to her expressive artistic choice. To put it differently, I wish to relate to the shadow side of hegemony that Arachne's story actually reveals, and to focus on the literary work of the Hebrew writer Shoshana Shababo, who also weaves her female characters' bodies into their life stories—particularly, I should say, their violated and sexually abused bodies. Unlike many of the male writers I have discused in the previous chapter, Shoshana Shababo does not use sexual violence as a metaphor, a symbol, or a rhetorical device. Rather, she presents it literally, as physical and sexual violation. Such an insistence on taking sexual aggression literally, explain Higgins and Silver, "often necessitates a conscious critical act of reading the violence and the sexuality back into texts where it has been deflected, either by the text itself or by the critics."[3] Unlike the literature presented by Higgins and Silver, in Shababo's case the representations of gender-based violence appear on the surface of the literary text; the text itself reads the sexual violence that was overlooked or repressed in early twentieth-century Hebrew literature back into itself.

Shababo's insistence on writing about the veiled side of hegemony is "a burden of representation," a deliberate and conscious decision, which carries within it a sociopoetic awareness and responsibility. It is a commitment to the understanding of the role of literature and representation in processes of social and national regulations. Shababo's work reclaims not just the material and emotional wounds of women, especially Middle Eastern and Sepharadi women,[4] from their symbolic or absent position but also exposes the ways in which gender-based violence marks the "Daughter of the East." Thus, sexual violence is the prism through which Shababo looks at her Sepharadi community; it is used as a litmus test to examine the norms, traditions, and ideologies that make up her subjectivity.

In this chapter I argue that in contrast to the norms of her time and to the conventions of the Hebrew canon at the time, Shoshana Shababo's work presents subjugation and sexual violence against women in a plainspoken yet critical way. By so doing she not only reproaches the common depiction of women as sexual objects but also, and more importantly, represents and constructs a bodily (at times sexually) eth-nogendered subjectivity. Shababo thus embodies an unusual option, at the time, of a woman writer who insists on disengaging from the general attitude of euphemism in regard to ethnicity, female sexuality, and sexual violence, as well on rejecting the common attempts to sweep ethnic- and gender-based aggression under the rug as part of the effort to join the revitalized Hebrew literature and the evolving national ideology.

Shoshana Shababo was born in Zichron Yaakov in 1910 to a veteran Sepharadi family that settled in Safed in 1840.[5] Her father came from a Moroccan family, and around the same time that her father's family settled in Morocco, Shababo's maternal great-grandfather, Isaac Shalom Cohen Carstani, who came with his family from Iran, also settled in Safed.

Shababo wrote and published in Hebrew in Mandatory Palestine, mainly during the thirties and forties. Her first of two novels was *Maria: A Novel Concerning the Lives of Nuns in the Holyland* (Marya: Roman mehayey hanezirot baaretz),[6] published in 1932. The second, *Love in the Town of Safed* (Ahava bitzfat), was published in 1942.[7] Between 1928 and 1942 she also published about forty novellas and short stories in reputable periodicals of the time, such as *Bustenai, Haaretz, Doar Hayom*, and *Hadoar*. Despite her relative success in the early stages of her literary career, an expeditious process of ignoring her work began in the midforties, and as a result, Shababo's literary work is currently virtually unknown to both readers and scholars of Hebrew literature. For decades now, Hebrew literary criticism has disowned her work, which was omitted from the major literary lexicons and leading anthologies of Hebrew literature.[8] Shababo's work regained some notoriety in 1996 with the publication of the eminent book by Yossef Halevi, *A Modern Daughter of the Orient: On the Works of Shoshana Shababo* (Bat hamizrach hahadash).[9] This book, published over two decades ago, was the first, and so far the only, monograph dedicated to the work of Shababo. In 2002, seventy years after its first publication, the novel *Maria* was granted the Ministry of Culture and Sport Award for

Literary Masterpieces, and in 2009 the Israeli periodical *Hakivun mizrach* devoted a special issue to a selection of Shababo's stories.[10] In spite of this recent acclaim, the literature of Shababo, a Jewish Sepharadi female writer in the old Yishuv,[11] still constitutes a largely overlooked and understudied chapter of Modern Hebrew literature.

It should not come as a surprise that scholars and readers have disregarded Shababo's work. Women's fiction in prestate Israel is a scandal of so-called forgetfulness,[12] or rather, neglect and intended omission. If this is the case in women's fiction generally, it is even more so the fate of Sepharadi women's literature. Moreover, the disappearance of Shababo from the public consciousness is also related to the fact that her work emphasizes and focuses on various elements, themes, and sensibilities often excluded from Hebrew literature due to the utopian nature of nation building, which tends to uphold a sense of high moral ground and aspires to model itself on admirable ethical standards, thus precluding representations of violence and oppression. Shababo's acute awareness of race, ethnicity, gender, class, sexuality, and gender-based violence goes far beyond the literary and ideological norms of the Hebrew literature and Israeli culture of her time. Shababo, then, is not merely engaged in "the question of the oppressed status of the daughter of the Orient"[13] but rather creates a radical discourse, idiosyncratic in its strangeness.[14]

The violated bodies of Shababo's female characters, mainly those of the "daughters of the East," slip "through the net of writing to baffle representation," as Terry Eagleton puts it in his analysis of Samuel Richardson's *Clarissa*.[15] The violated body, the "appropriable Other whose place is to be always elsewhere,"[16] reclaims not its otherness but rather its "elsewhereness." To borrow Teresa de Lauretis's notion, Shababo establishes "a view from 'elsewhere.'" That elsewhere "is not some mythical distant past or utopian future history; it is the elsewhere of discourse here and now, the blind spots, or the space-off of its representation."[17] This chapter is an initial quest into the depths of the "elsewhere" created in Shoshana Shababo's oeuvre.

The Daughter of the East: Writing Ethnicity

Immediately after the publication of Shababo's first novel, *Maria*, the well-established author Yehuda Burla (1886–1969) published a review that came out not only against the novel but also against the author, the publisher, and the editor, Asher Barash.[18] How can we understand the harshness and even maliciousness of this review, written by a man in his midforties, who had been Shababo's mentor only a few years earlier? Burla grounds his criticism in arguments related to the aesthetics of the literary act. Certainly, literary aesthetics are not gender neutral, and thus it can be argued that Burla's criticism is yet another suppression of women's literature by male writers in the name of "'universal" aesthetic criteria. However, in order to understand the depth of Burla's negative reaction to the novel, we must return to the younger Burla—the man who had not yet published his first short story, "Luna" (1918).[19] Burla writes about this period in his life, "At that time I got closer to Brenner and his influence on me was tremendous. I gave him not only my work, but also my fate. I decided in my mind: if he is fond of my story ["Luna"]—I will write, and if not—I will cease [writing]. And I thought to myself, if, God forbid, [he] rejects my debut creation, I will be miserable all my life, because writing has become 'as a burning fire shut up in my bones' [Jeremiah 20:9], and without it my life would not be called life."[20] For Burla the young writer, the opinion of a major figure of authority had the power to paralyze the act of writing.[21] It is striking, therefore, that when Burla himself became (at least in his mind) Shababo's authority (as a sort of Brenner to Shababo), he chose to implement its destructive potential. In other words, he chose to cut off Shababo's literary career and attempted to subdue her spirit. Shababo fully understood the significance of Burla's review, and in a private letter to him she wrote, "I will frankly inform you! I knew the malice of your heart! You tried to ostracize me from the literary arena [. . .]. Your review, as well as your letter, did not break my spirit and I would continue writing all the more forcefully quite a few large and small pieces, and the future will judge between us."[22] Indeed, the future favored Burla, but Shababo should be commended for her resistance and her willingness to pay the immediate price for her literary choices, and for not bowing to the authorities of the time—as Burla was prepared to do.

Yosef Haim Brenner (1881–1921), of whom Burla was in awe, was not just a literary father figure but also the quintessential representative of the Second Aliyah (immigration of Jews to the Land of Israel, 1904–1914).[23] In other words, he represents Zionist Ashkenazi ideology. As demonstrated by Burla's self-subjection to Brenner's judgment, in his self-image Burla was a writer born in the mold of national Zionist sensibilities. Shababo's novel, in contrast, does not comply with the typical norms of national Zionist Hebrew literature. By refusing to join as a successor to the Brenner-Burla dynasty and tradition, Shababo in fact highlights the path Burla did not take (and perhaps even repressed, being so anxious to gain Brenner's respect). In practice, then, the "guidelines" Shababo allegedly violated are what allowed Burla to ignore the inherent tension between the national experience and the ethnic one, and to establish his impressive career as a Zionist Mizrahi writer who subjugated his Sepharadi experience to Zionist ideology.[24] In this sense, Shababo was to Burla an image of a threatening "repressed."

Moreover, in his influential article "The Eretz Yisrael Genre and Its Artifacts" (1911), Brenner outlines what he views as the desirable and appropriate aesthetics of Modern Hebrew literature,[25] and no doubt Burla's criticism was deeply affected by Brenner's call. According to Nurit Govrin, Brenner's call favors the artistic aesthetic role of literature over its social role in creating a new national culture.[26] This, obviously, was not Shababo's choice.

Despite the fact that Burla applied Brenner's sensibilities to Shababo, in rejecting the potential social capital of literature, Burla actually imperceptibly altered the content of this social dimension. Brenner's article refers to the faults of literature aimed at promoting Zionist ideas, but Shababo does not fall into this category. The social dimension of her work is reflected in her—unique in its time—attempt to articulate ethnic-gendered subjectivity. By criticizing Shababo through Brenner's prism, Burla, in fact, eliminates (or simply does not see) this dimension and favors the Zionist discourse. In other words, while on the surface it seems that Burla's review adopts Brenner's mainstream approach, it instead reflects (perhaps unconsciously) an oppression of a different kind: ethnic-gender oppression, both his own and Brenner's. According to Hannan Hever, this repression reflects the oppression that stands at the core of Brenner's article: the suppression of the local, of the ethnic. Hever writes, "Brenner's universalism leaves no room for ethnicity as an independent voice [. . .]. Instead, the ethnic must subject itself to essentialist, universalistic representation. Nationality and ethnicity therefore exist in a state of mutual alienation and even conflict. As a result, authors seeking to produce ethnic writing are banished from the dominant canon."[27] Thus, ethnicity (as well as gender) upsets nationality—it must be erased from national sensibilities. By concentrating on ethnicity and gender (women of the local East), Shababo highlights a twice- (perhaps thrice-) marginalized identity vis-à-vis the canonized identity Zionism wished to promote: that of women of the East, of all nationalities, religions, cultures, and social environments.

The historical irony of Burla's attempt at oppression lies, in part, in the fact that Burla's work itself actually suffered a similar mechanism of exclusion. This exclusion denied his Sepharadi and non-Zionist roots, which actually characterized his early writing in the twenties.[28] In his discussion of Yehuda Burla, Gershon Shaked mentions that "while in contact with the foreign world, and while negotiating the Arab world, Burla's protagonists are going through processes similar to those experienced by the protagonists of Berdichevsky in their encounters with the Christian world [in Europe]."[29] For Shaked (born in Vienna in 1929), the Arab world is an alien one, and even when dealing with a Mizrahi writer, he cannot imagine the involvement of a Jewish writer in this Arab world. Moreover, Shaked reads Burla's work through his familiar prism of the literature of the Ukrainian writer Micah Joseph Berdichevsky (1865–1921). Shaked projects the Judeo-Christian European world onto the environment of the Jewish-Christian-Muslim Middle East. This lack of historical, geographical, and cultural grounding is not the result of ignorance but rather is a consequence of Shaked's own Zionist sensibilities. Zionist discourse, according to Ella Shohat, "has, in a sense, hijacked Jews from their Judeo-Islamic political geography and subordinated them into the European Jewish chronicle of shtetl and pogrom."[30]

According to Shohat, the Zionist concept of "Jewish History" assumes a unified and universal conception of history that is basically Euro-centered, rather than multiexperiential from different periods and diverse contexts. While the Zionist idea was constructed in its European context, Jews in the Islamic world had a different cultural interface, which did not necessarily require a national articulation of their identity. Thinking in terms of a unified (Zionist) Jewish experience allows little room for a comparative study of Jews in relation to other ethnic and religious minorities, particularly in Muslim environments. The Zionist vision of a singular Jewish experience leads to a historiographical narrative that has little room to overlap with non-Jewish communities and, as Shohat writes, "thus, this narrative rejects the idea of hyphenated and syncretic Jewish cultures, as well as the notion of linked and analogous oppressions between Jews and various communities. The selective reading of Judeo-Muslim history, in other words, makes two processes apparent: the unproblematized subordination of Jews within Islam to a 'universal' Jewish experience, and the rejection of an Arab and Muslim context for Jewish institutions, identities, and histories."[31] In this context, it is fascinating to note that by locating her first novel, *Maria*, in a Christian environment in 1920s Haifa, Shababo creates an alternative to this dominant approach. The Haifa of this novel is not the envisioned new Hebrew-Jewish city, and although it is located within the territorial borders of the Zionist enterprise, it is indifferent to Jews, both old and new, and their lives.[32] The protagonist of the novel, Maria Geda, who is the daughter of a wealthy aristocratic Christian Arab family, falls in love with George, a poor, handsome Christian dancer. She becomes pregnant following a night of passion, secretly gives birth in Beirut, returns to Haifa with her baby son and her beloved nanny, who raises him then locks herself away in a convent, loses her sanity, and dies. Shababo's identification with Maria is not based on religion (Jewish) or nationalism (Zionism) but on neutral geography (Palestine with its diverse occupants), ethnicity, and gender ("the daughter of the Orient"). This intersectionality is extremely foreign to Hebrew literature of the time.

Moreover, in contrast to two of her leading contemporaries, Yitzhak Shami (Hebron, 1888–1949), and Burla (Jerusalem, 1886–1969), whose writings address Zionism intensively, Shababo does not establish her poetic subjectivity as either embracing or rejecting Jewish nationalism. Zionism has very little presence in her two novels, and even in her stories it has no dominant presence. Indeed, although some significant exceptions exist, such as the stories Shababo published during and following the 1929 Palestine riots (Meoraot Tarpat) and the 1936–39 Arab revolt in Palestine,[33] most of her work is not embedded in the standard Zionist narrative of a singular Jewish experience. Shababo locates her work in various geographical, ethnic, and religious contexts. Her characters live in a Christian city and in a Jewish colony; they are Muslims, Christians, and Jews; they are ultraorthodox Jews from the Old Yishuv, as well as Jewish pioneers; they come from different socioeconomic backgrounds; they are robust or wounded in body and soul. In other words, Shababo does not directly articulate her agenda as pertaining to the repression of various gendered, ethnic, and religious aspects of her Sepharadi identity, but her work sets interrelated identity as an axis in a nonhierarchic way. None of these axes has a preferential status; rather, they interact on multiple and often simultaneous levels.[34]

Many times the multidimensional identities Shababo creates are defined by territoriality: her characters are related to geographic locations, especially Palestine and its surroundings (Damascus, Morocco, Beirut). Geopolitics, explains Indira Karamcheti, "determine the understanding of the terms Third World and woman: curiously, where you are is what you speak, and what you mean is where you are."[35] Through this geographical context, Shababo's work also perceives ethnoreligious identity, as well as socioeconomic status. Ethnicity, as well as economic affiliation, gender, or class, is not static but varies depending on the context. Shababo places her characters in different locations within this ethnic space. These positions lead, at times, to conflicts or struggles with their surroundings, and also, at times, to negotiations and dialogues with them. Exposing an ethnic-gendered experience (i.e., exposing the tension between ethnicity, religious, class, and gender) as one that, in its very definition, incorporates conflicting and sometimes contradictory entities enables Shababo to expand the boundaries of her own ethnicity. Not only is the Sepharadi woman's experience not seen as a stable and unified experience, it is also not perceived as being confined to any specific religion, nationality, or geographic location. It exists within a sphere of plurality and intersectionality.

Sexual Violence and Ethnogendered Subjectivity

Despite this experience of intersectionality, in Shababo's work, gender seems to function as the main anchor for much of the characters' identity. Shababo's fiction portrays ethnicity as dynamic and flexible, whereas gender (and class) is far more rigid, perhaps because gender is depicted primarily through the body—mainly women's bodies—which remains the site of oppression and abjection throughout. Further, Shababo's characters constantly struggle to find balance in diverse worlds. The manner in which they navigate their multiple and layered identities reflects the experiences and perceptions of sociocultural factors that influence their lives. The struggles faced by the characters occur through the vehicle of their bodies. In this, the body becomes a site of power and agency but also an arena of subordination.

More specifically, Shababo identifies gender-based violence as the main element that binds her various characters: male characters are its perpetrators, and female characters are its victims. In contrast to the predominant nature of Zionist literature, which perceives Judaism and national sentiment as the unifying elements of its community, Shababo portrays gender-based aggression as the scarlet thread that runs through her character's lives. This perspective allows for many different intersections of gender with geography, religion, ethnicity, and nationality. Shababo's "universalism" does not shape a coherent sequence of different Jewish communities but rather reveals the recurring gendered power dynamics present within diverse geographical, ethnic, and religious contexts. This does not diminish the impact of other dimensions of life experience; if anything, it probably has the opposite effect. As Kimberlé Crenshaw argues, the experience of intersectionality for black women is more powerful than the sum of their race and sex, and any observations that do not take this intersectionality into consideration cannot accurately address the manner in which black women are subordinated.[36] The same must be said for Shababo's characters.

Sexual violence thus reveals a widespread female experience, but at the same time, it exposes the ways in which specific social identities are connected with a specific social oppression that is manifested in different ways (e.g., racism, heterosexism, sexism, ableism). More specifically, it uncovers the point of intersection of gender with ethnicity (as well as with class, race, and religion).[37] To put it differently, sexual violence is a widespread female experience, and it is not an exclusive phenomenon to a particular ethnicity. Nevertheless, Shababo places the sexual violence in her writing mainly among the daughters of the East. Her choice in representing the Middle East might stem from her intimate acquaintance with this world, but more than that it is also a conscious sociopoetic decision. Despite the universality of sexual violence, and regardless of Western stereotypes of Eastern violence, Shababo represents the world of Middle Eastern women as an extreme case of social fringe: these women are abandoned to their fate because of the harsh social, cultural, and economic conditions that exist in the Middle East. Hence the intersection of ethnicity and gender in Shababo's work becomes remarkably powerful.

Furthermore, since sexual violence crosses ethnic boundaries, Shababo's literary depictions of sexual assault challenge ethnicity itself. The very act of creating a discourse about sexual violence against women, especially one emerging from women's perspectives, is in conflict with hegemonic approaches to Mizrahi femininity. Thus, the net of identities Shababo spins as a Sepharadi female writer in an eastern European masculine Hebrew culture raises questions that link gender to ethnicity, status, and power. Shababo's work does not create a hybrid identity but rather reveals the asymmetrical dimensions that construct female oriental subjectivity in Palestine between the two world wars. Likewise, Shababo does not present a simple fusion of various aspects that create a new identity (either oppressed or subversive) but rather exposes the forces and social constructions that establish various intersections of identity.

Shababo's story "Honeymoon" (Yerach-dvash, 1932) illustrates the dominance of the ethnic dimension in her work, as well as the inextricable relationship between gender, sexual violence, and ethnicity.[38] The story describes the short trip of Zalman, the son of Golda the widow, from his *moshava* (agricultural colony) to the city in search of a bride. Golda is a new immigrant, probably from eastern Europe, who, after the death of her husband "bought this land with her powers and her money. She planted an orchard, constructed a big farm, built a home . . . a home in Israel."[39] Golda the peasant woman represents the *halutz*, the Jewish pioneer, who settles and subsequently develops the Land of Israel. From a Zionist perspective, the gendered disruption—a female rather than male pioneer; a widowed single mother rather than a heterosexual nuclear family—threatens the idealized future of the (national and family) project. Other aspects of the story also go against the Zionist grain. The son Zalman, the next generation, "remains a cripple, his head smaller in comparison with his body. His brain is underdeveloped, and he is not too normal. Zalman is defective in his mind."[40] In the Zionist context, which linked the revival of the nation with its strength, disability (especially male disability) represents the ultimate failure and dooms its subjects to marginality.[41] Yet the solution to this "obstacle" appears in the form of Mazal, an orphaned Yemenite, who will marry Zalman.

Mazal's gendered, economic, ethnic, and cultural inferiority is prominent throughout the story. The power dynamics at play between Mazal and her new family are revealed in full force throughout the story, as the readers and Golda are exposed to the way Zalman and Mazal met. The story is told through the unreliable perspective of Zalman, and the bride seems, at times, actually to be a prostitute: she works at a French Hotel built by the deputy of Rimo, "who built a hotel in every city in which he visited."[42] Mazal "approaches the tables without shame" and "she is paid";[43] her lips are painted red and she wears "vulgar silk stockings and patent leather shoes."[44] The subtle suggestion as to Mazal's "occupation" is very significant in the discussion about sexual violence and ethnicity in the work of Shababo. Regardless of the different approaches to the question of choice and consent in prostitution, most current feminist scholarship recognizes the overwhelming physical, emotional, ethnic, and financial violence inherent in prostitution. Hence prostitution, by definition, is an act of gender-based violence.[45] Even what seems to be Zalman's marriage proposal is described in terms of a barter: the farm for sex. After they get married, Mazal's life continues as it had been previously: "The bride is busy with the housework, just the way she used to do in the hotel."[46] Marital life, then, is experienced as a variation on her work in the hotel, as either a prostitute or as a servant.

Just as in the story "Samson at the Harvest Season" (Shimshon beonat habatzir), which I will discuss soon, the Zionist pioneering dream (to "build a home in Israel"[47]) is exposed in its full concreteness as a web of intersecting exploitations. Shababo presents a so-called successful personal, ethnic, and national narrative. At the end of the story, Zalman is happy, his mother and his wife live in peace, "the heart of the widow is grateful to the giver of such happiness," and the earth is blessed—a hint at fertility in the marriage.[48] But this happy ending—just like most of Shababo's work—actually reveals the sexual, class, economic, ethnic, and gender oppression and exploitation that construct this idyllic scene.

"While Bending She Could Not Bring Herself to Grasp the Land": Zionism and Sexual Aggression

The story "Samson at the Harvest Season" (Shimshon beonat habatzir, 1932) describes the sexual exploitation of an Arab female laborer by a Jewish pioneer.[49] This sexual violence, followed by representations of (sexual and national) strength and arrogance on the pioneer's part, does not symbolize a romantic Orientalist desire for the Other, or a wish to immerse the foreign self in the authentic local. Rather, it represents a conquest among other conquests comprised of brutal force, aggressiveness, and invasiveness. The "desire of the pioneers" for the Land of Israel displays itself, according to Boaz Neumann and others, among other things, through erotic manifestations, such as lying on the ground, embracing, and kissing it.[50] Unlike Neumann, whose study emphasizes the pioneer's potency, Andrea Siegel, in her analysis of L. A. Arieli's and Aharon Reuveni's representations of rape and the "Arab question," rightly points out that the element of the latent sexual savagery in modern Jewish selfhood—"the intensely virile male, not the physically weak, enervated male—has largely been overlooked by scholars of gender and Zionism."[51] The aspects of brutality and coercion regarding Zionist "conquests" have been overlooked in favor of a romantic framing, whereas Shababo presents this savagery as unmitigated by national sentiments.

Shababo reveals the ethnogendered, oppressive, and noninnocent dimension of "the pioneer's desire," as if addressing in the thirties the points that Siegel would later argue.[52] Siegel also asks "what might be the sociopolitical ramifications of the New Jew's strength/weakness in terms of virility and sexual control."[53] It seems that Shababo was dealing with a similar question. She does not bow down to the sublimations that underpin the "desire of the pioneers," and instead of representing it as a romantic and erotic relationship between the pioneer and his virginal, beloved female land, she describes such "desire" in terms of concrete nakedness—namely, by representing a Jewish male pioneer sexually coercing a female Arab worker.[54]

The protagonist of "Samson at the Harvest Season" is characterized by a lack of education and wisdom: "He was a kind of Samson, burly violent, with brave arms, iron muscles, and a big hollow head."[55] His courage and passion for agriculture mark him as an appropriate pioneer, who "becomes cheerful at the sight of sweat, labor, and effort."[56] He is indeed the muscular Jew for whom Zionism was so desperate.[57] The rest of the description reveals the androcentric dimensions of such a concept: Samson does not speak much of his bravery, "but on one type of bravery he did like to talk: the bravery of conquering hearts." The euphemistic nature of conquering hearts is soon revealed: one of his "conquests" is the silent Arab worker Fatima, who "obeyed him out of surrender, did not defy Samson for his exploitation and did not slip away from his arms when needed. [She was] good and devoted."[58] Here the text seems to hint at a so-called egalitarianism, in which each participant in the brutal scene has a role to play, each a type of "devotion" suitable for his or her gender. Thus, the Arab's being "good and devoted" obscures her suffering and commits her subjectivity to performing her role in a national project that is completely alien and irrelevant to her.

The heroic act of pioneering in Shababo's story is written therefore as a narrative of sexual exploitation, in which the hero's point of view is heavily ironized. The Philistine Delilah from the biblical story of Samson (Judges 13–16), who caused the death of Samson, is reimagined in Shababo's modern variation as a powerless Arab worker. The biblical Samson was an unusual judge. He avoided the leadership of his people and acted alone against the Philistines, engaging in personal acts of conquest and revenge. Despite the negative messages hidden in the story, the biblical text, as well as the national memory of the story, do not condemn his actions. Shababo, however, joins the sages who condemned Samson for his persecution of women: "Samson followed his eyes, therefore Philistines put out his eyes."[59] In this way she further exposes the inextricable connection between sexual violence and national exploitation.

The biblical story of Samson and his Philistine women (the woman from Timnath, the whore from Gaza, and Delilah) links their betrayal to the national-military struggle of Samson with the Philistines. The motivation of the women's perfidy and of their violence, notes Ahuva Ashman, is confined in the biblical story to social and national interests, and is not linked to the potential anxiety of the women who are victims of violence and rape as a result of the victory of the enemy. Ashman indicates that it could be that perhaps money was not the main motivating factor that convinced Delilah to betray Samson—rather it was her fear of the "Philistines rulers" who came to her house (Judges 16:5), just as the Timnath woman fears the men who threaten to "burn you and your father's household to death" (Judges 14:15).[60] Despite this hidden aspect, the biblical story presents Samson as the one who is sexually vulnerable: by shaving his hair, Delilah removes his source of strength and potency. Thus, marrying a foreign woman is perceived not only as an attack on the social order that will cause Samson's downfall but also as an act that will reverse his gender.[61]

The Zionist Samson in Shababo's story converts this gender complexity and sexual vulnerability into simplistic and straightforward sexual aggressiveness. Daniel Boyarin argues that modern Jewish culture has assimilated the macho male ethos of Western civilization. The result is the creation of the "muscular Jew," which divorces Jewish men from a more traditional emphasis on study, prayer, and gentleness. The Zionist movement saw the "effeminized Jew" as a pathological product of the Diaspora. Zionism (and psychoanalysis) is guilty of inducing processes of westernization and modernization that set aside traditional feminized Jewish male paradigms for a vision of the "New Jewish Man."[62] Half a century before Boyarin formulated his argument, Shababo observed a similar conversion in the Zionist movement. Her story articulates a historic moment in which weakness and vulnerability are transformed into entitlement, aggression, and violence. Control and ownership are central values in that mindset, and that includes a masculine sense of entitlement over women. In this state of mind everything becomes subjugated to the success of the Zionist project and to the establishment of its male protagonist's identity. This dims and even justifies the aggressive dimensions of this stout new Jew.

As part of the mentality described by Boyarin, the biblical figure of Samson was warmly adopted by Israeli intellectuals and artists such as Abba Kovner, who, while serving as an education officer during the 1948 War, named his unit "Samson's Foxes." Shababo sheds a different light on that same Samson: neither his national heroism nor his sexual vulnerability is at the center of her exploration. Shababo, the Jewish daughter of the Orient, identifies with Fatima, the Arab daughter of the Orient (as well as with Delilah, the Philistine daughter of the Orient), who "while bending could not bring herself to grasp the land."[63] The Arab worker cannot obtain and own the land, neither in the sense of stability nor in the sense of national and personal safety. Her contact with the land passes through her agricultural services to the national enterprise, and through the violence of the "new owners" of the land: "Secretly, a little fear came into her heart, from this Jewish burly [Samson], who in one motion might squash her to the ground, and with one of his fingers could splash her blood."[64] Likewise, the Arab worker's relationship to the land is not through her nativeness, although she is a native, but rather through her violated body that nourishes the land for the benefit of others. She is conceived as a mere instrument, and is forced to comply with her instrumentalization.

Thus, in the very few times that Shababo does actually refer to the Zionist project, as in the story of Samson, she integrates the female body, especially the violated, abused, defeated female body, into the national story. She looks at it through an ethnogendered prism; what she sees is not a national *tkuma* (the revival of the Jewish people) but sexual and financial exploitation—namely, yet another variation of the way in which national/masculine interests establish themselves through gender-based violence. "The narrative, image, and story of female rape," claims Mary Layoun," is not exclusively a 'woman's' story. It is a social and political story."[65] Accordingly, Shababo's representation of desecrated female subjectivity (here and in many other examples, as I will later discuss) exposes bodily violation, and situates sexual violence as part and parcel of social and national power and agency.

Nativeness: Shoshanah Shababo and Esther Rabb

Shababo's intense preoccupation with gender, sexuality, and sexual aggression—as a native Hebrew speaker from a Sepharadi family of five generations in Eretz Israel,[66] "the first Israeli woman writer born in *Erez Israel*," and "a pioneer of female Hebrew Mizrahi writers, and perhaps the first *Eretz* Israeli writer"[67]—only heightens the comparison with Esther Rabb, the first female Hebrew poet born in the Land of Israel (1894–1981, Petach Tikkva), who also often engages with questions of sexuality and gender.[68] But despite some overlap, the differences between the two are enormous. Rabb came from an Ashkenazi family who emigrated to Palestine in 1876 from the Hungarian village of Szent István, whereas Shababo's Sepharadi family settled in Safed in the early nineteenth century.

While Esther Rabb's poetry describes a sunny, bright Eretz Israel (and not Middle Eastern) landscape, wild and awe-inspiring in its newness, as well as powerful female and androgynous figures, Shababo's novels take place in monasteries and the dark streets of Haifa and Safed, and depict oppressed womanhood and dominant patriarchy. Whereas Raab celebrates the experience of the new Jewish woman in the East, situating her in a primordial scene with open horizons and options, Shababo situates her women in enclosed and domineering confines. Furthermore, Raab identifies with the Zionist experience, and her poetry depicts the details of the landscape of Eretz Israel for its beauty, wilderness, cruelty, and charm. Jewish settling and belonging in the land stand at the center of her poetic agenda. Generally speaking, Zionist literature of the time tended to move away from the city and the urban, focusing instead on the new sights in which Zionism materialized and whereby the identity of the new Jew was constructed. Shababo, on the other hand, rejects this Zionist experience; it seems that the Zionist landscape of Jewish settlement, with its social configurations (the Kibbutz, the agricultural colony, the working group), are foreign to her, while the urban scenery, with its traditional configurations of family and society, are much more familiar.

Unlike her contemporaries, such as the poets Rachel Bluwstein Sela (known simply as Rachel), Nathan Alterman, and Avraham Shlonsky, all of whom immigrated to Palestine, Rabb represents the Zionist ideal of nativeness.[69] According to Dan Miron, unlike the abstract yearning of the immigrants for the Land of Israel and their anxiety about "belonging," Rabb's poetry reflects a natural connection to the Land.[70] Hamutal Bar-Yosef notes that Rabb has a corporeal connection to the Land of Israel that is related to her childhood memories, which makes her depictions of the land noticeably solid and vivid.[71] Indeed, Hannan Hever and Hamutal Tsamir criticize this romantic perception of nativeness, claiming that such a discourse veils the power dynamics that construct it.[72] Hever states that the discourse of Jewish nativeness insists on presenting Zionists' "natural" ownership of the land, and by so doing, works to obscure a colonial project. He also shows how nativeness itself marks the paradox of Zionism: on the one hand, it is a beginning, a new undertaking, a way of cutting off the past, and on the other, it is a continuation of the past. Hence Zionist nativeness is an element of a contradictory identity, marking itself as both an origin and an eternal presence simultaneously. Nevertheless, this issue is a major theme for Raab, who collaborates in the construction of this imagined nativeness as her authentic subject position, and offers an exemplary model of a new Jewish identity.

Unlike Rabb's Zionist nativeness,[73] Shababo's Sepharadi subjectivity does not act on behalf of the national interest and is not driven by the need to prove ownership of or belonging to the Land of Israel. Maybe this is the reason Shababo cannot (or does not wish to) join the eastern European obsession with conquering the Land. "*Kibush*" (conquest) was the slogan of the Zionist movement from its inception in regard to various projects, such as the conquest of the land, of labor, and of guarding.[74] In Shababo's writing, as I showed, the *kibush* has also become a sexual conquest. Shababo, whose subjectivity is not established on the negation of the Diaspora, wanders in the Land of Israel and its surroundings as a daughter of the East, with no ambiguity regarding her place. Raab, though born in Palestine, carries a Jewish postmemory of exile, and hence celebrates her so-called nativeness. In fact, Shababo is a very unique and unusual case of that time: a Hebrew writer who does not carry the burden of exile as a formative experience, and yet is not part of the Old Yishuv. In effect, she represents an unfamiliar model of a new Jewish woman.

Moreover, Shababo—as a Jewish Sepharadi woman—has been part of this place for five generations, so when she occasionally interacts with the literature of the pioneers and with Zionist attempts to mark the land as Jewish, she experiences the Zionist enterprise as invasive and aggressive. The Zionist project is perceived not as redeeming but as a yet another variation of (sexual) violence.

"Quivering and Withering in Her Lusts": Female Sexuality

Shababo's novel *Maria: A Novel Concerning the Lives of Nuns in the Holy-land* (Marya: Roman mehayey hanezirot baaretz) describes the alleged failed attempt of Maria to live her life according to her own standards, ignoring the strict norms and expectations of her surroundings. For class reasons, Maria, who comes from a wealthy and aristocratic family, cannot marry the simple man she loves. She gives birth to their son in secret, and in order to avoid a forced marriage or shaming of her family, she joins a convent. Generally speaking, patriarchy marks women's bodies and sexualities as the greatest threat to their subjectivity and cultural dominance; yet it also acts as the major "object" with which they can trade—whether as part of a marriage that will bring social and economic comfort or within the framework of prostitution.[75] Maria's decision to join the convent can be seen as a variation of this trade, because although her sexuality is neutralized, she still conforms to patriarchal systems through the symbolic act of marriage between nun and Holy Spirit. At the same time, the choice to join a monastery is also a choice that refuses marriage, as her symbolic marriage to God allows Maria to refuse to trade her body and her sexuality.

Furthermore, since Maria is unable to regain control of her life, she chooses (or is forced), perhaps paradoxically, to position her control (or imagined control) in relation to her body. At the monastery, her body becomes the main site of events, and controlling it enables her to shape her life. Life in the monastery allows her to remain loyal to her loved one (even if their love cannot rematerialize), to raise her son (albeit only partially and in secret), and even to partially fulfill her sexual desires, as I will soon show. Hence in some ways, despite the fact that she has exchanged one oppressive space (her father's house and her potential husband's house) for another oppressive space (the convent), she herself remains a desiring subject and is no longer simply an object of desire.

In other words, despite her rigid environment, Maria manages to break free and find a heterotopian space of existence that separates her from her oppressive environment. Moreover, by wandering the streets of Haifa, Maria actually evades the power of the monastery. Hence, one may argue that Maria in fact does not exchange her father's house for the monastery; rather, she has created an intermediate zone that is neither her father's house nor the monastery. I refer here to the space between the monastery and the slum where Maria's beloved nanny is raising her son. The novel reveals much about the actual and emotional adventures Maria experiences in those streets. Walking in the city, according to Michel de Certeau, is a speech act: "walking affirms, suspects, tries out, transgresses, respects, etc. the trajectories it 'speaks.' "[76] This urban space, hence, becomes a geo-mind space. Maria finds a way to do "poaching," to use de Certeau's notion, and to take advantage of loopholes and opportunities in order to express herself as an autonomous subject. This is an extraordinary subversive stratagem: an alleged nun, who is really a "perverse" woman, not a virgin, and even a mother—a so-called holy sister who secludes herself in a monastery but also constantly moves around the city.

In both of Shababo's novels, as in much other women's literature, the female body is represented in its duality, both as subject of patriarchal control and as an autonomous body (i.e., not as male property but as an actual material site of desire and action). Maria fulfills her desire with her lover, but social constraints drive her to escape to a convent, which, like any monastery, is a feminine space controlled by male power and authority but also a space that enables Maria to lead her idiosyncratic life. In a similar way, the protagonist of Shababo's novel *Love in the Town of Safed* marries against her will but refuses to consummate her marriage and eventually flees with her lover. Women's bodies are thus traded and objectified in patriarchal social context, but at times they also find ways to escape this oppression. This duality allows Shababo to formulate her criticism, and to work for social change at the same time.[77]

The duality of a subjugated subjectivity with a sense of agency, which, as stated, enables Shababo to convey her critique and to establish alternatives of action, experience, and identity at the same time, reflects, perhaps, her uniqueness in relation to Yitzhak Shami and Yehuda Burla, the two most prominent Mizrahi writers of her generation.[78] Shami and Burla also dealt with the status of women in the Middle East from a Mizrahi perspective,[79] but their literary work did not construct significant conceptual or material alternatives. Indeed we can find in some of Shami's and Burla's works an awareness and sensitivity to women's plight, but their work lacks a significant poetic, emotional, or concrete horizon for women to imagine and model their lives on.

Burla's renowned story "Luna" (1918) and Shababo's *Maria* (1932), for example, engage in a seemingly similar subject: the dismal situation of women in traditional patriarchal societies. "Luna" describes the miserable life of poor orphaned Luna, who is convinced to marry a man much older than herself who falsely presents himself as wealthy and generous. Two scenes in *Maria* seem to echo "Luna." At the beginning of the story, when Luna has not yet found her match, the narrator mentions that "she could, theoretically, take upon herself to become like one of the nuns—she supposedly does not desire any man. But how shall she bear the insult? She is a 'spinster,' who has not found her 'good fortune' [*mazal*—referring

here to finding a groom]."[80] Luna could have been "like one of the nuns,"
but she marries a much older man, suffers, and is left poor, divorced, and
with a child to raise.

Shababo implements Burla's proposal, and in the hope of a better
fate, Maria indeed becomes a nun. But this solution also fails in many
respects: Maria suffers and does not find peace in her life in the convent;
she dies, and is forced to leave her son with her parents. Thus, she seems
to not have been able to reap any reward from her decision to rid herself
of her oppressive family and society. However, the monasticism Shababo
presents from a female perspective is very different from that described
by Burla (that being a nun indicates lack of a desire for a man). This
difference is present not only in that the nun in Shababo's novel "vowed
on her virginity, while a mother"[81]—namely, she was a woman with sexual
experience—but also in how her monasticism does not counteract her
sexuality or suppress her rebellious spirit.

The fictional character of Sister Maria allows Shababo to articulate
one of the most radical scenes in Hebrew literature: a female masturbation scene. This scene corresponds with Burla's indirect description of
a male's orgasm in his story "Luna": "Sometimes when Luna stoops her
body and wipes the floor, it happens that a white-pinkish stripe gleams
and is revealed for a moment from under her dress—and a flow of warm
blood passes then through the body of Mula Ovadia; his heart quivers for
a few minutes with gentle and comfortable poundings that are followed
by weakness and fatigue in his entire body."[82] Both Burla's and Shababo's
descriptions of masturbation are radical for their times.[83] However, Burla
describes masculine sexual satisfaction while glancing at a young woman:
namely, he describes a voyeuristic erotic pleasure that stems from a
position of power. Hence, he does not in fact display a major deviation
from hetronormativity: it is "typical" for a man to experience sexual
satisfaction by viewing the "white and pink" underpants of a woman.
Shababo, on the other hand, represents female masturbation and desire,
and hence transcribes something that is culturally repressed by definition.
Her description reads,

A strange desire hit her [Maria]—to stay naked . . .

An inebriating smell faded from her flesh. Pleasant warmth
spread from it . . . all of her limbs trembled. Her heart strongly
throbbed . . .

She leaned back on the soft pillow and tickled her rosy nipples . . . she started burning up [with passion] . . . she sat upon the bed . . . then jumped up and sat upon the small statue of Jesus—quivering and withering in her lust . . .

[. . .]

While recalling that [her sex with George], she rolled up her nightgown over her white thighs. . . . Her trembling hand slipped slowly and softly on her small and erect breasts, on the soft pink nipples . . .

She entertained herself with stimulating and annoying imaginations that at times had quieted her storm a little.[84]

The posture of Jesus carrying the cross along the Via Dolorosa, or of Jesus on the cross, is converted in Maria's masturbation with her lying on the icon. This is a revolutionary imitatio Christi, during which Maria becomes Christ and the cross at the same time. Although Maria follows Christ's steps, her journey does not redeem her; despite her Via Dolorosa, she remains bound to her "cross": her body, her love, her background.[85]

What is unique in Shababo's writing, then, is not merely that she addresses Oriental female subjectivity, but rather that she incorporates female sexual desire, in her own time and place. She disregards or defies the social taboo about sexuality in general and female sexuality in particular. In her memoirs, Shababo testifies that they were five sisters, all who knew how to manage the household, "But about sex, *who knew*? Who dared to think? There was a taboo at our house about all sexual matters. I never saw my father kiss my mother, or put his hand on her. So I grew up with great ignorance about sex."[86] Yet Shababo's narratives do not take place in exotic, unfamiliar places, where unusual practices may occur. She places her characters in her own time and near her own environment. Needless to say that if sexuality in general is a taboo, female sexuality is all the more taboo in Shababo's sociocultural milieu. Therefore, the representation of female sexuality in the novel is of crucial importance, and it is a rare and extraordinary moment, with broad implications beyond Hebrew literature.[87]

Shababo portrays female sexuality as not structured around masculine desire. In a variation on Laura Mulvey's notion of the male gaze, Shababo's female Oriental character is not constructed for the pleasure of the (male/ Ashkenazi/Zionist) viewer.[88] Unlike Burla's Luna, who is displayed as an erotic object for the man whose sexual attraction is linked to voyeurism and scopophilia, Maria, as both the object and the subject of desire, is both subjected to her perspective and is the subject of her own desire. Maria herself is the object of the erotic description, the person looking on her body is she herself, and she is the one smelling her flesh and feeling the warmth of her body. Shababo, as if responding to Hélène Cixous's call four decades later, reveals that which is hidden in the "dark continent" of female sexuality, established by the male gaze as hidden in the dark due to the threat it carries.[89]

Moreover, Maria's masturbation is concentrated in the breast that is twice described as pink and rosy, just as in Burla's story "Luna." But while in Luna's case the pink refers to her vagina, the sexual organ that is related to man's penetration, and it is revealed to his desiring gaze, in Maria's case pink and rosy describe her breasts and nipples, and there is no male gaze involved in the scene. Maria herself takes her clothes off and rolls up her nightgown. Women's breasts, according to Luce Irigaray, are the erogenous alternative to the vagina. They express the "sex which is not one," namely, the diffusion and fluidity of female sexuality, which exists in various organs. Woman's breasts challenge the masculine central-ized phallicism and engender a different libidinal configuration as well as distinctly feminine knowledge.[90]

It is also important to note that the sexual description in the mastur-bation scene focuses neither on intercourse nor on the female genitalia as the main location of pleasure. While Shababo maintains the heterosexual structure of sexuality within a marriage, the "consummation" of this mar-riage between Sister Maria and Jesus takes place through female sexuality that does not define itself through the act of penetration.

Andrea Dworkin argues that the act of sexual penetration is one of major and grave social significance: "There is never a real privacy of the body that can coexist with intercourse: with being entered, the vagina itself is muscled and the muscles have to be pushed apart. The thrusting is persistent invasion. She is opened up, split down the center. She is occupied—physically, internally, in her privacy."[91] Intercourse, according to Dworkin, is a unique reality for women as an inferior class. It is a reality that includes, among other things, breaking boundaries, losing control, subjugation, and destruction of privacy, with all these built in as normal and even vital for the existence of mankind. Hence, "the political meaning of intercourse for women is the fundamental question of feminism and freedom: can an occupied people—physically occupied inside, internally invaded—be free; can those with a metaphysically compromised privacy have self-determination; can those without a biologically based physical integrity have self-respect?"[92] Shere Hite also makes a connection between the ability of women to be in charge of their (sexual) stimulation and their ownership of their own bodies, and to be autonomous human beings.[93]

Thus, while exposing the repressive dimension built into hetero-sexual intercourse, Shababo constructs a rare moment of Oriental female sexuality. The manner in which her characters (such as Maria and the protagonist of the novel *Love in the Town of Safed*) struggle over their sexualities is entwined with their ethnogendered political oppression.[94] Relinquishing intercourse and focusing on auto-erotic female pleasure through the masturbation scene both constructs female sexuality as a viable option and differentiates between repressed sexuality dominated by various elements (gender, ethnicity, class) and sexuality as an invigorating and liberating territory.[95]

Sexual Violence(s)

Like many radical stories, this rare moment of female sexuality in *Maria* is not rooted in some Sepharadi redemption but instead works to further the representation of yet another sexual repression. In one of her confessions to Father Gregor, the head priest of her monastery, Maria faints and then, "pale and trembling [Father Gregor] caught the fainting Maria and affectionately petted her shapely face. He caressed her gentle limbs and his heart pounded inside him. [. . .] His hands were lost in the thicket of her hair. [. . .] With trembling hands he removed his black robe and embraced her body to him: 'Why did you come to disturb me? Ah, a snake, a viper, came to seduce me!' [. . .] And he squeezed her with all his strength to his heart."[96] Maria wakes up and slowly understands the sexual nature of the situation: "She was horrified, it was the same fear that terrified her then, at the ball, while alone with George at the yard. 'You are terrible, my Father!' [. . .] 'It is beneath your dignity, Father!' She yelled and pulled back."[97] A little further in the novel, just after the masturbation scene, Maria herself initiates a sexual encounter with the priest ("'You come to me!' She dared utter"[98]), and, abusing his power, he accepts the invitation. Mary Gail Frawley-O'Dea explains that since priests and nuns are members of the inner family of the church, sexual relationships between them, even if they are consensual, represent incest.[99] Furthermore, in this case, because of the power dynamics between Maria the nun and her head priest, Maria, by status, is in a less powerful position than the priest. Hence, even if we do not accept the incest metaphor, and even if the relationship seems consensual, it is still sexual exploitation on the part of the priest because of their unequal status.[100] Maria's masturbation thus becomes a turning point—from the first sexual violence that she experiences with Father Gregor to an internalization of that violence in his second sexual violation.[101] In other words, female masturbation is positioned to duplicate sexual aggression, and it is unable to exercise female sexuality free of suppression.

The defeated site at the end of the Sepharadi-feminine trajectory is the result not of a wrong choice but of the failure built into this identity. In Catharine MacKinnon's words, "If sexuality is central to women's definition and forced sex is central to sexuality, rape is indigenous, not exceptional, to women's social condition. In feminist analysis, a rape is not an isolated event or moral transgression or individual interchange gone wrong, but an act of terrorism and torture within a systemic context of group subjection, like lynching."[102] The novel *Maria* presents several stories of sexual exploitation: the pastor rapes and harasses Maria, who also suffers from street harassment ("The whippersnapper continued to follow her. In the dark he began whistling with his lips and making masculine coarseness"[103]); Maria's brother takes their orphaned servant as his mistress, and after he impregnates her, he abandons her and travels to Paris, where he attempts to rape his cousin Lily;[104] and Syria, George's sister, is exploited emotionally and sexually by a rich young man and poisons herself when he leaves her.[105] Of the four women whose narratives tell the stories of sexual abuse, one loses her mind and dies in agony, another commits suicide, and two others disappear from the plot.[106] While the novel, then, explores the stories of different women, from various ages, ethnicities, classes, and religions, they all find themselves, at the end, in the form of the defeated and depleted body. These different identities intersect at the place where the female body appears as a site of male oppression and exploitation, and in moments of sexual violence. The various ethnic and gender-based assaults they experience shape the contours of their lives into a continuous sequence of oppression, invasion, and trespass, which seem to be pervasive in their Oriental ethnic and social milieu.

By focusing on those shared experiences, Shababo's work brings together the lives of women from different and seemingly distant milieus of the Orient between the two world wars. While MacKinnon reveals sexual aggression to be the universal experience of women, Shababo's work exposes the ethnic oppression and sexual violence as a systematic, paradigmatic expression of general violence in Sepharadi women's lives. Sexual violence is the extreme and harsh portrayal of the continuous and consistent control and oppression of women, which makes use of their bodies and their sexualities.[107] As such, it becomes a central prism through which the world is experienced in Shababo's work. This prism thus reveals the ethnic, national, religious, and familial systems as variations of gender-based oppression. In this way, sexual violence becomes the "Urtext" of Shababo's ethnogender subjectivity.

I wish to emphasize that I do not argue for a feminine experience per se but rather for an ethnic-gendered experience. Even though I have explored representations of sexual violence in Shababo's work in a way that might seem at times universal, Shababo, in fact, does not expand her gaze beyond the Orient she is familiar with. Most of her work deals with the "daughters of the East," and therefore the various representations of sexual violence and oppression portray these aspects as central to Sepharadi women's life. In that way the ethnic dimension is added to the seemingly "universal" representations of women. Thus, in the context of a Zionist society, as in the story "Samson at the Harvest Season," the inferiority and sexual exploitation of Fatima is depicted as related to her Arab identity, and even another (Western) woman, Rosa, participates in turning a blind eye to the sexual violence and exploitation of Fatima. But even where there is no Zionist gaze, such as in the novel *Maria*, in which the "daughter of the East" wanders within her own surroundings, she is a victim of exploitation and oppression. In other words, the exploited women and the Oriental environment converge and create a kind of ethnospecific femininity. The intersection between gender and ethnicity thus does not intend to obscure crucial differences between these identity categories, or to compare ethnic oppression to sexual subjugation. Rather it emphasizes both the interplay of various categories and the multidimensional experience of sexual violence and ethnic repression at the same time.

Conclusion

One of the scenes in the novel *Love in the Town of Safed* (Ahava bitzfat) occurs on the Jewish holiday Lag BaOmer, at the *hillula* (fest) of Rabbi Shimon bar Yochai—Mishnaic-era rebel against Rome and author of the

Zohar—on Mount Meron. Shababo does not take part in the Orientalist discourse, and she does not describe "the exotic" habits of the Orient, the melody prayers, the simple joy of dancing, or the traditional food. By contrast, she describes a very difficult and violent scene that takes place during the crowded celebration. Rabbi Yochanan sees the Sepharadi widow Yael, and "fishes her from the waves of women. He grabs her arm and pulls her after him, he pushes her into a hidden corner. And his hands, as usual, pinch and tickle between her shoulders and shins."[108]

Andrea Siegel mentions that "rape in late nineteenth-and early twentieth-century Jewish literature—as in many literatures—is often structured on hints, requiring the reader to fill in gaps, to focus on the unstated as much as on the author's words. Rarely can the reader arrive at a defined narrative of the events, which are signified by the absence of details."[109] In light of this, it is remarkable that Shababo depicts this sexual assault so directly. Moreover, in her oeuvre Shababo names and describes a wide spectrum of sexual violence against women in Mandatory Palestine. She portrays rape, sexual harassment, and gender-based aggression in many forms: sexual exploitation of Sepharadi women by Ashkenazi men ("Honeymoon"), of Jews toward Arabs ("Samson at the Harvest Season"), as well as sexual violence within the Sepharadi community itself (*Love in the Town of Safed*), and within the Christian community (*Maria*). Considering that writing about sexual violence "often means writing against the fear and pain that surround the topic; [and] also means acknowledging the anger,"[110] Shababo's writing is not just unique but also brave.[111]

But then again, the Mount Meron *hillula* is a Sepharadi-characterized domain, hence the violation of Yael the widow is not only a case of gender-based violence but also violence that relates to her ethnicity—to her experiences as a woman living in a traditional Sepharadi community. Feminists of color criticize the idea of "womanhood" as a universal subject and challenge the ontological and epistemological premises of Western feminism, which claim to be blind to color.[112] Identities are viewed as multiple, often characterized by an intersectional experience. A GendeRace approach advances the view that identities are constantly influenced by social relations based on gender and race.[113] Most of the discourse on gender focuses on white women while it conceives of itself as universal. The main failure of white feminism, according to feminism of color and Third World feminism, is its inability to acknowledge the racial-class-ethnic element of gendered identity. White gender studies conceptualize the experience of (white) women without seeing how race, class, and sexuality construct gender. Moreover, critical race theory suggests abandoning the idea of gender as the major axis of analysis and suppression, to which further suppressions are added later. Feminism of color thus rejects the focus on a disguise of "color blind" gender and instead highlights the complex intersections of sexuality, ethnicity, and femininity in various sociocultural margins, dismantling the centrality of (white) gender.

The intersection of various axes of identity allows one to address the complexities that slip away when focusing only on gender (in that way, for example, from a national and militaristic perspective, Jewish female settlers are in a better power position than Palestinian men, but from a gender perspective they might be in a more vulnerable position). Through the prism of sexual violence and sexual abuse, Shababo exposes various points on the spectrum of power relationships, thereby highlighting multiple experiences of oppression. In that way, for example, while Yael the widow is in a GendeRace inferior position, Golda the widow is in a gender inferior position in the face of the Zionist enterprise, but at an ethnic and economic advantage in relation to the Yemenite Mazal. At the same time, by focusing on sexual violence, Shababo depicts the complex array of Sepharadi and Oriental women's experiences in racialized and gendered sites, situating them as within their class, religion, and ethnicity as well. Within this complex space, women negotiate their own subjectivity and mediate social definitions. Their gender and ethnicity, as well as their violated bodies, create their biographies. Shababo tells these biographies, so to speak, of her female characters—unique and private stories that are also always communal.

Chapter Three

"Do Not Bandage the Wounded"

*Wounded Soldiers and Nonconsensual Relations
in Israeli War Literature*

~~~~~~

Man, damn it, is born to die and not to be paralyzed. A good soldier,
a soldier loyal to his people and his homeland, must return home
healthy, or be killed on the battlefield. A wounded soldier, crippled,
paralyzed—only complicates life for everybody.

—Dan Ben-Amotz, *I Don't Give a Damn*[1]

Who thought, even for a moment, that I would find myself in hospital. During the days of anticipating [the war] I thought of only two
possibilities: death or return home [from the war] unscathed. But
not of any intermediate road. What do people who've never been
hospitalized in their lives know about hospitals and what it means
to be wounded? When they announce on the radio or in the paper
some incident or accident, and follow with numbers of dead and
wounded, we only pay attention to the dead. Nobody takes much
note of the injured. I was no better than the rest.

—Yaacov Haelyon, *A Doll's Leg*[2]

How can we avoid the disabled? They exist!

—Dan Ben-Amotz, *I Don't Give a Damn*[3]

In 1969, the writer Uriel Ofek edited an anthology titled *From the War: Fiction and Poetry* (Min hamilchamah: Siporet veshirah). In his introduction, he explains that the book includes literary works about "the wars of the IDF [Israel Defense Forces] in its twenty years," and he presents the list of topics that appear in those writings: "love of the homeland, friendship and comradeship, adherence to the mission, the conquest of fear, the yearning for peace, and the grief over fallen comrades."[4] This topical summary holds nothing unexpected, except for that which is notably absent from the themes Ofek covers: the subject of the wounded soldiers.[5]

Certainly, readers of Hebrew literature are familiar with the wounded soldiers—both male and female—in Gershon Shofman's short story "A Sanatorium for Soldiers" (Beit havraah lehayalim, 1952). More specific characters, such as Michael, who was injured during the 1948 war from Yehudit Hendel's story "His Memory Was Damaged" (Zikhrono nifga, 1950) and Nissim, the disabled veteran from Yehudit Hendel's novel *Street of Steps* (Rehov hamadregot, 1955), might also be recognizable.

But these characters do not stand at the heart of the plot and they are not well-developed characters. Until the publication of Yoram Kaniuk's novel *Himmo, King of Jerusalem* (Himmo, melech Yerushalayim) in 1966, Hebrew literature was almost devoid of major representations of wounded soldiers. *Himmo*, along with several successive texts that brought issues of injury and disability to the fore, such as Shalom Babayoff's *The Seventh Glory: A Fighter's Story* (Hazohar hashevii: Sipuro shel lohem, 1968), Dan Ben-Amotz's *I Don't Give a Damn* (Lo sam zain, 1973), and Yaacov Haelyon's *A Doll's Leg: A Story of a War Injury* (Regel shel bubah, 1973), will serve as the focal point of this chapter.

In Yaacov Haelyon's essay "That's How I Was Injured," which was written while he was still in the hospital recovering from wounds sustained during the Six-Day War, he recounts the moment of his injury, and writes that "from the moment I was injured, I felt like I was subordinate to the war; as a disturbing factor. In the battle, there is no time for the wounded. As horrifying as it sounds, they disturb, keep other fighters busy, and may even endanger them. So I felt lonely."[6] Haelyon explores the cold pragmatism of the inability to tend or relate to the soldiers that were injured during the war, but his words are also representative of a wider cultural attitude toward the wounded. In a short story about the 1948 war, published by Amitai Etzioni, the narrator is left to wrestle with the implications of being given a military order "not to bandage the wounded."[7] The command stems from pragmatic reasoning: the soldiers in battle must concern themselves with fighting, conquering, and staying alive themselves, and not lett anything—or anyone—stand in the way of that goal. However, the order haunts the story's narrator, not allowing him peace, as it contradicts basic ethical and moral humanistic standards in a world that stands apart from the cold determined rationale of war. The story prompts a direct discussion about morality and behavior in times of war but also bears deeper implications about the issues surrounding the exposure and concealment of those soldiers wounded in war. Hebrew literature has traditionally conformed to the national tendency to glorify war and those who conduct it, and therefore often plays into more lauded and iconic images of war by depicting mainly the heroes—and the fallen— of battle. Hebrew literature itself fails to bandage its wounded; it ignores and marginalizes them in an attempt to keep the glorifying rhetoric of war straightforward.[8]

Hebrew literature is rife with stories of fallen soldiers. Moshe Shamir's *He Walked Through the Fields* (Hu halach ba-sadot, 1947), S. Yizhar's *Days of Ziklag* (Yemei tziklag, 1958), and Yehudit Hendel's "The Sons' Grave" (Kever banim, 1950) are a few of the well-known examples of canonical texts that tackle this subject as a central theme. In a culture that centralizes war and the role of the military, one may ask why literature ignores the soldiers that were injured in the war and treats them as a "disturbing factor." Are they, too, not examples of the heroic spirit that is demanded and heralded regarding soldiers on the battlefield? Who exactly are they disturbing, and what is the nature of that disturbance? Moreover, in Zionist literature that prefers its soldiers either counted among the heroes or counted among the fallen, what meaning is conveyed through the rare representation of wounded soldiers, and what intention, if any, can we discern through these patterns? These questions are underscored by a trend that seems to accompany the representation of war injury, involving questions of sexuality after physical injury,[9] and, more specifically, the development of sexual relationships with nurses and caregivers.

When a nurse-patient relationship develops into a personal and sexual relationship, it becomes, by definition, inappropriate, violating ethical obligations in regard to crossing professional boundaries and sexual misconduct. The National Council of State Boards of Nursing defines sexual misconduct as "engaging in contact with a patient that is sexual or may reasonably be interpreted by the patient as sexual; any verbal behavior that is seductive or sexually demeaning to a patient; or engaging in sexual exploitation of a patient or former patient."[10] Sexual misconduct can also

apply to additional behaviors as well, including kissing, suggesting or discussing the possibility of dating, having a sexual or romantic relationship
prior to the end of the professional relationship, or soliciting a date with
a patient, client, or key party (immediate family members).

And while noting the professional obligations of medical or caregiving staff, it is important to note that workplace violence and predatory
behaviors *toward* health care professionals is much more common than
the reverse. Healthcare workers (particularly nursing staff) are most frequently the object of patients' violence, including sexual harassment and
gender-based violence.[11] And indeed, with the exception of *Himmo, King
of Jerusalem*, in all other representations of the war-wounded in Hebrew
literature, the injured soldiers are the ones who sexually harass the nurses.
Further exploration into the intersection of disability and sexual violence
in Israeli war literature of the 1960s and early 1970s is critical, and this
chapter seeks to interrogate the various problematic aspects of this particular dynamic.

"In a World of Dark Horrors"

Hebrew literature often deals with Israel's wars, and with soldiers as its main
characters. Therefore, the scarce representation of IDF soldiers wounded or
injured is puzzling.[12] This omission bears out a profound cultural repression, with deep and abiding ramifications as to how disability is viewed
culturally. It might be explained in several ways, all related to "a world
of dark horrors," to use Yaacov Haelyon's turn of phrase,[13] whether that
be the threat of disability in general or the potential threat that it poses
to militaristic Zionist ideology.

Rosemarie Garland-Thomson suggests that disability gathers us
into the everyday community of embodied humankind. It forces people
to confront potential vulnerability and mortality, as well as the fact that
disability is inherent to the human condition.[14] Furthermore, Martha Albertson Fineman explains that disability exposes the connection between
vulnerability and dependency, defining dependency more broadly as a
human need for care. In a liberal social order founded on the myth of
the autonomous subject, bodily, mental, or intellectual vulnerability is
intimidating. Recognizing that all human beings need some form of care
and might experience it in differing ways becomes a threat, a fact of life
that society seeks to repress, for its own comfort.[15]

In a national context, this generalized anxiety becomes embodied in a different way, especially as the wounded become a concrete visual reminder of the lingering costs of war.[16] Ortsion Bartana claims that the novel *Himmo, King of Jerusalem* communicates "the feeling that the [new] state [of Israel] not only solved problems but also created problems,"[17] and Yael Munk notes that the novel "depicts the slaughterhouse of the War of Independence, [. . .] and points an accusing finger at the government, which is interested in creating a heroic text for the Israeli ethos."[18] Cultural representations tend to dichotomize the sacrifices made in war into two distinctive categories: the dead (i.e., fallen heroes who gave their lives and service to their nation) and the wounded (the living reminders of potential lost). In other words, while the figure of the *living-dead*—the youthful warrior sacrificed on the national altar, who haunts the nation's consciousness—emphasizes pain, guilt, gratitude, and acceptance of the unpreventable sacrifice on the altar of the nation, the image of Himmo as a *dead-living* emphasizes "the account of disappointments versus promises,"[19] namely, the frustration and dire consequences of the political situation.

Yaacov Haelyon fought in the War of 1967 in the Golan Heights and was wounded in the battle of the Tel Faher outpost.[20] He survived his initial wounds as an amputee, now blind in one eye, and with temporary trauma covering the rest of his body. Yaacov Haelyon documented his personal experiences of the injury, his adaptation to his prosthesis, and his rehabilitation process in his book *A Doll's Leg: A Story of a War Injury* (Regel shel bubah).[21] After the book was published in June 1973, it immediately became a bestseller and an iconic heritage book of the Six-Day War. In the book, Haelyon addresses the sense of anxiety that his disability provoked among his friends, and the myriad of ways it confronts common cultural narratives about the cost of war. He writes, "I didn't know whether anybody would be interested in the story of how I was wounded. Perhaps people preferred the drunkenness of victory, without its by-product called: the price."[22]

This tension isn't limited to Haelyon's friends; Haelyon recounts a conversation between his daughter, Tami, and his wife, Yael, writing, "In an hour-long intimate tête-à-tête with Yael, who is sitting next to her [Tami's] bedside before she falls asleep, [Tami] confesses her fears: 'I don't want what happened to Daddy to happen to me. I will never, never, be a soldier.' "[23] This scene appears immediately after the description of Tami's first encounter with her father's prosthesis. The prosthesis, which functions as a visible symbol of disability, is an accessory that is simultaneously an integral part of his functionality while also being literally external and detached from him; it is also something that tries its best to mask that which is now clearly gone (a limb), and in doing so, it becomes a sort of symbol. The wounded soldier's body becomes a site for unconventional attitudes regarding national discourse that regrets the "price" of the war but does not question its necessity.[24] Tami's anxiety in her conversation with her mother is a simple truth about how societies disguise or obscure the wounded after war; the very existence of injured soldiers not only raises questions about the "price" of the war but also possesses the potential to disrupt narratives about the justification of war.

In her book *States of Injury: Power and Freedom in Late Modernity*, Wendy Brown explores how a sense of woundedness might become the foundation for politicized identity.[25] Thus, paradoxically, the presence of wounded soldiers in Hebrew literature—even if it is limited—can also be understood as literary rhetoric that constructs the Israeli soldier as vital and just, and not only as a victim of war or the price the nation must pay for survival. Judith Butler, who was deeply influenced by Brown's book, suggests that a violent act is, among other things, a way of relocating the capacity to be violated elsewhere, in perpetuity, thereby producing an appearance that the subject who enacts violence is then impermeable to violence. The accomplishment of this invulnerability becomes one aim of violence; by injuring the other and then noting the injured *as* other, one can scaffold a rhetoric of superiority and invincibility while further marginalizing the other. This specific process of normalization occurs when the violence is "justified" as "legitimate" and even "virtuous," even though its primary purpose is to secure an impossible effect of mastery, inviolability, and impermeability through destructive means.[26]

The representation of the disabled soldiers in Hebrew literature facilitates two distinctive moves: that injuring the other "passes off" vulnerability and confers immunity, and simultaneously, that in injuring another, a mirror is held up to reflect back inevitable vulnerability. In reading narratives containing disability representation, the Israeli reader subconsciously wards away potential injury, while at the same time, the presence of the disabled—and the great anxiety it confers—allows the reader to confront and perhaps even help process this anxiety. In other words, the literary text enables its readers to become "defined by its injury (past) and injurability (present and future),"[27] that is, to be in an omnipotent position of invulnerability in thinking about their own futures, while also possibly risking acknowledgment of their inevitable mortality. Either way, as Butler reminds us, "the production of the subject on the basis of its injured status then produces a permanent ground for legitimating (and disavowing) its own violent actions."[28]

"You Easily Fall in Love with the Nurse"

It's a strange world—a hospital. A miniature world. It's all contained in the room where they put you. There is no status, or differences, between patients. A nurse is an angel. A doctor—a supreme being. You easily fall in love with the nurse, and esteem the doctor for every tiny little thing.

—Yaacov Haelyon, *A Doll's Leg*[29]

Yoram Kaniuk's novel *Himmo, King of Jerusalem* (Himmo, melech Yerusha-layim), published in 1966, takes place in St. Hieronymus's monastery in Jerusalem, which is converted into a military hospital during the siege of the city in 1948–49. The novel tells about the young nurse Hamutal Horowitz, who falls in love with Himmo Farrah, one of her patients. Himmo is a soldier suffering from grave wounds, who does not speak other than to murmur "shoot me" over and over. Throughout the novel, Hamutal's feelings toward Himmo become complicated and entwined with questions of the ethics of euthanasia, until, at the end of the novel, she administers his fatal injection.[30] The novel gained tremendous popularity in Israel, and in 1986 was even adapted for a film directed by Amos Guttman and starring Alona Kimhi and Dov Navon.

In the novel, Himmo is described as someone who has lost human semblance as a result of his mortal injury: "Right leg missing, left leg missing, one arm missing from the elbow, the other hand missing from the wrist; lacerated belly; a madman's drawing of a human form; crushed stumps of limbs; a trunk swathed in bandages; blue shrapnel marks, some embedded in the flesh and some skin-deep; red, gaping wounds, and the stink of rotting flesh [. . .] yes, and his eyes were missing, too. [. . .] two empty, crumpled sacs. [. . .] *God, what's holding all these shattered fragments together? What's keeping this dismembered body alive?*"[31] Himmo is initially objectified and reduced to a literal list of his body parts—those that remain, as well as those that are missing. Throughout the novel he is depicted as being "as good as dead all along,"[32] and thus seems to lack any agency whatsoever. Intense and life-threatening war injury is often seen as a liminal area between life and death. The sense of threat to life, which was real in the battle (imagined or real), is preserved in the cultural representation of the injured even when their lives are no longer in imminent danger. This position may express the horror in the face of human vulnerability, and preserves the ableist attitude that assumes that abled-bodied identities and bodies are preferable, and thus, is what all people truly desire. The "broken body," according to this ableist reasoning, makes life incomplete and therefore comparable to—if not worse than—death. To use Robert Murphy's words, "The notion that one is better off dead than disabled is nothing less than the ultimate aspiration against the physically impaired, for it questions the value of their lives and their very right to exist."[33] Therefore, the death of Himmo by euthanasia is seen as an act of kindness: the nurse's final act of benevolent grace, rather than murder.

Like other wounded soldiers in Hebrew literature, Himmo is portrayed as a helpless sick person more than an injured person. Haelyon describes this feeling during his rehabilitation after being injured, writing, "You're in a degrading situation in which everybody can give you orders. Your voice or opinion carries almost no weight. 'A Case'—not a man with senses, desires, a soul and pride. You must wear the pale blue pajamas, the uniform—I almost said convict garb—of patients, which blurs any sign of personal identity."[34] Hebrew literature focuses on the stages of suffering within the hospital: blood, surgeries, medications, and attempts at healing rather than the posthospitalization or recovery phase, in which someone is working to integrate back into their life. Hebrew literature addresses soldiers working hard to regain their autonomy and independence (and thus "humanity") after injury. What we lack are characters (and real-life role models) who have moved passed this "rehab" stage and are doing other things. Hebrew literature thus preserves disability in a state of dependency and helplessness, even when the disabled people themselves are no longer experiencing their disability in such an immediate and painful way. For example, we do not know anything about Ben, the protagonist of Shalom Babayoff's novel *The Seventh Glory: A Fighter's Story*, or Yaacov Haelyon after they left the hospital. Since in Hebrew literature, as mentioned above, there are almost no wounded soldiers, it is interesting that when we finally find some, they seem to lack agency in their own experiences of injury and then fade into the background when they might instead be working to reclaim or redefine their own embodied experiences. What does this representation serve? Why does Hebrew literature insist on treating disability as a life "less than" that is situated in a constant state of helplessness or as an additional hurdle to be overcome rather than relating to disability as a collection of complex and multifaceted experiences?

Since disability is perceived as a disease, and as a state of helplessness and lack, it is rooted in descriptions associated with being childish and feminine.[35] Mitchell S. Tepper explains that "disabled populations are not viewed as acceptable candidates for reproduction or even capable of sex for pleasure. We are viewed as child-like and in need of protection."[36] This view of effeminized and asexualized characters with disabilities also has a long history in Hebrew literature. In Devorah Baron's story from 1909, "Leizer-Yessel," for example, Leizer-Yessel has only one hand and no facial hair. His disability is depicted as linked to his impotence and is perceived as harming both his learning and his sexuality.[37] Similarly, in Shmuel Yosef Agnon's story "Ovadia the Cripple" (Ovadia baal mum) from 1921, Ovadia is limping, amputated, and using a crutch. His limp symbolizes his impotence, and it enables the effeminization of his masculine disabled body and the subsequent mockery that he endures, signified in passages such as the following: "Immediately two young men came and took the crutch out of the amputee [Ovadia], and put it in between his legs."[38]

Due to the sociocultural links between disability, effeminacy, and infantility, the disability of wounded soldiers in Hebrew literature seems to be examined and evaluated through the lens of male sexual potency. In most cases, sexual potency quickly becomes warped, manifesting itself in chauvinism and sexual exploitation and, more specifically, through sexual relationships between the wounded soldiers and the female characters around them . . . most often their nurses.

Israel Hameiri's 1972 story "Beer Sheva Is Close" (Beer Sheva krova) describes two soldiers, a driver and a paramedic, who are transporting a wounded soldier from the battle zone to a hospital in Beer Sheva and on the way pick up a young female hitchhiker. The wounded soldier is described as slowly losing his life: his pulse is weakening, his lips are frothing, and his hand is cold. As the wounded soldier's life drains away, however, the sexual tension in the car between the three "lovers"—the driver, the paramedic, and the hitchhiker—increases and builds. When the hitchhiker first gets into the car she is unaware of the injured soldier, but when she becomes aware of him, the paramedic is quick to allay her anxieties. This moment, however, becomes the first time that the paramedic (speaking in first person in the following passage) views the hitchhiker in a sexual way: "The girl keeps looking at me. Her breasts are pressed against the back of the chair. I glance over at the wounded [soldier], check his pulse again, touch his bandage that has moved. But as if remembering something, I suddenly come back abruptly and look at her. Her parted lips, her firm neck. Long and firm. Flexible. Her T-shirt, tattered stripes of blue and red, carelessly wraps her firm breasts. The dark, delicate slit went a little down her neck, into the opening of her shirt, inside. [. . .] Slowly I reach out and touch her cracked lips."[39] The sexual tension in this scene is literally mediated through the presence and the body of the dying wounded soldier. The paramedic's touches to check the wounded man's pulse and his bandage are distracted by an urge to reach out and caress the woman's lips; as the wounded man's pulse weakens, the paramedic seems filled with his own sense of virility, life, and sexuality with each heartbeat. In this way, the medic's sexuality becomes symbolically linked to the helplessness of the wounded soldier. It is as if he is reassuring himself—and the female character—that although a corrupted male body is present, it does not mitigate the other whole and able male body. It is a form of distancing himself from the wounded soldier.

This short story, and others like it, only augments my preoccupation with questions about the wounded and disabled body in Hebrew literature. Why are wounded soldiers largely ignored in favor of heroes—both living and dead—and when an exceptional reference is made, what purpose does this representation serve? Furthermore, what lies at the root of the poetic choice to associate representations of disability with sexuality, especially when desire and sexual tension is so often tied up with the role of caregiver or nurse?

I am interested in the "fantasy of disability," to use Jeffrey Preston's term, that is, not the true lived experience of people with disability but rather the dominant cultural projections on disability, "the unconscious fantasies circulating in representations of disability,"[40] and the role these fantasies play in Israeli culture. In other words, I am interested in the connection between heterosexuality and abled-bodied identity—"compulsory able-bodiedness," as Robert McRuer suggests[41]—in general, and more specifically, in the juxtaposition of gender-based violence and disability in the representation of wounded soldiers.

Disability in the Heterotopian Hospital

At the center of this investigation stand three works of literature concentrated on physically wounded soldiers that I have referenced above: Yoram Kaniuk's *Himmo, King of Jerusalem* (Himmo, melech Yerushalayim,

1966), Shalom Babayoff's *The Seventh Glory: A Fighter's Story* (Hazohar hashevii: Sipuro shel lohem, 1968), and Yaacov Haelyon's *A Doll's Leg: A Story of a War Injury* (Regel shel bubah, 1973). All three books are set within a hospital. This fact in itself is not surprising, because, as various scholars have shown, Israeli cultural images of people with disabilities are largely seen through a medical model of disability.[42] Disability is perceived, above all else, as a personal tragedy, and the images focus on the efforts to integrate back into "normal life," which often simply seems to be code for "able-bodied life."[43] Therefore, these representations generally offer a narrative of overcoming disability (instead of accepting, embracing, or celebrating it), often reliant on the virtue, courage, and determination of the disabled person. This underscores disability's representation as a personal issue rather than a broader social or political one, and situates an individual's willpower at the center of their recovery narrative.

Saying that, considering the hospital as a liminal space for such narratives opens up other possibilities. The hospital functions as a uniquely heterotopian space that contains a paradoxical capacity to be simultaneously bounded and permeable.[44] It becomes a site of social control where alternative and transgressive social orders emerge and are contested. As Russell West-Pavlov explains, "The hospital is a discourse-generator, a place where the 'truth' about disease is engendered—and not revealed, or found, as common sense would suggest. The relationship between the institution, the architectural space, the discourses which circulate around that institution and the knowledge produced there and taking effect upon the inmates is a complex and multi-directional one."[45] Acknowledging the hospital as a heterotopian space, then, enables the novels to construct and express a variety of approaches to disability within a uniquely formulated social order.[46]

Not only do all three novels find common ground in their setting, but they also all depict sexualized gender-based violence, related to the relationships between the wounded soldiers and their nurses. The heterotopian nature of the hospital as a space of multiple orderings unveils the myriad of ways in which Hebrew literature imagined disability and sexuality in the late sixties and early seventies. Although most of the texts discussed in this chapter were written by disabled authors who were wounded in wars—Kaniuk was injured during the 1948 war, and Babayoff and Haelyon during the 1967 war—disability is discussed here solely as a narrative device rather than a matter of personal identity, thus becoming what David T. Mitchell and Sharon L. Snyder have termed a narrative prosthesis.[47] In other words, I do not explore disability as a concrete life experience but rather as a symbolic figure that enables culture to define and validate its norms. As Sarah Rainey notes, "Representations reflect social attitudes, but they also set limits of possibility—they help define what is socially imaginable."[48] Accordingly, the following discussion will also address how sexual exploitation, via the "romantic" relationships in these books, prevent the subject of disability, as a multifaceted and lived experience, from entering into the public consciousness of Israeli society.

Himmo, King of Jerusalem

"LIKE A YOUNG GIRL BEFORE HER FIRST INTIMACY"

As previously mentioned, the novel *Himmo, King of Jerusalem* (Himmo, melech Yerushalayim) depicts Himmo, a severely injured and disabled man, in hospital after battle and the nurse Hamutal, who falls in love with him and eventually ends his life. The book describes Hamutal's emotional and sexual attraction to Himmo as an almost naïve infatuation. After the initial shock from the sight of his critically wounded body, Hamutal does not look at Himmo with the eyes of a nurse but rather as a young woman almost hoping to fall in love:

> It was a dismal scene [. . .] and she, who only a moment ago had been counting [Himmo's] missing limbs like an undertaker, all at once became oblivious of the dismembered trunk and was entirely captivated by [Himmo's] open mouth [. . .]. It was a beautiful mouth (to her last day, Hamutal would blush whenever she recalled how beautiful it was). Her horror at the sight of the body quickly dissipated as the mouth, to her eyes, turned into the acme of perfection [. . .]. *A mouth dripping kisses!* [. . .] A delicate mouth, somewhat feminine [. . .]. She felt a touch of utter purity, as though she had stripped herself of her material being, leaving herself naked like a young girl before her first intimacy.[49]

The novel continues with equally vivid imagery of not only Hamutal's love and sexual attraction to Himmo but also her eventual sexual encounter with him, as Kaniuk writes,

He saw Hamutal lay a trembling hand on [Himmo's] strip of forehead exposed between the bandages and leave it there a moment or two, and then, as though she was struggling between a dream and reality, between reverie and wakefulness, she slipped her hand slowly down to the mouth and let it hover the contour of the lips. With infinite gentleness she parted the lips, delicately probed for the tongue with her fingers, stroked the smoothness inside the mouth, passed a barely touching finger over the white teeth. In the pale glow of the kerosene lamp the act seemed to stretch out endlessly [. . .]. "The mysterious paths," she inwardly called [the cleft between Himmo's lips], just as she called the junction of the lips at each corner "the mouth's secret" and the tiny triangle "the crown."[50]

By sexually penetrating her finger into Himmo's mouth, Hamutal is sublimating a heterosexual act of penetration, during which she enacts gender role reversal: Hamutal's fingers become phallic, and the lips around Himmo's mouth turn into a kind of female genitalia.[51] Adia Mendelson-Maoz suggests that this gender role reversal enables Hamutal to break out of her own otherness as a woman.[52] However, it seems to me that this reversal is meant to emphasize a change to Himmo's positionality, rather than Hamutal's, as Himmo's disability culturally effeminizes him, and makes him someone who can be penetrated, and even assaulted.

Throughout the novel, as mentioned, the relationship between Hamutal and Himmo is described in relatively typical terms as one of falling in love, attraction, sexuality, and marriage. On the face of it, the novel relates neither to the fact that Hamutal exploits her position as a nurse and in fact sexually harasses Himmo, nor to the fact that she has sex with him despite his inability to refuse or consent to it. Himmo never actually expresses his consent to the relationship with Hamutal, though it is unclear whether or not the disability itself is what is fully preventing him from doing so. Scholars of Hebrew literature also do not address these dimensions in the novel. Mendelson-Maoz, for example, claims that "within the temporary and bizarre space of St. Hieronymus's monastery, the novel succeeds in presenting a wonderful reciprocal relationship between Hamutal and Himmo."[53] Describing the relationship between Hamutal and Himmo as "reciprocal" ignores the depiction of Himmo throughout the novel as lacking agency, and hence overlooks both the nonegalitarian power relations between the (abled-bodied) nurse and her (disabled) patient, and the sexual exploitation inherent in their sexual encounters.

However, the novel itself does not completely ignore these complicated dynamics. Himmo's bed is called *mitat sdom* (Sodom's bed; a procrustean bed). Sodom's bed is an expression that refers to a condition that limits the possibilities of action, derived from the biblical story from Genesis that tells of God's decision to destroy the city of Sodom and its inhabitants because of their great wickedness, which is expressed in various social sins, from homosexual relations to sexual violence to a lack of hospitality.[54] Himmo is in a hospital bed, but the image of the bed as a Sodom's bed immediately renders him as a victim akin to the victims of violence in Sodom, thus painting the nurse as one of the victimizers. Thus, while Hamutal's devotion to Himmo is seen on the surface of the novel as "a paragon of womanhood and motherhood,"[55] and as the embodiment of a "holy martyr,"[56] in a deeper layer of the novel, when Hamutal sleeps with Himmo on his Sodom's bed, she sexually exploits him because he cannot express consent, and the novel presents this as sexual violence that turns Himmo into someone who can be penetrated.

The invocation of the term *Sodom's bed* itself immediately places the reader in the mindset of homosexuality, based on the context of the biblical story. In the Bible, homosexual violence is depicted not only as a crime against an individual but also an inversion or perversion of social gender standards and expectations. A sexual encounter between men in the bible, explains Ahuva Ashman, seemingly changes the gender of the penetrated man, forcing him to perform a victimized, feminine position. The masculinity of the active/penetrating man is proven through the denial of their rival's masculinity, as the man has been humiliated and defeated as a woman through the rape. Thus, homosexuality in the ancient world is a code of violence and submission. Biblical homophobia does not stem from concerns about the otherness of a different sexual orientation but rather reflects anxiety about violent servitude of men by other men.[57]

Hence, when Hamutal violates Himmo on his Sodom's bed, she not only transforms herself into a Sodom man (i.e., a violent man), but she also "degenerates" him into the status of a woman and intensifies his otherness.[58] The sexual violence against Himmo, then, reinforces the femininity of the disabled body. While this depiction ostensibly allows for a surface reading of sexual violence, it simultaneously codes the sexual violence in a way that exposes the novel's ableist attitude of disability as a feminine and vulnerable position. Similar to the scene in which Hamutal penetrates Himmo's mouth with her finger, the use of the image of Sodom's bed depicts disability as inherently lacking agency. It is this fear of "becoming" Himmo and being passive, penetrated, and humiliated that creates a cultural standard for aggressive chauvinism for wounded male soldiers in other literary representations.

The fear of feminization and exclusion from the national discourse and sphere becomes realized as Himmo, the ultimate wounded soldier, himself is excluded in the most obvious of ways. His supposedly inherent vulnerability does not allow him to take part in the development of the relatively new state he has fought for or to become emblematic of Israeli masculinity more broadly. Therefore, even when the siege of Jerusalem opens and the novel ends, Himmo remains in siege, vulnerable to attack, and Hamutal gives him a lethal injection, thus permanently isolating him from the life of the Zionist state.

"Break through the Siege": Himmo's Death

The wounded in Yoram Kaniuk's novel often joke at their own expense, thinking up derisive nicknames for themselves, such as "the lost prize-winners," which refers to the fact that "these fellows won't get any awards. No awards or medals are handed out for what they've done. Wounds burn and smart, Mister. For a moment we were heroes on the battlefield—redemption on a silver tray, rebirth of the nation, our reply to the ghettos of Europe, a two-thousand-year-old hope, and all that—and just look what's become of us! Damned souls sacrificed to Dr. Abayoff's Moloch!"[59] The novel pulls its focus from the so-often-featured *living-dead*, as fallen war heroes, to a description of a *dead-living*. The notion of the living-dead is hinted in the reference to Nathan Alterman's poem "The Silver Platter" (Magash hakesef), first published in *Davar* newspaper on December 19, 1947, which became an iconic symbol of sacrifice for the emerging Jewish state, and the concept of the dead-living is embodied in Himmo's character.[60] The fundamental difference between the two is central to the novel: while the living-dead may (and even should) return to the life of the nation in order to enable its existence and justify the sacrifice, the dead-living functions as an image to be forgotten, and thus inevitably ends up excluding the experience of disability from the national sphere.[61] This exclusion functions in a wider context as well, as the existence of the dead-living would be an inexcusable threat to three cultural motifs that serve to justify a societal self-identification with war: the chosen Zionist body, the finite experience of siege warfare, and conceptions of personal independence as a reflection of national independence.

Meira Weiss examines how Israeli society is articulated through the body. She explores the ways in which the Israeli body is chosen and regulated as part of the production of the Zionist project, idealizing health, power, and perfection. This "chosen body," to use her language, lauded visions of the hypermasculine, the Jewish, the Ashkenazic (eastern European Jews), and the wholesome—all of these being, without exception, physically able.[62] Himmo—the wounded, effeminized Mizrahi soldier[63]—is, in essence, a fundamental exception, an outlier, in the image of the chosen body, and must therefore be excluded from the emerging state.[64] To be more precise, Hebrew literature introduces a character like Himmo into the text in order to enable his exclusion. Thus, the physical and social condition of the disabled soldier sheds light on the abled-bodied soldier's (and civilians') relationship to the state.[65] Himmo's image as a wounded soldier does not serve the national project per se, but his sexual victimization and death establish clear boundaries between proper and improper masculinity in Israeli society.

While the siege of Jerusalem during the War of Independence serves as a realistic background for the novel, it also functions to characterize disability: physical disability is perceived as a siege in and of itself. The "maimed and wretched" soldiers are depicted as being "chained to their hopeless situation."[66] Thus the novel actually parallels Jerusalem under siege to disability, which represents a body and soul constantly under siege. The injured soldiers "know full well—feel it in their maimed bodies—that they are trapped . . . [while] their weary abled-bodied comrades are trying to break through the siege as it relentlessly closes in."[67] Given this comparison, it is no surprise that when the siege breaks, the novel kills the disabled. The overcoming of the siege constitutes a national military victory, and therefore requires overcoming disability through the vehicle of Himmo's death, as his disabled body inherently preserves the state of siege, which counters rhetoric about the defined limitations and finite nature of siege warfare.

Furthermore, various societies, including Israeli society, give primacy to the value of independence. It is enshrined in various social policies, legal mechanisms, and philosophical understandings of personhood.[68] Given the value and emphasis of independence in national dialogue, the representation of a wounded soldier's dependency—a living reminder of the interdependent nature of society in general—is often erased from cultural narratives, except in circumstances that lead to disability deletion or death. The soldier who is dependent on another is doomed to die on the page, as the very position of dependency cannot overcome the borders of siege to enter into a literal state of personal independence.

Literature and other cultural platforms have a long history of erasing the assistance that allows its wounded and disabled subjects to thrive. In contrast to this tradition, *Himmo, King of Jerusalem* emphasizes not only the body that needs assistance but also the complicated array of care that goes into treatment. Scenes of care, according to Rachel Adams, are a valuable index for understanding cultural assumptions, desires, and anxieties.[69] As a result, *Himmo, King of Jerusalem* becomes an object lesson in cultural attitudes toward dependency and self-reliance in Israel in the 1960s.

"Dependency work" is the labor of caregiving that goes into ensuring the comfort and well-being of the wounded soldiers.[70] The problem at hand is that, generally speaking, literary depictions of a dependence on caregivers creates a divide between givers and receivers of care, suggesting that a person may occupy only one of these roles. Therefore the soldier, who serves the nation as a protector and caregiver, cannot be a recipient of help, especially when that assistance is mandatory for survival. A disabled soldier like Himmo, who cannot conceal or overcome his disability, cannot be integrated into nascent national society; Himmo's existence and the fact that he has both given and received care make him an uncomfortable reality, which is difficult to situate politically.

Representations of injured soldiers allow for movement between "permitted dependencies" and those that are "pathological."[71] The glorification of war allows the wounded soldier to be in the position of dependency, but only if it is temporary and eventually leads to the desired rehabilitation, that is, to the erasure of the disability, as is the case in Yaacov Haelyon's *A Doll's Leg*. But when the injury is permanent and ongoing, and the state of dependence threatens to exceed the boundaries of the hospital and invades the protected and established spaces of the national home, it becomes pathological. Himmo is a hybrid representation of permitted and pathological dependence. The novel's representation of Himmo's injuries as an ongoing, chronic condition that involves care and vulnerability challenges the foundations of war culture, which can function only in binaries of victory and loss, life and death. By this logic, there is no space for a character such as Himmo, whose injury exposes the failures and limitations of medical treatment that visualizes a complete recovery as its only goal. In order to maintain the supposedly irreconcilable difference between the living-dead and the dead-living, Himmo must die.

ACCESS TO PLEASURE

The relationship between Hamutal and Himmo in *Himmo, King of Jerusalem*
received scholarly attention not because of the abusive power dynamics
at play but simply because scholars couldn't seem to comprehend the
possibility of a relationship between a disabled soldier and an able-bodied young woman. Gershon Shaked, for instance, claimed that Hamutal's
love "expresses an unbridled attraction to death,"[72] and Mordechai Avishai
doubted Hamutal's feelings, "because all we know about ordinary love is
not relevant to this case [. . .]. Clearly, this is not a relationship similar
to any type of love that is created between a man and a woman, with its
emotional and sexual implications."[73] Avishai even concluded by claiming
that this "weird and supernatural" relationship could not have happened in
real life. His position is not unusual; it expresses a widespread perception
that an abled-bodied person would not be interested in a relationship with
a person with disabilities. Furthermore, this perception is also predicated
on the desexualization of disabled bodies.

    Within this cultural context, the novel opens a rare discourse about
sexuality and disability. Anne Finger claims that "sexuality is often the
source of our [people with disabilities] deepest oppression; it is also
often the source of our deepest pain. It's easier for us to talk about—and
formulate strategies for changing—discrimination in employment, education, and housing than to talk about our exclusion from sexuality and
reproduction."[74] For that reason, access to pleasure, according to Tepper,
is the real accessibility issue for disabled people. True integration means
accessibility to pleasure.[75] Without minimizing the extent of ableism in
the novel—and no doubt *Himmo, King of Jerusalem* couches disability
in profoundly negative terms—as an injured soldier, Himmo occupies a
cultural space of dislocation, one where his disability provides a unique
lens through which ableist discourse on desire can be reevaluated.

    Despite the effeminization of Himmo, in contrast to the cultural
tendency to desexualize disability, Hamutal's sexual attraction to Himmo
actually preserves his sexuality and vitality, in a fashion. Hamutal experiences Himmo as a sexual man. Thus, for example, "she yearns to tell him
what she looked like, describe her graceful neck, her ebony-dark hair [. . .].
She wanted to tell him about her firm, erect body, about her full, well-
formed breasts that lay with her on her lonely pallet."[76] She also imagines
Himmo's sexual desire "and she imagined that he, Himmo Farrah, was at
that instant waiting to hear the [erotic] description she denied him. She

was sure that Himmo [. . .] was fully perceptive of what she had been waiting to do."[77] In other words, Himmo is imagined by Hamutal to be sexually desirous and capable.

The discourse about sexuality and disability, which appears implicitly, and perhaps even unconsciously, in the novel *Himmo, King of Jerusalem* develops into a kind of a call for accessibility to pleasure almost a decade later in Dan Ben-Amotz's best-selling novel *I Don't Give a Damn* (Lo sam zain), published in 1973. The latter novel describes the entanglement of the love story between Rafi and Nira, following Rafi's injury in the War of Attrition. Himmo's and Rafi's disabilities thus might offer a strategic location through which the novels could articulate a radical perspective about the "missing discourse of pleasure."[78] Even if the novel *I Don't Give a Damn* offers a chauvinist representation of sexuality that applies only to physically disabled male veterans, it is still one of the first novels in Hebrew literature that not only deals directly with questions of disability and sexuality but does so by concentrating on something other than the fertility of the disabled. The entire novel revolves around Rafi and Nira's relationship, and despite the fact that they break up, the novel depicts a candid sex scene between the abled-bodied Nira, and Rafi, who uses a wheelchair after his injuries.

While discussing sexuality and disability, it is interesting to compare the novel *Himmo, King of Jerusalem* to its cinematic adaptation, directed by Amos Guttman in 1987.[79] The film minimizes the sexual dimension in the "relationship" between Hamutal and Himmo, and it does not describe Hamutal as taking advantage of Himmo. However, Himmo's sexuality, as well as his attraction to Hamutal (which has no basis in the novel) is more prominent in the film than in the novel. This is especially evident in the cinematic scene in which when Hamutal lies down next to Himmo, his hand reaches for her, and he actually initiates the first moment of physical intimacy between them. While in the novel his hand is amputated, the film depicts him as having full control over his hand. It is reasonable to assume that Himmo's cinematic depiction as having agency over his sexuality was influenced by the discourse about sexuality and disability in the novel *I Don't Give a Damn* published fourteen years before the movie was released.

The novel *I Don't Give a Damn* was also adapted into a film, directed by Shmuel Imberman in 1987.[80] Access to pleasure is also more prominent in the cinematic adaptation of *I Don't Give a Damn* than in the novel. This may be the reason that, while the novel ends with Rafi and

Nira's breakup, the film ends with the two of them happily back together. Additionally, and more significantly, the cinematic adaptation brings the discussion about the sexuality of injured soldiers back into the space of sexualized violence. The cinematic adaptation added a scene that does not exist in the novel. In this scene, Rafi's disabled veteran friend Amnon invites him to his apartment to convince him that he could return to normal life after his rehabilitation; as if to demonstrate, Amnon freely rolls his wheelchair around his apartment, cooks dinner, and talks about his work and hobbies. At the peak of this "normality show" Amnon invites two women prostitutes to "help" Rafi regain his sexuality.[81] Rafi does not participate and leaves the apartment, but this scene becomes the catalyst for two of the most sexualized scenes in the movie: the scene in which Rafi takes erotic photos of his sister-in-law, and the sex scene with his former girlfriend, Nira.

Despite the fact that the call for accessibility to pleasure does not recur in Hebrew literature after the 1970s, it does continue to develop in Israeli cinema. But just as the discourse on the subject in Hebrew literature evolved through the representation of sexual exploitation, Israeli cinema too addresses this issue mainly through representations that preserve the juxtaposition of disability and sexual vulnerability, as seen in movies such as Shmuel Hasfari's *Shchur* (1994), Asaf Korman's *Next to Her* (At li layla, 2014), and Nitzan Gilady's *Wedding Doll* (Hatuna meniyar, 2015).[82] Thus, and perhaps paradoxically, ableist representations of sexual violence in Israeli culture generate access to pleasure for people with disability.[83] It is quite tragic that rehabilitating the male character demands demeaning and humiliating the female character, and that even a positive development is actually a reinforcement of sexual and gender stereotypes.

A Doll's Leg: A Story of a War Injury

The hospital conceived as a heterotopian space allows for a variety of disability manifestations, that is, for different "fantasies of disability." The fantasy of disability "is a net of ideas, created by no single individual but perpetuated and circulated between subjects, which seeks to contain the danger of limitation, to subject it to a set of social preconceived notions about what it means to be disabled and how a person is expected to act and react to the diagnosis of disablement."[84] While the previous section dealt with the exclusion of the disabled body from the national space, in the present section I shall focus on the way in which the Israeli fantasy of disability works to reappropriate and repurpose the disabled body to fit its own agenda.

The autobiographical book by Yaacov Haelyon, *A Doll's Leg: A Story of a War Injury*, is a story of rehabilitation—both physical rehabilitation and also the "blurring" of disability that comes with adapting to day-to-day life. In Haelyon's book, disability does not change or challenge heterosexuality, family structure, or national perceptions. The injury is seen as a temporary disturbance that must be managed and overcome, and not as a potential for the reexamination of values.

Haelyon's book ends with a scene in which during a stay in Paris he decides to go down the steps of the Eiffel Tower "from the beginning to the end. And without stopping." Haelyon writes, "Standing at the bottom, between the spread-eagled legs of the tower, shaking as though from malaria and pouring with sweat, I knew I was victorious: over the tower, over my leg, over the first Syrian shell, and the second Syrian mortar bomb."[85] The victory is described in decidedly erotic terms as a sexual interaction with a woman: Haelyon stands between open legs, trembling and sweating. It is interesting that the Eiffel Tower, a distinctly phallic symbol, becomes a feminine symbol in describing the sexual vigor and the rehabilitation of the disabled person. The heterosexual act becomes the marker of victory and a sign of masculinity in spite of disability.

In an earlier passage in *A Doll's Leg*, Haelyon hints at the fear that a soldier's disability would undermine heterosexual conventions. He discusses a sort of internal negotiation regarding heterosexual normative boundaries, writing, "The conversation [among the injured] turns round to the question of whether a man who is paralyzed can make love to his wife. And the corollary, can he father children? The answer is in the affirmative. There are those who have investigated. It turns out that his partner must be the active one in bed."[86] Heterosexuality is preserved and fulfilled in the grandeur of having children, but with the price of giving up the symbolism of power relations in bed: the disabled man must be passive, and his (abled-body) partner active. The fact that the book ends with the Eiffel Tower sexual experience, therefore, is significant. It not only preserves heteronormative sexuality but also restores the speaker to his active position, and his partner to her passive one, in a sort of ultimate objectification: a silent, still tower.

It is important to clarify that heterosexuality, which is used to help symbolize Haelyon's triumph over his disability and facilitates his return to normalcy, passes in the book through sexual violence.[87] *A Doll's Leg* is interwoven with an unmistakably aggressive male gaze. When Haelyon describes the nurses approaching him to take care of him, he attests that "at first I see a waist. Then my eyes ascend upwards and identity its owner. [. . .] I like the nurses in Hut 25. They almost all share an aura of patience and goodwill. Each in her own way. Fair Bina Palgi; dark-skinned Hannah Eliahu with her white teeth; Aliza, the masseuse, her magic hands soothing aching backs. [. . .] There's also golden-haired Rivka Bott."[88] Elsewhere he recounts, "Women were our first and most important subject of discussion. Especially at night, after lights out, when slumber was in no hurry to come and lusts awaken. There was not a single girl—nurse, volunteer or even visitor—who wasn't examined closely, and undressed by hungry stares. In the nightly symposiums we would dissect in great detail their physical assets, and debate them with great enthusiasm. One remembered brown eyes, while his colleague contended that they were blue. One said that her legs were exceptional, and the other that 'they were not good.' "[89] The objectifying gazes exceed the boundaries of the conversations between the wounded, and the nurses are consistent victims of sexual suggestions and harassment.[90] For example, one morning, when the nurse Zahava arrives to wash Haelyon, he strokes her hand and suggests, as if jokingly, that "perhaps we should change place? I'll vacate the bed—and you rest on it. If you behave nicely, I'll even wash you."[91] And then he makes suggestive comments to the nurse Lisette as well, who "was giving me an injection, I declared that it wasn't antibiotics that I needed but wine, women and song."[92] Haelyon is apparently unaware of the extent of the harassment and cheerfully refers back to the extent of his own wit, while contrasting the behavior of the nurse, who, "[being] of English origin and educated to good manners and restrained behavior, for a moment froze."[93] Similarly, Haelyon laughingly comments on the behavior of Yisrael, another wounded soldier in the ward, who has sexual relations with his physiotherapist: " 'I missed you, my adopted brother,' he [Yisrael] said, exposing his shining teeth as usual, and winking towards the girl [his physiotherapist] who had pushed his wheelchair from the hospital as though to say: 'And what do you think of her?' "[94]

Recuperating and regaining a sense of agency, then, passes through offensive jokes, verbal humiliation, and the sexual harassment of women, mainly nurses and other caregivers in the hospital. The disabled masculinity, which, as noted, is always suspect of femininity and weakness, restores its gender and national privileged status through the sexual harassment of female caregivers. While the sexual abuse of the wounded soldier by the abled-bodied nurse in the novel *Himmo, King of Jerusalem* enabled the exclusion of disability from the national project, the sexual harassment of female abled-bodied caregivers by disabled male soldiers in *A Doll's Leg* enables them to overcome their disability and return to the loving embrace of nationalism. According to this "fantasy of disability," disability can remain present in Israeli culture only when the subject camouflages it through violent and chauvinist masculinity. So although these works seem to present two opposite ends on a spectrum of sexuality and disability, both end up forcing disability itself out of the narrative: once by the extinction of the disabled body, and once by overcoming, actually or imaginary, disability and neutralizing its subversive force.

A *Doll's Leg* ends with the statement "The war isn't over. [. . .] But the tin soldiers, standing on their one leg, are as steady as their comrades on two. Not only in fairy tales."[95] The war that hasn't ended isn't only the ongoing war in Israel but also the arduous rehabilitation process of disabled or injured soldiers. Thus, the victory of Haelyon and his injured comrades is both a national victory (a military victory) and a gendered one (as depicted in the Eiffel Tower scene). This double victory is embodied in the reaffirmation of the national discourse, in overcoming disability and in social appropriation: "Shuki Kaufman finished the Technion with honors. Without a hand and without a leg. Yisrael Cohen, without both hands, graduated in economics and holds a senior position in a co-operative. [. . .] Gadi Refen, who should have received mention in dispatches for his bravery in hospital, won [. . .] a medal for valour in battle. He returned to the army."[96]

The tin soldier from Hans Christian Andersen's 1838 fairy tale does not attempt to prevail over his disability. He experiences various adventures and falls in love with a dancer, whom he believes has one leg, just like him, but at the end of this tragic fairy tale, he is thrown into the fire, according to Mitchell and Snyder, as a punishment "for his willingness to desire someone physically perfect and therefore unlike himself."[97] Unlike Anderson's tin soldier, Haelyon's injured soldiers steadily "[stand] on their one leg." They are rewarded with fame and glory, and "return to the army"; they are adopted anew by the nation, and their masculinity, which was threatened by their injuries, is restored by their acts of aggression against women as they recover.

As can be seen in the epigraph for this chapter, Haelyon refers to the injury as an "intermediate road" between falling in the battle and returning home unharmed. Accordingly, the hospital's heterotopian universe is perceived as an intermediate space, serving solely as a means to return home: "So there's nothing left but to bite your lips and keep reminding yourself that the purpose of these tyrants [the medical personnel] is to get you better, cure and return you healthy and in one piece to your home—to the life beyond the walls of the hospital."[98] The hospital is a transitional space, a road leading back to normalcy. Although the hospital in the book contains various kinds of power dynamics—men and women, injured and abled-bodied, patients and caregivers—it is not experienced as a promising liminal space in which normative power struggles are undermined and new social understanding may arise but as a place where the potential for change must be cured. The image of Haelyon and his disabled friends as supercrips that overcome and defeat their disability via heroic efforts ends up strengthening the conviction and confidence of able-bodied narratives in the context of a stable, able social system, rather than doing anything to undermine common conventions of disability.[99] Thus, on the face of it, the book describes a physical process of healing through surgery and physiotherapy, but inadvertently, the book also exposes national and gendered "healing," and an indoctrination process that seems to socially require, and indeed to even advocate, the sexual harassment and subjugation of women.

The Seventh Glory: A Fighter's Story

Shalom Babayoff's novel *The Seventh Glory: A Fighter's Story* (Hazohar hashevii: Sipuro shel lohem) tells the story of Ben, a soldier who was blinded in the 1967 war, and Mia, the nurse who took care of him at the hospital following his injury.[100] Throughout *The Seventh Glory*, Ben and Mia fall in love, and the novel ends with their marriage. This romantic narrative obscures the fact that by definition, since it is a relationship between a nurse and her patient, it is built on sexual impropriety and harassment. When considering the power structure that positions Ben, as a patient, under the care of Mia, as a nurse, it is undeniable that their intimate relationship is fashioned on a foundational abuse of hierarchical power.[101]

However, the very fact that a love story depicting a relationship between a disabled man and an able-bodied woman exists is unusual. As Sarah Rainey mentions, love in cultural representations is an abled-bodied institution, and in the rare cases in which love between disabled/nondisabled people comes across a larger cultural radar, "it is almost always the stuff of drama," and it is represented as a tragedy.[102] Therefore, the representation in *The Seventh Glory* of a romantic love story between a blinded soldier and an abled-bodied woman raises some questions, including, but not limited to: Why, despite the fact that ethically (and in Israel, since 1988, also legally[103]) we are still dealing with persistent issues around sexual harassment, does the novel present this as a beautiful relationship? And who or what does this positive image serve, in the context of a nationalistic and ableist culture?

While lying in the hospital, Ben observes his injured comrades and notes that with the transition from the battlefield to the hospital, their thoughts of the battlefield disappear, and in the company of nurses and friends, "little by little, the thought of what was is pushed to a remote corner, and a glorious light of eternal hope and peaceful coexistence emerges from it."[104] The hospital thus enables the injured soldiers to repress the injury and neutralizes the transition from an abled-bodied soldier to a disabled veteran. The wounded in this novel "were not guys who were hurt in their spirit; they did not relate to their condition [. . .], and it made me [Ben] think that they were heroes [. . .]. They were the ones who redeemed Israel from a total destruction."[105] In this, any and all injury is perceived as a physical injury with no emotional, psychological, or political consequences.[106] The injury does not raise questions about the necessity of war and its price, and it does not challenge the national discourse: "Months ago they [the enemies] threatened to destroy us [Israelis] and now we stand in territories where the struggle of a people is expressed—a struggle of a people that has not known what rest is since it was chosen at Mount Sinai."[107] In the translated word "territories" here, Ben refers to the territorial expansion of Israel during the 1967 war. In this war, the State of Israel seized the Gaza Strip and the Sinai Peninsula from Egypt, the West Bank (including East Jerusalem) from Jordan, and the Golan Heights from Syria. In fact, Ben creates an unconscious link between the wounded and the borders of the country, so that to the reader, the success of the occupation of those territories seems like proof of righteousness in the Zionist struggle. While having no land—prior to the establishment of the State of Israel, or while controlling only part of The Land of Israel (Eretz Israel) prior to the 1967 occupation—the nation is perceived as disabled, as missing organs. The occupation is thus part of the nation's rehabilitation process, and its "healing" supposedly proves that the nation's disability is not permanent and eternal. The wounded thus participate in the general healing process, that of making the national self whole again.

From the early stages, Zionism has tried to "rehabilitate the Jewish people from their seemingly disabled state in the diaspora to a new healthy and 'normal' nation in Palestine."[108] As part of this mission, Sandy Sufian argues, disability "operated on two, perhaps paradoxical ties: one of collective disability able to undergo a curative transformation, and one of individual pathology deemed as incapable of changing and therefore lacking the potential of ever becoming the autonomous ideal."[109] A rather similar process occurs throughout the course of the narrative in *The Seventh Glory*. Disability as a concrete, individual experience has no place in the rehabilitation of the nation. Thus, just as the fallen soldiers sacrificed their lives for the homeland, so too the wounded who "do not relate to their condition" sacrifice their disability for the sake of the nations' rehabilitation. It should be noted that this sacrifice is not the disability itself but the willingness of the wounded to overcome disability and neutralize its subversive potential.

The danger inherent in the representation of a disabled soldier who is unwilling to sacrifice these things, who wishes to identify with disability in some way, is expressed in Dan Ben-Amotz's novel *I Don't Give a Damn*. Not only is Raffi, the disabled veteran, not actively trying to conceal his disability, but he devotes his time and energy to photographing "only the wounded and the disabled."[110] This causes discomfort to those surrounding Rafi. His father, for example, who was himself wounded while serving in the Haganah, is angry and barks at Rafi, "When will you stop messing with yourself, with your wounded, with your disabled people and with those fallen soldiers?"[111] While this reaction marks and glorifies the expected path of the wounded soldier, Rafi continues to photograph the wounded, in open opposition to societal norms.

Rafi's gaze on the injured body through his camera is not exclusively focused on his own wounded body. Rather than attempting to hide away his otherness, his camera actually solicits stares and looks from others around him. Unlike the gaze that is "an oppressing act of disciplinary looking that subordinates its victim,"[112] Rosemarie Garland-Thomson proposes that we think about staring not as a one-way act but rather as a starer/staree interaction, as "an intense visual exchange that makes meaning."[113] While for Garland-Thomson staring enables the (usually abled-bodied) observer and the (disabled) observant to communicate, Rafi calls for a sort of social staring through his camera lens, which not only makes disability visible in a culture that tries to conceal its presence but actively focuses in on such difference. Rafi explains his photographs simply, asking, "How can we avoid the disabled? They exist!"[114] He refers to his photographs not as art but rather as sources of information, saying, "I'm talking about information. About facts that people refuse to see. Because seeing these photographs, precisely at a high concentration, and precisely not as aesthetic photographs but as difficult ones, means to think, means to draw conclusions."[115] The novel implicitly presents its conclusions: it is saturated with questions about political leadership in Israel, it doubts the necessity of war, and it is skeptical of Israel's image as a peace-seeking nation dragged into war against its will. Thus, as filmmaker Judd Ne'eman claims (while referring to the film and not to the novel), Rafi is a posttraumatic fighter who undermines the sanctification of modern nationalism and is not committed to the normative identity of the fighting man.[116] What is significant here is that Rafi's distance from national values results from his injury and is related to his disability. In fact, Rafi articulates a critically disabled position that calls attention to the ways in which disability experiences "might resist the demands of compulsory able-bodiedness and have demanded access to a newly imagined and newly configured public sphere."[117] Thus, because of this kind of subversive potential of disability, Israeli culture invests so much effort in corralling disability and neutralizing its rebellious potential . . . which brings us back to the love story of Ben and Mia from *The Seventh Glory*.

In the midst of falling in love, Ben feels that Mia looks at him with her innocent eyes, while thinking about his qualities, "the qualities of a young man who has long ceased to think about his maim."[118] This thought gives rise to a desire to "grasp her virgin body, kiss her divine lips, and express my deepest gratitude."[119] Ben experiences himself as someone who is not affected by his injury. His disability does not shift his perspective on his life or his connections to anything cultural or political. It is his disregard for his disability that enables his sexual desire. Therefore, although the novel presents the sexual desire and marriage of a disabled man, it does not offer a discussion about disability and sexuality (as we saw in *Himmo, King of Jerusalem* and *I Don't Give a Damn*). Rather, it presents a process of overcoming disability, of ceasing to contemplate disability and of shrugging off its consequences. Perhaps this is why the book has so few overtly sexual descriptions, and apart from one kiss at the end of the novel, we are not exposed to descriptions or discussions about the sexuality of the newlyweds.

Later in the novel, when Mia's mother becomes aware of her daughter's love, she objects to the marriage, claiming that Mia is destined for better and that this kind of marriage will ruin her life. Mia's brother, however, who was also wounded in the war, supports his sister and claims that she is about to do something noble. He tries to convince their parents, explaining, "I understand Mia's feelings. I witnessed something similar in the hospital where I lay. There, too, there were cases when a nurse fell in love with a wounded soldier she was taking care of. If Mia wants [to marry] Ben, we should not prevent her from doing so. She is smart, intelligent, and old enough to know what she wants. And I thank my dear sister for her beautiful thought. We have to bear in mind that thanks to Ben and dozens of men like him, we won the war. We must be grateful to them, dear parents."[120] The sister/nurse (in Hebrew, it is the same word, *ahot*) is given, as though a prize, to the wounded soldier. Therefore, despite the fact that the sexual harassment between an abled-bodied nurse and her injured patient in a hospital appears to be similar to the model in the novel *Himmo, King of Jerusalem, The Seventh Glory* is closer in its spirit to *A Doll's Leg*. While the sexualized gender-based violence in *A Doll's Leg* is used to reeducate and "domesticate" disability, marrying the nurse in *The Seventh Glory* is presented as a reward for both bravery in battle and the willingness to disregard or unquestioningly accept disability. Thus, the supposedly abled-bodied status of the wounded solider is achieved through either heterosexual exploitation or heteronormative romance.

"Only a Brief, One-Time Baptism by Fire": Conclusion

Representations of disability in general, and of wounded soldiers more specifically, in Israeli literature, cinema, art, and popular culture are still very rare.[121] The ones that emerge from time to time into culture move, as Michael Oliver pointed out, between two extremes, couched in politically and socially charged motives. On the one hand, the disabled are described as worthless, miserable, and unfortunate victims (like Himmo), and on the other, they are admired for their ability to successfully cope with their challenges, ideally without complaint (like Haelyon and Ben).[122] Moreover, the few representations of disabled characters often consist of those who were once abled-bodied and were injured in an accident, a sports event, or a battle. These stories are presented as sorrowful but also as somewhat heroic. The disabled person is perceived as the victim of a cruel world, which of course presents the disability in a tragic light rather than as an inescapable part of life, and lauds those who manage to suffer or adapt quietly, rather than inconveniencing an able-bodied world with their narratives and experiences.

As a traumatic experience, injury prompts change in the injured soldier, which might threaten both his masculinity and the national project.[123] Despite this threat, in a society saturated with wounded, the injured cannot be completely eliminated from cultural representations, and so instead, they are closely monitored; mainstream culture tends to appropriate disruptive elements and internalize them for its own needs. Just as fallen soldiers are embraced in the arms of grieving nature, their deaths acquiring meaning through nationalistic platitudes, disability must be conquerable, transformed and adapted to fit certain national and gendered norms, in order to survive as representation within Hebrew literature. While much has been written about the gendered and heteronormative dimensions of the masculine Zionist body, of no less importance is the compulsory able-bodiedness inherent in it, which, in the case of wounded soldiers in Israeli literature, is constructed through the vehicle of sexual violence.

Wounded soldiers as central figures in Hebrew literature do not voice their experiences in ways that create or sustain disability culture, celebrate the uniqueness of disability, or aim for anything more than integration into mainstream culture. Vic Finkelstein, who strives to create a thriving alternative culture of people with disabilities, takes issue with the attempt of disabled people to integrate into the dominant culture, arguing that it actually preserves hierarchical power relations.[124] In Israeli society, the narrative of integration is dominant, and in rare cases, the texts themselves attest to the process of erasing the actual experience of disability or its subversive potential, as can be seen in the 1975 book *Injury* (Ptsia), written by Yoram Avi-Tamar (Yoram Tzafrir's pseudonym),[125] who was severely wounded in the Six-Day War. The book is based on notes and recordings made during Avi-Tamar's hospitalization, and it describes his injury and rehabilitation. At some point in the book, Avi-Tamar asks himself: "Is there specificity or uniqueness in seeing things and presenting them in the eyes of a disabled or wounded person? To ask it differently, what is legitimate and what is not legitimate to say on behalf of the wounded? Sometimes, as is known, there are in literature, or even in political articles, attempts to reconstruct what appears or needs to be known as a collective opinion or collective disappointment of war injured and disabled veterans. From my wording, one can of course understand that I deny this right."[126] Avi-Tamar not only denies the generalization of positions that may characterize wounded soldiers but also rejects the possibility that the experience of disability might bring with it a different positionality. To him, physical disability does not change anything in the essence of his abled-bodied identity; it is merely something to work around or overcome. Disability is a temporary disturbance to able-bodiedness, rather than an alternative to it. In the words of Moshe Admon, who was also wounded in the 1967 war, "The war did not affect me, since it was only a brief, one-time baptism by fire. [. . .] The injury does not bother me. [. . .] In a few weeks, I'll be back to myself."[127] From this position, as stated, wounded soldiers in Hebrew literature do not establish cultural alternatives but rather their disability reassures and consolidates heterosexual, abled-bodied, Zionist culture.

Wounded main protagonists in Hebrew literature mainly appear to serve or expand on a culturally approved able-bodied identity; they are therefore depicted in a way that neutralizes their disability. They are either excluded from society, as in *Himmo, King of Jerusalem*, or overcome their disability, as in *A Doll's Leg* and *The Seventh Glory*. Furthermore, since "heteronormative epiphanies are necessarily able-bodied ones,"[128] the process of overcoming disability hinges on the abuse and subjugation of female caregivers, either through harassment or through their depiction as a reward at the end of a long trial. In other words, sexualized violence in the rare books that portray wounded soldiers as central characters serves as a way to suppress the presence of disability and war injury in Israeli culture. Disability and its interface with sexual violence (either as victims or as perpetrators) is used to preserve the national chosen body in Hebrew literature.

Chapter Four

"Subduing the Terrible Sound of Silence"

Memoirs of Incest Survivors

‿⤬⤬‿

As if I asked that my voice will manage this time to subdue the terrible sound of silence.

—Dorit Avramovitch[1]

Introduction

The novel *Shira and Hiroshima* (Shira vehiroshima, 2003) was written by Ofra Offer Oren, who was raped by her father when she was approximately fourteen years old.[2] The novel opens with the suicide of a teacher who seemed to have had quite a regular life, but the novel later reveals a story that the teacher wrote but never published, describing her father's abuse. The current chapter returns metaphorically to this incest story that was told and written, unpublished and rediscovered. This chapter thus deals with the autobiographical writing of women whose childhoods involved the trauma of incest.

Oren's next novel, *I Feel Good, I Feel Good—A Letter to Mother: The Memories of the Survivor of Incest* (Yofi li, yofi li, 2006), also contains many autobiographical details, but in contrast to the previous novel, it follows a protagonist who manages to recover from her incestuous past and rebuild her life.[3] While in the first novel the victim of incest commits suicide and can be heard only through other characters and through the letter she has left, in the second novel the victim survives and has the opportunity to speak for herself and tell her own story. Accordingly, though this chapter analyzes themes such as the fear of annihilation, silence, and silencing, it also centers on the voices of incest survivors who managed to bring their stories to light. Until recently, the voices and experiences of these women were hardly heard in Israel—neither in literary representations and visual culture nor in film and popular media. The work of listening to these voices and making their stories known, then, is not trivial; it is an endeavor of tremendous social and political importance.[4]

The memoirs discussed in this chapter depict incest from the perspective of the victim. Even though the incest took place in the author's childhood, the memoirs enact the perspective of adult women who are (or were) in therapy and are aware of their trauma.[5] In addition, the memoirs are well situated within the psychological and feminist discourses around incest. Most of them correspond directly with psychological treatments and present a wide spectrum of therapeutic experiences—some supporting and empowering, others intrusive and offensive. They all forego the cultural norm of ignoring sexual violence in favor of directly addressing the trauma; none of the memoirs cooperates with the cultural aestheticization of sexual violence or with its concealment.[6] On the contrary, each memoir contains graphic and detailed descriptions of sexual acts, of the abuser's manipulations, and of the physical dimensions of the incestuous abuse.

Most of the memoirs also share other key aspects related to the experience of incest: they describe the opacity and denial of the victim's supposed support systems (mothers, neighbors, educators, and therapists), and they depict the connection between an abusive home and a variety of other forms of sexual violence experienced by the victims outside home. The texts describe a range of psychological responses experienced by the victims, such as dissociation, a sense of defilement, self-hatred, and uncontrolled aggression, as well as passion and love for the abuser. The memoirs blur the binary distinction between enemy and loved one, abuser and protector—and the abuser's family relationship to the abused only adds to the confusion. Despite the writers' awareness of the many ways in which their abusers exploited their power and influence to harm them, they all also emphasize experiences of emotional dependence on the abuser, and at times, reflect on their love—and desire—for them. They describe the pleasure of being "the chosen one" from among other members of the family, and they recognize that, at times, the abuser is an integral participant of the few positive memories of their childhoods; in some cases, the abuser is the only witness to their cherished pretraumatic existences.

Despite the enormous importance of such memoirs for the personal and collective cleansing of cultural discourse and real life, it is important to note that even the most intense and vulnerable incestuous experiences that the authors may share with their readers are only a partial account of the actual reality of incest. In other words, while the published memoirs open an important and rare window onto the world of incest victims, it is a window that enables only an incomplete—and, at times, unrepresentative—glimpse of actuality. This is not, as one may assume, the result of the inherent impermeable and individual nature of each author and each situation, or of the fictive or artistic representations of this trauma in literature. Rather, this is mainly because, at least so far, authors within this genre are all adult Jewish-Israeli women who suffered incest in their childhood,[7] mostly from men (often fathers, uncles, or brothers). They are educated women who are aware of their abuse and have the eloquent theoretical, literary, or psychological language to articulate their trauma. Also, these are all women who feel they—at least somewhat—overcame their past abuse. Thus, a vast range of voices still remains silent: the voices of Arab-Israeli victims of incest; the voices of children, boys, and men;[8] the voices of those exploited by women;[9] the voices of young and adolescent girls; the voices of women who cannot overcome the devastating effects of the abuse in order to voice it; and the voices of women who are not certain about what did or did not happen to them. Moreover, the written texts do not represent the voices of those who flatly refuse to discuss the trauma or who, for many reasons, simply cannot do so. The memoirs do not reflect the experiences of women whose stories are being told and retold by their bodies and behaviors: women in prostitution, incarcerated women,[10] incest runaways and homeless girls, women hospitalized in psychiatric facilities, and women facing continued sexual abuse.[11] Additionally, the memoirs discussed in this chapter were all written by women who had the emotional, social, and financial wherewithal to publish their stories; these are the narratives that editors found worthy of publication. As such, they represent, at least in part, attitudes that the public can and is willing to hear, contain, and confront. Therefore, although these voices are those of marginalized and excluded women, and thus may be expected to some degree to uphold an oppositional stance aimed at undermining social, cultural, and even national conventions, they still nonetheless operate from the contained social margins and from within the social order. They are certainly employing an accepted apparatus (published documents, and printed and marketed matter) for making themselves heard. In this sense they are somewhat privileged in comparison to women whose stories remain untold and untapped. It is also noteworthy that these memoirs describe the incestuous experience from a relatively safe perspective, in terms of time and space; that is, they are mediated through the writer's organization of information (affected by memory, protective mechanisms, etc.), and as such, they represent neither the experience per se nor the emotional and cognitive mechanisms that were in motion during the traumatic events.

Intertwined Narratives

The first collection of articles on incest in Hebrew, *The Secret and Its Breaking: Issues in Incest* (Hasod veshivro, 2004), opens with the growing interest in the phenomenon of incest in Israeli discourse. Among various examples of this trend the editors write, "There is even a new genre of survivors' stories in Hebrew."[12] Without getting into the various moral, ethical, and therapeutic meanings of the term "survivors," the characterization of "survivors' stories in Hebrew" is accurate in a sense, because the narrative of "survivors" (and not "victims") implies overcoming, strength, and empowerment. This is in fact the main narrative that comes out in Israeli memoirs that seem to present a conservative, continuous, and coherent therapeutic narrative of "from harm to growth." However, the writing itself, as well as certain elements of the stories, reveal different narratives, which even while upholding the same conservative sequence at times also simultaneously present options for different emotional and poetic chronicles of the incest experience.

   In accordance with this direction, the subtitle and the foreword of the memoir *When Time Stood Still: Incest—from Harm to Growth* (Keshe hazman amad milechet: Giluy arayot—mepgiah letzmicha), cowritten by incest survivor Ziv Koren and her therapist Rachel Lev-Wiesel, draws a unidirectional narrative from trauma to recovery. By so doing, it credits Koren with the position of survivor, which seems to implicate healing and overcoming. Lev-Wiesel writes in her foreword,

> Ziv decided that she would not spend the next 30 years living under the shadow of her abuse. When she was six the abuse began, and for 30 years she lived with the scars[,] and the

whole world was perceived through the lens of her abuse. She was in therapy for six years. The therapy was perceived as a contained, safe place, yet, in a sense, it was another entrapment. Now she was able to decide that the next 30 years would not be wasted being stuck in the past. The present and future would no longer continue to be a reflection of the past.[13]

Lev-Wiesel, the therapist, herein indicates that incest is something that one should and can overcome. The trauma becomes "digested" into the victim's posttraumatic subjectivity, and it transforms into an inherent part of her self-growth. Trauma that is not channeled into healing or growth is seen as "a waste" of a kind. In other words, it is not only that the trauma does not delay, break, or prevent the process of growing but also that it may cease to exist as a presence and is no longer experienced in and of itself, regardless of its posttraumatic implications.[14]

Although the book attempts to describe the incest itself and not just the way it is experienced and transcribed in retrospect, most of it is devoted to the aftermath, the therapeutic processes, and the effects of childhood incest on Koren's adulthood: "People think that if the abuse finishes, then it is done. But, in a way, that final moment is exactly the moment that everything starts . . . that is exactly the moment that consequences of abuse begin."[15] What is hinted at is that therapy deals with the consequences, and may do so successfully, as exemplified in the latter part of the book's subtitle: "from harm to growth." Therapy seems to promise growth even if there was a time when "time stood still."

With that said, the title of the book is *When Time Stood Still*, which immediately indicates that incest is not experienced as a finished business, as something that is completed or can be left behind, but rather as an experience that remains present in the life of the victim. The decision to give the book a title that focuses specifically on the traumatic moment is what allows the reader to also think about it in a way that is different from Lev-Wiesel's stated intention, especially given that Koren herself implies that time has never resumed its course: "People always ask me why I keep going back there. As if I have control. And who ever said that I left it, so that I would have to return?"[16] Thus, the very act of unifying the two voices in the book overshadows Koren's voice and underlines Lev-Wiesel's. Since there is no symmetry between Lev-Wiesel and Koren in terms of status, class, or power, the rational and confident voice of the therapist takes over Koren's voice.

Moreover, the book opens with a scene in which Koren gives her therapist a painting that she has done, and in response the therapist takes it and places it at a different angle. In other words, the book opens with the therapeutic suggestion to turn the picture over: "Look at this picture upside down. What do you see?"[17] The idea is to change the victim's perspective, but also, I would argue, to resituate the direction of the narrative itself, in a way that complies with the idea of healing via therapy. Koren's text, however, contains poignant moments that rage against this linear narrative of growth: "It sucks that I feel that I am back at the beginning . . . what frustrates me the most is that every stop makes me go back to the beginning. . . . I am not able to start where I stopped. . . . Sometimes I feel that I have started the process many times because I could not finish it."[18] The excessive use of ellipses in this short e-mail expresses obfuscation of the mind, a sort of emotional stutter, or perhaps an inability to express feelings that are inconsistent with the general spirit of the memoir. The multiplicity of ellipses is a linguistic sign that infers a refusal to accept the authority of syntactical logic, and one that contradicts the narrative of closure and coming to terms with trauma. Interestingly, Lev-Wiesel, Koren's therapist, added a footnote to this particular e-mail, which reads, "Another cycle begins towards lifting the veil."[19] This footnote intends to interpret the victim's frustrated experience, as well as to explain her painting, but it assumes and imposes a premise of rehabilitation ("lifting the veil"), of the repetition being meaningful and constructive, as opposed to it being meaningless, frustrating, fruitless, or hopeless. In other words, the memoir presents a linear narrative of overcoming trauma, but at the same time it also establishes a chaotic, rhizomatic option.[20]

While the therapist constantly tries to arrange and discipline Koren's rhizomatic chaos into a neat, linear narrative, Koren indeed collaborates in this attempt, but at times she also raises resistance to this rigid framework and tries to escape from it. Thus, I suggest reading this book, as well as the other memoirs discussed in this chapter, as a rhizomatic text. Such a reading may emphasize the degree of the victim's refusal to tell their incest story in a conventional way. Indeed, they might be interested in healing, and they may at times surrender to the logic of "the drug of speech," but the remnants of their story constantly undercut the restrained narrative—and bring the narrative back to its starting point in order to reexamine (probably unsuccessfully) the possibility of mastering the trauma by organizing it logically.

A Rhizomatic Story

The rhizome is a philosophical concept developed by Gilles Deleuze and Pierre-Félix Guattari, mainly in their book *A Thousand Plateaus* (1980).[21] "Rhizome" was originally a botanical term. A rhizome is a modified stem of a plant that sends out roots and shoots from its nodes. It connects the parts horizontally and not vertically; it is a grid without a center. The rhizome stands in opposition to the arborescent model, which represents a vertical relationship between stem and branches radiating out from the root. While analytical, rational, and logical thinking approaches reality from top to bottom, using generalizations and a bird's-eye view, the rhizomatic approach aims to set a different metaphor based on a net-oriented image, in which various levels of thought are constantly connected to each other. The general idea of the rhizome, then, is to stay away from clear-cut definitions and the logical and rational analysis we tend to impose on the topics we discuss. The alternative is a model developed in many directions and on different levels of meaning, a system based not on fundamental principles and inferences but on various nodes of ideas that have relationships with each other and that feed off each other. The rhizomatic notion has no singular basis and no original moment or point of inception: it is nonlinear, anarchic, and nomadic. It defies the conventions of Aristotelian narrative. As a result, the same idea might have different aspects and shades in different points of the complex web of interconnected experiences.

The rhizomatic nature of *When Time Stood Still* is apparent in its nonconventional style: it is a therapeutic memoir and a coauthored book that edits and arranges the testimony of the victim. It combines e-mails, written interpretive texts, drawings, photographs, and footnotes. It is Koren's memoir, but also Lev-Wiesel's academic research work, dealing with incest in childhood, as well as with art therapy. It is important to clarify that the book is not constructed as a Talmudic text that presents a main text at the center and several interpretations around it. Rather, *When Time Stood Still* can be described as spatial: various texts, experiences, and meanings written by both authors spread over the pages, inviting the reader to peruse them chronologically, page after page, one e-mail after the other (all the e-mails are dated), or to engage in them in a mode of disarray. This disarray is possible since there is no hierarchical relationship between the various parts of the text, and certain paintings, emotions, and events keep coming back in different contexts.

The rhizomatic dynamic is also suggested by Koren in her complaint about having to start from the beginning at every go, and her frustration at not being able to produce a continuous narrative when her efforts are constantly subverted by an alternative dynamic that refuses linear sequence and, eventually, closure. Her story in the memoir is thus a sort of a rhizome. It moves from a logocentric, arborescent way of thinking about incest (which seems to be the therapist's approach) to a branching-out, rhizomatic type of thought, thus expressing again the limits of language and writing as offered by therapy.

The rhizomatic alternative abolishes the model of center versus margin. It allows elimination of the mindset that seeks exclusion within a tradition of "either-or"; it enables escape from the binary psychoanalytic pendulum regarding trauma between the "trauma and recovery" narrative and the "hopelessness and imprisonment" narrative. The memoir *When Time Stood Still* thus includes in its totality at least these two narratives, and it disturbs and disrupts any closure that could comfort the victim.[22]

Whereas the arborescent system is one-dimensional in its structure and procession, the rhizomatic system is multidimensional. Various changes and metamorphoses—which at times lack exact location, and which may not have self-restoring forces—take place within that multiplicity. Accordingly, an incest survivor's repetitive symptoms can express changing situations simultaneously, with no value judgment of "progress" or "regression." Shez's semiautobiographical novel *Away from His Absence* (Harchek meheadro, 2010) tells the story of an adult woman who has an incestuous "relationship" with her father. The protagonist, Ofra (whose name is revealed only on the last page of the novel), age thirty-four, has a friendly relationship with Shez, a sixty-four-year-old poet. While one might refer to Ofra and Shez as two different figures, they can also be two dissociative embodiments of the same character—one of them young and troubled, and the other older and self-controlled. One of the scenes in the novel describes an encounter between the two on a train. On the eve of Passover, Shez comes from Tel Aviv to Haifa to take Ofra with her, but Ofra does not open the door for her. When Shez returns to the train station, Ofra, pretending to be a meticulously dressed woman, follows Shez, and finally sits down in front of her on the train, without Shez recognizing her. When they arrive at Tel Aviv, Ofra narrates, "the train stops. Shez gets off before me [. . .] I watch her as she leaves the train station [. . .] gets into the backseat of a cab that begins to drive, moves away and disappears." In contrast, Ofra sits on a bench: "For a while I sit motionless, staring at the empty air [. . .]. Again, I go up the stairs, buy a ticket to Haifa, enter the train and go back again."[23] Unlike Shez, who actively, logically, and productively proceeds to her destination, Ofra stares into space and travels aimlessly in a journey that takes her back to her starting point.

Seemingly, although the encounter between the two characters takes place on a train—a symbol of movement and progress—this is actually a regressive and failed engagement. However, reading it through the rhizomatic model of narration, it is not necessarily regarded as such. The rhizomatic model does not situate the scene within a hierarchical scheme of ascribing "progress" to the adult and rehabilitated Shez versus "regression" to the young and "messed up" Ofra. Rather, it enables one to come into contact with the multidimensional nature of the experienced encounter, with various emotional and poetic dimensions that function simultaneously. The rhizomatic interpretation transcends the limits of time, place, and emotional barriers, and it connects the two supposedly separate dissociative personalities, Ofra and Shez. It thus allows the character/s to act (travel, write), as well as to cease and become mute, to remain lonely and sorrowful in Haifa, while being supported and embraced in Tel Aviv. The two haunt each other equally, without giving preference to one performance over the other, without placing them unequally on a linear time scheme of progress. For every instance of Ofra's life, there is a Shez, and vice versa.

"New Language":[24]
An Alliance between Writers and Readers

Contemporary therapeutic approaches dealing with victims of sexual abuse stress the importance of a collaborative relationship between therapist and patient for the empowerment of the patient. Since a lack of power and agency, as well as detachment from others, were the focus of the traumatic experience, recovery is based on the creation of new relationships. It is the therapist's responsibility to establish a therapeutic alliance built on a mutual and cooperative working relationship and not on authority or control.[25] Whether this is really possible or is simply a repressive fantasy of the therapy industry is a separate question. But if we adopt such insights from the practice of therapy when reading incest memoirs, the memoirs' rhizomatic structure—which, as mentioned, has no single authoritative

source and offers a nonhierarchical method of constant deterritorializa-
tion—constructs a kind of alliance between the writers and their readers.
This alliance aims to communicate the harm and create an environment of
joint exploration and mutual influence, which does not deny the built-in
alienation and asymmetry between writers and readers.[26]

In her memoir *As Though Nothing Happened* (Klum lo kara . . . ,
2015), Shoshan Rotem describes decades of failed psychological and
psychiatric treatments, ranging from the ignorance of therapist to the
imperviousness of official mental and legal institutions regarding her
rape and incest trauma. At the age of fifty-two, Rotem started therapy
with Sheri Oz, an expert in treating trauma victims of sexual abuse and
incest, and for the first time in her life she felt understood and important.
Among a variety of differences between her treatments prior to that with
Oz, Rotem describes the dimension of equality between the two—"Sitting
in the room with Sheri is different from anything I have known before.
We are both sitting opposite each other, with nothing separating us, no
table to hide behind. We are both equal, both equally vulnerable and
the conversations are eye to eye"[27]—as well as the encouragement of the
therapist to respond, ask questions, and express herself: "Suddenly I find
myself sitting with a therapist who encourages me to ask, say, shout, yell,
protest; the same points where with previous therapists I was paralyzed.
In the places where Shoshi [Shoshan Rotem] stayed polite, looking out for
what is nice and not nice to say or ask or comment, I find myself learning a new language."[28] The memoirs share this "new language" with their
readers. They invite the readers to ask questions, to express themselves,
and to engage and listen from a place that is interested and sensitive to
the nuances of pain, as well as to its enormous range.

It is important for me to emphasize that I do not claim that there is
a therapeutic dimension to the alliance between the memoirs' writers and
readers. What I am trying to argue is that the memoirs reflect insights
about—and awareness of—the emotional and social needs of the writers,
as well as the challenges and barriers of the readers, and they generate
creative (rhizomatic) spaces that enable communication with their world,
engendering a social impact. In other words, the memoirs act as fields
of opportunities that are directed at different audiences under different
cultural and emotional circumstances. Rotem tells about the effect of the
supportive therapy she received: "So for the first time I am experiencing
(*hova*) having a voice. Fulfilling my requests [by the therapist Sheri Oz]
enables me to feel safe and extend my small radius one centimeter after

another and another and another."[29] Her voice gets a kinesthetic existence ("I am experiencing having a voice") that slowly allows her to portray and expand the boundaries of her subjectivity. Her "small radius" grows into a memoir, which continues to expand that same radius. Expanding the radius is not a trivial option in the world of one for whom escape is her mother tongue: "I was flooded by images from my past—the numerous times when I/we, mother and I, fled. And the times when I didn't flee—but was made to leave (kicked out); 'fleeing' [*brichot*] as a mother tongue."[30] The writing-reading alliance is an act that transcends this mother tongue of fleeing, dissociative escapes, and silencing evasions; the memoirs crave a listening ear and are aware of the power of both telling and listening.

"The Person That Murdered You Is Also the Person That Made You the Best"[31]

As part of the alliance the memoirs construct with their readers, they are inherently revealing. At the same time they do not enable voyeurism, and they clarify the boundaries of the intimacy of writing, the margins of the self, and the privacy of the writers. The role of the readers in that alliance is also not simple. Even though the traumatic event hurts first and foremost the survivor, it also threatens (although in a very different way) not only the immediate surroundings but also those who are interested in supporting the survivor and listening to her.[32] As such, it requires a constant examination of the readers' vulnerability as well as their strengths. At times it also calls for a dimming—even if temporary and partial—of their defense mechanisms. In other words, while the rhizomatic structure of the memoirs enables listening to the story of the victims, it might also disrupt the reader's socioemotional organizing mechanisms, because it contains options that might seem incoherent: "Everybody around me is willing to listen as long as it fits their definition of the world. But with incest, it does not fit anyone's natural definition of the world."[33] One of those aspects that does not fit the readers' "definition of the world" is the complex connection of the victims to their abusers, a connection most of the memoirs insist on addressing in a sharp and uncompromising way.

　　Koren's therapeutic memoir contains many pictures she painted during her therapy with Lev-Wiesel but only one photograph. It is a photo of Koren as a child, taken by the uncle who sexually abused her. The photograph is accompanied by an e-mail she wrote to her therapist:

I remember this picture . . . here already he was abusing me. This was a trip he took me on . . . He took a picture of me . . . I look at this picture and I don't know how to react to it . . . You see how small I am? How can you abuse something that small? [. . .] Just look at how she, sorry, I, look at him? This is a glimpse of love . . . [. . .] I remember that day he walked with me, and played with me, and we had a picnic together. I remember I had fun with him . . . [. . .] That day he did not touch me, just love . . . I loved these days. . . . Despite the constant fear that something could change, I still loved them . . .[34]

The photograph evokes diverse and conflicting feelings, which are expressed verbally in the e-mail. Combining the visual medium with the written one—the photograph with the e-mail, and all those with the memoir itself—enables Koren to express the various emotional contradictions and complexities related to her relationship with her abuser, and to the way the adult child remembers him. This fusion reveals perhaps one of the most counterintuitive aspects of the memoirs: listening to the voice of the victims requires us to abandon the polarized division between ally and foe. One of the challenges of our society is the love of the victim for her abuser. Although it is very clear in all of the memoirs who is the culprit (or culprits), and who the victim, they all describe the inability to absolutely and unquestionably hate the victimizer, often in fact also expressing love for them. Maya Reed writes the following in her memoir *Captive: Chronicle of Professional Incest—An Autobiographical Story* (Shvuya, 2002):

I used to love my dad, because he was my father, and because he always was. He woke me up in the mornings and dressed me and made me breakfast and brought me to kindergarten, and when I grew he walked me to school. He brought me back home in the afternoon and washed me and combed me and made my braids and prepared lunch and fed me when I was little and played with me. He always was, my mother always was not.

You have to know my father to really not believe that he was capable of doing what he did. When he was wearing the mask of sanity there wasn't a nicer and lovable and more entertaining person than him: He drew with me and read me stories and sat with me on the floor and we built towers of blocks together and we went to the pool and to the beach and we built magnificent sand palaces.[35]

The various portions within the rhizome do not seek to match each other, which enables seemingly contradicting and unrelated experiences to coexist. This quality allows expressing that which would be inconceivable and incomprehensible in a nonrhizomatic system. Reducing the experience of incest to a narrative of a diabolical father, brother, or grandfather on the one hand, and an angelic child on the other, is indeed accurate in terms of values, moral, and legal statutes, but it misses the emotional experience of the victim. In any case, the binary distinction between good and evil, love and hatred, is not the one that emerges from the memoirs. In addition to the fear and pain, the memoirs also describe feelings of love, affection, desire, dependence, and closeness to the abuser.

In addition to the mature and accepting voices heard in the memoirs, there is also a voice that locates the victim and her abuser on the same side, since both are excluded from their family and society, share a common secret and "sin," and supposedly deserve the same punishment. In Koren's words,

> I'll tell you why I'm mad . . . because I tell the truth and I share the biggest secret . . . [. . .] I think that the girl [Koren in her childhood] is just angry that we see him [the abusive uncle] all the time as a monster . . . [. . .] He wasn't just a monster and for me, he wasn't a monster at all . . . Yes, there was evil. And yes, a part of him was a monster, but not all of him . . . [. . .] You know, all my childhood I had to conceal, to hide, to lie, to manipulate. And to be exploited . . . and therefore, I've been trying to break free and get the truth out . . . they tell me indirectly to shut up . . . and again, I feel like they do not see me and they do not see the girl . . . the girl loves him and I will not take that away from her. . . . No one expects to be thought of as an angel, truly they don't, because he was not . . .
>
> But when the girl experiences the reactions against him, this hurts her . . . they do not harm only her, but how she relates to him . . . [. . .]. You know what, I will not quiet it and I will not shut up . . . whoever is unable to accept it, they

shouldn't be there . . . [. . .]. When I defend him, I defend myself as well. When they are attacking him, they are basically telling me that I am not good enough . . . if my identity was created through him, then I'm also a monster . . . when they have this attitude towards him, they take away from me all of the good things too . . . the good things that enabled me to survive him . . . to alleviate the feeling of the girl . . . The girl cannot tolerate this attitude against him, because he is all that she had . . .[36]

In this nightmarish world, where everything is reversed, the abuse is perceived by the victim as evidence of love, and so, paradoxically, there is fear not only of the thing itself but also of its absence. To use the words of the protagonist of Shez's *Away from His Absence*, "I'm soft. Soft and far. Far away from my father. As far away from him as the distance between Tel Aviv and Haifa. But at the same time I am also far from my father's absence. Infinite distance away from his absence."[37] The distance from the father's absence contains both the unwillingness to be separated from the abusive father and the recognition that the abuse is forever engrained in her, finding herself with no way out.

The emotional complexity is also reflected in the fact that sometimes, perhaps in a paradoxical way, the abuser is the only witness to the pre-traumatic world of the victim,[38] and in this case, he was also the bearer of her few positive childhood memories:

Believe me, it is hard for me to think about it in good terms. It is not easy for me to say there were good things about him [the abusive uncle] or that I felt love for him. That I depended on him. That, at some point, I really needed him. That he was all that remained from my childhood and that was all that was within it. They do not understand that I do not remember anything else other than him. I also have difficulty with this. I know that if I take him out of me, I have no past! [. . .] The truth is, he also was good to me, not just bad. You know how hard it is to live with the feeling that the person that murdered you is also the person that made you the best?! It's very easy to judge from the outside, but I have to live with it, not anyone else.[39]

Hanging on to the stereotype of the loving, caring, and protecting parent or relative is often a booby-trapped illusion of the child-victim. The need to be loved by parents and relatives is enormous, and it does not stop or disappear as a result of abuse, as evidenced by the description of Lior Gal-Cohen in her memoir *Dad's Gift* (Hamatana shekibalti meaba, 2012) about her life as a victim of incest in a kibbutz: "Love with a hit is better than no hit and no love. The concepts get confused. The search for love is endless and one will pay a heavy price for it."[40] Incest thus actually teaches the child that love and humiliation are intertwined, and that pleasure and pain are one and the same. The memoirs describe in detail these dynamics, and the duality of the terrified infantile soul that holds on to the abuser's love while being betrayed again and again.

Gal-Cohen's *Dad's Gift* addresses also the nonintuitive connection between writing, recovery, and the positive impact of the abusive father: "My father loved me and was very proud of me. His love and pride gave me the strength to go through this difficult and long lasting journey: to speak the secret, to tell it, to openly deal with it in my life. [. . .] His love gave me the strength to deal with his deeds [. . .]. His love gave me the power to cut off my life from his life and pay the price for it."[41] Despite her awareness throughout the memoir of the inherent contradiction between love and abuse, Gal-Cohen insists on the love and affection that she and her father shared. Love, anger, and pain do not deny each other's existence. The eulogy she wrote to her father (before his death) opens with her statement, "I learned a lot of things from you [. . .]. I loved walking with you, playing with you, and listening to stories you read to me." It continues with the blame, "You broke my heart Daddy," and ends with the sober understanding that "the world without you would be a better world. "[42] This eulogy does not reflect a linear progression of disillusionment but instead reveals a rhizomatic emotional experience that embraces (rather than solves or organizes) the tension between different insights and emotions that appear incompatible with each other. The various feelings toward the father are organized as a structure of networks operating in different directions and on different levels at the same time, a model that allows a fluid relationship between the different relations and responses to the father. This is an obituary that contains the father's death during his lifetime, as well as his vitality postmortem; it expresses denunciation of the father and separation from him, as well as the sense of an unresolved debt to him. This serves as an accusation of the father as well as a declaration of love for him.[43]

"Although the Selection and Fragmentation Err Reality, It May Actually Reinforce It"[44]

Much has been written about the social, political, legal, and psychoanalytic inability (or lack of motivation) to contain and to account for a variety of violent events, especially—but not only—against women and children. The voices of many survivors of sexual abuse in general, and of domestic sexual violence in particular, are not being heard and are still not fully comprehended. As a society we still suffer "an episodic amnesia," to use Judith Lewis Herman's term, in relation to women's sexual trauma.[45] Koren articulates similar feeling: "Society is like the family—silencing, exclusionary, and abusive."[46] More specifically, Effi Ziv claims that incest is marked in the public sphere and consciousness as an abject. She argues that alongside the visible consensus about social and moral prohibition of incest, there is a hidden social consensus about the avoidance of discussion and the exposure of its details and measures.[47] Anat Gur argues that incest and the sexual abuse of women and children is a cultural secret that—by using various mechanisms of collective and personal denial—our society tries not to unveil. She calls on us to learn the language and silence of sexual trauma: "A world that is not willing to accept the reality of survivors of traumatic abuse produces one of the templates for re-victimization [. . .]. Recognizing traumatic disorders must involve the brave initiative of remembering, feeling, and witnessing."[48]

The memoirs discussed in this chapter also express a concern about the unintelligibility of their own voice, and of survivor's voices in general. So, for instance, Koren writes in her memoir, "Wow, I do not know if what I have written here makes any sense. Truly, I tried. It is really difficult to explain something that seems impossible to explain in words. [. . .] I will try to draw for you what I wrote. Perhaps through the painting it will become clearer."[49] I don't really know how we should listen to the voices of women and children who were sexually abused, but I think that we might conclude from Koren's words that when dealing with the voice of victims, and when attempting to decipher the language of pain, it is important to understand not only the visible content but also the mechanisms that are acted out in the writing itself, that is, in the stylistic (conscious and unconscious) decisions of the memoirs' authors. For example, the literal attempt to describe the experience and the painting of that experience are not separated from each other in Koren's memoir. Leora Somer argues that the visual expression in painting enables one to express unarticulated experiences. She explains that since visual art skips verbal and cognitive barriers, it enables the one who paints to access subconscious emotions.[50] Even if this may be true in some cases, it seems that the memoirs present another option, whereby the interface, the encounter between writing and painting (and in other cases, between photos and written text or between different genres), enables one "to explain something that apparently is impossible to explain in words."[51]

One of the main stylistic characteristics of the memoirs, as I mentioned above, is a mixture of genres. Ruti Shalev incorporates illustrations (probably her own), a psychological questionnaire from her childhood, documents from her various treatments (including her Rorschach questionnaire), and some of her childhood paintings in her memoir *Belly* (Beten, 2000). Reed's *Captive* (Shvuya) combines a formal complaint letter, diary segments, quotes from her psychological treatment, a letter that was not sent, and quotes from her phone call to the rape center hotline. In *The Naked King* (Hamelech eirom, 2004), Dorit Avramovitch tells her personal story in an almost-academic format, often relying on scholarly explanations drawn from gender studies. Koren's memoir is coauthored with her therapist, Lev-Wiesel, and it brings together paintings from her therapy, interpretations of these paintings, and e-mail correspondence between Koren and Lev-Wiesel. Rotem's *As Though Nothing Happened* (Klum lo kara . . .) is interwoven with quotations from therapy reports she had over the years, a letter from one of Rotem's doctors, as well as a letter she wrote as a child to her beloved uncle.

Hybridity of genres and mediums is not a new cultural phenomenon—certainly not in the context of Israeli culture or in representations of trauma. However, I believe the fact that almost all of the memoirs use hybrid writing is significant and worthy of exploration. Therefore, I would like to offer a few ways of understanding this conscious or unconscious choice by the memoirs' authors, and mostly to try to "listen" to what hybridity has to tell us about the experience of incest.

In her memoir *Belly* (Beten), Shalev says of her writing, "When told precisely, the entire story seems to me as weakens itself. The high dose of evil makes the details so wretched and pitiable. Although the selection and fragmentation err reality, it may actually reinforce it." [52] Shalev separates "accuracy" from reality, which paradoxically can be accessed only through the renunciation of accuracy. The traumatic reality contains experiences that cannot find their place in any language other than an unruly and disruptive one. Following Shalev's insight, I would like to refer to the mix writing as a rhizomatic variation and as a writing strategy that enables survivors of incest to express in writing that which evades direct description.

To return to the question of pain's capacity to be expressed and heard, Elaine Scarry in her study of pain and torture claims that one of the features that characterizes pain is its inability to be shared, since it defies language. Scarry posits that "physical pain does not simply resist language but actively destroys it."[53] She argues that pain, at its worst, numbs the person and destroys his or her language. The inability to articulate to others the depth of feeling and sensations related to the pain, as well as the helplessness of others in light of the pain of the individual, isolates the sufferer.[54] In her study about illness narratives, Shlomith Rimmon-Kenan challenges Scarry's argument and claims that despite the fact that pain might destroy language, it can also motivate it.[55] In other words, while pain might mute language, it can also generate a desire for it and a search for new ways of expression. In fact, she argues, the complexity of many illness stories stems from the coexistence of that which cannot be articulated, and its very articulation.[56] Incest memoirs exist within this spectrum of the meager and limited power of language, but nonetheless a pressing desire to utilize writing to convey these experiences fuels many authors. Thus, I would argue that while the crossbreed writing acts out the victims' lack of confidence in language and its fundamental failure in expressing their incestuous experience, it simultaneously allows the writers to deal with their desire to tell their story.

In *Alice Doesn't: Feminism, Semiotics, Cinema* (1984), Teresa de Lauretis articulates a fundamental paradox for feminist theorists: "The only way to position oneself outside of [dominant, constructive] discourse has been to displace oneself within it—to refuse the question as formulated, or to answer deviously (though in its words), even to quote (but against the grain)."[57] The hybridity of the memoirs can therefore be understood as a deliberate or inadvertent distortion. As such, the hybrid approach enables the writers to exist on the margins, to be in constant friction with the edges of their experience and language, and to conduct a dialogue with the personal and social unconscious. The writers embroider and rip apart their memories, cut and paste their experiences in an attempt to extract some meaning, on the one hand, while also sabotaging the possibility of a comprehensive interpretation, on the other. The mixed writing defies any immediate, one-dimensional, and monotonous message about incest, as was seen, for example, in memoirs' description of the complex love for an abuser, and, as I will soon show, with respect to their representation of the experience of dissociation.

In addition, the reality of child sexual abuse in general, and incest in particular, is based, among other things, on exploitation, betrayal of trust, and crossing borders. Childhood incest survivors live in chaos; all the boundaries of their world have been breached: bodily borders, mental boundaries, and family frameworks. In her memoir *The Naked King* (Hamelech eirom), Avramovitch testifies that "incest is not a single event and not even just an act of a father, but rather a whole life dynamic that has no limits and in which everything is allowed."[58] The hybridity of the incest memoirs can thus be understood as a reflection, a product, or a celebration of the volatile borders of the self, namely, the lack of conventional boundaries. The hybridity externalizes the lack of boundaries, the noncompliance to conventional and more organized kind of writing (and existence), and it becomes an unwritten component of the implied alliance between the writers and their readers. At the same time, the hybrid writing also allows itself the freedom to "rehabilitate" borders and thus to produce unexpected emotional and intellectual encounters.[59] More specifically, as part of the desire to express incest from the victim's perspective, the crossbreed writing enables the authors to deal with various aspects of the harm and its consequences in a nonstereotypical way, one that at times contradicts the popular representations of posttraumatic symptoms, as can be seen, for example, in victims' representations of dissociative behaviors.

"To Be Made Up of Separate Parts"[60]

Trauma survivors often employ dissociation as a protective mechanism that enables them to block out their awareness of the abuse. Dissociation is thus a situation in which events and experiences that normally are connected and integrated have been separated and divided from each other. Symptoms of dissociation resulting from trauma may include splitting, depersonalization, psychological numbing, disengagement, fragmentation, and denial or amnesia regarding the events of the abuse. In incest the abuse of a (usually) older member of the family is emotionally and intellectually incomprehensible for the abused child, hence dissociation and fragmentation mechanisms allegedly allow annulling the distressing event and the intolerable hardship. Much has been written about the dissociation mechanism and dissociative identity disorder (DID) (known in the past as multiple personality disorder, or MPD), as well as about their relation to severe and repeated physical, sexual, and/or emotional abuse in early childhood. In the present context, I am not interested in the rich and valuable psychological discourse about the disorder but rather in three separate subjects related to it: the ways in which the authors of the memoirs experience their dissociation and splitting, the psychoideological position they establish through it, and the connection between dissociation and their hybrid style.

Anat Gur interviewed victims of incest with eating disorders. She notes that one of the narratives about beneficent and healing treatment that came out of the interviews was associated with a depathologization of the traumatic symptoms. Gur notes that the interviewees positively mentioned treatments that gave meaning and significance to their severe symptoms, and that rather than referring to the symptoms as pathology, offered a new understanding of them as mental strategies of dealing with their childhood sexual abuse.[61] A similar effort at depathologizing the dissociation and understanding it as a symptom related to the abuse is apparent also in the autobiographical writing of the incest survivors. In this context it is important to listen to the ways in which the writers of the memoirs experience their dissociation and splitting.

In her article "Dissociative Identity and Its Representation in Contemporary Media," Maya Reed (the author of *Captive* mentioned above) emphasizes that contrary to popular representations of dissociative identity disorder (such as in the American sitcom *United States of Tara* from 2009 and the Israeli documentary *The Girl with the 30 Identities* from 2012), and contrary to what is implied by the past term "multiple personality disorder," the dissociative processes are taking place in one's identity and consciousness, and are not separated personalities. The different "personalities," which are called this because of historical convention, are in fact split components of a single personality that were personified in an untypical manner that created an interidentity amnesia, or a dissociative amnesia, namely, the inability to recall or relate to important personal information.[62] Etzel Cardeña stated that the memory discontinuities characteristic of dissociative identity disorder "produce a lack of self-integration, experienced by DID patients as the coexistence of diverse identities that exist more or less independently from the stream of consciousness and bank of memories of the presenting identity or alter."[63] Reed mentions that one of the first impulses of doctors and therapists is an attempt to document the differences between the alternative "personalities" of their patients. She quotes Frank W. Putnam, who argues that overemphasis of the multiplicity per se is a common error among therapists who are new to DID. Putman warns about a fascination with the differences between the personalities, which sends a clear message to the patient that the split personalities (and not the patient herslf) are the ones who fascinate the therapist and others. He mentions that patients with DID seek treatment not only because they have various identities within themselves; rather, at the heart of their distress are dissociative symptoms such as flashbacks, loss of time, memory lapses, hearing inner voices, and other conversion symptoms. They need treatment in a wide range of pathology that manifests itself, among other things, in psychosomatic symptoms and behaviors such as self-harm, suicidality, addictions, depression, and anxiety.[64]

The memoirs themselves—in their content, as well as their constant movement between genres and styles—replicate the structure of dissociative states, but contrary to the popular and therapeutic representations that Reed criticizes as extreme and dramatic, they reflect varied and more moderate experiences that are mainly internal, and do not occur like some circus act with prominent external expressions.

Shez's pseudomemoir novel *Away from His Absence* (Harchek meheadro) is written in first person and present tense. Born Efrat Yerushalmi, she changed her name to Shez, which is a contraction of *shem zmani*, or "temporary name." Ofra, the protagonist of *Away from His Absence*, and her friend Shez, who is thirty years older, are supposedly two distinct characters, and perhaps they are indeed two separate beings, but at the same time they are also the same figure. Moreover, even though in various interviews Shez—an incest victim—emphasizes that the novel does not reflect her autobiographical story, one might see in the duplication of Ofra and Shez an embodiment of both the fictional figure of Shez and her autobiographic representation in the character of Efrat Yerushalmi, who was fifty-one when the novel was published. "My other name [Efrat Yerushalmi] is the name of the girl I was, and she still lives in me. [. . .] There is the then and there, and there is the here and now," says Shez in an interview.[65] Ilan Sheinfeld notes that the writing in first person and present tense, together with the split between the narrator and Shez, is indeed the result of an emotional dissociative disconnect that is related to the incest, but in the novel it becomes "not only a horrifying outcome of incest, but also a literary device [. . .] that enables the author to split herself between several characters [. . .] in order to be able to write about those difficult things from a distance within reach, one that allows [her] to

touch them through a mask in the form of another character."[66] In other
words, Sheinfeld sees in the split a mediating device that allows for the act
of writing. Returning to Reed's observation about popular representations
of dissociative identity, we can understand Shez's novel as an attempt to
write the dissociation from her own (or her character's own) perspective.
Thus Shez's novel reveals the complex mechanism of an individual who
was—and still is—abused. The novel uncovers the cognitive and emotional
mechanism of a personality that is comprised out of various parts that
seem disconnected from one another, and that are embodied in the character of Ofra/Shez (sometimes also called "I/she" in the novel [67]). Each
part has its own reactions, feelings, thoughts, perceptions, and physical
sensations. But just as in the inner world of the dissociative personality,
there are various interactions between the different parts of her personality,
so too Ofra and Shez maintain a complex relationship in the novel. The
organization of the characters in a literary narrative highlights the fact
that even if the parts are experienced as separated to some degree, they
are not different "people" or altered "personalities" but rather different
expressions of the same woman:

> I [Ofra] look at that Shez, who does not realize who she is,
> what her story is, what this woman's story is, sixty-four years
> old and acting as if she was twenty. As if she is my age [. . .].
> I say these words out loud: "I am a stranger to you, why are
> you being so nice to me?" "You are not at all a stranger to
> me," Shez says. [. . .] "You are like a daughter to me," she says
> softly. "I know where you come from. Don't ever say to me
> that you are a stranger."[68]

People with dissociative disorders often feel as if they are split into
different personalities, because they have memories, thoughts, feelings,
and behaviors that might not be typical to them and that they have not
identified with themselves; at times they might feel that they are strangers
to themselves. Shez's novel expresses this feeling and even exaggerates it
through the choice of two different characters, but at the same time, the
dual deployment of Ofra's and Shez's personalities throughout the novel
allows for their eventual integration, enabling them to remain known to
one another as two parts of one being.

   Away from His Absence, as well as the other autobiographical writings,
therefore, establishes exchanges between identities that are not necessarily

experienced as complete "personalities" that take possession of the body but rather as "inner voices that affect feelings and behaviors."[69] To use Koren's language, "I do not have figures; I have parts. I have never felt that this is not me. My dissociation never has completely detached me from myself. I do not have multiple identities. [. . .] These are the different parts in the captivity and socialization process. [. . .] It is very difficult to explain that I consist of different parts and that I am [a] different version of them. [. . .] This is what it is like to be made up of separate parts."[70] This articulated statement demonstrates that the hybrid writing and integrated styles might be understood as a performance of dissociative states but also as overcoming the split. Sheri Oz explains that the multiple identities do not enable the dissociative personality to obtain a holistic perception.[71] Thus, as mentioned, on the one hand the multiplicity of genres act out the various emotional roles, namely, the split as the only way to experience the whole, but on the other hand it may also express the stage in which the victim overcomes the split, that is, an emotional stage that is able to experience the different genres (different roles) as part of an overall personality.[72]

Koren's memoir brings together e-mails and paintings in order to process, as well as to describe and explain, the splitting between the mature Ziv Koren and, the child she was, Zahavit, the dissociative character of Koren. The e-mails explain the paintings and respond to them directly. While the e-mails reveal the painting's agency, they also relate the visual image to the written text, hence creating an interpretative place in itself, a rhizomatic space that enables representation of the dissociative characters as simultaneously separate and consolidated, as both escapist and protective. In one of the e-mails the therapist Lev-Wiesel asks Koren about her relationship with Zahavit the child she was, and Koren answers that "now that she [Zahavit] paints through me, it gives her a place that I perhaps cannot give her. I facilitate, but it is not enough for her. The painting is a way for her to go back to her childhood and speak [ledaber] about what is happening to her."[73] The wording here is fascinating. First, for Koren some of the paintings that were drawn by her in her adulthood were drawn by Zahavit the child and not by Koren the adult. Secondly, the painting is a way to talk about (and not to articulate or express) the trauma. Thus, the dissociative text should be deciphered through the interface between the various dimensions of the self, as well as between the different media. In other words, the verbal and visual texts do not have a hierarchical relationship, and one does not come to explain or describe the other (as research about art therapy often tends to assume[74]), but rather their joint presence in the memoir, as well as in the emotional space of the writer/painter, is a dynamic intersubjective presence.[75] When Koren goes back to talking about herself as an adult, she writes, "Ziv is the assembly of all the parts together, with very strong control over them . . . she is the whole of all the parts . . . if each string of a violin is a part, then Ziv creates the melody."[76] Seven pages and five days later, the memoir presents Koren's painting of a violin with unraveled strings surrounded by musical notes. Next to this painting we see Koren's e-mail:

> This is a type of process that I can play. I play until they begin to break. The strings are torn . . . therefore, they need to be fixed. This is the cycle . . . I think that I tried to reflect through the painting the sensation that I perform and then I create the cutting . . . it is not simple; I need to connect them all and then continue from the place that the cutting was created. . . . Did I explain this well? This is the dissociation. The strings are the feelings and they are not connected and therefore I need all the time to connect the strings over and over again.[77]

This text explains the painting, and the painting both supports and contradicts the explanation. The painting precedes the description, while responding to earlier variations of the description. In other words, Koren expresses the dissociation through a hybrid representation that does not force her or her readers to choose between words and images or between early and late forms of self. Rather, this hybrid portrayal lets the survivor experience, process, and share the complex experience of splitting with her readers. Thus, *When Time Stood Still*, as do the other memoirs, reclaims the representations of their authors' suffering. They present a spectrum of distress, and different levels of anguish, and by so doing reject the appropriation of it by the therapist, the public, and the media, which tend to refer (if at all)—voyeuristically—only to the most extreme cases.

Summary: The Cliché of the Memoir

All of the memoirs discussed in this chapter present feminist approaches to sexual trauma. Most of them mention the enormous impact feminist therapy and rape crisis centers had on the authors' recovery and on their understanding of their personal experience within a wider social context. If there is anything common to all of the memoirs—which differ from each other in many aspects—it is that they all acknowledge the transition of pain into a text, and into a culture. These memoirs do not refer to the body as an essential and autonomous unthinkable and unarticulated area but rather relate to personal physical and emotional pain and abuse as a cultural and social product that should be deconstructed and questioned. Hence they raise questions such as how to talk about pain, how and why incest is silenced, what enables the exploitation, and so on.

Moreover, the autobiographical writings discussed here were all *published*, meaning they have passed into the public domain, and as such, they have become political speech. Writing the experience that (perhaps) has no words not only intends to describe the abuse and the experience of being a victim but also places it in an array of social power relations. In her memoir *Dad's Gift* (Hamatana shekibalti meaba, 2012), Gal-Cohen deals with the political dimension of testifying about sexual abuse: "To try to connect life experiences with the theory of social behavior, to try to combine the personal and the social. Perhaps a kind of 'the personal is political.' My experiences are mine alone, but if it happens to one more and to many more, it's something general that is going on here. The phenomenon of 'sexual violence' and 'incest' are general in any society, and then it is already a social phenomenon, a topic worth political pursuing. [. . .] It is really hard to understand talking about general social phenomenon and that's why I'm telling [it] through my personal experience, which I publish."[78] Personal experience is at the core of the events, but it is also a kind of a necessary rhetorical tool for the success of the political struggle. This struggle is present in different degrees of intensity in all of the memoirs, and in all of them writing itself is seen not only as a way of achieving the social objective but also as an evidence of personal or social—significant or modest, temporary or sustainable—triumph.

This position of overcoming difficult life circumstances and of not succumbing to the violent burden is admirable, and its personal, cultural, and political importance should not be underestimated. However, it is difficult not to also think about this narrative of "from trauma to recovery" as a cultural cliché. Just as nearly every American TV series character who has been raped or abused recovers, so do the memoirs narrate the difficulty and pain, but from the perspective of someone who not only managed to personally overcome it but is also in a position to make a personal and social change.

It is important for me to emphasize that even though the cliché is perceived at times as a form of expression that indicates a poor or mediocre way of thinking, one can also see it as a sophisticated rhetorical device that has the power to deliberately conceal and distort truths.[79] Therefore, Nana Ariel suggests that in order to understand the power of the cliché, we should ask what it does—how it operates and what functions it fulfills—instead of trying to understand what it says.[80] Roland Barthes sees in clichés measures that serve ideology, which present the historical as natural. Hence he claims that in order to unload the clichés from their power we should not only read them critically but also establish a new neologist language.[81]

According to this approach we should examine why the discussed memoirs were actually published, and in what ways their publication serves the same culture that allowed the incest in the first place. In other words, the cliché might be a red flag signifying the suspicion that the publication of the memoirs is not indicative of social change. In addition, it might not be a primary signal of social recognition of the massive dimensions of incest and sexual violence against children and women but rather its opposite, and the voices of the survivors might resonate in the public sphere because what they reveal does not in fact have a destabilizing effect on the social and cultural space around them. In this sense, the cliché dimension of the memoirs may be perceived as (yet another) defense mechanism of the survivors, a kind of variation of dissociation (i.e., by performing an act of speech the victim in fact covers up her story). As such, even though the memoirs protect their writers, they also hinder their capacity to cope with their pain. In other words, despite the fact that the memoirs reveal difficult elements of the survivors' lives, paradoxically they also conceals them and allows their personal and social concealment and repression.

Moreover, the stories of growth and triumph present a narrative in which, against all odds, the survivors manage to overcome their difficulties, thanks to their determination and willpower. This narrative implies a singular responsibility of the individual over his or her fate, and expropriates the social or political responsibility for the violence.[82] Thus, even though the memoirs present important and new voices that were unheard before, it might be argued that, in a sense, they are actually voicing hegemony and not the survivors, who are repeatedly stumbling in a world lacking compassion.

Without underestimating the huge importance of this critical suspicion, Irit Rogoff raises the following question: "But what comes after the critical analysis of culture? What goes beyond the endless cataloguing of the hidden structures, the invisible powers and the numerous offences we have been pre-occupied with for so long? Beyond the process of making and making visible those who have been included and those who have been excluded? Beyond being able to point our finger at the master narratives and the dominant cartographies of the inherited cultural order? Beyond the celebration of emergent minority group identities as an achievement in and of itself?"[83] Perhaps in order to address this question in the context of incest victims' memoirs we should reject Barth's position, which sees the cliché as a negative and dangerous element that contributes to the conservation of ideologies. Refraining from value judgments of clichés and perceiving them as constructive devices will enable us to understand the important role of the cliché in the reception of the memoirs, namely, we will be able to think about the cliché as essential for the communication between the authors and their readers. Generally speaking, while the critical approach refers to the clichés as a phenomenon that involves symbolic violence, the constructive approach refers to the use of clichés as an essential means of social interactions that rely on shared understandings and thus sees the cliché as a necessary substitute for chaos and violence.[84] Therefore, by the very act of being cliché, the narrative of overcoming the trauma enables the writers to communicate their painful experiences. Ruth Amossy and Terese Lyons explain that since clichés emerge through an act of recognition, they are actually rhetoric devices that enable communication: "The cliché is a familiar element encompassing the realm of '(every)one'; it insures a circular relationship between 'I' and 'you.' It is a common place in which emotional identification can occur."[85]

Memoirs about sexual violence in general, and incest in particular, are a relatively new phenomenon—and still quite a rare one—in Israeli culture. Thus to speak of what might be considered a cliché has in fact great significance both to the authors, who have no literary tradition to follow, and to the readers, who are new to these kinds of texts. In fact, it is hard to determine whether the cliché allows a nonthreatening dialogue between the memoirs and their readers, that is, that the cliché mediates the silenced experience, or whether the cliché is masking the dialogue, namely, the authors cannot imagine a different kind of dialogue, or they do not trust their readers to be able to engage in a nonbanal conversation. To be loyal to the rhizomatic structure of the memoirs, these options are probably taking place simultaneously.

In addition, the clichés play an important role in the construction of subjects as part of a social order. They function as a means of authorizing the subject to be a part of society, defining the subject as a member of society.[86] Accordingly, the cliché structure of the memoirs enables the excluded victims to be included (to some extent at least) in society. Moreover, the capacity to understand and relate to this almost-worn-out narrative of "from harm to growth" has the ability to define membership in the community and to mark the boundaries of its discourse.

Yet where the cliché is present, there is also a possibility of refuting it. And, indeed, in addition to the complexity that already exists in the use of a cliché narrative, the memoirs also draw a multidimensional rhizomatic formation that contradicts or opposes the cliché of "trauma and recovery." Thus, the memoirs adopt and replicate the cliché characteristic of the hegemonic, feminist, and psychoanalytic discourse of incest, while deconstructing and challenging it. The memoirs depict a layered and often-contradictory array of sexual abuse and its aftermath. Thus, in order to communicate this complexity and to be able to not only tell the truth of themselves but also to produce that same truth, they construct rhizomatic memoirs that establish anarchic structures that prevent one-dimensional statements or reductive generalizations about incest.

Unlike the other memoirs mentioned in this chapter, which were written by adults who are survivers of incest, Shirley's Diary: From the World of a Child Survivor (Miyomana shel Shirley, 1999) describes a series of incestual and other sexual abuses from the naïve perspective of Shirley, the child experiencing the abuse. Without understanding what happens, Shirley reveals a variety of feelings related to her abuse: her dislike of the rapes, the awakening of her sexual desire, her disappointment in her mother, her fears, the abuser's mechanisms of intimidation, the blindness of her teachers, and her death wish and attempted suicide, as well as her loneliness, eating disorders, dissociation disorders, and shame. All this is paired with a narrative of her vast emotional strength: "I just want to be similar to myself, and I have found that I am not so ugly."[87] On one page Shirley briefly refers to an episode related to her writing: "Today I wrote a poem, but it was so sad that I threw it away. In this poem I described the way I see myself: black as a raven that eats rotten things, or like clouds when there is a storm, or like a plague."[88] Shirley writes a poem, trying to express herself artistically and sublimate her pain, but she is unable to cope with the emotional intensity of the poetic outcome. At the same time, she also does not want to destroy or ignore the deep layer of the poem—or rather, of the writing process. Therefore she speaks about the poem in her diary. The diary thus becomes a kind of an unconscious intermediate stage between direct writing (her diary) and a poetic process (her poem).

Symbolically, and in retrospect, this moment becomes a kind of writing instruction to the adult survivors that will publish their autobiographical writings. In her unripe language Shirley urges the older writers not to give up their voice or the complexity of the experience, and not to set down their experience in a fixed or one-dimensional way. Indeed, the authors of the memoirs we have considered continue what Shirley started. Without having to hide their writing or throw away the fruits of their creation, they describe their lives in a multidimensional way, without guiding their narrative to a predetermined destination point. To end with the language of Avramovitch, "As opposed to a culture of a society that cherishes one single identity, and which aims to organize the world in a clear ranking [. . .], there are other spaces in which precisely the seemingly confusion and the lack of vertical order enables life in them. I wish to call each and every one to join my journey to the never ending book that has so far crystallized into an abundance of essays."[89]

Chapter 5

"The Girl with the Billy-Goat's Hoof"

Parental Abuse, Metamorphosis, and Poetics in the Poetry of Tsvia Litevsky

❧

Dionysus never had the pleasure of a mother's gaze, and his father's gaze terrified him.

—Tsvia Litevsky[1]

From the Album
The man
who was my father who wasn't
my father
The woman
who was my mother who wasn't
my mother
The girl
with the billy-goat's hoof,
the bull's testicles
and the cat's throat[2]

מִן הָאַלְבּוֹם
הָאִישׁ
שֶׁהָיָה אַבָּא שֶׁלִּי שֶׁלֹּא

הָיָה אַבָּא שֶׁלִּי
הָאִשָּׁה
שֶׁהָיְתָה אִמָּא שֶׁלִּי שֶׁלֹּא
הָיְתָה אִמָּא שֶׁלִּי
הַיַּלְדָּה
בַּעֲלַת טֶלֶף הַתַּיִשׁ,
אֶשְׁכֵי הַפָּר
וּגְרוֹן הֶחָתוּל

On the cover of Hebrew poet Tsvia Litevsky's second book is part of a photo depicting a girl-woman-doll. It was taken by American photographer Ralph Eugene Meatyard (1925–1972), a resident of Lexington, Kentucky, who is known for his experimental photographs. Among his crowning achievements is his 1960 "No Focus" series, in which blurring, the deliberate obfuscation of the photographed subject, and, more fundamentally, the subversion of the photographic technique itself—the power of the lens and the realism that it appears to create—unremittingly test the limits of the artistic medium, as well as the limitations of the gazing eye. Meatyard's camera lens focuses, among other things, on children on the verge of adolescence making their first painful contacts with violent sexuality and emotional bereftness. His photographs create what look like hybrid images of elderly children, doll-children, and adolescents with animal bodies. Like Meatyard, Litevsky too deals with the psychopoetic juncture of abuse, metamorphosis, and ars poetica. The present chapter aims to examine these issues, focusing on the speaker's relationship with her father, who sexually abused her when she was young, and on her mother, who refuses to look her in the eye.

Tsvia Litevsky's voice burst onto the Israeli poetic scene two decades ago. She has been warmly and collegially embraced by such mainstream poets as Maya Bejerano, Nurit Zarchi, Efrat Mishori, and Rafi Weichert.[3] She has participated in mainstream poetry festivals and been published in Israel's leading literary journals. Her first book, *In Grace of Darkness* (Bahoshekh hameitiv, 1998), was awarded the Israel Education and Culture Ministry's prize for a best first book. Since then she has published six more books of poetry—*Don't Point Your Finger at Me* (Al tatsbia alai, 2003), *The Green towards the Green* (Hayarok bedarko el hayarok, with drawings by Tamra Rickman, 2006), *One Wall I Called Home* (Lekir ehad karati bayit, 2007), *Liturgy* (Liturgiya, 2010), *I Shall Die as Born* (Amut kenoledet, 2013), and *Fields of Infinite* (Arugot haeinsof, 2016)—and two books of essays, *Everything Is Full of Gods: Self and World in Myth* (Hakol male elim, 2013) and *Ascending to Light* (Migufo shel olam, 2019). Her poems set out a broad spectrum of experiences and impressions, from invocations of everyday events to coping with being a child of Holocaust survivors to ars poetic discussions, existential musings, and spiritual contemplations of nature.

In light of the poetic richness of Litevsky's oeuvre, I wish to clarify that in focusing on her treatment of parental abuse, I am not claiming that this is its overarching feature. I hope, rather, to shed light on a particular facet of her writing that is important both to gaining a deeper understanding of it and to broadening our insight into the complex relationship between creative writing and emotional distress. Moreover, insofar as it is possible to separate extra-poetic reality from poetry itself, I intend to deal not with Litevsky's biographical experience in the simple sense but with its embodiment—or reincarnation—in her poetry. Without entering into the multifaceted theoretical discussion of the relationship between biography and writing, or the relatively slim scholarly work on biographical writing by victims of sexual abuse, this chapter centers on Litevsky's poetic and expository writing on parental abuse. The poetic act, by nature and at its best, builds worlds that transcend the boundaries of the real world; it sets itself up not as a mirror to reflect what actually happened but as a space to set down and verbalize complex emotional processes and responses that are not necessarily those that might be expected. I wish to explore these poetic sites, as they are embodied in Litevsky's poetry. Moreover, in light of the silence surrounding incest, and how rare it has been in Israeli culture for incest survivors to find a literary voice (until very recently), it is important to concentrate on this aspect of Litevsky's poetry, and to make it more visible.

"Being Your Daughter": The Father Figure

From the point of view of the desirous god, metamorphosis is merely a prop picked out from the never-ending stock of the possible, which is at his beck and call, while from the point of view of a rape victim, metamorphosis is a last refuge before annihilation.

—Tsvia Litevsky[4]

"Rebirth"

> When the name "sexual abuse" was first given to the experience that
> molded my life, my world fell apart, and I began to grow.
>
> —Tsvia Litevsky[5]

> The cult of Dionysus: abandonment of the home as the embodiment
> of order and culture; going out into the wild; ecstasy (which means
> going beyond the self so as to merge with the god); loss of awareness;
> blindness; giving oneself utterly over to attentiveness; reduction of
> language to *call* and *echo* alone (the wild orgiastic cries)—with the
> victim at its center. The god in the image of the wild animal torn
> to pieces in order to be resurrected and reborn—this cult embodied
> my heart's desire.
>
> —Tsvia Litevsky[6]

Tsvia Litevsky's poetry is replete with mythological figures and archaeo-
logical sites. Not for naught is the cover of her first book adorned with
a detail from the wall paintings in the Grotte de Lascaux in the south
of France, perhaps the world's most famous cave of paintings by early
humans, dating from the Magdalenian period, some 12,000 to 17,000 years
ago. Litevsky turns these ancient works of art into a visual manifesto of
ars poetica. Like historical sites, mythology enables movement between
past and present. Litevsky's poetry is transfixed by (and sometimes also
fixated on) the past—both autobiographical (her own and her mother's)
and mythological. In a note to the cycle "Dionysus: Chapters of a Biography" (Dionysus: Pirkey biographiya), Litevsky explicates her project:
"The names of the poems in this cycle denote stations in the life story of
Dionysus, which begins with a traumatic birth."[7] Apart from announc-
ing a mythological biography, the title could also be taken as a guide to
reading Litevsky's own biography. If so, it is worth our while to examine
how mythology serves Litevsky's psychopoetic world.

In Litevsky's poetic autobiography, mythology offers a space of
exaltation, a "storm concealed in the heart of transparency."[8] In a 2012
video interview for the Hebrew "Writers Read" Internet project, Litevsky
relates an experience going back to her girlhood, of seeing the sun one
rainy winter day and thinking to herself, "I shall never give up on perfection."[9] Mythology, with its all-too-human gods, is rife with imperfection,

but it also holds up an ideal of perfection, of an exaltation to which one may aspire. Transgressions, errors, vengeance—all these take place in the supernal world. Litevsky's poetry is an ongoing effort to situate affliction in a world of perfection and exaltation.

Mythology also provides Litevsky with one of her most sophisticated psychopoetic tools: the metamorphosis. Metamorphosis enables its subject to oscillate between life and death, sleep and wakefulness, and femininity and masculinity, and to be reborn into different soul states. It offers a cogent poetic tool for writing about sexual abuse, as forms assumed and shed become the embodiments of fears, desires, and defense mechanisms for the individual who has been violated in body and soul.

In Ovid's *Metamorphoses* we learn of Actaeon, the hunter who became the hunted. Actaeon spies naked Diana (or Artemis, in Greek mythology), and she, as punishment, transforms him into an antelope who will be torn to pieces by his own hunting dogs. The mythological narrative joins forbidden (sexual) ogling with muteness and body battering. In Litevsky's rendering of this mythological tale, it is hard not to think of it in the context of sexual trauma.

Actaeon
Your eyes are ensnared by gleaming thighs,
a line of moistened hips,
a breast, a raised arm,
Their gaze disappearing everlastingly into the forested armpit.

Bristly hair bursts out
upon your joints, your nape, your back
your tailbone—
Your ears are raised to overtones
beyond human hearing,
openning as cathedral arches.
Your skin responds with trembling
to the insects suddenly smitten with you.
You do not feel the dogs' ravaging.[10]

אקטיאון
עֵינֶיךָ לְכוּדוֹת בְּלֹבֶן יְרֵכַיִם,
קַו מָתְנַיִם לַח,

שָׁה, זְרוֹעַ מוּרֶמֶת,
לָעַד נֶעְלָם מַבָּטָן בְּיַעַר בֵּית הַשֶּׁחִי.

שֵׂעָר נִחָר פּוֹרֵץ
בְּמִפְרַקְתֵּךְ, עָרְפֵּךְ, גַּבֵּךְ,
בְּעֶצֶם הַזָּנָב –
אָזְנֵיִךְ נִזְקָפוֹת לַצְּלִילִים הָעֶלְיִּים
שֶׁמֵּעֵבֶר לִשְׁמִיעַת אָדָם,
נִפְתָּחִים כְּקַשְׁתוֹת קָתֶדְרָלָה.
עוֹרֵךְ עוֹנֶה בְּרֶטֶט עַז
לַחֲרָקִים שֶׁהִתְאַהֲבוּ בָּךְ לְפֶתַע.
אֵינֵךְ חָשׁ בִּנְשִׁיכוֹת הַכְּלָבִים.

The poem presents a sharp transition from Actaeon's gaze on Diana's body to a description of his own changing body. In contrast to the sexual gaze on Diana that captures the eyes of the viewer and leads him to his loss ("Their gaze disappearing everlastingly"), the description of Actaeon's transforming body is accompanied by vital—almost erotic—verbs: his hair bursts out, his ears prick up, and his skin trembles to the extent that he does not feel the devastating bites of the dogs. His metamorphosis is described as a moment of extreme alertness and vitality leading to destruction; a kind of *petit mort* or *jouissance* in its Lacanian sense, that is, a lethal delight, a phallic pleasure that is related to the urge to conquer and achieve, and that paradoxically contains an almost unbearable level of excitation. And if so, then in Litevsky's poem, Actaeon's transformation from man to animal is not a punishment (as described in the mythology) but a result of his forbidden peephole, of his intrusive erotic excitement.

What is interesting, however, is that the poem could have focused on the intrusive eroticism of peeping, or, alternatively, it could have presented a kind of journey of vengeance for the sexual invasion, but instead it actually focuses on the process of Actaeon's detachment from his human body, namely on the metamorphosis itself. Actaeon becomes a figure that embodies the psychosomatic response to a difficult experience: despite his sharp senses, his emotional state prevents him from feeling the pain caused by the predatory dogs. The poem's narrator thus identifies not with Diana, who is as it were the victim, but with the mechanism by which the body assumes the quality of woundedness, of being torn asunder.[11] It is this identification that enables the connection between Actaeon, the victimizer, who undergoes a metamorphosis, and Litevsky's poetic persona that adopts metamorphosis as a mechanism for responding to sexual violence.

Greek mythology, as we know, is replete with stories of women who were raped and consequently metamorphosed,[12] including Philomela, raped by Tereus and turned into a nightingale; Io, raped by Zeus and turned into a cow; Arethusa, turned into a stream in her attempt to flee Alpheus; and Daphne, transformed into a laurel tree in order to get away from Apollo. The metamorphoses to which these are subjected constitutes an (unsuccessful) effort to maintain the rape victims' silence. But their silencing comes not only from outside; it is also an expression of the victims' inability to verbalize their trauma, to express it, or, as Litevsky puts it, "to call it by name."[13] Moreover, as "a last refuge before annihilation,"[14] metamorphosis expresses the incest victim's sense of an alteration of body and soul. It is a psychopoetic variation of the mechanism of detachment or dissociation, of the emotional disconnection that occurs in the course of a traumatic experience.

Dissociation is a mental process in the course of which a disconnection is created in the subject between different aspects of the self that are ordinarily integrated with one another. It is a state of inability to integrate information, experiences, or emotions that appear to be threatening. Eli Somer, following John Briere, lists several common types of dissociative behavior occurring in abuse victims: disengagement, numbing, observation, and amnesia. There is a mental disengagement from one's surroundings; a numbing mechanism by which the subject dilutes the strength of the negative emotions bound up with the traumatic event; an experience of becoming an external observer of the events rather than the one caught up in them; and a repressive amnesia aimed at forestalling contact with memories too hard to bear.[15] Metamorphosis—poetic dissociation—thus enables one, cognitively, to survive the abuse, but at times at the price of a loss of subjectivity. In her autobiographical essay "Calling It by Name" (2004), which describes the process of her rehabilitation from the sexual abuse she endured, Litevsky elucidates this loss: "Eliminating the dimension of consciousness from language means eliminating its vital foundation, eliminating the creative dimension of reality. It therefore led to a state of incoherence, a one-way metamorphosis of life into death, of the world into chaos."[16]

Litevsky's reading of mythology as a narrative of sexual victimization also comes to expression in the poem "Aphrodite," in which the goddess of love is figured not as a seductress but as the victim of nonverbalized trauma.

The poem rails against the oversight of painters who see only Aphrodite's beauty without understanding how "in my [Aphrodite's] shrouded nights I was violated over and over."[17] Their artistry blinds them to the travesty. In the poem "Tammuz," we return to the image of Aphrodite, this time by way of the story of Adonis, the god of fertility. Aphrodite punishes Smyrna, daughter of King Theias, by making her lust for her father. When her father realizes that she has seduced him, he wants to kill her, but the gods transform her into a myrrh tree. Adonis is born of the tree and entrusted to the care of Persephone. Years later, he meets his death when Artemis, seeking revenge on Aphrodite—who loves Adonis—sends out a wild boar, who, according to some accounts, gores him in the groin. From his blood springs the crimson anemone. Litevsky's poem is hypnotized by the moment of the blood's transformation: "Right here, close up, / My blood is sprouting anemones."[18] The poem's female speaker identifies with bleeding Adonis, with the boy born of sin. At the same time, going back to poems such as "They Left Me Lying There," and "The Circle Line,"[19] which deal with paternal abuse, "Tammuz" also expresses identification with Smyrna, the daughter who, as it were, seduces her father. The story of Adonis enables the speaker to express the duality of the daughter's experience in being both victimized and pervaded by feelings of guilt and desire for the father who ravaged her.

Calling It by Name: From Trauma to Art

While Aphrodite in Litevsky's early poem was unable to vent her distress and so represented the failure of creativity in the face of sexual trauma, the speaker in "Tammuz" returns to the mythological possibility of transforming blood (pain, the violated body) into anemones (flowers, beauty, vitality). The act of writing comes not to verbalize the traumatic event but to transform certain aspects of it. The creative process demands the channeling of pain into the realms of writing and of spiritual and cognitive exploration.

In the essay "Calling It by Name," Litevsky describes her emotional coping with her father's sexual abuse. Six years later, in her book *Liturgy*, she published the poem "Calling by Name" (Likro bashem), in which she writes of her progenitor (*molidi*): "And to me he passed down the pain / of calling by name all the things surrounding."[20] Thus she signaled the transition from calling her trauma by name to the naming that lies at the heart of the creative process.

This transition is also the moment when the transformation occurs from the image of the specific, flesh-and-blood father to the great, symbolic Father, the patriarch, the God, the Progenitor and world-Creator. Patricia Yaeger and Beth Kowaleski-Wallace have discussed the wholesale adoption by Western culture in general and by feminist readings in particular of the Lacanian theory regarding the "Law of the Father and the Phallus." This theory, they argue, separates the concrete, physical, embodied father (who by virtue of this, argues Elaine Scarry, is vulnerable and ephemeral, that is, in possession of a historical body[21]) from the symbolic Father, the Phallus, representing patriarchal power. They elaborate that by suppressing the father's body, the Lacanian conception necessarily suppresses his historicity, for the symbolic Father operates beyond the limits of time and space. Consequently, they call for recognizing the father both as a product of history and as an ideological construct.[22] Shira Stav has shown how incest "is the very (suppressed) reality that underlies any attempt to represent the father-daughter relationship."[23] In order to free the daughter from this hermetic construct, she calls for recognition—on the father's part, but mainly on the daughter's—of the father's existence as a body. Following scholars such as Yaeger, Kowaleski-Wallace, Jane Gallop, and Nancy Miller,[24] who saw the suppression of the fatherly body as a principal foundation of his power, Stav, too, argues that restoring the father's historical concreteness is a way of undermining his symbolic power and opening the door to new directions of thought and communication.[25]

Although the movement in Litevsky's work is mainly from the concrete father to the symbolic one (and from wounding to creativity),[26] her sojourns in the world of the concrete father do not allow for any sharp separation between him and the symbolic father. They also don't yield the relief, mutuality, and compassion that Scarry attributes to the possessor of a body. Descriptions on the order of "You withdrew your hand from my pants. / I brought you a towel from the kitchen"; "Soft and vulnerable as a baby / is your masculinity against my thigh";[27] or "the curve of your pinion sucks / into itself the force of gravity"[28] leave the speaker in the realms of terror and horror: "Will the threat be fulfilled? / Will I die?"[29]

Moreover, the restoration of the father's body, for Litevsky, extinguishes the speaker's own existence. The poem "The Gully of Zin" (Naḥal Zin) opens with a Darwinist perspective: "Who lives here, / who eats whom? / How is that project of sustenance and extinction accomplished?" In this context, the daughter hasn't got a chance, and she disappears, turning into a hollow in a stone "into which your groan will inject itself, my father / and the groans of all your fathers' fathers," or a crease in a hand "whose

deep, arid crevices / you will flood, my father, with the torrents of your
eyes, you and your fathers' fathers." The father's groans and tears—inherent
to his denial to himself of his own violence but simultaneously the palpable
manifestation of his embodiment and his vulnerability—extinguish the
daughter's existence: "I am the end of a thousand years of wandering."[30]

The call to recognize the father's physicality and historicity is indeed
fascinating from a theoretical point of view and exciting for the variety of
emotional, cultural, and poetic options that it opens up. At the same time,
the call to embrace the historical father (even if he comes in addition to
the symbolic one) does not, I believe, come to grips with one of the more
tortuous and widespread mechanisms associated with incest—that of the
victim's identification with the victimizer. Anna Freud argued that in order
to cope with the external threat, the subject internalizes the figure that
roused her to terror and so converts the passivity of being a victim into
activity; that is, in her inner world, she changes the power arrangements
between herself and the aggressor.[31] Sándor Ferenczi, relating specifically
to child victims of sexual violence, understands identification with the
victimizer as allowing the child an illusion of control, of being prepared
for danger.[32] But what is important to him is not the motivation for
identifying with the victimizer but that in the course of it the daughter,
though she identifies with the father's power, simultaneously endows him
with her physicality. In other words, the cultural separation between the
penis and the phallus, between the concrete and the symbolic father—of
such critical importance in the modern Western experience—is not part
of the daughter's usable emotional heritage. In the daughter's experience of
pain and betrayal, the body's power (both her father's and her own), along
with its weakness and vulnerability, are not separated from her feelings
of annihilation, or of being singled out, or of omnipotence.

Moreover, Litevsky's poems express a variety of relationships between
the father's consciousness and that of the daughter. At times the daughter
identifies with the father, while at others she endeavors to preserve her
own consciousness. Ferenczi—like Yaeger and Kowalesky-Wallace—pre-
supposes a separation between the consciousness of the victim and that
of the victimizer. But that separation, even if it is sought or desired, is
not always attainable in the worlds of literature and of trauma, especially
in the context of incest, since the familial relationship between father
and daughter makes it even harder to separate their consciousnesses.
Litevsky's metamorphoses enable her to express the multifacetedness of
these identifications, and the complex interrelationship between the need

for the father and the daughter to separate and the need to preserve their closeness (both because of the need for identification with the aggressor in order to anticipate his behavior, as Ferenczi argues, and because he is the father—the symbolic order—that same order from which one must separate in order to establish the self; but in order to separate from it one must first identify with it).

The poem "The Circle Line" (Kav hama'agal) opens with a scene of abuse and the identification that comes as a consequence: "You circle around me / blinding me with a high beam of terror / we are accomplices." The poem continues with a description of the breaking of the taboo: "What is forbidden to see / gleams at me from all sides"; and with the chilling question: "What is this profound obedience engendered in me by your gaze?"[33] Slavoj Žižek, following Lacan, distinguishes between two types of identification. The first, the type discussed by Anna Freud and Ferenczi, is identification with what we would like to be. The second is the internalization of the abuser's gaze, that is, identification with "the very place *from where* we are being observed, *from where* we look at ourselves so that we appear to ourselves likeable, worthy of love."[34] If the "worthy" is what is capable of being seen, what can be marked by the gaze, then this mechanism of identification, by definition, is doomed to failure in the incest victim. The daughter never experiences or internalizes being seen as worthy of love, both because in sexual abuse the father, by definition (again: as an individual and as a cultural representation) does not see his daughter ("How can I know I exist, if no one sees me?"[35]), and because of the compounding, in the incestuous relationship, of the contention and conflict bound up with the notion of "love," problematic and suffused with sexual tension as it already is. The daughter's inability to wholly internalize the father's gaze—or his language, to invoke Ferenczi's conceptual realm—creates a disturbing, unbridgeable, and omnipresent gap between the daughter's perspective and that of the father. Thus, the need to be both worthy and visible—that is, the unquenchable desire for the father's gaze, both external and internalized—engenders that "profound obedience" to him, to both the concrete and the symbolic father. "Would that I could extract you / from my bloodstream," cries the daughter in the poem that opens with the line "If being your daughter" (Lu heyoti bitekha), expressing both the internalization of the father figure and the need to separate from it.[36]

This twilight world between the daughter's gaze and the gaze that seeks to be worthy of the father's gaze allows no escape from that "profound obedience." The only opening, at this stage, for escape from the emotional trap is by way of blindness, of obliterating the gaze: "My gaze seeks a hiding place / but I see only him. How shall I say I saw— / How shall I say I didn't see— / Who will believe me— / God, strike me blind";[37] "Come with your finger, Daddy / and poke out my eye";[38] "I need nothing but flesh / to feed / my blindness."[39]

Establishing a gaze that is not a variation of the father's is the project of every daughter in a patriarchal culture,[40] the psychopoetic project of every artist daughter, and certainly the main project in the experience of a writing daughter who is an incest survivor. The speaker in the poem "The Minotaur's Daughter" (Bat haminotaur) who kills her half-man, half-bull father is left with emptied eyes.

The Minotaur's Daughter

I cannot say
"My father's hands were a murderer's hands."
The fear in his gaze—
my reflection.
I just can't.

The clamor of invisible stands
deafens my ears.
An inhuman crowd
surrounds the labyrinth arena
emitting a loud, rhythmic whispering
like the blood *rushing* in my head.
I can't take it anymore.
I split the Minotaur's heart
with the blade
my soul shrinking into its tip.
His corpse is exposed to all.
Nothing can stop me anymore.
I exit,
my body is spent.
My eyes are empty.

The sides of Rothschild Boulevard
wrap me in the depth on the surface of depth.
The treetops of depth.

Houses of depth.
I stop walking.
I listen.[41]

בַּת הַמִּינוֹטָאוּר
אֵינֶנִּי יְכוֹלָה לוֹמַר
«יְדֵי אָבִי הָיוּ יְדֵי רוֹצֵחַ».
הָאֵימָה בְּמַבָּטוֹ–
בְּבוֹאָתִי.
אֵינֶנִּי יְכוֹלָה.
הֵמַלַּת יְצִיעִים סְמוּיִּים מִן הָעַיִן
מַחֲרִישָׁה אֶת אָזְנִי.
קָהָל בִּלְתִּי אֱנוֹשִׁי
סְבִיב זִירַת הַלַּבִּירִינְתְּ
מַשְׁמִיעַ לְחִישָׁה רָמָה ,קְצוּבָה
כְּמַשַּׁק הַדָּם בְּרֹאשִׁי.
אֵינֶנִּי יְכוֹלָה עוֹד.
אֲנִי מְפַלַּחַת אֶת לֵב הַמִּינוֹטָאוּר
בַּלַּהַב
שָׁאַל חַדּוּ נִצְטַמְצְמָה נַפְשִׁי.
גְּוִיָּתוֹ גְּלוּיָה לְעֵין כֹּל.
דָּבָר אֵינוּ עוֹצֵר עוֹד בַּעֲדִי.
אֲנִי יוֹצֵאת הַחוּצָה,
אִיבְרַי רֵיקִים מִמַּאֲמָץ.
עֵינַי רֵיקוֹת.

צִדֵּי שְׂדֵרוֹת רוֹטְשִׁילְד
עוֹטִים עָלַי עֹמֶק לְפָנִים מֵעֹמֶק.
צַמְּרוֹת עֹמֶק.
בָּתֵּי עֹמֶק.
אֲנִי עוֹצֶרֶת מִלֶּכֶת.
מַאֲזִינָה.

The daughter's murder of her father lacks the power to establish a nonpatriarchal gaze. Moreover, murdering the father constitutes an internalization of the male position, both in the Freudian sense of killing one's father as a male fantasy, and because of the daughter's identification with the mythological Theseus, killer of the minotaur, who was considered Athens' primal lawmaker (his name derives from the Greek word *thesmos*, or "institution"; in other words, he is the very embodiment of the symbolic order). At the same time, however, the speaker is identifying with the only mythological figure endowed with the power to escape the labyrinth built by Daedalus, using the ball of twine given him by Ariadne. The father's murder in Litevsky's poem is thus not only an attempt to extinguish him but also, simultaneously, a fantasy of escape from the familial and emotional maze.

The journey of flight from the father and the process (with its successes, failures, and struggles) of establishing the daughter's gaze are bound up with the writing act; it is they that constitute the deep-seated transition from "calling it by name"—an act of designation focused on verbalizing the sexual abuse—to "calling by name"—the ability to verbalize the world in all its various dimensions. Designation, the writing act, thus involves both approaching the father's gaze and the effort to escape that very same gaze, but it neither unravels the snarl nor does it necessarily free the gaze's owner from her bonds. In the poem "Gazelles" (Ayalot), the speaker's gaze becomes a yoke on its object. Here is the poem's opening verse:

> What are the gazelles trying so hard to flee?
> What is it they want to throw off their backs?
> It's my gaze they're fleeing
> It's my gaze they want to throw off
> their slender, curvaceous backs, oh so lovely
> my covetous gaze
> resting on their lovely backs—to throw off.[42]

מִמָּה נִמְלָטוֹת הָאַיָּלוֹת בִּמְרוּצָתָן
מָה תִּרְצֶינָה לְהַשִּׁיל מֵעַל גַּבָּן
מִמַּבָּטִי הֵן נִמְלָטוֹת
אֶת מַבָּטִי תִּרְצֶינָה לְהַשִּׁיל מֵעַל
גַּבָּן הַקָּמוּר וְהַצַּר הַיָּפֶה מִכָּל יָפֶה
מַבָּטִי הַחוֹמֵד
הַשָּׁוּרֶה עַל גַּבָּן הַיָּפֶה לְהַשִּׁיל

"What do the gazelles do at night?" asked the highly acclaimed Hebrew poet Leah Goldberg; "Who is the keeper of their sweet dreams . . . What do the gazelles dream of at night? . . . Who wakes them at dawn from their sleep?"[43] Her questions bridge between the poetic world and the world outside it, while attributing to words the ability both to describe and to create worlds. In her late poem "Returning" (1969), which sets out to answer "the questionnaire on 'why are lyric poems written,' " Goldberg has no doubt of the power of the written word: "So what to do with horses in the twentieth century / and with the gazelles / and with those big stones / in the Jerusalem hills?"[44] Litevsky, however, wonders, "What are the gazelles trying so hard to flee?"[45] Her question expresses not only a sense of being pursued, but also, primarily, her consciousness of their flight, that is, of their movement and their anticipated disappearance. The speaker's answer is unambiguous: "It's my gaze they're fleeing," the speaker's gaze, the very foundation of the poetic act, which has become violent and threatening in coveting the gazelles' rippling beauty and threatening to imprison it within the walls of the poem. The connection between gazelles (*ayalot*) and poetry echoes the biblical blessing of Jacob to his son Naphtali: "Naphtali is a hind [*ayala*] let loose, which yields lovely fawns" (Genesis 49:21). This blessing has received a wide variety of interpretations, and although its meaning is not entirely clear, one can see a link in the verse between the blessing, the nimbleness of the hind, and the establishment of a poetic statement. In Litevsky's poem, however, the gazelles that have been let loose are not a stimulus for creativity but rather are fleeing in an attempt to evade their poetic fate and the speaker's gaze.

The paralyzing force of the gaze underlies Lacan's discussion of the gaze and art. In Seminar 11, he relates to painting as a "terminated gesture," one that freezes movement.[46] Lacan describes the paradoxical situation of the painter vigorously at work on a maneuver that actually freezes movement—and as such, kills. Cezanne's paintings, according to Lacan, allow one to track this dialectic of motion (associated with the symbolic), on the one hand, and stopping or suspension (associated with the imaginary), on the other.[47] Similarly, Litevsky's poetry, too, oscillates between a conception of the poem (language, the word) as an attempt to grasp something that by definition eludes one and the realization that the artistic deed is a foredoomed effort to grasp something that is elusive by nature: "I saw an antelope in the field / a memory that resembles forgetting / a forgetting that is an antelope."[48] Already in her first book of poems, it emerges that the only way to do art is not to be concerned with memory and not to fear forgetting.[49] In "Conversation with Borges" (Siḥah 'im Borges), the speaker declares, "Already in high school, I traded memory for the possible. / Just be, I said to it, / the taste of a cake that I've never encountered."[50] Although "even a dream hasn't the guts,"[51] one must replace the pain of concrete reality with something better. Thus, a painting must be conceived not as an artistic creation that succeeds in capturing something on a small scale but as an expression of blindness, of the limitations of the artist. The only beauty that exists is that "which I knew not from sight."[52] Thus, in the transition from "calling it by name" to "calling by name," traumatic blindness is converted into blindness as a poetic stance. Just like Tiresias, the blind seer of Thebes, whose blindness gave him the capacity for profound insight, for Litevsky, too, unseeing becomes an isle of seeing; darkness, *nihil*, is the source of creativity. "For me, darkness is the condition for rebirth," she wrote in an essay marking the publication of her book *Liturgy*. "To be reborn as much as possible— that is my desire."[53] Metamorphosis as a vessel for expressing the body and subjectivity of abuse victims is itself metamorphosed, to create a poetic voice that not only does not fear confronting its own death ("and everything I write is absorbed into you and vanishes"[54]) but also arises courageously to hope and joy, as attested in the poem "Chorus" (Zimrah):

Birds obscured by splendor
plead to be born.
Lightly nodding, I assent.
A quick flutter, and they emerge from my vents
bundles of bursting energy, joy.[55]

זמרה
צִפֳּרִים סְמוּיוֹת בַּזֹּהַר
מְבַקְּשׁוֹת לְהִוָּלֵד.
בְּנִיד רֹאשׁ קַל אֲנִי נֶעְתֶּרֶת.
בְּפִרְפּוּר מָהִיר וָעַז הֵן נֶחֱלָצוֹת מִפִּיּוֹתַי,
פְּקָעוֹת שֶׁל כֹּחַ מִתְפָּרֵץ, שִׂמְחָה

"Any Distance / Is the Thrill of My Returning to You"[56]: The Mother Figure

The red-hot feeling, so dominant in my life, that I felt towards my mother, I called "love." My mother was never gone from my thoughts. My joy in my achievements and talents was the joy of laying them at her feet. From when I was a little girl, I had raised myself for her sake. [. . .]

Her sadness stirred me to dread. Her happiness was the project and purpose of my life. . . . Is that love? Is that constant certainty, even in my adult years, that I cannot live without her, to be interpreted as love? How sad, though also enlightening, to find that these feelings are represented in the world by the word "anxiety." The linguistic signification, and so also the cognitive-emotional signification, was lacking. That wasn't love, but a terrible cry of privation, an abnegation of my own self in order to maintain my mother, for her collapse or abandonment would have left me alone against my father.

—Tsvia Litevsky[57]

A CRY OF PRIVATION

In Litevsky's poetry, the father's assault takes place within the domestic, familial realm. The home, Litevsky reminds us, is "the representation of the soul, with its burden of significances—territory, borders, protection, intimacy—it is the un-homely (*unheimlich*) place."[58] More specifically, in Litevsky's psychopoetic world, the sordid family story is embodied in a complex dynamic of gazes, identities, and expectations. In decoding the figure of Dionysus, one of Litevsky's principal objects of identification,[59] it is the various gazes that shape both the traumatic experience and the struggle to come to terms with it. As she wrote, "Dionysus never had the pleasure of a mother's gaze, and his father's gaze terrified him. His primal need for a confirming gaze was never answered and remained a constant privation. [. . .] Everywhere he had to fight for recognition."[60]

The first part of this chapter was concerned with the father's terrifying gaze; the second will be devoted to the mother's absent one. By examining the poem cycle "Give Me a Face" in Litevsky's book *One Wall I Called Home*, I wish to inquire into the implications of the mother's missing gaze and the dynamic between the daughter crying out for it and the mother who looks aside.

The poem cycle "Give Me a Face" (Teni li panim),[61] dedicated "To Mom" (Le'ima), describes the relationship between the speaker—the daughter—and her Holocaust survivor mother. Its time frame is bounded at one end by the mother's childhood and at the other by her funeral. It exposes a complex relationship, straddling geographical and emotional realms and dealing with the speaker's loss of her mother as an adult. Compounding this complexity, the mother herself, having lost her own mother at a young age, knows well the experience of parental abandonment.

The title "Give Me a Face" exposes the core of the mother-daughter relationship: The daughter experiences herself as faceless, as lacking an identity, and her mother as the only figure capable of correcting that deformity. Moreover, the call to "give me a face" intimates the bitter truth of the mother's "concealed," missing face. But just as the notion of the "concealment" of God's face (*hester panim*) does not contradict its presence, so, too, does the "concealed face" of the mother not only not cancel out its presence, it also, primarily, highlights its centrality to the daughter's life:

In your embrace is no shelter from the terror of your absence.
See how my skin, in your bosom, grows
ranks of scales,
in my mouth, a forked tongue.
Yellow gazing slits
open up slowly beneath my eye membranes.
In a little while, from in your arms,
I shall leap out into the thicket,
my breath setting fire to the grass.[62]

אֵין בְּחִבּוּקֵךְ הֲגָנָה מֵאֵימַת הֶעָדְרֵךְ.
רְאִי אֵיךְ מַצְמִיחַ עוֹרִי בְּחֵיקֵךְ
שׁוּרוֹת קַשְׂקַשִּׂים,
בְּפִי לָשׁוֹן מְפֻצֶּלֶת.
חֲרִיצֵי מַבָּט צְהֻבִּים
נִפְקָחִים לְאַטָּם תַּחַת קְרוּם עֵינַי.
עוֹד מְעַט וּמִבֵּין זְרוֹעוֹתַיִךְ
אֲזַנֵּק אֶל הַסְּבַךְ,
נְשִׁימָתִי שׂוֹרֶפֶת אֶת הָעֵשֶׂב.

The fear of the mother's disappearance is the principal stimulus for the metamorphosis that transforms the speaker from a human figure into a kind of beast, a dragon or salamander. The lack of maternal protection forces the daughter to develop a protective armor (the "ranks of scales"), but, paradoxically, that armor signifies the annihilation of her self, her transformation from a human subject into a mythological beast. Moreover, that metamorphosis is also a fantasy—at once desired and terrifying—of a journey of separation from the mother, of leaving the maternal embrace ("In a little while, from in your arms / I shall leap out into the thicket").

The fantasizing itself, along with the recognition of the limitations of the maternal embrace, mark the separation between mother and daughter, but it also simultaneously expresses the symbiosis at the base of their relationship, the inability of the daughter to break away from her mother. Realizing the fantasy will lead to the grass being set afire. But, just as in Dahlia Ravikovitch's poem "The Dress," the burning dress— the danger, the terror—cannot be distinguished from the speaker who wears it ("I'm not wearing a dress at all, can't you see / what's burning is me"[63]), so too the grass burned by the daughter's breath is not outside her but is bound up with her own childhood: "Deep in the tall grass, I recognized a three-year-old girl / ablaze wholly to give. To be given [to her mother]."[64] It is out of that recognition—of the three-year-old, who is also the metamorphosing girl and the adult woman experiencing her mother's death—that the speaker declares to the mother: "You are my adventure. / Any distance / is the thrill of my returning to you."[65] The only possible distance/space for the daughter is that which is constructed and bounded by the limits of her need for her mother. In contrast to the Freudian *fort/da* game (away!/back!), in which the infant copes with the process of separation from its mother by rehearsing the painful experience of separation while also controlling it,[66] the *fort-da* in Litevsky's poetry expresses failure to cope with the separation and marks the limits of that leap out of the maternal arms.

The failure to separate from the mother, and the daughter's constant yearning for her, turn the metamorphosing situation of self-annihilation and rebirth into the mother's embrace in an unrelenting existential-emotional condition. For Litevsky, it is inextricably bound up with her mother's traumatic past as a Holocaust survivor who had lost her own mother even before the war, when she was only five years old. Allusions to that past appear in only two of the poems:

. . .
Ice.
On the face of it you wound your way each morning
from the orphanage to school
in a coat too large for you.
On the face of it you fled the Germans.
. . .[67]

. . .
קֶרַח.
עַל פָּנָיו שֶׁרַכְתְּ דַּרְכֵּךְ בַּבֹּקֶר
מִבֵּית הַיְתוֹמִים לְבֵית הַסֵּפֶר

בִּמְעִיל גָּדוֹל מִמִּדָּתֵךְ.
עַל פָּנָיו בָּרַחְתְּ מִפְּנֵי הַגֶּרְמָנִים.

. . .

*

At five you swore never again to say "Mommy"
after tearing your lips
on the frozen iron railing.

From the other side of your orphanhood
I come knocking.

A word searches for a mouth
Mommy[68]

*

בַּת חָמֵשׁ נִשְׁבַּעַתְּ לֹא לוֹמַר עוֹד "אִמָּא"
לְאַחַר שֶׁקָּרַעַתְּ אֶת שְׂפָתַיִךְ
מִמַּעֲקֵה הַבַּרְזֶל הַקָּפוּא.

מִן הָעֵבֶר הַשֵּׁנִי שֶׁל יַתְמוּתֵךְ
אֲנִי מִתְדַּפֶּקֶת.

מִלָּה מְחַפֶּשֶׂת לָהּ פֶּה
אִמָּא

What is the other side of orphanhood? On what door, partition, wall is it that the daughter comes knocking?

The experience described in the last verse of the poem may be ascribed to the mother: in the mouth of the little girl orphaned of her mother, the word "Mommy" has been emptied of substance. But the verse can also be read as referring to the speaker, the daughter of that orphaned girl, wandering in search of her mother, seeking a way to break through the wall of her mother's orphanhood. This twofold ending expresses a kind of double orphanhood: the orphaned mother, by her truncated functioning, passes the orphan experience on to her daughter, infusing her with the sense of parental deprivation. Daughter and mother come together in their longing for the mother of which each is bereft—the one orphaned and the other abandoned.

The mother's incapacity for emotional functioning as a mother and her stunted emotional presence in her daughter's life, a recurrent trope in Litevsky's poems, produces in the daughter a sense of being "wildly unmothered," of an orphanhood deriving not only from the mother's actual death but from maternal abandonment in various forms. "If a mother had deserted us," writes Adrienne Rich, "whatever our rational forgiveness, whatever the individual mother's love and strength, the child in us [. . .] still feels, at moments, wildly unmothered."[69] This as-it-were orphanhood and the mother's problematic motherhood are bound up with each other in a tangled, unyielding knot that cannot, it seems, be unraveled and endlessly turns back on itself.

The image of the daughter knocking on the wall of the mother's absence ("From the other side of your orphanhood / I come knocking") may remind us of another orphaned girl whose effaced subjectivity is one of her most salient features: Tirtza, the heroine of Shmuel Yosef Agnon's influential novella "In the Prime of Her Life" (Bidmei yameha) and probably one of the most prominent female characters in Hebrew literature.[70] The bond between Tirtza and her mother, Leah, is at the center of the emotional drama sketched by Agnon. The extent to which Tirtza lives her own life or tries to reconstruct, rehabilitate, or replicate her mother's is a focal question, one that cannot be extricated from Tirtza's own process of establishing her identity or of separating—actually and emotionally—from her mother. Her enormous identification with her mother is of course one of the principal drivers of the story's development, and it is also a formative element in establishing Tirtza's voice.

The mother's voice is recalled in Agnon's novella mainly in its absence ("Lying on her bed my mother spoke scarcely a word,"[71]), and the memory of her illness is wrapped in the silence that enwrapped the house ("Our house stood hushed in its sorrow";[72] "A carpet was placed in the hallway to absorb the sound of each and every footfall"[73]). Tirtza, already in her mother's lifetime, yearns to hear that absent voice, and tries, almost without success, to reach it and touch its frayed edges: "But when she [Leah] spoke it was as though limpid wings had spread forth and led me to the Hall of Blessing. How I loved her voice. Often I would open her door just to hear her ask, Who's there?"[74]). Tirtza's sense of her own self-annihilation and of her lack of visibility and presence in the lives of her loved ones was constant in her childhood. Rattling the door in order to hear her mother ask "Who's there?" is an attempt to make herself present in the mother's life, even as she knows, unconsciously, that when her mother asks this question, it is not she, the daughter, who is its desired object. It is a touching attempt by Tirtza to impose her own existence, an attempt that in fact attests to her self-image as absent from the sphere of her mother's desires.[75] In her own moments of knocking at her mother's orphanhood, Litevsky is back in the same emotional space as Tirtza, rattling the door.

This foundational experience of ravenous hungering for that sheltered place that the mother does not provide, while changing the focus of identification, returns in Tirtza's adult years when she herself falls ill after her meeting with Akavia Mazal (her mother's love): "And whenever the door turned on its hinges I asked, 'Who's there?' My heart beat feebly and my voice was like mother's voice at the time of her illness." The little girl yearning for her mother's voice herself becomes that voice; the voice absent from the child's life becomes a critical presence in her adulthood. The type of erasure lurking in Tirtza's voice is multidimensional. Not only has it become the mother's voice, the one that was lacking, but by taking it on, Tirtza also erases the option that had yet been open to her as a child—that she herself might be the question's object. Now, in the mouth of the adult Tirtza, the question can no longer be directed at herself. This positioning erases the childlike desire to be the object of the question. It constitutes a kind of unconscious recognition—piercingly cruel—that the mother's question, too, was never really meant for the daughter.[76] The mother asking "Who's there?"—just like Tirtza at the stage when she takes over her mother's question—is not awaiting or expecting her daughter; she waits, it seems, for her lover. Thus, Tirtza not only wipes out her own voice by taking on her mother's, she also wipes out her own existence as the object of her mother's desire by taking on the position of desiring.

It was not Tirtza who was the object of her mother's desire and longing but Akavia Mazal. Tirtza, in several senses, completes the harsh process (of her own effacement) set in motion toward her by her mother by identifying with her mother and taking on the same object of desire (Akavia Mazal). It is as though the failure to be the wanted person— Akavia Mazal, or a beloved child—leaves her no room but to be the one who wants him.[77]

Litevsky, unlike Agnon, does not convert her desire for her mother into the desire for a man,[78] but she preserves in her poetry Tirtza's emotional-poetic model of the daughter's unquenchable desire for her mother's presence, and of self-effacement as a way of remaining present in the mother's life. Tirtza's knocking on the partition behind which her

mother's voice is hiding is the poetic-emotional position of the daughter
in Litevsky's poems: "From the other side of your orphanhood / I come
knocking."

The complexity of this position is palpable in the following untitled
poem:

I am the chamber of your memories.
They creep along my walls
in search of skin
and hair

I am the shadow that edges your smile
the unrelenting inside
holding on to your heels

I am the throng of crows
nesting
at the base of your childlike sleep
arms flung out—

Ah, let the children come and do not hinder them,
for to them belongs the kingdom of heaven.[79]

אֲנִי חֲדַר הַזִּכְרוֹנוֹת שֶׁלָּךְ.
לְאֹרֶךְ קִירוֹתַי הֵם זוֹחֲלִים
לְחַפֵּשׂ לָהֶם עוֹר
וְשֵׂעָר

אֲנִי הַצֵּל בְּשׁוּלֵי חִיּוּכֵךְ
הַפָּנִים הָעִקֵּשׁ
הָאוֹחֵז עֲקֵבַיִךְ

אֲנִי קְהַל הָעוֹרְבִים
הַמְּקַנֵּן
בְּתַחְתִּית שְׁנַת הַיֶּלֶד שֶׁלָּךְ
פְּרוּשַׂת הַזְּרוֹעוֹת –

הוֹ הַנִּיחוּ לַיְלָדִים וְאַל תִּמְנָעוּם,
כִּי לְאֵלֶּה מַלְכוּת הַשָּׁמַיִם.

This self-image as "the shadow that edges your smile" takes us back to the annihilation of self, the diminution stemming from life in the shadow of the mother's trauma, of being a "memorial candle."[80] Not only does the daughter experience herself as her mother's echo rather than as a subject in her own right, but it is a discordant echo, darkening her smile. It is a kind of burden; the daughter's very existence is a painful reminder of the mother's long-gone, lost childhood.

The daughter's description as "the unrelenting inside / holding on to your heels" exposes even more complex dimensions to her relationship with her mother, in that it voids the parental bond altogether by turning mother and daughter into twins; as it were, they are Jacob and Esau: "When [Rebecca's] time to give birth was at hand, there were twins in her womb. The first one emerged red, like a hairy mantle all over; so they named him Esau. Then his brother emerged, *holding on to the heel of Esau*; so they named him Jacob" (Genesis 25:24–26, CJPS translation). The poem's speaker draws her mother into the womb together with herself and so turns her mother simultaneously into mother and infant. The daughter is born as though holding on to the heel of her mother, who is also her twin. This is a neediness that will never be fulfilled, an existential position of holding on to a mother who has herself remained a child. It is holding on to the mother's Achilles heel—her weakest point. But, to go back to the mythological story of Achilles, the daughter is also holding on to what will ultimately produce her own vulnerability, her own point of weakness; for Achilles's mother, Thetis, we recall, immersed him in the river Styx to make him invulnerable, but because she was holding him by the heel as she did so, she unwittingly also created the point of vulnerability that would bring on his death from Paris's poisoned arrow.

The poem's speaker goes on to identify herself with the "throng of crows / nesting at the base" of her mother's childlike sleep. Here, too, as in the preceding verse, the speaker suppresses the basic mother-daughter relationship and locates herself in the mother's childhood, in her preparental stage. In her need to be assimilated into her mother, the girl-child who is to be born of the woman still immured in her own childhood turns herself into her mother's throng of crows, into that inconceivable Gothic cloud of darkness, the potential for destruction that surrounds the innocently sleeping little girl. Yona Wallach's poem "Cassius" opens with the realization that "the crows call to you / to leave the land and rebuild" and closes with the terrible certainty that "you will hear crows till the end of your days."[81] In between, in Wallach's poem, stands "crazy girl," who indirectly takes us back to Agnon's Tirtza, the "girl-child of ancient demons." The daughter, then, sets herself at the core of her mother's hurt and identifies with her orphanhood. In so doing, she effectively establishes her own seeming orphanhood.

But what is perhaps the most important context for the crows is the raven of rabbinic literature.[82] To be sure, the sages taught that the raven, for all its roughness, feeds its young; it makes an effort for the sake of its children, and all the more so must a person feed his or her sons and daughters.[83] However, according to the sages, ravens are also paradigms of creatures who disdain their own offspring and do not raise and nourish them: "when they bear their young and see that they are white—they fly from them."[84] Thus, for example, the sage Rava speaks of "him who can bring himself to be cruel to his children and household like a raven."[85] The daughter's emotional journey in Litevsky's poem leads her to nest in her mother's childhood, to forge for herself a place in her mother's pretraumatic stage. In so doing, she annihilates herself, both by ceasing to be a daughter and by identifying with the "crow" in her mother, with the fixation that will not allow the orphaned girl to grow up to be her daughter's mother, with the raven that abandons its young—that is, her own self.

"Ah, Let the Children Come"[86]

Unlike the daughter who is the mother's chamber of memories, the shadow edging her smile and her throng of crows, the mother herself is described in the poem as sleeping: "your childlike sleep, arms flung out—." This Jesus-like image draws us to the poem's climactic lines, to Jesus's command in Matthew 19:14, and to the speaker's own plea: "Ah, let the children come, and do not hinder them, for theirs is the kingdom of heaven." Although the daughter looks at her mother as the latter ought to be looking at her daughter, this is not only a role reversal between mother and daughter. It is also an emotional scheme in which the daughter sees the mother before her in the image of Christ on the cross, suffering and anguished, while she herself becomes Jesus extending his compassion and shelter to the children—to her mother and, simultaneously, to herself, since the children who will gain the kingdom of heaven in Litevsky's poem could be both the mother, whose orphanhood and flight "from the Germans" have allowed her no escape from her childhood, and the daughter, crying out for her mother.[87]

In an untitled poem evincing a fragment of a palpable, emotional memory, the daughter-speaker's identification with the image of Jesus is amplified:

> Embalmed, I lie in the cave sepulcher.
> You shall stand on its threshold,
> marveling at the beauty of the wall paintings.[88]

חֲבוּשָׁה אֲנִי שׁוֹכֶבֶת בְּמְעָרַת הַקֶּבֶר.
עַל סִפָּהּ תַּעֲמְדִי,
נִפְעֶמֶת מִיָּפְיָם שֶׁל צִיּוּרֵי הַקִּיר.

Like a mummy, the daughter lies in what might be the Holy Sepulcher, the tomb of Jesus. Like Jesus—the dead man who came back to life, who was not alive but also not dead, so, too, the daughter exists in the twilight zone of being present but unseen. The mother, who was asleep in the previous poem, does not see her daughter in this poem, either. Marveling at the beauty of the wall paintings, she fails to see her daughter, entombed, embalmed, annihilated. The daughter, by contrast, is sensitive to the faintest undulation in her mother's tones. She not only senses her mother's marveling at the paintings, but, mainly, she is aware of her standing at the cave's threshold. The mother's emotional stance is, indeed, a luminal one: she is not a mother but also not a child; she is not present but also not absent; she oscillates between the beauty of the wall paintings and the extinction of the burial cave.

The daughter's self-annihilation, like the Jesus imagery used of both mother and daughter, elucidates her desperate plea—"seeking a gaze: // Give me a face. Give me a name!"[89] In keeping with the Lacanian conception of the gaze, according to which it is the gaze of the other that enables the subject to conceive of him/herself as an object of desire,[90] the daughter, too, seeks out the mother's gaze for the sake of constructing her own face. It is the mother's gaze that affirms the daughter's face—her identity is a distinct subject. The absence of that gaze—the mother who lies sleeping or does not see her daughter—prevents the daughter's separating from her mother and affirming herself as a discrete entity, with a name.

The mix of self-affirmation and self-annihilation that is bound up with the desire for a face is associated in the tradition of Christian asceticism with love for Jesus's face. Saint Thérèse de Lisieux speaks of this in her autobiography, first published in 1898: "Until then I had known nothing of the richness of the treasures of the Holy Face . . . you were first to explore the mysteries of love hidden in the Face of Jesus. . . . He whose kingdom is not of this world showed me that the only condition worth coveting is 'to want to be ignored and regarded as nothing, to find joy in contempt of self.' I wanted my face, like the Face of Jesus, to be, as it were, hidden and unrecognized. I longed to suffer and be forgotten."[91] Identification with Jesus's face is associated with self-effacement, disappearance, being forgotten. To be assimilated (though not swallowed up) into the other (Jesus, the mother) is also, for Litevsky, the daughter's desire.[92] Jesus's face, for Saint Thérèse de Lisieux, embodies a present/absent entity, like the mother in Litevsky's poetry. For Litevsky, too, as we have seen, the bond with her mother passes through the image of Jesus as a figure of suffering and forgiveness, as one who shelters the sufferers. Being assimilated into the dual image of Jesus enables the daughter to be both Jesus taking pity on the defenseless (the mother, the orphaned girl) and the suffering Jesus (the abandoned daughter). Moreover—and far more significantly—this dual image of Jesus enables the speaker to mark the parental lack, to demand what she deserves as a daughter, to fantasize a motherly sheltering and simultaneously to forgive her mother. The mother, in her distress and, primarily, in her fixation in the traumatic moment of her childhood, is a child and a victim. She is Jesus and the child needing Jesus's compassion. At the same time, Jesus-like, she can also (at least potentially) offer protection. The dual image of Jesus, then, enables the speaker simultaneously to experience a broad range of feelings toward her mother: to verbalize the parental lack, to demand what she deserves as a daughter, to fantasize about a mother's protection, and, simultaneously, to absolve her mother.

In addition, to stay within the bounds of the Christian associations in Litevsky's poetry, the demand for a face hints at the Christian symbolism of the veil of Veronica.[93] Veronica, seeing Jesus struggling and suffering as he bore the cross from the place of his trial to the site of his crucifixion, offered him her veil to wipe the sweat streaming down his face. Jesus accepted the offer, and when he returned the veil, it had his facial features imprinted on it. Thus was Veronica called Vera Icon, the "true image." In contrast to the numerous cases in Western literature in which the moment of the daughter's birth marks the death of the mother,[94] in Litevsky's poetry that moment establishes the daughter's own need for self-effacement, for disappearance. The daughter, for Litevsky, is born into her own annihilation, just as the moment when Jesus's face is impressed on the veil heralds the moment of his disappearance in the flesh, the demise of his body. Where Veronica's veil was impressed with Jesus's perspiring face as he walked the Via Dolorosa, in Litevsky's poetry the impression is of a faceless, nameless entity that begs, "Give me a face! / Give me a name!" The daughter's entreaties for a face and a name are not only a call for a discrete identity but also a painful recognition of her own emotional position, in the existential stance of a daughter for whom any distance is the thrill of returning to her mother.

But within this emotional (vicious) cycle lies yet another stratum involving Veronica's veil. The notion of *vera icon*, the true image, refers us to issues of representation, primarily in the artistic, aesthetic-poetic context. Let us return to the poem "Calling by Name," which I dealt with above in the context of the daughter's relations with her (concrete and symbolic) father; this time, I shall focus on its ars poetica from the perspective of the daughter's relations with her mother.

Calling by Name
Is this the garden with the four rivers flowing around it
in which my progenitor called names to all the things
surrounding
And to me he passed down the pain
of calling by name all the things surrounding,
the name from which there is no going back to all the things
surrounding
And to me he passed down the longing to return
to the horse the glorious terror of his snort,
to the stones their silence,
to loose the laws of Name and of Heaven,[95]
the reins of the stars

And to me he passed down his empty place in the space in
    between
me and all the things surrounding.
The space in between me and myself.
The space of me.[96]

לקרוא בשם
הֲזֶהוּ הַגָּן שֶׁסְּבָבוּהוּ אַרְבָּעָה נְהָרוֹת
וּבוֹ קָרָא מוֹלִידִי בְּשֵׁמוֹת לְכָל
אֲשֶׁר סָבִיב

וְלִי הוֹרִישׁ אֶת הַכְּאֵב
לִקְרֹא בְּשֵׁם לְכָל אֲשֶׁר סָבִיב,
הַשֵּׁם שֶׁאֵין מִמֶּנוּ חֲזָרָה אֶל כָּל
אֲשֶׁר סָבִיב
וְלִי הוֹרִישׁ אֶת הָעָרְגָּה לְהָשִׁיב
לַסּוּס אֶת הוֹד אֵימַת נַחְרוֹ,
לָאֲבָנִים דְּמִמְתָן,
לְהַתִּיר חֻקּוֹת שֵׁם וְשָׁמַיִם,
מוֹסְרוֹת הַכּוֹכָבִים

וְלִי הוֹרִישׁ אֶת מְקוֹמוֹ הָרֵיק שֶׁל תָּוֶךְ
בֵּינִי וְכָל אֲשֶׁר סָבִיב.
הַתָּוֶךְ שֶׁבֵּינִי וּבֵינִי.
הַתָּוֶךְ שֶׁאֲנִי.

The heritage in the poem "Calling by Name" is the junction of pain and name giving; that is, writing is a replication of the speaker's childish state (the heritage of pain) in the body of an adult woman, a woman who can give a name, whether that woman is the speaker herself, in writing the poem, or the mother, who has the power to give her daughter a name. In other words, in the act of writing, too, the daughter identifies with her mother (and not with the phallic aspect of writing[97]) to create a mythological, hybrid image. This is in fact the metamorphosis that takes place in the earlier poem opening with the words "In your embrace is no shelter."[98] In this sense, "my progenitor" in "Calling by Name" is both God and the primordial Adam in the biblical story, but it is also the mother. Unlike Adam, who summoned up the wisdom to call by name "all the things surrounding," the mother, as we have seen, has failed in her task of giving her daughter a name. In this sense the act of writing is one of rectifying the mother's failure and of androgynous identification with the ability to beget—in both the male sense (of creativity, name giving, giving life through writing) and the female sense (of giving life).[99]

Moreover, while the daughter in Litevsky's poems cries out for a face and a name, her entreaty itself actually begets her a face and a name—her name as a woman and a poet. Even as she beholds her mother's retreating back—to quote Litevsky, "Every morning in kindergarten, facing your retreating back / the world is born of chaos"[100]—she assimilates on her mother's back not only her gaze but also her unique poetics. The mother failed to give her daughter a name, but the daughter's act of writing—of chronicling their relationship, and of metamorphosing the father's abuse into an act of writing—is in itself an act of name giving on the daughter's part. Although it will not save the daughter from her need for her mother or from her father's violence, it enables her, if only for a while, to get out of her mother's "chamber of memories" and establish her own transcendent voice—the poetry of Tsvia Litevsky.

Conclusion

"Silence Cries Out"[1]

⁓⸎⸙⸎⁓

The Untold Stories

On International Women's Day 2016, one of Israel's most popular lifestyle magazines, *La'Isha* (literally translated as "for the woman"), featured a cover story that documented the experiences of twenty-two "courageous women" (to use the magazine's language) who told their stories of rape and sexual assault, including their full names and photographs.[2] The cover photograph was accompanied by the statement "They are no longer victims, but strong women who survived and won." This cover photograph and the photograph of each woman were taken from a project spearheaded by the Association of Rape Crisis Centers in Israel in 2012. The project was titled "Heroines" and featured the work of photographer Alicia Shahaf. "Heroines" is a gallery comprised of portraits of women, from all different ages and backgrounds, who were subjected to sexual violence.

Photographer and activist Alicia Shahaf initiated "Heroines" to encourage women who have been sexually assaulted to break their silence, and to help overcome feelings of shame or guilt that followed in the wake of their trauma. The "Heroines" initiative is one of tremendous importance in working to undermine the social conventions that keep women trapped in silence by suggesting that, after an attack, a woman's identity—and therefore her story—must be concealed in order for her to be protected and to recover. The project implicitly claims that hiding women's identities (in all forms, from the blurring of their faces to the distortion of their voices in interviews) actually contributes to the systemic suppression of sexual violence and its marginalized position in forums of public discussion and debate. Moreover, the crux of the "Heroines" project lies in the reversal of the traumatic relationship between the attacker and the victim; survivors expose their identities and thus raise awareness of the wide-ranging demographics and the far-reaching consequences of this phenomenon. In each photograph, the woman gazes directly at the camera, a challenge and a reclamation of identity that has been ignored by both public discourse and media, while literally giving a face to the victims of sexual violence.

The project itself stands as an important testament to one of the various attempts of survivors and activists to influence and more actively engage in larger narratives about sexual assault. Recent years have seen the emergence of more survivors of gender-based violence giving a public voice on these issues, to the extent that Rotem Elisha, one of the women in the "Heroines" initiative who was raped at the age of twelve, was chosen as one of the torchbearers at the 2016 Torch-Lighting Ceremony (Tekes Hadlakat Hamesuot) that marks the end of Israel's Memorial Day and the beginning of Independence Day.

Thus the feminist movement has had an undeniable positive influence on personal, social, and therapeutic approaches to sexual violence in Israel and around the world. Rape crisis centers were opened throughout Israel in the late 1970s,[3] followed by the development of treatments anchored in feminist ideologies that generated increased visibility in the media and national public discourse that eventually led to the legislation of new laws (such as the Prevention of Sexual Harassment Law in 1998).[4] Visual art and cinematic representations have also shown an increased interest in gender-based violence as a topic, providing yet another means of representation.

Saying that, while in fields such as psychology, law, and cinema one can point to a development in awareness about the subject and its subsequent increased popularity as a topic of conversation and analysis, the same is not true for the representations of sexual aggression and violence in Hebrew literature. As demonstrated throughout this book, Hebrew literature is void of the clear linear development of progression from silence to speech, for example, or from objectification of women to depictions of women's agency. Early texts offer a wide range of representation of sexual assault and rape *and* the varied responses to that violence, sometimes even representing more graphic and daring expressions than those offered by texts written decades later. While Israeli literature from the 1980s on explicitly tackles these issues far more often and in more direct ways, the range of possibility for processing and coping with the aftermath of sexual trauma is surprisingly limited. While writers such as Gershon Shofman, Shoshana Shababo, Dahlia Ravikovitch, and Amalia Kahana-Carmon struggled with questions situated in vulnerability, victimhood, and silence, the representation of sexual assault in contemporary literature is more occupied with empowering women, overcoming trauma, finding a means to voice and transcribe trauma, and exploring the subversive power of survival.

Along the same lines, the "Heroines" project, while immensely important, highlights the relevance of discourses around heroism in relation to victims of sexual violence. The project is embedded in a judgmental cultural dichotomy between *victims* and *survivors* of sexual violence; victims are often seen as lacking control over their lives and imagined as destined to lead lives immured in trauma and self-destruction, while survivors manage to successfully combine elements of power, control, and agency within their aftermath experiences, thereby creating a potentially damaging narrative of what transcending or overcoming must look like.[5]

Since speech acts and cultural representations not only reflect our subjectivity but also work to both mediate and affect it in political and metaphysical ways, it is crucial to understand not just the important nuances of the current discourse around sexual violence but also its risks and limitations. More than two decades ago, authors Linda Alcoff and Laura Gray warned us about the potential danger survivors face within the discourse of confession as a means to healing: "When breaking the silence is taken up as the necessary route to recovery or as a privileged political tactic, it becomes a coercive imperative on survivors to confess, to recount our assaults, to give details, and even to do so publicly. Our refusal to comply might then be read as weakness of will or as reenacted victimization. But it may be that survival itself sometimes necessitates a refusal to recount or even a refusal to disclose and deal with the assault or abuse, given the emotional, financial, and psychological difficulties that such disclosures can create."[6] As a society, we have not been sufficiently sensitive to this risk.

One cannot deny the tremendous achievements of the feminist movement and the many ways in which it has enriched and broadened the critical discussion of gender-based violence. Therefore, it is important to emphasize that I do not take issue with the act of speech as a means of processing but rather with its cultural dominance in relation to other voices and experiences of victims. The current writings (and other forms of expression) from survivors representing sexual aggression have significantly undermined patriarchal conventions and reduced the effectiveness of silencing techniques in Israeli society, but at the same time, their dominance may overshadow or stifle other experiences of sexual abuse victims. Feminist scholarship explored the varied ways in which discursive strategies operate to preempt or to dismiss the speech of women and children—particularly if they are survivors of sexual trauma. Scholars have shown that "if survivor speech is not silenced before it is uttered, it is categorized within the mad, the untrue, or the incredible."[7] My argument focuses not on this mechanism of silencing but rather on how expectations around the form of "proper" or "appropriate" feminist speech—in which victims are encouraged by wider society to articulate their trauma as the sole means of overcoming or coping with it—have become a more pervasive form of oppression in the current Israeli discourses around sexual violence.

The demand for another to speak, along with a strict sense of what this speech should look and sound like and what emotions or reactions it should solicit from others, has become a dominating and coercive force that works against the transgressive nature of victims' speech. Within the last few decades, Israeli society appears to have deemed that the most acceptable—if not sole—option for coping with sexual aggression is through a direct verbal or artistic expression of the trauma. Options such as partial repression or coping through silence are not part of the cultural-literary discourse, which narrows the scope of the conversation in both volume and variety. The language most prevalent in these conversations, such as use of the word *heroines* or suggesting that the word *victim* should always be replaced with the word *survivor*, feeds into a discourse of empowerment and the overcoming of sexual trauma that marginalizes a great number of women. In other words, survivors' voices, as well as other representations of sexual violence, are inscribed into a dominant discursive structure. So although literary representations of sexual violence indeed make it possible to "break the silence" and explore various aspects of sexual abuse, they are also co-opted and manipulated in a way that greatly limits the opportunities for more voices within the discourse about gender-based violence. It seems as though, paradoxically, raising awareness around gender-based violence in Israel has also led to the creation of new mechanisms of social control over victims of sexual violence.

One of the most potentially problematic and harmful approaches to feminist studies on sexual violence is that the primary objective of victims—and of society—is to be rid of negative emotions associated with experiences of assault or abuse. As a result of this framework, most scholarly and creative energies are channeled toward neutralizing negative emotions and strengthening positive ones; expressions of powerlessness, uncontrollable rage, and other "negative" emotions that find their way into the larger cultural conversation are seen as a transitional step toward overcoming these feelings, with the end goal of empowerment. This becomes consistent with cultural conventions about the beneficent power of optimism and positive thinking, as well as the unquestioned utility of total rehabilitation.

This more contemporary take on social narratives, in which victims process their emotions after a traumatic experience, is actually at odds with earlier examples of literature dealing with these same questions, in which a wider, more complicated range of responses is perfectly accept-able. In its early stages, Hebrew literature—like other literatures that, at times, undermine social and emotional conventions—casts doubt on the very idea that difficult or challenging feelings need to be conquered or overcome in the aftermath of sexual trauma. Many early Modern Hebrew texts assume there is a reason for the existence of a variety of emotions, whether positive or negative, and do not work to indoctrinate its readers to elicit a certain emotional response. This openness and flexibility undergoes a massive socialization process that results in a relatively limited range of narratives about sexual violence and its consequences.

Hebrew literature is saturated with descriptions of sexual violence, often conducting multiple sociopoetic discussions about it. Given the sheer number of depictions and instances of violent imagery, the absence of certain types of narratives is conspicuous and damning. Contemporary Israeli literature rarely tells the stories of women who are still suffering from abuse, women involved in sex work or prostitution, or incarcerated women. It hardly ever represents women who live fulfilling lives despite not coping with their trauma, or about women who are not sure about what happened, or about women who cannot—or choose not to—express their stories. Furthermore, contemporary Hebrew literature rarely explores the connection between sexual violence and the Israeli occupation,[8] and it seldom addresses the diversity of the victims, or the uniqueness of sexual vulnerability in different minority communities within Israeli society. For instance, depictions of sexual assaults of Palestinians, LGBTIQ people, men and boys, people with disabilities, and migrant workers are largely absent. When seen in contrast with the sheer abundance of literary descriptions taking up the discussion of sexualized gender-based violence in Hebrew literature, the deafening silence is resounding.

This divergence in representation begs multiple questions: What causes this collective mental block in the writing about sexual violence? What are the cultural barriers that prevent the inspection and contemplation of this phenomenon in different ways? Why, despite the enormous contribution of rape crisis centers and feminist discourse on sexual violence that have helped many survivors, is current literature so relatively narrow-minded when it comes to the scope of those affected? Why does contemporary Hebrew literature distance itself from silence, weakness, and speech that does not lead to progress and "healing"?

Sexual violence provokes anxiety in those who experience or witness it, both directly and indirectly. It awakens angst because it is a constant reminder of the vulnerability of our bodies and souls, and it forces us to confront how ultimately helpless and uncontrolled certain aspects of our existence are. By addressing sexual aggressiveness so openly and with so many examples, Hebrew literature seems to confront this fear with bravery and aplomb. But the missing links in this representation are manifold—from the untold stories of women who did not extricate themselves from the position of victimhood to those who internalized their own vulnerability—and conceal much deeper anxieties about sexual violence. Vulnerability and the randomness of victimhood become an ever-present cloud of cultural fear that Israeli society has been incapable of dealing with for the last four decades; it has been unable to confront the potential of uncontrolled destruction. Thus, when it comes to sexual violence, contemporary Hebrew literature simply cannot cope with helplessness and hopelessness. Susan Brison explains that shame, guilt, and the feeling that if you had done something differently, you might have prevented the sexual assault, are easier to accept and understand than living with the recognition that the assault was arbitrary, unpredictable, and independent of you or your behavior, and as such, it is an experience that might happen again at any given moment.[9] Internalizing a sense of guilt, or in the case of Hebrew literature, focusing on the narrative of the "survivors" rather than the "victims" (an accurate term that seemingly strips agency and empowerment from those who have experienced the trauma) is more comforting than living with the terror of the uncontrollable.

The narrowed range of possible expressions and representations of sexual violence in recent decades could also very easily be explained by the shifts in Israeli political contexts. It is one of the missing links that connect political violence and sexual brutality, if only evidenced and underscored by its varied presence in prestate Modern Hebrew literature. The few texts that deal with this connection, such as Michal Zamir's novel *A Ship of Girls* (Sfinat hababot, 2005),[10] focus on subjects such as the Israeli Defense Force's (IDF) sexism and the sexual harassment experienced by women during their military service; what is not discussed are the potential ramifications and intersections of the Israeli occupation on sexualized gender-based violence in Israel and in the Palestinian occupied territories.[11] This disregard is part of a broader, deeper silence about the violent effects of the occupation, and specifically, its implications regarding sexual violence against women and children in particular.[12] Thus, Hebrew literature in recent decades, as well as Israeli academic scholarship and media, ends up overlooking the fateful effects of the occupation on issues of sexual trauma—not only in Israel but also in the Palestinian occupied territories.[13]

The focus on empowerment within Hebrew literature thus ends up neglecting the effects of the occupation on Israeli society—as well as the reality of the lives of Palestinians under occupation—which perpetuates and intensifies the potential for sexual violence. The deep anxiety inherent in this concealment is not limited to general concerns about human vulnerability or to the randomness of evil that exists as part and parcel with the presence of sexual violence, but rather, this sociocultural anxiety is also related to the direct or indirect accountability of Israeli society for the existence of certain sexual abuses and traumas within the occupied territories and Gaza.

In this context, it is interesting to reconsider Rotem Elisha's involvement in the 2016 Torch Lighting Ceremony. Her lighting of the torch creates a symbolic parallel between a woman who survived sexual violence as a child and the State of Israel that grew out of difficulties and losses. This parallel unconsciously preserves a national sense of victimhood and the self-perception of Jewish Israelis as having moved from the position of victims to being a state of survivors. But more significantly, the violence Rotem Elisha experienced being put on public display emphasizes the randomness not just of the evil she personally experienced but supposedly of any evil, thus divorcing such things from their political context during a fixedly political event at the central ceremony of Israel's Independence Day.

One might find it ironic that, almost a century after writers such as Henya Pekelman, Rivka Alper, and Shoshana Shababo exposed the unspoken connection between Zionist ideology and violence against women, a survivor's status and experiences would be used to smooth over or cover up similar unconscionable connections. Just as Hebrew literature exposes the fact that sexual violence is inherent in and does not contradict patriarchal thinking, focusing on sexual violence in the context of the Israeli-Palestinian conflict carries the risk of exposing and highlighting the sexual aggressiveness inherent in Israeliness itself. In other words, exploring multidimensional aspects of sexual violence in writing has the radical potential to expose the gender and national power relations embedded in the Israeli-Palestinian conflict, as well as to help unveil the moral, ethical, and legal implications of Israeli supremacy.

An Apologetic Note

In the final stages of writing *Flesh of My Flesh*, I find myself in a somewhat frustrating position. While throughout the book I have depicted unique and courageous voices that were, at times, excluded from Jewish and Israeli communities, and that articulated previously untold experiences, I concluded the book by pointing out a most certain blemish of absence within a crucial and creative literary discourse that has developed over the course of a century.

Although contemporary Hebrew literature has an almost singular model for representing sexual violence, exploring Modern Hebrew literature from its initial stages has exposed a much more complex and multifaceted approach to gender-based sexual violence. Thus, I wish to finish this book with a story of silence that offers an ideological element that is slowly being extracted from Hebrew literature. My hope is that it can—and will—function as poetic inspiration for unconventional ways of composing stories of sexual trauma. The story was written in the 1950s, and it is the first story written by the as-of-yet-unknown author Amalia Kahana-Carmon, who later became one of the major voices of Israeli fiction. The story doesn't portray a survivor who overcomes the assault, nor does it describe a process of working through the traumatic event. Rather, it portrays the harm in "a soft murmuring sound" and therefore offers a uniquely poetic approach to the representation of sexual violence in literature.

Amalia Kahana-Carmon:
"Beer Sheva, the Capital of the Negev"

Wartime Sexual Violence

On June 29, 1956, Amalia Kahana-Carmon published her first story, "The Whirling Sword" (Hacherev hamithapechet) in *Masa*, the literary supplement of the daily newspaper *Lamerhav*. The story was reprinted (with some significant omissions) in 1966 in her collection of stories *Under One Roof* (Bikhefifah ahat) under the name "Beer Sheva, the Capital of the Negev" (Beer Sheva birat Hanegev).[14] The story describes the experience of Ilana, a young signal operator in the Palmach's Negev Brigade during the days of Operation Yoav (the conquest of Beer Sheva), and focuses on her relationship with Noah, a Palmach soldier who was killed during that operation.[15] The story briefly describes a sexual encounter between Noah and Ilana, which takes place on the first day of their acquaintance, while sharing a tent near the battlefield. The story provides very little information about their sexual encounter, which appears as a single sentence in the story:

> [Ilana] turned her head again. As a result, her hairpin fell off and got lost, and her hair fell across her face. The young man [Noah] moved her hair to the sides—straightened it on her temple, and clearing her forehead with his palm—and looked at her while leaning on his arm.
> "What are you looking at?" She asked brokenly.
> "What are you looking at?" He repeated her words mumbling, and Ilana saw the flash of a row of bright teeth in the darkness of the tent and then, like a bird of prey, he plunged his head into the cleavage of her thin khaki shirt.[16]

Yair Mazor understands the relationship between Ilana and Noah as a love story,[17] and Hannah Herzig reads this sexual scene as a scene that describes "the devotion of Ilana to Noah."[18] Lily Rattok even claims that "the erotic love story" between Ilana and Noah might be understood as an outspoken critique by Kahana-Carmon. This is because it breaks the typical dichotomous polarization between the female virgin warrior and the sexual woman; the protagonist of the story is a loving girl but also a fighting young woman, as she is described as "soft in her love but determined in her military role."[19]

However, I find it difficult to ignore the fact that this scene can also be read as depicting sexual violence or at least "as containing an element of coercion."[20] Noah is described as a bird of prey, which hints at the violence inherent in the act, especially since the bird of prey in Jewish tradition is linked to impurity.[21] Additionally, later in the story Ilana thinks of Noah in unflattering terms, describing him as "not from here, but of the night,"[22] and when she sees him she describes his hair as growing "in strange primitiveness" and his hands as too long, "like monkey's hands."[23] Furthermore, when she sees him in the dining room the story relates that "among all the people, a mark shone on his forehead, like the mark of Cain, like a frontlet between his eyes."[24] Herzig explains the symbolism of seeing the mark of Cain as Ilana's sense of guilt for her devotion to Noah, a sense that engenders embarrassment in her.[25] However, it seems to me that the mark of Cain on Noah's forehead may also testify to his guilt of sexual coercion in their encounter.

In addition, certain parts of the story that refer to Ilana's emotional state of mind—parts that appeared in the first version of the story and were later taken out—support the reading of sexual violence in the story. For example, when Ilana and Noah are in the tent, the readers become privy to Ilana's inner feelings: "Good God!—thought Ilana, and did not know what she was thinking about. What was this lump pressing and moving inside her? Her body, her obedient, tolerant body, was suddenly at the mercy of this stranger, dependent on him and his good graces. And none of it made sense. But her body wept and wept, a fool of a body, longing for attention, longing for meaning and magic."[26] Following the sexual encounter, the original story also describes Ilana's fear: "The storm is beyond the windows. The storm cries wildly [. . .]. A concealed fear attacks her."[27] While Hannah Herzig understands these omitted descriptions as a way of presenting the new and naïve erotic sensations that arise in Ilana,[28] and Rattok sees it as a self-censorship that has to do with the literary norms of Kahana-Carmon's fiction at the time,[29] I believe those descriptions reinforce an interpretation that speaks to sexual aggression. Likewise, Yael Levi Hazan claims that "this omission emphasizes the power of Noah's act and its deviation from the boundaries of good taste, and it all serves as criticism of the disintegration of moral values that occurs during war."[30] More broadly, reading the sexual scene between Ilana and Noah as a scene of sexual coercion enables us to understand the story as one that reveals the sexual vulnerability of young adults, and especially female soldiers, within the framework of the Zionist project.

In the early version of the story Noah and the conquest of the Negev (the implementation of the Zionist project) are one and the same: "And he was the Negev to me."[31] In the later version, while Noah continues to represent the New Jew whose "two legs are planted in the ground,"[32] and is "like a juniper in the desert [Arava],"[33] his vitality (almost animalism) is more prominent. His power is not perceived as a legitimate force channeled to a military conquest and victory but rather as violence directed against Ilana. In other words, in the later version of the story Kahana-Carmon creates a stronger link between national violence and sexual violence, thereby reinforcing certain readings of the text.[34]

With this understanding of a potential motivation behind the alterations to the story, it is important to note another significant addition. Ilana's first flashback to the days when she was a soldier participating in the conquest of Beer Sheva ends with two seemingly unrelated references: "At midnight they came and woke me up: 'Ilana, here is the key to the radio room.' Darkness. Where is the right side? Where is the left side? Where is the wall? Where is the entrance? In my sleep I reached out my hand: 'Whoever is there, find my hand.' My hand was found in the darkness. The key was placed in it. The fingers were folded over it. And my hand was not left. It was held for a moment. [. . .] And the Arab captive who watches the engine room, is humming in his corner."[35] The Arab captive did not appear in the first version of the story. The later version of the story, then, draws an initial connection between Ilana's vulnerability ("And my hand was not left") and the presence of the Arab captive. In a public talk Kahana-Carmon gave in honor of the publication of her book *Up on Montifer* (Lemala Bemontifer), she explained the meaning of captivity in her writing, and claimed, "You are in captivity when someone else determines, according to his will, the nature of your existence."[36] This broad definition refers to captivity as the embodiment of power relations and not merely as a sole physical experience, and it might explain Ilana's identification with the Arab captive. Thus, the story shapes national and gendered imprisonments as related entities, despite their differences.[37]

Shimrit Peled claims that the forced sexual relations between Ilana and Noah replace the national physical and territorial confrontation over Beer Sheva.[38] However, the presence of the Arab captive in the story, in my opinion, allows Kahana-Carmon not to convert one violence into another but rather to depict their *simultaneous* occurrence. If the story were simply about a replacement, it would in effect cooperate with the concealment of national violence, and at the same time also turn the sexual violence into no more than a national symbol. Thus, while Peled offers a reading that swaps national violence with sexual violence, it seems to me that the story actually offers a dynamic of two-dimensional violence. Instead of the rhetoric of repression and conversion, Kahana-Carmon exposes the various branches of violence, that is, the insidious nature of national and gender-based trauma.

A POETIC OF DISPERSIONS

The fact that the sexual assault in the story was excluded from most academic readings tells, of course, more about the research and the interests of scholars of Hebrew literature than about the literature itself and its areas of interest. However, this "blindness" can also be attributed to Kahana-Carmon's deliberate poetics. In other words, the double meaning inherent in the nature of the relationship between Noah and Ilana may be interpreted as a subversive stylistic decision of Kahana-Carmon. On the one hand, by blurring the violent nature of their relationship, the story accedes to the literary-ideological norms of the time by overlooking injustices in the Zionist project; in this case, it showcases the wrongs of the Sabra (native-born Israeli Jew) soldier against women who shared the same Zionist ideology. On the other hand, the very decision to write about this subject puts Kahana-Carmon in line with her pioneering predecessors—Rivka Alper, Henya Pekelman, and Shoshana Shababo—who revealed in their literary work what was silenced in their seemingly egalitarian surroundings.[39]

The story "Beer Sheva, the Capital of the Negev" (i.e., the later version) opens with Ilana at a restaurant in Beer Sheva, as her "heart wrapped [nitatef] itself around her. She wanted to be in Tel Aviv, with her husband and child." The use of the verb nitatef (to be enwrapped) reminds readers of the biblical story of Jonah, the prophet who refused to prophesy and desperately tried to escape his role as prophet. During one of his most difficult moments of crisis, when he was in the belly of the fish, he turned to God in prayer: "When my soul fainted [behitatef] within me I remembered the Lord, and my prayer came in unto thee, into thy holy temple" (Jonah 2:8). This intertextuality implies Ilana's mission—the story's mission, to be more precise—to tell about women's experiences that were often ignored within the Zionist movement, as well as the mission to create a nontrivial space for a poetic expression of those experiences. The two versions of the story, as well as the meticulous editorial work in the transition from the first to the second, testify to the difficulty in fulfilling this ideological and literary mission underlying the story.

While the ideological mission of writing about sexual violence is widely expressed in feminist research, the literary mission and responsibility gets less attention. Not only does the story draw on a wider range of emotions in relation to the assault (Noah, for instance, is both loved and repulsive, charming and violent), but, more significantly, it offers only ambiguity about the nature—and even the very existence—of the sexual aggressiveness itself. As stated, while this ambiguity might represent the literary norms of the time in relation to sexual violence, it may also be a conscious poetic choice—that is, a fictional or poetical means of voicing an experience of sexual violence. In contrast to contemporary discourse that directs writing about sexual aggression to areas of certainty and empowerment, Kahana-Carmon creates a different kind of space that sets up an uncommon discourse about sexual violence; it is a space of conscious silence, of repressed memories, of uncertainty about the nature of the trauma, and of a lack of processing. It is interesting to note that in the early version of the story the narrator asks, "How does silence cry itself out?"[40] Even though the later version might also be read as a story that expresses the poetics of silence, the direct question about that poetics was erased, as if Kahana-Carmon predicted in this erasure the dominance of the discourse in the decades following the publication of her story.

It is important for me to stress that while the silence and the indirect description of the sexual aggression in the story might be understood as articulating a posttraumatic state or as a poetic way to express that which cannot be expressed in words, it strikes me that Kahana-Carmon offers a much more radical option. Her story is about sexual violence that has no words, not because words are limited in their ability to describe the harm but rather because the story deals with the essence of vagueness itself, with the emotional and mental state in which the victim herself is not sure about what exactly happened and even whether or not there was sexual coercion at play during their encounter. Kahana-Carmon thus actually shapes the poetics of that ambiguity, and the movement between a variety of feelings and attitudes regarding Noah and the relationship between him and Ilana. The story has an element of stylistic restraint, and a sense of stream-of-consciousness technique in the seemingly free associations from Ilana's past. It uses an implicit and somewhat somnambulant language, and it is written in a nonlinear way, with a kind of mental hop and fragments of memories, embodied in the transitions from third-person present tense to first-person present tense and third-person past tense.[41] It is tempting to read these literary devices as poetics of trauma that act out emotional triggers, unorganized memories, dissociations, and disruptions of linear stream of consciousness. Leora Bilsky explores the incompatibility between the language of the court, a logical and rational language, and the language of survivors' testimonies, an emotional language, at times fragmented and nonlinear.[42] The traumatic speech is perceived among survivors, therapists, and feminist scholars as reliable in terms of acting out the traumatic experience and its aftermath, but nevertheless as a speech that at times deviates from rational language. The traumatic speech is perceived (and constructed) as fragmented, inconsistent, and disrupted, as well as unreliable, self-contradictory, and uncontrollable.[43] Although the story's style implements some of these characteristics, it seems that it actually shapes a different representation of the posttraumatic experience, which rejects any monolithic position regarding sexual violence.

In "Beer Sheva, the Capital of the Negev" there is a sentence that Ilana speaks in her mind to Noah (notably absent in the first version): "On the faces of all people I will seek for your dispersions [pzurotecha]."[44] This sentence might express Ilana's longing for Noah; years after his death, she looks for his image etched on her surroundings.[45] At the same time, this sentence might also communicate her anxiety, a kind of a nightmare that expresses a loss of confidence in men, as if every man were a potential aggressor. But since, to use Esther Fuchs's language, "Kahana-Carmon's poetics is inseparable from her interest in the female condition,"[46] we might also understand this sentence as a sort of reading instruction, as a way of drawing our attention to a poetics of dispersions, so to speak, to an insistence on a story that is indeed coherent and carefully structured, but one that is not embedded in a confined, one-dimensional narrative of either a downfall or a recovery following the assault.

Even though the story is told from Ilana's subjective perspective, this subjectivity neither detaches Ilana from reality nor distorts her capacity to recall her past events.[47] This stylistic mode goes hand in hand with the Hebrew tradition of writing about sexual violence, a tradition that demonstrates logical and structured discourse around sexual violence. While all of the examples in *Flesh of My Flesh* show the sensitivity of writers and survivors to the harsh effects of gender-based violence, they all also reveal a rational and self-conscious speech. It is thus hard to know whether these sound representations of sexual violence in literature reflect the atypical experience of victims of sexual aggression (that is, survivors who do not respond to typical posttraumatic symptoms), or if in practice they unconsciously cooperate with oppressing mechanisms that judge posttraumatic expressions. However, it could be that literature enables a glance into a world that deviates from the typical sociological experience.

Either way, Kahana-Carmon stands out in her difference from the literary tradition that was presented throughout this book, because her story expresses a unique poetic position regarding sexual violence that has not been assimilated into Hebrew literature. Kahana-Carmon tells us a story in which not only is it unclear whether the relationship was consensual or not, but even if it was not consensual, the way the protagonist processes her experience is not channeled into any familiar—poetic, psychoanalytic, or national—narrative. The story ends with the abstract thought of Ilana, now a mother and a wife, sitting in a restaurant: "In the strong light, everyone's faces look like portraits in the dark."[48] The story may reveal repressed or unclear traumatic events, as well as complex emotions, but it leaves the faces of its characters in the dark.

Notes

❦

Notes to the Introduction

1. Nano Shabtai, *The Book of Men* [Sefer hagvarim] (Jerusalem: Keter, 2015), 171. Please note: translations throughout the book are mine, unless otherwise noted.

2. Shabtai, *Book of Men*, 171.

3. Judith Lewis Herman, *Trauma and Recovery: The Aftermath of Violence—From Domestic Abuse to Political Terror* (New York: Basic Books, 1992), 73.

4. Shoshi Hatuka, "Women's Day 2016: 'Heroes and Brave Despite the Bleeding Wound" [in Hebrew], *Mako*, July 3, 2016. https://www.mako.co.il/news-israel/local-q1_2016/Article-8478cd53fc15351004.htm.

5. Rotem Izak, "Nano Shabtai Thought She Was Writing about Love" [in Hebrew], *At Magazine*, March 31, 2016.

6. Even though the diagnosis of PTSD "is one of the few diagnoses within the DSM-IV system that acknowledge an outside environmental event as the cause of the psychological distress"—and as such, it moves away from the individual model of responsibility—the very definition of PTSD entails a depoliticization of trauma. This is because "posttrauma" is an expression that, by virtue of the language used, delineates a trauma in the past as a closed phenomenon. Maria P. P. Root, "Women of Color and Traumatic Stress in 'Domestic Captivity': Gender and Race as Disempowering Statuses," in *Ethnocultural Aspects of Posttraumatic Stress Disorder: Issues, Research, and Clinical Applications*, ed. Anthony J. Marsella, Matthew J. Friedman, Ellen T. Gerrity, and Raymond M. Scurfield (Washington, DC: American Psychological Association, 1996), 374.

Treatment that acknowledges PTSD was also criticized from a therapeutic perspective. Patrick J. Bracken argues that focusing on the traumatic memory of the individual not only leads to the isolation of the traumatic event from its social context and from the political circumstances in which it was created but also contributes to isolating the treatment from the patient's deep personal emotional context. Patrick Bracken, "Hidden Agendas: Deconstructing Post Traumatic Stress Disorder," in *Rethinking the Trauma of War*, ed. P. Bracken and C. Petty (London: Free Association Books, 1998).

7. Arthur Kleinman, *Writing at the Margin: Discourse between Anthropology and Medicine* (Berkeley: University of California Press, 1997), 177; emphasis in source.

8. Liisa H. Malkki, "Speechless Emissaries: Refugees, Humanitarianism, and Dehistoricization," *Cultural Anthropology* 11, no. 3 (August 1996): 378.

9. Root, "Women of Color," 374.

10. Effi Ziv, "Insidious Trauma" [in Hebrew], *Mafteakh: Lexical Review of Political Thought* 5 (2012): 55.

11. Here and throughout the book, I refer to sexual violence as part of a larger discourse on trauma, but it is important to note that, as Joanna Bourke shows, "unlike most other 'bad events,' which were incorporated within trauma narratives from the 1860s, the ascription of psychological trauma was only applied to rape victims a century later." One example she provides is that, prior to the 1970s, psychiatric texts ignored the long-term psychological effects of rape. Joanna Bourke, "Sexual Violence, Bodily Pain, and Trauma: A History," *Theory, Culture & Society* 29, no. 3 (May 2012): 25.

12. Judith Lewis Herman, *Father-Daughter Incest* (Cambridge, MA: Harvard University Press, 2000), 62.

13. Tori A. H. McNaron and Yarrow Morgan, eds., *Voices in the Night: Women Speaking about Incest* (Minneapolis, MN: Cleis Press, 1982), 15. McNaron and Morgan go as far as to argue that "there is not a taboo against incest, merely against speaking about it." Shira Stav connects Hermann's and McNaron and Morgan's arguments and claims that Western patriarchal society is not based on the prohibition of father-daughter incest but rather is based on the absence of this prohibition and on its position as a "present-absence." McNaron and Morgan, *Voices in the Night*, 15; Shira Stav, "Fathers and Daughters: The Entrapment of Incest" [in Hebrew], *Teorya u-vikoret* 37 (Fall 2010): 71.

14. Shira Stav claims that incest "is not a cultural pathology" but rather stands at the heart of our sociocultural norms, and therefore is deeply rooted in patriarchal relations between fathers and daughters, and between men and women. Stav, "Fathers and Daughters," 75.

15. Stav, "Fathers and Daughters," 71.

16. Rivka Alper, "Mistake" [Shgaga], unpublished story, GI 472/68508, n.d., 14. I would like to thank Orian Zakai for sharing this manuscript with me.

17. Rivka Alper, "Mistake." Orian Zakai alludes to this story in her pioneering article "A Uniform of a Writer: Literature, Ideology and Sexual Violence in the Writing of Rivka Alper," *Prooftexts* 34, no. 2 (Spring 2014): 232–70. Additionally, an excerpt from the story was published online. See Ruth Bachi Kolodny, "Like a

Beast Devouring Her Blouse" [in Hebrew], *Haaretz*, May 22, 2007. https://www.haaretz.co.il/.premium-1.2291395.

18. Orian Zakai claims that the intermediate level of proficiency in Hebrew in the story indicates that it may have been written in Rivka Alper's early years in Palestine. Zakai, "Uniform of a Writer," 267.

19. Zakai, "Uniform of a Writer," 257–58.

20. Alper, "Mistake," 14.

21. Tsvia Litevsky, *Don't Point Your Finger at Me* [Al tatsbia alai] (Tel Aviv: Helicon, 2003), 31.

22. Henya Pekelman, *The Life of a Worker in Her Homeland* [Hayey po'elet ba-aretz] (Beer Sheva, Israel: Kinneret, Zmora-Bitan, Dvir, 2007).

23. Tamar S. Hess, "Henya Pekelman's Memories" [in Hebrew], in Pekelman, *Life of a Worker*, 219–35. See also David De Vries and Talia Pfeffermann, "The Ordeal of Henya Pekelman, a Female Construction Worker," in *Struggle and Survival in Palestine/Israel* (Berkeley: University of California Press, 2019), 125–40.

24. Pekelman, *Life of a Worker*, 163. Although the rape is not marked by words, it remains as a concrete and material presence in the text. It is not a verbal presence, but it is a space that resists the elimination and exclusion of the violent act. The two lines of hyphens are not to be understood as silence; if anything, we might think about them as acting out the insufficiency of language to express the traumatic event. Thus, talking about the rape is a necessity for Pekelman at the same time that language becomes an insufficient tool for communicating its effects.

Moreover, Pekelman sought methods of articulating her experience of sexual assault, but was met, time and again, with society's refusal to acknowledge her narrative. The very existence of the hyphens indicates the erasure itself. Since throughout her autobiography Pekelman criticizes the various mechanisms of gender oppression surrounding her, we might understand the hyphens not only as her way of expressing the insufficiency of language to address her traumatic experience but also as referring to social mechanisms that erase her rape story, and enable her rapist to continue his life as if nothing had happened. Thus, it could be that the hyphens indicate not only the rape but also the context within which the rape took place. In other words, the hyphens may refer to the ways in which Pekelman's particular rape is related to intersectionality, privilege, and positionality within the larger structure of her environment in mandatory Palestine.

25. Tamar S. Hess, "Henya Pekelman: An Injured Witness of Socialist Zionist Settlement in Mandatory Palestine," *WSQ: Women's Studies Quarterly* 36, nos. 1 & 2 (Spring/Summer 2008): 208.

26. Kimberlé Crenshaw coined the term "intersectionality" in her renowned paper "Demarginalizing the Intersection of Race and Sex" as a way to explain the multilayered oppression of women of color. Kimberlé Crenshaw, "Demarginalizing the Intersection of Race and Sex: A Black Feminist Critique of Antidiscrimination Doctrine, Feminist Theory, and Antiracist Politics," *University of Chicago Legal*

Forum 140 (1989): 139–67. See also Kimberlé Crenshaw, "Mapping the Margins: Intersectionality, Identity Politics, and Violence against Women of Color," *Stanford Law Review* 43, no. 6 (1991): 1241–99.

Notes to Chapter One

1. David Vogel, *Married Life* [Ḥayei nisu'im], trans. Dalya Bilu (New Milford, CN: Toby Press, 2007), 319–20.

2. Emma Liggins has shown how sympathy for the prostitute in Victorian literature was often attained at the price of acceptance and replication of stereotypes of working-class women and female sexuality; the same is true of Hebrew literature of the revival period. See Emma Liggins, "Prostitution and Social Purity in the 1880s and 1890s," *Critical Survey* 15 (2003): 39–55.

3. For a detailed analysis of representations of prostitutes in literature, theater, cinema, and law, see Shulamit Almog, *Prostitution: Cultural and Legal Aspects* [Nashim mufkarot] (Tel Aviv: Ministry of Defense–Modan, 2008).

4. Walter Benjamin, *Charles Baudelaire: A Lyric Poet in the Era of High Capitalism* (London: New Left Books, 1973), 171. Quoted in Deborah Epstein Nord, *Walking the Victorian Streets: Women, Representation, and the City* (Ithaca, NY: Cornell University Press, 1995), 5.

5. Timothy J. Gilfoyle notes that although many people attribute the association of prostitution, sexuality, and modernity to Foucault, it was already articulated a century earlier by the British psychologist and doctor Havelock Ellis. See Timothy J. Gilfoyle, "Prostitutes in History: From Parables of Pornography to Metaphors of Modernity," *American Historical Review* 104, no. 1 (1999): 135.

6. Nord, *Walking the Victorian Streets*, 2–3.

7. Much has been written about the connection between the writings of the *telushim* and the autobiographical experiences of the writers themselves. See, for example, Gershon Shaked, *Hebrew Narrative Fiction, 1880–1980: In the Land of Israel and the Diaspora* [Hasiporet haivrit, 1880–1980] (Tel Aviv: Hakibutz hameuhad-Keter, 1983); and Nurit Govrin, *Reading the Generations: Contextual Studies in Hebrew Literature* [Keri'at hadorot: Sifrut 'ivrit bema'agaleha], vols. 1–2 (Tel Aviv: Gevanim, 2002), and vols. 3–4 (Jerusalem: Carmel, 2008).

8. See Aminadav Dickman, "Tirgumim Basifrut Ha'ivrit Bitkufat Hatehiah" [Translation in Hebrew literature during the Revival Period], in *New Jewish Time: Jewish Culture in a Secular Age* [Zman yehudi ḥadash: Tarbut yehudit be'idan ḥiloni], ed. Dan Miron and Hannan Hever (Tel Aviv: Lamda, 2007), 3:94–98.

9. The sensitivity of the Talmudic and midrashic literature toward prostitutes is encapsulated in their use of the word *mufkeret* (loose woman) to refer to them, as opposed to *perutsah* (harlot) or *yats'anit* (streetwalker). For a discussion of the language issue and the connection between names for prostitutes and ideological attitudes toward them, see Almog, *Prostitution*, 11–21.

10. See Tali Artman-Partock, "Erua Sifruti Vesiper Histori: Ben Hazal Le'avot Haknesiah" [Literary event and historical narrative: Between Rabbinic and Patristic literature], *Mekharei Yerushalaim besifrut 'Ivrit* 24 (2011): 23–54; and "Haznut: Ben Yahadut Lenatsrut" [Prostitution: Between Judaism and Christianity], *Adken* 56 (2012): 24–29.

11. For a general survey of representations of prostitutes in Jewish sources, see Naomi Graetz and Julie Cwikel, "Trafficking and Prostitution: Lessons from Jewish Sources," *Australian Journal of Jewish Studies* 20 (2006): 25–58.

12. Thomas Heise, *Urban Underworlds: A Geography of Twentieth-Century American Literature and Culture* (New Brunswick, NJ: Rutgers University Press, 2011), 9.

13. Gershon Shofman, *Collected Works of G. Shofman* [Kol kitvei G. Shofman] (Tel Aviv: Am Oved, 1945), 1:89–95, 176–79, 307; 2:38–39, 138–42.

14. Joseph Klausner, "G. Shofman," in *G. Shofman: A Selection of Critical Essays on his Literary Prose* [G. Shofman: Mivḥar ma'amarei bikoret al yetsirato], ed. Nurit Govrin (Tel Aviv: Am Oved, 1978), 75.

15. Shalom Kraemer, "Darko Be'omanut Hasipur" [His way in the art of storytelling], in Govrin, *G. Shofman: A Selection of Critical Essays on His Literary Prose* [G. Shofman: Mivḥar ma'amarei bikoret al yetsirato], ed. Nurit Govrin (Tel Aviv: Am Oved, 1978), 145.

16. Yeshurun Keshet, "Nefesh Hador o Nefesh Hayahid?" [The generation's soul or the individual's soul?], in Govrin, *G. Shofman*, 94.

17. Rivka Gorfein quoted in Govrin, "Mavo: Mahalakhah shel habikoret al sipurei G. Shofman," in Govrin, *G. Shofman*, 28.

18. The abolitionist approach to prostitution, which is rooted in the struggle for the abolition of slavery in the United States, sees prostitution as a form of sexual slavery. Consequently, this conception not only sees prostitution as the objectification of women's bodies but it also, by definition, rejects the notion that it could be a choice. It follows that a woman engaged in prostitution is always to be seen as a victim. Moreover, this approach sees in prostitution a violation of elementary human rights and an unmitigated expression of men's domination of women. Accordingly, as mentioned, prostitution is not a choice and cannot be defined as "work." It is not work, not only because trafficking in any other bodily organ is not legitimate, but primarily because prostitution, according to this conception, is understood as an addiction and as a symptom of weakness and distress. For more on the abolitionist position, see Melissa Farley, *Prostitution, Trafficking and Traumatic Stress* (New York: Psychology Press, 2003); Gilfoyle, "Prostitutes in History," 33; Andrea Dworkin, "Prostitution and Male Supremacy," in *Life and Death: Unapologetic Writings on the Continuing War against Women* (New York: Free Press, 1997), 139–51; Catharine MacKinnon, *Toward a Feminist Theory of the State* (Cambridge, MA: Harvard University Press, 1989), 138; Kathleen L. Barry, *Female Sexual Slavery* (New York: New York University Press, 1984); and Eli Sommer, "Hatotsa'ot Hanafshiyot shel Ha'isuk Bezanut" [The devastating

consequences of engaging in prostitution], lecture given at the conference "Sakhar Benashim, Zanut Uma Shebeineihem" [Trafficking in women, prostitution, and everything in between], Tel Aviv, September 22, 2000).

19. My colleague Amos Goldberg suggests broadening this argument to see in Shofman's stance a critique of the concept of choice that is so central to the liberal worldview. I am grateful to him for the comment and for his intellectual daring. In my book *A Poetics of Trauma: The Work of Dahlia Ravikovitch* (Lebanon, NH: University Press of New England, 2013), I discuss how Ravikovitch's writings challenge the concept of choice in Western culture in general and in the Zionist enterprise in particular.

20. Shofman, *Collected Works*, 1:176–79.

21. Edward J. Bristow, *Prostitution and Prejudice: The Jewish Fight against White Slavery, 1870–1939* (Oxford: Clarendon Press, 1982); Jo Doezema, "Loose Women or Lost Women," *Gender Issues* 18 (Winter 2000): 23–50.

22. H. N. Bialik, "In the City of Slaughter" [Be'ir haharegah], in *The Complete Works of H. N. Bialik* [Kol shirei H. N. Bialik], ed. Yitshak Fiksler (Tel Aviv: Dvir, 1973), 358.

23. Shofman, *Collected Works*, 1:179.

24. Bialik, *Complete Works*, 350.

25. See Alan L. Mintz, *Hurban: Responses to Catastrophe in Hebrew Literature* (New York: Columbia University Press, 1984), 131; Anita Shapira, *Land and Power: The Zionist Resort to Force, 1881–1948* (Oxford: Oxford University Press, 1992); Michael Gluzman, "'Hoser koah: Hamahalah hamevishah beyoter': Bialik vehapogrom beKishinov," in *In the City of Slaughter: A Late Visit upon the Hundredth Anniversary of Bialik's Poem* [Be'ir haharegah: Bikur me'uhar bemel'at me'ah shanah lapoemah shel Bialik], ed. Michael Gluzman, Hannan Hever, and Dan Miron (Tel Aviv: Resling, 2005), 14; Hannah Naveh, "Migdar Vehazon Hagavriyut Ha'ivrit" [Gender and the vision of Hebrew masculinity], in *New Jewish Time: Jewish Culture in a Secular Age* [Zman yehudi hadash: Tarbut yehudit be'idan hiloni], ed. Dan Miron and Hannan Hever, 3:117–18 (Tel Aviv: Lamda, 2007); David Roskies, *Against the Apocalypse: Responses to Catastrophe in Modern Jewish Culture* (Syracuse, NY: Syracuse University Press, 1999), 86; and Mikhal Dekel, "'From the Mouth of the Raped Woman Rivka Schiff,' Kishinev, 1903," *Women's Studies Quarterly* 36, no. 1/2 (2008): 199–207. See also articles by Alan L. Mintz, Dan Laor, Michael Gluzman, Iris Milner, Sara R. Horowitz, Anita Shapira, David G., Roskies, Arnold J. Band, Lawrence Kaplan, and Asa Kasher in "Kishinev in the Twentieth Century," a special issue of *Prooftexts* 25 (Winter/Spring 2005).

26. Gluzman, Hever, and Miron, *In the City of Slaughter.*

27. Gluzman, Hever, and Miron, *In the City of Slaughter*, 74.

28. Michael Gluzman points out that the gap between the worldviews evinced, respectively, in "On the Slaughter" and "In the City of Slaughter" is also expressed in the difference between the two suppressed poems "To the Martyrs"

(Lakedoshim), written in the aftermath of the anti-Jewish violence in Odessa in 1854, which expresses identification with the victims, and "Be Strong and Brave" (Ḥazak ve'emats), commemorating the victims of the Białystok pogrom in 1907, which condemns the weakness of the victims; see Gluzman, "Hoser koaḥ," 28–29. Mikhal Dekel has also discussed the differences between "On the Slaughter" and "In the City of Slaughter." She notes that in the former poem, the speaker identifies with the victims, while in the latter the act of spectatorship creates a distance between the speaker/witness and the readers, on the one hand, and the victims, on the other. Dekel attributes this attitude of distance to Bialik's representation of the witness as an emergent tragic figure. See Mikhal Dekel, *The Universal Jew: Masculinity, Modernity, and the Zionist Moment* (Evanson, IL: Northwestern University Press, 2010), 142–43.

29. Steven L. Jacobs, trans., *Shirot Bialik: A New and Annotated Translation of Chaim Nachman Bialik's Epic Poems* (Columbus, OH: Alpha, 1987), 154.

30. On the posture of witnessing in Bialik's writing, see Dan Miron, "Me'ir haharegah vehal'ah: Hirḥurim al hapoemah shel Bialik bimil'at me'ah lehofa'atah," in Gluzman, Hever, and Miron, *In the City of Slaughter*, 74–154. And see Lilach Lachman, "The Reader as Witness: 'City of the Killings' and Bialik's Romantic Historiography," in *The Jews and British Romanticism: Politics, Religion, Culture,* ed. Sheila A. Spector (Basingstoke, UK: Palgrave Macmillan, 2005), 211–32.

31. Gluzman, "Hoser koaḥ," 27.

32. Jacobs, *Shirot Bialik*, 134.

33. Sara R. Horowitz points out that the critical and ironic gaze directed at the men in "In the City of Slaughter" does not apply to the images of the raped women. See her "The Rhetoric of Embodied Memory in 'In the City of Slaughter,'" *Prooftexts* 25 (Winter/Spring 2005): 81, 84.

34. Mikhal Dekel offers an intriguing analysis of "In the City of Slaughter," according to which the poem establishes a masculinity based on a model of mythical tragedy. Reading the poem through the prism of tragedy allows her to expose a complex masculinity, a Jewish masculinity that is not active, violent, or vengeful. This masculinity stands ready to act but is simultaneously held in; it is passive but deeply committed to the nation. See Dekel, *Universal Jew*, 166.

35. David Vogel, *Collected Poems* [Kol hashirim], ed. Aharon Komem (Tel Aviv: Hakibbutz Hameuchad, 1998), 120. I thank Deborah Greniman for this beautiful translation.

36. I am not arguing that Vogel reflects a feminine attitude or expresses a female voice, either in "I've Butchered My Wife" (Tavaḥti ishti) or in his other texts. As against Dan Miron, who argues that the poetic format of Vogel's "feminine" poems is no different from that of his "masculine" poems, Naomi Seidman offers a more complex view, arguing that femininity and masculinity in Vogel's works should be read as meeting points between gender and poetics. In other words, femininity and masculinity in Vogel's work raise questions about gender identity and

about the various types of modernist poetics. See Dan Miron, *Founding Mothers, Stepsisters: The Emergence of the First Hebrew Poetesses* [Imahot meyasdot, achayot chorgot] (Tel Aviv: Hakibbutz Hameuchad, 1991), 93; and Naomi Seidman, " 'It Is You I Speak from within Me': David Fogel's Poetics of the Feminine Voice," *Prooftexts* 13, no. 1 (January 1993): 87–102.

37. Mintz, *Hurban*, 129–54; Dan Miron, *H. N. Bialik and the Prophetic Mode in Modern Hebrew Poetry* (Syracuse, NY: Syracuse University Press, 2000).

38. Horowitz, "Rhetoric of Embodied Memory," 75.

39. Glenda Abramson, *Hebrew Writing of the First World War* (London: Vallentine Mitchell, 2008), 231.

40. Dan Miron draws our attention to the stratum of Jewish national meaning in Vogel's *Married Life* (Ḥayei nisu'im), pointing out that "here the two protagonists who come into conflict are not only a man and a woman, but a Jew and a Gentile." Miron reads this theme in the context of the erotic complex of the Jew's love for the non-Jew, referring in this regard to Agnon's "The Lady and the Peddler" (Ha'adonit vaharokhel) and Smolenskin's "The Reward" (Hagmul). See Dan Miron, "Matai nehdal 'legalot' et Vogel?" in his *The Blind Library: Assorted Prose Pieces, 1980–2005* [Hasifria ha'iveret: Proza me'urevet, 1980–2005] (Tel Aviv: Yediot Aharonot, 2005), 102–24.

41. Hamutal Tsamir, "Lilit, Ḥava Vehagever Hamit'apek: Hakalkalah Halibidinalit shel Bialik Ubnei Doro" [Lilith, Eve, and the self-restraining man: The libidinal economy of Bialik and his contemporaries], in *Mehkarei Yerushalaim besfrut 'ivrit* 23 (2009): 151–63.

42. Jean Laplanch and Jean-Bertrand Pontalis, "Fantasy and the Origins of Sexuality," in *Formations of Fantasy*, ed. Victor Burgin, James Donald, and Cora Kaplan (London: Methuen, 1986), 26.

43. Amalia Ziv, "Ben Sehorot Miniyot Lesovyektim Miniyim: Hamakhloket Hafeministit al Pornografiya" [Between sexual goods and sexual subjects: The feminist controversy over pornography], *Teorya u-vikoret* 25 (Fall 2004): 183.

44. Laplanch and Pontalis, "Fantasy and the Origins of Sexuality," 22.

45. Laplanch and Pontalis, "Fantasy and the Origins of Sexuality," 22–23.

46. Teresa de Lauretis, "On the Subject of Fantasy," in *Feminisms in the Cinema*, ed. Laura Pietropaolo and Ada Testaferri (Bloomington: Indiana University Press, 1995), 75.

47. Patricia Yaeger and Beth Kowaleski-Wallace point out that, as feminists, we are attuned to the way cultural construction produces a multifaceted female identity, at times infused with splits and contradictions. They argue that we are far less attuned to the way cultural construction dismantles and challenges the image of both the concrete and the symbolic father. See Patricia Yaeger and Beth Kowaleski-Wallace, eds., *Refiguring the Father: New Feminist Readings of Patriarchy* (Carbondale: Southern Illinois University Press, 1989), x.

48. L. A. Arieli, *Collected Works* [Kitvei L. A. Arieli: Sipurim, mahazot, hagadot, ma'amarim, igrot], ed. Michael Arfa (New York: Israel Metz Foundation Press–Dvir, 1999), 1:71–86.

49. Arieli, *Collected Works*, 1:73–74.

50. Shofman, *Collected Works*, 1:89–95. According to Gershon Shaked, the story "Trifles" is an example of a "leitmotif sketch." The recurrent leitmotif is that of "the erotic negation, the erotic disorder that ensues when the lover is unloved and the beloved, unloving." See Gershon Shaked, *Dead End: Studies in J. H. Brenner, M. J. Berdichevsky, G. Shofman, and U. N. Gnessin* [Lelo motsa: Al Y. H. Brenner, M. Y. Berdichevsky, G. Shofman, ve U. N. Gnessin] (Tel Aviv: Hakibbutz Hameuchad, 1973), 136.

51. Shofman, *Collected Works*, 1:95.

52. For more on gender performativity, see Judith Butler, *Gender Trouble: Feminism and the Subversion of Identity* (New York: Routledge, 1990).

53. It is interesting to note, on a purely anecdotal level, that the Hebrew verb *merashresh* ("rustle, tinkle") makes its first appearance in Shofman's story "Trifles." Bialik, editor of *Hashiloaḥ*, the literary journal in which the story was first published, attests in a 1922 letter to the writer Daniel Persky (published in *Hadoar*, September 7, 1934) that it was he who coined this word and inserted it into Shofman's story; see Eilon Gilad, "Gilgulah Shel Milah-'Rishrush': Me'eifo Hegi'a La'ivrit Hatslil Hamatok Shel Hakesef?" [The incarnation of the word "rustling": Where did the sweet sound of money come to the Hebrew?], *Haaretz*, February 22, 2013. https://www.haaretz.co.il/magazine/the-edge/mehasafa/1.1934286. The addition of *merashresh* enhances the hedonistic dimension of Hillel's character, with the aim of highlighting his frustration; see Shofman, *Collected Works*, 1:90. Symbolically, it is not coincidental that Bialik, in his editorial role, contributed his linguistic wisdom toward balancing Hillel's impotence and shoring up his clout.

54. It may be the fundamental difference between identification and empathy that underpins these dissimilar attitudes. There is a dimension to identification with weakness that is threatening to the male speaker, while empathy allows not only for a defensive distance but even for a kind of patronizing that protects Shofman's speaker from the subversion and distortion of gender relations. On the differences between identification and empathy, see Dominick LaCapra, *History in Transit: Experience, Identity, Critical Theory* (Ithaca, NY: Cornell University Press, 2004); and Carolyn J. Dean, *The Fragility of Empathy after the Holocaust* (Ithaca, NY: Cornell University Press, 2004).

55. The axe reaches its apotheosis as a phallic symbol in Shofman's story "The Axe" (Hakardom), in Shofman, *Collected Works*, 1:25–31. The axe as a symbol of ethnic violence also appears in Brenner's "He Sent Me a Long Letter" (Mihtav arokh shalaḥ li, 1906): "Anyone who bears in his body the weakness of the Jew—will fall by the axe, by the fist"; in Y. H. Brenner, *Collected Writings* [in

Hebrew] (New York: Shtibl Press, 1937), 6:28. Brenner, like Bialik before him, makes rhetorical use of the phallic quality of the axe to create an association between sexual vulnerability and ethnic violence.

56. David Vogel, *Viennese Romance* [Roman vina'i] (Tel Aviv: Am Oved, 2012), 236.

57. Yosef Haim Brenner, *Around the Point* [Misaviv lanekudah], (1904), in *Collected Works* [Ktavim] (Tel Aviv: Hakibbutz Hameuchad, 1977), 1:504–5.

58. It is hard not to see a connection between Brenner's cry of "my sister" and Yehuda Leib Gordon's poem "Aḥoti Ruḥamah" (My sister Ruhama), first published in *Hamelitz* in 1882, which was one of the major responses in Haskalah literature to the rape of Jewish women in the pogroms. For discussions of "Aḥoti Ruḥamah," see Andrea Siegel, "Women, Violence and the Arab Question in Early Zionist Literature" (PhD diss., Columbia University, 2011), 52; Michael Stanislawski, *For Whom Do I Toil? Judah Leib Gordon and the Crisis of Russian Jewry* (New York: Oxford University Press, 1988), 198–99, 204; and Alan Mintz, "The Russian Pogroms in Hebrew Literature and the Subversion of the Martyrological Ideal," *AJS Review* 7/8 (1982/1983): 264.

59. That Abramson pays the prostitute without using her services is fascinating. According to Freud, the prostitute enables the client to fantasize about an all-powerful mother, but the payment simultaneously protects him, in letting him to maintain his position of power. In this context, Abramson's deed may be understood as a desperate effort to maintain a position of power and agency in relation to his own life. See Sigmund Freud, "Fetishism" (1927), in the *Standard Edition of the Complete Psychological Works of Sigmund Freud* (New York: Vintage, 1999), 11:152–59.

60. Vogel, *Viennese Romance*, 239.

61. Vogel, *Viennese Romance*, 240.

62. Vogel, *Viennese Romance*, 240.

63. The Hebrew writer's self-image as a whore is connected to the autobiographical experience of having been supported by rich Jews, to the trade in the words of the sacred tongue, as well as to the feminine image of the *galut* (Diaspora) Jew. It may also be read in relation to the wider question raised by Catherine Gallagher regarding the relationship between art and prostitution. See her "George Eliot and Daniel Deronda: The Prostitute and the Jewish Question," in *Sex, Politics, and Science in the Nineteenth-Century Novel*, ed. Ruth Bernard Yeazell (Baltimore, MD: Johns Hopkins University Press, 1985), 54. I am grateful to Mikhal Dekel for this reference.

64. Vogel, *Married Life*, 25.

65. The speaker in Vogel's poem "I Said to the Men" (Amarti lagvarim, 1920) would seem to be a prostitute; through her voice, Vogel expresses the fear she arouses in the "respectable" women who "quaked and fled away" from her (Vogel, *Collected Poems*, 272). Although the speaker's identity as a prostitute is

uncertain, it is certainly not unreasonable to suppose so. According to Miron, the poem "expressed the prostitute's sense of alienation; no man wants her or her tender ministrations, and everyone shuns her." Miron, *Founding Mothers, Stepsisters*, 93. Naomi Seidman accepts the view that the poem's speaker is a prostitute; see her "It Is You I Speak," 100.

66. Vogel, *Married Life*, 29.

67. Vogel, *Married Life*, 280.

68. Vogel, *Married Life*, 281.

69. Vogel, *Married Life*, 281.

70. See Sigmund Freud, *Three Essays on the Theory of Sexuality*, trans. James Strachey (New York: Basic Book, 1962); and David D. Gilmore, *Misogyny: The Male Malady* (Philadelphia: University of Pennsylvania Press, 2001), 41–43. Feminist theorist Susan Griffin argues that men's repulsion toward women's bodies stems from fear of loss of control during sexual relations. The woman's body reminds the man of his own body and its attachment to nature, of his lack of control over it. See Susan Griffin, *Pornography and Silence: Culture's Revenge against Nature* (New York: HarperCollins, 1981), 202.

71. Roland Barthes was among the first to expose the illusory mechanism at work in striptease performances. He argued that striptease is based on a contradiction: the nullification of the woman's sexuality at the very moment when it is laid bare. A striptease performance, according to Barthes, is not an expression of autonomous female sexuality or of female creativity; it is a performance that uses the female body to make a presentation to male eyes, for the purpose of gratifying male appetites. The woman in the performance is conceived not as a subject with a personality, opinions, wishes, desires, and so on but as an object meant to serve such male purposes as power, possession, and sexuality. See Roland Barthes, *Mythologies*, trans. Annette Lavers (New York: Farrar, Straus and Giroux, 1972), 84–87.

72. Vogel, *Married Life*, 223.

73. Vogel, *Married Life*, 221.

74. Vogel, *Married Life*, 224.

75. Vogel, *Married Life*, 227.

76. The novel does not relate directly to this event as an attempted rape. The principal hint at sexual violence comes in the sentence "but the man thrust both his hands at her as though to fondle her, and his cane fell to the ground" (Vogel, *Married Life*, 172). I agree with Menahem Peri's argument in his afterward to the novel that the reference is to an attempted rape; see Menahem Peri, "He'ara al nosah hasefer" [A comment on the book's style], in Vogel, *Married Life*, 332. Interestingly, the character of Lotte, who suffers from her unrequited love for Gurdweil and from depression and ultimately takes her own life, is formed on the Freudian model that sees a direct connection between hysteria and childhood experience of sexual violence. In "The Etiology of Hysteria" (1896), Freud argues

that at the bottom of every case of hysteria lies a premature sexual experience. Freud later changed his position, replacing his theory of infantile seduction with that of infantile sexuality, according to which hysteria derives not from real occurrences but from fantasies of sexual relations with the father. See Freud, *Three Essays*, 78; Elizabeth Grosz, *Jacques Lacan: A Feminist Introduction* (London: Routledge, 1990), 50–81. Sandor Ferenczi rejected Freud's change, arguing in a 1933 article that childhood sexual traumas are far more prevalent than one might think; see Sandor Ferenczi, "Confusion of Tongues between Adults and the Child," in *Final Contributions to the Problems and Methods of Psycho-Analysis*, ed. Michael Balint, trans. Eric Mosbacher (London: Hogarth Press, 1955), 161. Ferenczi's point of view is widely accepted today.

77. Vogel, *Married Life*, 225.

78. Vogel, *Married Life*, 501.

79. Eric Zakim locates Gurdweil within the modernistic context of Vogel's writing, arguing that he is simultaneously both victim and victimizer. See Eric Zakim, "Between Fragment and Authority in David Fogel's (Re)Presentation of Subjectivity," *Prooftexts* 13, no. 1 (January 1993): 107.

80. Vogel, *Married Life*, 39.

81. Melanie Klein, "Notes on Some Schizoid Mechanisms" (1946), in *Envy and Gratitude and Other Works, 1946–1963* (London: Hogarth Press / Institute of Psycho-Analysis, 1975).

82. For a discussion of paranoid anxiety in Bialik's writings, see Mikhal Dekel, "From Where Have I Eaten My Poetry? On Bialik and the Maternal," *Shofar: An Interdisciplinary Journal of Jewish Studies* 31 (Fall 2012): 104–5.

83. See Jay R. Greenberg and Stephen A. Mitchell, *Object Relations in Psychoanalytic Theory* (Cambridge, MA: Harvard University Press, 1983), 126.

84. See Daniel Boyarin, *Unheroic Conduct: The Rise of Heterosexuality and the Invention of the Jewish Man* (Berkeley: University of California Press, 1977); Naveh, "Migdar vehazon hagavriyut ha'ivrit"; Gluzman, *The Zionist Body: Nationalism, Gender, and Sexuality in Modern Israeli Literature* [Haguf hatzioni: Le'umiut, migdar uminiut basifrut ha'israelit hachadasha] (Tel Aviv: Hakibbutz hameuchad, 2007); Hamutal Tsamir, *In the Name of the Land: Nationalism, Subjectivity, and Gender in the Israeli Poetry of the Statehood Generation* [Beshem hanof: Le'umiyut migdar vesobyektiviyut bashirah hayisraelit bishnot haḥamishim vehashishim] (Jerusalem: Keter Books / Beer Sheva, Israel: Heksherim Center, 2006); and Amnon Raz-Krakotzkin, "Galut Betokh Ribonut: Lebikoret 'Shelilat Hagalut' Batarbut Hayisraelit" [*Exile* within sovereignty: Critique of "The Negation of *Exile*" in Israeli culture], *Teorya u-vikoret* 4 (1993): 23–55, and 5 (1994): 113–23.

85. Robert Cover writes of the terror underlying the process of establishing juridical sovereignty, in connection with the recognition that judicial authority will bring with it conflicts with the sovereign over against which its judiciary autonomy has been established. Similarly, the moment when the Zionist com-

munity declares its national independence is (also) one of terror. The thought of
sovereignty over themselves aroused fears in members of the revival generation
that came to expression in their literary works. See Robert Cover, "The Folktales
of Justice: Tales of Jurisdiction," in *Narrative, Violence, and the Law: The Essays
of Robert Cover*, ed. Martha Minow, Michael Ryan, and Austin Sarat (Ann Arbor:
University of Michigan Press, 1993), 173–202.

86. Gluzman, "Hoser koah."

87. Tsamir, "Lilit, Hava."

88. In what follows I shall focus on the conceptions of power emerging from
"In the City of Slaughter" and "Al hashehitah," but, as Tsamir showed in "Lilit,
Hava," a sense of power courses through many of Bialik's poems, such as "Don't
Wipe" (Lo timah, 1899, 108), "In the Field" (Basadeh, 1893, 36), "Harbingers of
Spring" (Pa'amei aviv, 1900, 96), and "Winter Poems" (Mishrei hahoref, 1902, 136).
Ziva Shamir and Ruth Shenfeld have discussed the elements of national freedom,
power, and autonomy in Bialik's works; see Ruth Shenfeld, *Metamorphosis of a
Story: The Formation of Bialik's Stories* [Gilgulo shel sipur: Al darkei hahithavut shel
sipurei Bialik] (Tel Aviv: Katz Institute, Tel Aviv University, 1988); Ziva Shamir,
No Story, No History: Bialik's Stories from Texture to Context [Be'ein 'alilah: Sipurei
Bialik bema'agaloteihem] (Tel Aviv: Hakibbutz Hameuchad, 1998). Hannah Naveh,
by contrast, in her discussion of "Aryeh the Muscleman" (Aryeh ba'al guf) and
Bialik's conception of power, emphasizes Bialik's skepticism as to the chances of
"muscular Judaism" inheriting the place of the "old-time" Jew; see Naveh, "Migdar
vehazon hagavriyut ha'Ivrit," 119. Hannan Hever, too, reads "The Trumpet Was
Abashed" (Hahatsotsrah nitbaishah) as a text that poses an option for the Zionist narrative and actually affirms Jewish existence as a national minority in the
diaspora; see Hannan Hever, "Gerush behag haherut: Al 'hahatsotsrah nitbaishah'
leH. N. Bialik," in *The Narrative and the Nation: Critical Readings in the Canon of
Hebrew Fiction* [Hasipur vehale'um: Kri'ot bikortiyot bakanon hasiporet ha'ivrit]
(Tel Aviv: Resling, 2007), 99–106.

89. "The necessity of looking like an upstanding citizen wears down one's
selfhood," wrote Vogel of himself in his diary entry for May 25, 1919, quoted in
Dan Pagis, "Kavim Lebiografiah" [An outline for biography], in *Collected Poems*
[Kol shirei David Vogel], ed. Dan Pagis (Tel Aviv: Agudat Sofrim, 1966), 13.
This surely relates to the need to function within bourgeois European society,
but it can also be understood as relating to a wider variety of social and national
expectations, such as those of the Zionist enterprise. In a rough paraphrase, then,
this multivalent quotation may be understood as saying something along the lines
of this: the necessity of looking like an upstanding citizen—that is, hardworking
and solid—wears down one's selfhood, with the weakness at its core.

90. David Vogel, "'Ari ne'urai," *Kol hashirim*, 207, suppressed poem written
September 29, 1941, traslated by A. C. Jacobs, in *Collected Poems and Selected Translations* (London: Menard Press, 1996), accessed July 14, 2020. https://www.poetry

international.org/pi/poem/22499/auto/0/0/David-Vogel/Now-I-have-forgotten/
en/nocache.

91. Jessica Benjamin, *The Bonds of Love: Psychoanalysis, Feminism, and the Problem of Domination* (New York: Pantheon Books, 1988), 100.

92. J. Benjamin, *Bonds of Love*, 101.

93. Tsamir, "Lilit, Ḥava," 137.

94. Consciously or not, Tsamir herself alludes to this option. In a footnote, she circumscribes her argument that the poetry of the revival generation was entirely concerned with various ways of maintaining desire and masculinity: "Although it seems to me that only in Bialik does the *processing* of weakness and its transformation into strength and desire come out so clearly"; Tsamir, "Lilit, Ḥava," 169n89; emphasis in source.

95. Raya Morag, "Kol, Dimui, Vezikaron Hateror: Hakolno'a Hayisraeli Ha'alilati Bitkufat Ha'intifadah Hashniyah" [Sound, image, terror, and memory: Israeli narrative cinema in the age of the second intifada], *Yisrael* 14 (2008): 71–88. See also Libby Saxton, "Anamnésis: Godard/Lanzmann," *Trafic* 47 (Autumn 2003): 48–66.

96. Julia Kristeva, *Desire in Language: A Semiotic Approach to Literature and Art,* trans. Thomas Gora, Alice Jardine, and Leon S. Roudiez (New York: Columbia University Press, 1980).

97. Théodule-Armand Ribot, *Diseases of Memory: An Essay in the Positive Psychology,* trans. William Huntington Smith (New York: Appleton, 1887).

98. Naveh, "Migdar vehazon hagavriyut ha'Ivrit," 119. It is interesting in this context to recall Gershom Scholem's characterization of the Zionism reflected in Agnon's works, particularly *Tmol shilshom*: "Zionism in Agnon's writings is basically a noble failure, whereas everything else in Jewish life is a sham." Gershom Scholem, "Reflections on S. Y. Agnon," *Commentary*, December 1967, accessed July 1, 2020. https://www.commentarymagazine.com/articles/gershom-scholem/reflections-on-s-y-agnon/?utm_source=copy&utm_medium=website&utm_campaign=SocialSnap.

99. Naveh, "Migdar vehazon hagavriyut ha'Ivrit," 122.

100. Pagis, "Kavim lebiografiah," 35.

Notes to Chapter Two

1. Nitza Keren, *Like a Sheet in the Hand of the Embroideress: Women Writers and the Hegemonic Text* [Kayeria beyad harokemet] (Ramat Gan, Israel: Bar-Ilan University Press, 2010). Keren's approach is influenced by feminist scholars such as Elaine Showalter, Susan Gubar, Sandra Gilbert, and Nancy K. Miller, who posit that mythological and classical women associated with textile production (Arachne, Ariadne, and Penelope) act as symbols of the woman-as-artist and feminine authorship.

2. Lynn A. Higgins and Brenda R. Silver, eds., *Rape and Representation* (New York: Columbia University Press, 1991), 3.

3. Higgins and Silver, *Rape and Representation*, 4.

4. Sepharadi Jews are the Jews of Spain, Portugal, North Africa, and the Middle East and their descendants. The adjective "Sepharadi" is derived from the Hebrew word *Sepharad*, which means "Spain." In an Israeli context, Sepharadi Jews are at times subdivided into *Sepharadim*, from Spain and Portugal, and *Mizrachim*, from Northern Africa and the Middle East. The term "Arab-Jews" is sometimes used as an alternative to the Zionist perspective implied in the term *Mizrachim*.

5. Safed, also known as *Tzfat*, is one of the four Jewish holy cities, which is located in the northern region of Israel/Palestine.

6. Shoshana Shababo, *Maria: A Novel Concerning the Lives of Nuns in the Holyland* [Marya: Roman mehayey hanezirot baaretz], ed. Orna Levin (1932; repr., Tel Aviv: Bimat Kedem Lesifrut, 2002). The original title reads *Marya: A Novel from the Lives of Nuns in the Land of Israel*. Note that the Hebrew word for "novel," *roman*, also means "a romance" or "a love affair."

7. Shoshana Shababo, *Love in the Town of Safed* [Ahava bitzfat] (1942; repr., Tel Aviv: Bimat Kedem Lesifrut, 2000).

8. For a list of lexicons and anthologies of Hebrew literature that omitted Shababo's work, see Yossef Halevi, *A Modern Daughter of the Orient: On the Work of Shoshana Shababo* [Bat hamizrach hahadash] (Ramat Gan, Israel: Bar-Ilan University Press, 1996), 15n17 and 17n13; as well as Yaffah Berlovitz, "Prose Writing in the Yishuv: 1882–1948," in *Jewish Women: A Comprehensive Historical Encyclopedia*, Jewish Women's Archive, last modified March 1, 2009. http://jwa.org/encyclopedia/article/prose-writing-in-yishuv-1882-1948.

9. Halevi, *Modern Daughter*.

10. Gormezano-Gorfinkel and Bat-Shachar, eds., *Hakivun Mizrach* [Eastward: Culture and literary journal] 19 (2009).

11. The "Old Yishuv" is the community of Jews already living in Eretz Israel when the Zionist movement began encouraging immigration to Palestine.

12. Yaffah Berlovitz, ed., *Tender Rib: Stories by Women-Writers in Pre-State Israel* [She-ani adamah ve-adam] (Jerusalem: Hakibutz Hameuhad, 2003), 9.

13. Halevi, *Modern Daughter*, 10.

14. Yitzhak Gormezano Goren and Ketzia Alon offer several explanations for the vanishing of Shababo's work from literary canon. Gormezano Goren and Alon place the blame on two individuals: the writer Yehuda Burla, who nourished Shababo in her early years but later turned his back on her and published a virulent and deadly critique of her first novel, and David Carstani, whom she married at the age of thirty-two right before she stopped producing her own writing. Gormezano Goren also suggests sociological and psychological reasons for Shababo's absence, but focuses on the thematic and stylistic issues that isolated Shababo from her literary surroundings: writing about Christians in a period in which

literature in Eretz Israel concentrated primarily on pioneering and occupation of land, her linguistic verity (Hebrew, Arabic, French, and English), and her daring descriptions of sexuality. Yitzhak Gormezano Goren, "My Journey with the Rose: An Encounter with Shoshanah Shababo's Work" [in Hebrew], *Hakivun Mizrach* 19 (2009): 8–12; Ketzia Alon, "Shoshanah Shababo: About Fracturing and Collapse, Disappearance and Evading" [in Hebrew], *Hakivun Mizrach* 19 (2009): 13–20.

15. Terry Eagleton, *The Rape of Clarisse: Writing, Sexuality, and Class Struggle in Samuel Richardson* (Oxford: Basil Blackwell, 1982), 61.

16. Eagleton, *Rape of Clarisse*, 62.

17. Teresa de Lauretis, *Technologies of Gender: Essays on Theory, Film, and Fiction* (Bloomington: Indiana University Press, 1987), 25.

18. Yehuda Burla, "Marya" [in Hebrew], *Moznayim* 4, no. 8 (1932): 11–12. Yossef Halevi notes that although some brief but positive reviews of the novel *Maria* appeared, Burla's response was heavily influential to the minds of readers and many literary critics. Halevi, *Modern Daughter*, 15.

19. Gershon Shaked mentions that the story "Luna," which was written in 1913, was first published in *Haezrach* (edited by S. Ben-Zion) in 1918. The story "Bein Shivtay Arav," written after "Luna," was published before it, in 1917, in *Al hasaf* (edited by Yaakov Shteinberg). Gershon Shaked, *Hebrew Narrative Fiction, 1880–1980: In the Land of Israel and the Diaspora* [Hasiporet haivrit, 1880–1980] (Jerusalem: Hakibutz hameuhad, 1983), 84.

20. Yehuda Burla quoted in Shaked, *Hebrew Narrative Fiction*, 83.

21. Batya Shimony claims that "Burla's entry into the Hall of Hebrew literature is accompanied from the first moment by a fear of rejection." Batya Shimony, "Identity under Trial: Yehuda Burla's Fiction between Sepharadi Manners and Zionist Existence" [in Hebrew], *El Perizente* 1 (2007): 45.

22. Shoshana Shababo, "Authors and Poets: Shoshana Shababo, 1932" [in Hebrew], *Do'ar Yisrael* [IsraelPost.co.il], accessed June 25, 2020. http://www.israel post.co.il/unforget.nsf/lettersbycategory/5857FA97C3CE396E42256C1A003457 71?opendocument.

23. Nurit Govrin, *Brenner: "Nonplussed" and Mentor* [Brenner: Oved 'etsot u-moreh derekh] (Tel Aviv: Misrad ha-bitahon, 199), 1.

24. Batya Shimony explores the dual identity of Burla, ranging from his Jewish-Sepharadi roots to the new Zionist experience, and analyzes Burla's work through his complex relationship with the dominant Zionist group, a relationship of simultaneous acceptance and rejection. Shimony, "Identity under Trial," 45–60.

25. Y. H. Brenner, "The Eretz Israel Genre and Its Artifacts (1911)," in *The Collected Works of Y. H. Brenner* [Kol Kitvei Y. H. Brenner] (Tel Aviv: Hakibbutz Hameuchad, 1985), 569–78. Nurit Govrin insists that despite the huge impact of the article "The Eretz Israel Genre and Its Artifacts," in other writings, and particularly in Brenner's role as a critic and editor, he expresses an entirely different position in relation to the literature of Eretz Israel. Nurit Govrin, "In Praise of

the 'Genre': Brenner as the Supporter of the 'Palestinian Genre'" [in Hebrew], *Dappim: Research in Literature* 3 (1986): 97–116.

26. Govrin, "In Praise of the 'Genre,'" 101.

27. Hannan Hever, "Yitzhak Shami: Ethnicity as an Unresolved Conflict," *Shofar: An Interdisciplinary Journal of Jewish Studies* 24, no. 2 (2006): 126–27.

28. Yochai Oppenheimer recounts the change in the writings of Yehuda Burla. Although the early stages of his literary career (namely his work in the twenties) does not reveal a Zionist agenda, from the thirties onward, his literature expresses Zionist canonical norms. Yochai Oppenheimer, *Barriers: The Representation of the Arab in Hebrew and Israeli Fiction, 1906–2005* [Meever lagader: Yitsug ha'aravim basiporet haivrit vehayisraelit, 1906–2005] (Tel Aviv: Am Oved, 2008), 82–109.

29. Shaked, *Hebrew Narrative Fiction*, 97.

30. Ella Shohat, "Rupture and Return: Zionist Discourse and the Study of Arab Jews," *Social Text* 75 21, no. 2 (2003): 59.

31. Shohat, "Rupture and Return," 60.

32. Yosef Haim Brenner and Shmuel Yosef Agnon also often describe mixed cities, especially Tel Aviv-Jaffa and Jerusalem, as can be seen, for example, in Brenner's *Breakdown and Bereavement* (1920) and Agnon's *Only Yesterday* (1945). But unlike Shababo, their works do not deal at all with the local Arab and Christian population. The mixed cities that interest them are Jewish towns, and not places where other populations live or where Jewish and Arab communities reside alongside one another.

33. See, for example, "Klavim leor shalhevet" (1929), "Almana" (1930), "Bishfot ha-shoftim" (1930), "Brachah" (1932), "Ha-ugah shenitbayshah" (1936), "Hashviah" (1936), and "Pliah" (1936).

34. This is not the position of Ronit Matalon, who views Levantine subjectivity in a different way. Matalon suggests that being Levantine is not a particular discrete identity but rather, to use Gil Z. Hochberg's language, "a marker of *the instability of identity*. Less an identity than a position of ambiguity"; Gil Z. Hochberg, *In Spite of Partition: Jews, Arabs, and the Limits of Separatist Imagination* (Princeton, NJ: Princeton University Press, 2010), 72. In her essay "My Father at Age Seventy-Nine," for example, Matalon deals with the complicated dialectic of the Mizrahi voice in the context of the Zionist project, and places her father and Jacqueline Kahanoff as two alternative models to Ashkenazi Zionist oppression. In other words, Matalon enters into a direct dialogue with Zionism. Shababo, however, does not establish her multilayered subjectivity as an interface with the Zionist project but rather simply acts out her Sepharadi experience. This is not an idealization of the past nor of a future utopia, as Matalon would have it; Ronit Matalon, "My Father at Age Seventy-Nine," trans. Mikhal Dekel, *Callaloo* 32, no. 4 (2009): 1182–88. The main difference is in the ongoing engagement of Matalon with the Zionist discourse, which is different from Shababo's indifference to it. While Matalon struggles to justify the Levantine subjectivity and to include it in

the Israeli discourse, Shababo disclaims canonic expectations and writes about her characters without fawning; she ignores the differences and the limits set by the patriarchal, national, ethnic, and religious discourse. Matalon points out the discriminatory nature of the Zionist/Western discourse, which needs a defined and distinct identity, and is not able to accommodate different and fluid identities. What seems to be an infected identity for the hegemony is understood by Matalon as actually a more flexible and productive subjectivity. In some ways, this is also the position of Shababo. The question is whether Shababo is aware of the dominant discourse, and whether her indifference to it stems from her naivety or is, rather, a conscious position.

35. Indira Karamcheti, "The Geographics of Marginality: Place and Textuality in Simone Schwarz-Bart and Anita Desai," in *Reconfigured Spheres: Feminist Explorations of Literary Space*, ed. Margaret R. Higonnet and Joan Templeton (Amherst: University of Massachusetts Press, 1994), 130.

36. Kimberlé Crenshaw, "Demarginalizing the Intersection of Race and Sex: A Black Feminist Critique of Antidiscrimination Doctrine, Feminist Theory, and Antiracist Politics," *University of Chicago Legal Forum* 140 (1989). See also Victoria Pruin DeFrancisco, Catherine Helen Palczewski, and Danielle D. McGeough, *Gender in Communication: A Critical Introduction* (New York: SAGE Publications, 2013), 10; and Angela Y. Davis, "Rape, Racism and the Capitalist Setting," *Black Scholar* 12, no. 6 (1981): 39–45.

37. Much has been written about the relationship between gender, race, ethnicity, class, and power. See, for example, K. Walseth, "Young Muslim Women and Sport: The Impact of Identity Work," *Leisure Studies* 25, no. 1 (2006): 75–94; C. F. Pelak, "Negotiating Gender/Race/Class Constraints in the New South Africa," *International Review for the Sociology of Sport* 40, no. 1 (2005): 53–70; Floya Anthias and Nira Yuval-Davis, "Contextualizing Feminism: Gender, Ethnic and Class Divisions," *Feminist Review* 15 (1983): 62–75.

38. Shoshana Shababo, "Honeymoon" [Yerach-dvash], in Halevi, *Modern Daughter*, 218–28.

39. Shababo, "Honeymoon," 218.

40. Shababo, "Honeymoon," 219.

41. From its inception, the Zionist movement has created a conceptual connection between the revival of the nation and the well-being and prosperity of its people. Much has been written about the juxtaposition of nation building and the body in a Zionist context, as well as about the gendered aspect of this "muscular Judaism." Yet most of the critical discourse about the formative years of the Zionist movement and Israeli society ignores the idealization of the abled body. See Meira Weiss, *The Chosen Body: The Politics of the Body in Israeli Society* (Redwood City, CA: Stanford University Press, 2002); Ilana Szobel, "Choreographing the Disabled Body: Performing Vulnerability and Political Change in the Work of Tamar Borer," *Journal of Jewish Identities* 12, no. 1 (2019): 55–74.

42. Shababo, "Honeymoon," 222.

43. Shababo, "Honeymoon," 223.

44. Shababo, "Honeymoon," 226.

45. See, for example, Melissa Farley, *Prostitution, Trafficking, and Traumatic Stress* (New York: Psychology Press, 2003); Andrea Dworkin, "Prostitution and Male Supremacy," in *Life and Death: Unapologetic Writings on the Continuing War against Women* (New York: Free Press, 1997), 139–51; Kathleen L. Barry, *Female Sexual Slavery* (New York: New York University Press, 1984).

46. Shababo, "Honeymoon," 227.

47. Shababo, "Honeymoon," 218.

48. Shababo, "Honeymoon," 228.

49. Shoshana Shababo, "Samson at the Harvest Season" [Shimshon beonat habatzir], in Halevi, *Modern Daughter*, 229.

50. Boaz Neumann, *Land and Desire in Early Zionism* (Waltham, MA: Brandeis University Press, 2011).

51. Andrea Siegel, "Rape and the 'Arab Question' in L. A. Arieli's *Allah Karim!* and Aharon Reuveni's *Devastation*," *Nashim* 23 (2012): 117. In her discussion of Rivka Alper's novel *Quivers of Revolution* (Pirpurey mahapekha, 1930), Orian Zakai also points out that sexual aggression against Jewish women in Alper's novel derives not, as with Bialik's "In the City of Slaughter," "from the traditional weakness of Jewish men, but from violence associated with the modernization and masculinization of the Jewish man." Orian Zakai, "A Uniform of a Writer: Literature, Ideology and Sexual Violence in the Writing of Rivka Alper," *Prooftexts* 34, no. 2 (Spring 2014): 241. The connection between rape and occupation, and in particular colonialist occupation, is not unique to the Zionist project. While analyzing sexual violence endured by Native American communities, Sarah Deer depicts the development of colonist rape culture and shows how again and again rape has been a weapon in the colonial effort. Sarah Deer, *The Beginning and End of Rape: Confronting Sexual Violence in Native America* (Minneapolis: University of Minnesota Press, 2015).

52. Ronit Gez claims that Shababo inserted associated antinationalistic overtones with the desire of the Jewish protagonist, and was therefore criticized by her contemporaries, who advocated writing in the spirit of nationalism and Zionism. Gez analyzes the story as an exploitation narrative but reads it in the context of literature about "forbidden love" between Arabs and Jews, thereby ignoring or undermining the sexual nature of this violation. Ronit Gez, *Women's and Men's Fiction in the Yishuv Period: Negotiations over the National Narrative* [in Hebrew], unpublished PhD diss. (Beer Sheva, Israel: Ben-Gurion University of the Negev, 2001), 193, 201.

53. Siegel, "Rape and the 'Arab Question,'" 111.

54. In her analysis of Alper's unpublished story "Mistake," Orian Zakai claims that "sexual violence is reproduced rather than repudiated in the Zionist

space" (Zakai, "Uniform of a Writer," 257). Zakai further demonstrates the way in which "sexual violence is transposed to the national setting and becomes part and parcel of the making of Zionist masculinity" (Zakai, "Uniform of a Writer," 258).

55. Shababo, "Samson at the Harvest Season," 230.

56. Shababo, "Samson at the Harvest Season," 234.

57. See Michael Gluzman, *The Zionist Body: Nationalism, Gender, and Sexuality in Modern Israeli Literature* [Haguf hatzioni: Le'umiut, migdar uminiut basifrut ha'israelit hachadasha] (Tel Aviv: Hakibbutz hameuchad, 2007); Todd Samuel Presner, *Muscular Judaism: The Jewish Body and the Politics of Regeneration* (New York: Routledge, 2007).

58. Shababo, "Samson at the Harvest Season," 234.

59. Mishnah Sotah 1:8.

60. Ahuva Ashman, *The Story of Eve: Daughters, Mothers, and Strange Women in Bible* [Toldot Ḥavah: Banot, imahot, ve-nashim nokhriyot ba-Miḳra] (Tel Aviv: Miskal, 2008), 132. Mieke Bal also analyzes the biblical stories of the murder of men by women as a fantasy of revenge for violence against women. See Mieke Bal, *Death and Dissymmetry: The Politics of Coherence in the Book of Judges* (Chicago, IL: University of Chicago Press, 1998), 230.

61. Bal (*Death and Dissymmetry*) notes that Sisra, Abimelech, and Samson, the three biblical men who were killed by women, were murdered using tools that penetrated their heads. The murder, then, not only took their lives but also sexually humiliated them. See also Ashman, *Story of Eve*, 125, 132.

62. Daniel Boyarin, *Unheroic Conduct: The Rise of Heterosexuality and the Invention of the Jewish Man* (Berkeley: University of California Press, 1977). Unlike the "new Jew" that was a negation of the diasporic Jew (described in stereotypical ways as pale, gaunt, and helpless), the new Zionist woman was not freed from the "chains" of the Diaspora, and was seen primarily as a helpmate to the new Jew. On a symbolic level, a study of visual imagery of the early years of the new state reveals that the new Jew was depicted as a young Jewish idol with a handsome face and shapely body that symbolized his spiritual virtues. Compared to the new Jewish men, women are rare in those images, and they usually occupy only a marginal role. See Yaron Peleg, *Homoeroticism in Modern Hebrew Literature, 1880–2000* [Derech Gever] (n.p.: Shufra Publications, 2003), 25.

63. Shababo, "Samson at the Harvest Season," 230.

64. Shababo, "Samson at the Harvest Season," 234.

65. Mary Layoun, "The Female Body and 'Transnational' Reproduction; or, Rape by Any Other Name?," in *Scattered Hegemonies: Postmodernity and Trans-national Feminist Practices*, ed. Inderpal Grewal and Caren Kaplan (Minneapolis: University of Minnesota Press, 1994), 73.

66. Halevi, *Modern Daughter*, 13.

67. Halevi, *Modern Daughter*, 9, 17, 20. Shababo's daughter also mentions that her mother is "the first Hebrew writer born in the *moshava* (agricultural

colony) Zichron Yaakov" (Shababo, *Love in the Town of Safed*, 118). Moshe Behar points out that, as far as we can know, Shababo is the first Mizrahi woman writer who published stories and novels in Hebrew. He mentions the name of the feminist intellectual Esther Azhari Moyal (1873–1948), who indeed published in Jaffa from 1909 until she lost her husband and became destitute in 1915, but she wrote mostly scholarly, nonfiction work, and mainly in Arabic and French, not in Hebrew. See Moshe Behar, "The Centennial of 'Flora Saporto': Thoughts on the Possibility of a Mizrahi-Feminist Alliance," *Pe'amim: Studies in Oriental Jewry* 139–40 (2014): 43.

68. Yossef Halevi argues that Shababo continues the literary and ideological project of the first Aliyah female writers Hemda Ben-Yehuda (1873–1951) and Nehama Puhachevsky (1869–1934), who were dealing with nationalism and the status of women in the Land of Israel (Halevi, *Modern Daughter*, 118–19). For a discussion about the literary connections between Shababo and Devorah Baron (1887–1956), who is considered the first female to write Modern Hebrew literature, see Alon, "Shoshana Shababo," 16–18.

69. The traditional approach to immigration and human-place relations is based on a clear division between the "country of origin" and the "destination land." Various historical changes, such as the collapse of major colonial regimes and economic globalization, challenge this clear-cut division. Contemporary understanding of spatial relations and the position of the subject is more flexible and focuses on the "in-between": tourism and migration, transmigrants, life on the borderland, temporary and diasporic communities, and more. This focus has spawned new concepts of identity, culture, and belonging. Thus, instead of former concepts such as "society" or "culture," Arjun Appadurai offers the idea of the "ethnoscape," which explores fundamental disjunctures of global cultural flows. See Arjun Appadurai, *The Future as Cultural Fact: Essays on the Global Condition* (London: Verso Books, 2013); Smadar Lavie and Ted Swedenburg, eds., *Displacement, Diaspora, and Geographies of Identity* (Durham, NC: Duke University Press, 1996); Nina Glick Schiller and George E. Fouron, "Terrains of Blood and Nation: Haitian Transnational Social Fields," *Ethnic and Racial Studies* 22, no. 2 (1999): 340–66.

70. Dan Miron, *Founding Mothers, Stepsisters: The Emergence of the First Hebrew Poetesses* [Imahot meyasdot, achayot chorgot] (Tel Aviv: Hakibbutz Hameuchad, 1991).

71. Hamutal Bar-Yosef, "Sanctity of the Holy Land: Reflections on Three Poems of the Third Aliyah," in *The Land of Israel in 20th Century Jewish Thought* [Eretz Israel bahagut hayehudit], ed. Aviezer Ravitsky (Jerusalem: Yad Izhak Ven-Zvi, 2004), 388–98.

72. Hannan Hever, *From the Beginning: Three Essays on Nativist Hebrew Poetry* [Mereshit: Shalosh masot al shira ivrit yelidit] (Tel Aviv: Keshev, 2008); Hamutal Tsamir, *In the Name of the Land: Nationalism, Subjectivity, and Gender*

in the Israeli Poetry of the Statehood Generation [Beshem hanof: Le'umiyut migdar
vesobyektiviyut bashirah hayisraelit bishnot haḥamishim vehashishim] (Jerusalem:
Keter Books / Beer Sheva, Israel: Heksherim Center, 2006).

73. For more about the complexity of Rabb's nativeness, see Hamutal Tsamir,
"Love of the Homeland and a Deaf Dialogue: A Poem by Esther Raab and its
Masculine Critical Reception" [in Hebrew], *Teorya u-vikoret* 7 (1995): 124–45.

74. See Anita Shapira, *Futile Struggle: Jewish Labor, 1929–1939* [Hama'avak
hanikhzav: Avoda ivrit, 1929–1939] (Tel Aviv: Hakibutz Hameuhad and Tel Aviv
University, 1977); Hannah Naveh, "A Group Portrait *Agav Orha*: Was It Or Was It
Not? More of Y. H. Brenner," in *Literature and Society—Studies in Contemporary
Hebrew Culture, Papers in Honor of Gershon Shaked*) [Sifrut ve-hevra ba-tarbut
ha-ivrit ha-hadasha], ed. Yehudit Bar-El, Yigal Schwartz, and Tamar Hess (Tel
Aviv: Hakibbutz Hameuchad and Keter, 2001), 82–100.

75. Orly Lubin, "From Territory to Site: The Oriental Woman in the Film
Jacky" [in Hebrew], *Bikoret veparshanut* 34 (2000): 177–93.

76. Michel de Certeau, *The Practice of Everyday Life* (Berkeley: University
of California Press, 1984), 99.

77. This argument is deeply influenced by Orly Lubin's brilliant analysis
of representations of Orient femininity in the movie *Jacky*. See Lubin, "From
Territory to Site."

78. According to Gilah Ramras-Rauch, "Along with Smilansky and Shami,
Burla expanded the horizons of Hebrew fiction: [. . .] Burla and Shami depicted
Jewish Sepharadi society and Arab society in Palestine and Syria, as well as the
broad milieu of the Orient, the Levant, and the Balkans." Gilah Ramras-Rauch,
The Arab in Israeli Literature (Bloomington: Indiana University Press, 1989), 22.

79. Batya Shimony offers an interesting interpretation of Burla's choice to
include female protagonists in some of his work. Burla's work implements Mizrahi
identity into Ashkenazi Zionism. Focusing on women allows Burla to doubt the
success of this process because it does not take place in the centers of power of
the Spanish community (i.e., men in the old Jewish settlements), but rather in
marginal sites (women in Zionist spaces such as a kibbutz or Tel Aviv). Shimony,
"Identity under Trial," 52, 55, 60.

80. Yehuda Burla, *His Hated Wife: Luna* [Ishto hasenuah: Luna] (Tel Aviv:
Am Oved, 1959), 197.

81. Shababo, *Maria*, 50.

82. Burla, *His Hated Wife*, 192.

83. Nitsa Ben-Ari describes the repression of the erotic in Hebrew literature
and the puritan ideology on Hebrew culture in its formative years. See Nitsa Ben-
Ari, *Suppression of the Erotic in Modern Hebrew Literature* (Ottawa: University
of Ottawa Press, 2006).

84. Shababo, *Maria*, 152–53.

85. During her act of masturbation, Christ the martyr becomes an object
of sexual desire. In other words, Maria experiences Jesus at the juxtaposition of

his suffering and his sexuality. This juxtaposition might create a radical interpretation of the Christian stigmata as an ultimate representation of the integration between suffering and penetration.

86. Shoshana Shababo, "Memories," in Shababo, *Love in the Town of Safed*, 129–30.

87. Michelle Fine claims that the educational discourse on the subject of girls' sexuality is mainly a supervising discourse, which creates moral panic and silences girls' sexual subjectivity. Twenty years after publishing her prominent article, Fine claimed in another article that despite the years that have passed, the achievements of the feminist movement, and alleged sexual freedom, educational discourse still denies the possibility that girls are having, or could have, sexual desire. See Michelle Fine, "Sexuality, Schooling, and Adolescent Females: The Missing Discourse of Desire," *Harvard Educational Review* 58 (1988): 29–53; Michelle Fine, foreword to *All about the Girl: Culture, Power, and Identity*, ed. Michelle Fine and Anita Harris (New York: Routledge, 2004).

88. Laura Mulvey, "Visual Pleasure and Narrative Cinema," *Screen* 16, no. 3 (1975): 6–18.

89. "The sexual life of adult women is a 'dark continent' for psychology." Sigmund Freud, "The Question of Lay Analysis" (1926), in *Standard Edition of the Complete Psychological Works of Sigmund Freud* (New York: Vintage, 1999), 20:212. See also Helene Cixous and Catherine Clement, *Newly Born Woman*, trans. Betsy Wing (Minneapolis: University of Minnesota Press, 1986). On the manner in which sensuality and sexuality is constructed as dangerous in the Middle East, see Jean George Peristiany, ed., *Honor and Shame: The Values of Mediterranean Society* (Chicago, IL: Chicago University Press, 1966); Daisy H. Dwyer, *Images and Self-Images: Males and Female in Morocco* (New York: Columbia University Press, 1978); Fatna A. Sabbah, *Woman in the Muslim Unconscious* (New York: Pergamon Press, 1984); Nancy Lindisfarne, "Variant Masculinities, Variant Virginities: Rethinking 'Honor and Shame,'" in *Dislocating Masculinity: Comparative Ethnographies*, ed. Andrea Cornwall and Nancy Lindisfarne (New York: Routledge, 1994), 82–96; Charles Lindholm, *The Islamic Middle East: An Historical Anthropology* (Cambridge, MA: Blackwell, 1996); Ipek Ilkkaracan and Gulsah Seral, "Sexual Pleasure as a Woman's Human Right: Experiences from a Grassroots Training Program in Turkey," in *Women and Sexuality in Muslim Societies*, ed. Pinar Ilkkaracan (Istanbul: Women for Women's Human Rights, New Ways, 2000), 187–98; Arsalus Kayir, "Women and Their Sexual Problems in Turkey," in *Women and Sexuality in Muslim Societies*, ed. Pinar Ilkkaracan (Istanbul: Women for Women's Human Rights, New Ways, 2000), 253–68.

90. Luce Irigaray, *This Sex Which Is Not One*, trans. Catherine Porter, with Carolyn Burke (Ithaca, NY: Cornell University Press, 1985).

91. Andrea Dworkin, *Intercourse* (New York: Free Press Paperbacks, 1987).

92. Dworkin, *Intercourse*, 156.

93. Shere Hite, *The Hite Report* (New York: Macmillan, 1976), 196.

94. bell hooks examines the cultural representations of the black female body, and draws connections between black female sexuality and Western racist and sexist culture. See bell hooks, *Yearning: Race, Gender, and Cultural Politics* (Boston, MA: South End Press, 1990); see especially the chapter "Third World Diva Girls: Politics of Feminist Solidarity," 89–102.

95. Catharine MacKinnon argues that in order to gain control over their sexuality, women should establish their sexuality from within the oppressive discourse. Women should understand the violence and inequality that construct their sexuality, and by acknowledging it—and not by denying it—thereby work to create an alternative sexuality that will undermine this oppressive discourse. See Catharine MacKinnon, "Rape: On Coercion and Consent," in *Writing on the Body: Female Embodiment and Feminist Theory*, ed. Katie Conboy, Nadia Medina, and Sarah Stanbury (New York: Columbia University Press, 1997), 42–58.

96. Shababo, *Maria*, 60–61.

97. Shababo, *Maria*, 62.

98. Shababo, *Maria*, 157.

99. Mary Gail Frawley-O'Dea, *Perversion of Power: Sexual Abuse in the Catholic Church* (Nashville, TN: Vanderbilt University Press, 2007), 97–98.

100. Frawley-O'Dea, *Perversion of Power*.

101. Maria eventually gains back her ability to reject the sexual exploitation, but it leaves her powerless and voiceless (Shababo, *Maria*, 167).

102. MacKinnon, "Rape: On Coercion and Consent," 42.

103. Shababo, *Maria*, 192.

104. Shababo, *Maria*, 217.

105. Shababo, *Maria*, 246–47.

106. To use the language of Linda Higgins and Brenda Silver, these characters who disappear from the novel encourage us to read rape and sexual violence in ways that involve "listening not only to who speaks and in what circumstances, but who does *not* speak and why." See Higgins and Silver, *Rape and Representation*, 3.

107. For a fascinating analysis of Alona Kimchi's novel *Lily la Tigresse* in the light of similar approaches to rape, see Roni Halpern, *Body and Its Discontents: Israeli Women's Literature from 1985 to 2005* [Guf belo nahat] (Tel Aviv: Hakibbutz hameuchad, 2012), 192–219.

108. Shababo, *Love in the Town of Safed*, 79.

109. Siegel, "Rape and the 'Arab Question,'" 120.

110. Higgins and Silver, *Rape and Representation*, 7.

111. In this context, it is important to mention Rivka Alper's first novel, *Quivers of Revolution* (Pirpurey mahapekha), which was published in 1930 under the pseudonym Ella R. The scholar Orian Zakai discusses "the novel's uneasy critical reception and the Zionist critics' denial of and/or resentment toward Alper's bold representations of rape, incest and abuse" (Zakai, "Uniform of a Writer," 237).

112. Pnina Motzafi-Haller, "Reading Arab Feminist Discourses: A Postcolonial Challenge to Israeli Feminism" [in Hebrew], *Hagar: International Social Studies*

Review 1, no. 2 (2000): 63–89; Uma Narayan, "Towards a Feminist Vision of Dignity, Political Participation, and Nationality," in *Reconstructing Political Theory: Feminist Perspectives*, ed. Mary Lyndon Shanley and Uma Narayan (University Park: Penn State University Press, 1997), 48–67; M. Jacqui Alexander and Chandra Talpade Mohanty, eds., *Feminist Genealogies, Colonial Legacies, Democratic Futures* (New York: Routledge, 1996); Chandra Talpade Mohanty, "Under Western Eyes: Feminist Scholarship and Colonial Discourses," in *Third World Women and the Politics of Feminism*, ed. Chandra Talpade Mohanty and Ann Russo (Bloomington: Indiana University Press, 1991), 51–80; M. Jacqui Alexander, "Not Just (Any) Body Can Be a Citizen: The Politics of Law, Sexuality and Postcoloniality in Trinidad and Tobago and the Bahamas," *Feminist Review* 48 (1994): 5–23.

113. For a GendeRace analysis of current Israeli society, see Smadar Lavie, *Mizrahi Wrapped in the Flag of Israel: Mizrahi Single Mothers and Bureaucratic Torture* (Oxford: Berghahn Books, 2014).

Notes to Chapter Three

1. Dan Ben-Amotz, *I Don't Give a Damn* [Lo sam zain] (Tel Aviv: Bitan, 1973), 260.

2. Yaacov Haelyon, *A Doll's Leg: A Story of a War Injury*, trans. Louis Williams (Cape Town: John Malherbe, 1974), 64.

3. Ben-Amotz, *I Don't Give a Damn*, 195.

4. Uriel Ofek, *From the War: Fiction and Poetry* [Min hamilchamah: Siporet veshirah] (Tel Aviv: Ministry of Defense, 1969), 9.

5. Uriel Ofek's disregard for the wounded in this anthology is rather puzzling in light of the fact that he served as a paramedic in the *Palmach* during the years 1944–49, and given his poem "Military Hospital" (Beit cholim tzvaei) published in *Written in 1918: A Collection of Stories and Poems Written during the War of Independence* [Nikhtav betashah], ed. A. B. Yaffe (Tel Aviv: Reshafim, 1989), 314–15. The topic has since been regularly disregarded in Hebrew literature in the five decades since Ofek's initial introduction; for example, Uri S. Cohen's book *Security Style and the Hebrew Culture of War* contains more than four hundred pages and includes a twenty-page index . . . but not a single reference to war-wounded or disabled veterans. Uri S. Cohen, *Security Style and the Hebrew Culture of War* [Hanosach habitchoni] (Jerusalem: The Bialik Institute, 2017).

6. Yaacov Haelyon, "That's How I Was Injured" [Kach niftzati], in Ofek, *From the War*, 314; translation mine.

7. Amitai Etzioni, "Do Not Bandage the Wounded" (Lo lahbosh et haptzui), in Ofek, *From the War*, n.p.

8. Ignoring the representation of the wounded is not unique to Hebrew fictional literature. Dalia Gavriely-Nuri and Tiki Balas examine Israeli television coverage of wounded soldiers during the 2006 Lebanon War and discuss how it

obfuscates the topic of wounded soldiers in their article "'Annihilating Framing': How Israeli Television Framed Wounded Soldiers during the Second Lebanon War (2006)," *Journalism* 11, no. 4 (2010): 409–23.

9. The present chapter focuses on physical disability, although there are also some representations of posttraumatic stress disorder (previously often labeled "shell shock") in Hebrew war literature, including Yitzhak Orpaz's *Daniel's Trials* [Masa Daniel] (Tel Aviv: Am Oved, 1969) and Yoram Kaniuk's novella *Vultures and Villainy* [Etim unevelot] (Tel Aviv: Yediot Aharonot, 2006). While addressing The Yom Kippur War (1973), Avner Holtzman argues that the heroic perspective that characterized early Israeli war fiction gave way in the 1990s to a narrative that focuses on the traumatic dimension of the war. This "literature of the mentally injured," to use Holtzman's phrase, is characterized by representations of mental and physical trauma, outrage over the political and military leadership, and the inability to break free from the traumatic war experiences. Avner Holtzman, "The Mark of Fire: Forty Years of Writing about the Yom Kippur War" [in Hebrew], *OT: A Journal of Literary Criticism and Theory* 4 (2014): 66.

10. National Council of State Boards of Nursing, *Practical Guidelines for Boards of Nursing on Sexual Misconduct Cases* (Chicago, IL: National Council of State Boards of Nursing, 2009).

11. D. M. Gates, E. Fitzwater, and U. Meyer, "Violence against Caregivers in Nursing Homes: Expected, Tolerated, and Accepted," *J Gorontol Nurs.* 25, no. 4 (1999): 12–22. See also Branko Gabrovec and Ivan Eržen, "Prevalence of Violence towards Nursing Staff in Slovenian Nursing Homes" *Zdravstveno varstvo* 55, no. 3 (May 2016): 212–17.

12. There is a sizable gap between the presence of wounded soldiers in Israeli society and their respective lack of representation in Hebrew literature. To illustrate this point, a weekly report dated January 30, 1949, from the Military Casualties Division sums up the casualties of the War of Independence until the end of January 1949 and places the number of injured soldiers at 4,226. Baruch Hurwich, *"The Fifth Front": The Israeli Soldier Military Medicine in Israel: The War of Independence, 1947–1949* [Kol hayal hazit] (Jerusalem: Misrad habitahon, 2000), 398–99.

13. Haelyon, *Doll's Leg*, 161.

14. Rosemarie Garland-Thomson, "Misfits: A Feminist Materialist Disability Concept," *Hypatia* 26, no. 3 (2011): 591–609.

15. Martha Albertson Fineman, *The Autonomy Myth: A Theory of Dependency* (New York: The New Press, 2005). See also Garland-Thomson, "Misfits."

16. I am addressing here physical and visible disabilities, even though wounded soldiers experience an extremely wide range of hidden—or partially hidden—injuries, such as depression or PTSD. On the relationship between the experience of nonvisibly disabled veterans and notions of sacrifice during the Civil War, see Sarah Handley-Cousins, "'Wrestling at the Gates of Death': Joshua

Lawrence Chamberlain and Nonvisible Disability in the Post–Civil War North." *Journal of the Civil War Era* 6, no. 2 (2016): 220–42.

17. Ortsion Bartana, *Fantasy in Israeli Literature in the Last Thirty Years, 1960–1989* [Hafantasya besiporet dor Hamedina] (Tel Aviv: Hakibbutz Hameuchad, 1989), 64.

18. Yael Munk, "Actualization of Political Protest—Between Literature and Film," *Resling* 3 (1997): 44.

19. Munk, "Actualization of Political Protest, 67.

20. Also referred to as the Six-Day War; terms are often used interchangeably, though the moniker Six-Day War is often specific to Jewish-Israeli sources.

21. The title of Haelyon's book, *A Doll's Leg: A Story of a War Injury*, refers to the amulet he took when he went into battle: the leg of a doll belonging to his young daughter.

22. Haelyon, *Doll's Leg*, 101.

23. Haelyon, *Doll's Leg*, 199.

24. In this scene, there is a concrete realization of the metaphor "narrative prosthesis" that David T. Mitchell, and Sharon L. Snyder offer, as they write, "Our phrase *narrative prosthesis* is meant to indicate that disability has been used throughout history as a crutch upon which literary narratives lean for their representational power, disruptive potentiality, and analytical insight." David T. Mitchell and Sharon L. Snyder, *Narrative Prosthesis: Disability and the Dependencies of Discourse* (Ann Arbor: University of Michigan Press, 2000), 49.

25. Wendy Brown, *States of Injury: Power and Freedom in Late Modernity* (Princeton, NJ: Princeton University Press, 1995).

26. Judith Butler, *Frames of War: When Is Life Grievable?* (New York: Verso, 2009), 178.

27. Butler, *Frames of War*, 179.

28. Butler, *Frames of War*, 179.

29. Haelyon, *Doll's Leg*, 64.

30. Yoram Kaniuk was born in Tel Aviv in 1929. He was wounded in 1948, during the War of Independence. After his injury he was hospitalized in a monastery that was converted into a military hospital; Yitzhak Bezalel, "The Stories, the Roots, the Fate: An Interview with Yoram Kaniuk" [in Hebrew], *Masa*, January 13, 1967, 1–2. According to Tom Segev, a man named Amnon Vigolik, who was wounded in the War of Independence, was the inspiration for the character of Himmo. Tom Segev, "A Story of Love and Death" [in Hebrew], *Haaretz*, April 16, 2008. https://www.haaretz.co.il/misc/1.1319327.

31. Yoram Kaniuk, *Himmo, King of Jerusalem*, trans. Yosef Shachter (New York: Atheneum, 1969), 34–35.

32. Kaniuk, *Himmo, King of Jerusalem*, 200.

33. Robert F. Murphy, *The Body Silent: The Different World of the Disabled* (New York: W. W. Norton, 2001), 230.

34. Haelyon, *Doll's Leg*, 64–65.

35. On *childish*, Yosefa Loshitzky claims that *Himmo, King of Jerusalem* "creates an almost explicit analogy between the state of the infant during the pre-Oedipal stage and the state of the wounded soldiers." Yosefa Loshitzky, "The Bride of the Dead: Phallocentrism and War in 'Himmo, King of Jerusalem,'" *Literature/Film Quarterly* 21, no. 3 (1993): 221. On *feminine*, in their article "The Dilemma of Disabled Masculinity," Russell Shuttleworth, Nikki Wedgwood, and Nathan J. Wilson rightly claim that most of the studies about gender and disability focus on masculinity and how it intersects with disability "as an almost generic category, rather than on how masculinity (or masculinities) intersect(s) differently with various types of impairment." Although I focus on physical disability as a result of injury in the battle, this chapter additionally reflects the same issues that they so rightly identify. Russell Shuttleworth, Nikki Wedgwood, and Nathan J. Wilson, "The Dilemma of Disabled Masculinity," *Men and Masculinities* 15, no. 2 (2012): 174.

36. Mitchell S. Tepper, "Sexuality and Disability: The Missing Discourse of Pleasure," *Sexuality and Disability* 18, no. 4 (2000): 285.

37. Nurith Govrin and Avner Holtzman, *Devorah Baron: The First Half* [Devorah Baron: Hamaḥatsit harishonah, hayehah viyetsiratah] (Jerusalem: Mosad Byaliḳ, 1988), 457–64.

38. Shmuel Yosef Agnon, *At the Handles of the Lock* [Al kapot hamanul: Sipure ahavim] (Berlin: Jüdischer Verlag, 1922), 411.

39. Israel Hameiri, "Beer Sheva Is Close" [Beer Sheva krova], in *Wildness* [Praut] (Tel Aviv: Hakibbutz Hameuchad, 1972), 41–42.

40. Jeffrey Preston, *Fantasy of Disability: Images of Loss in Popular Culture* (London: Routledge, 2018), 9. Ellen Samuels terms a somewhat similar phenomenon as "fantasies of identification," which she defines "seek[ing] to definitively identify bodies, to place them in categories delineated by race, gender, or ability statues, and then to validate that placement through a verifiable, biological mark of identity." Ellen Jean Samuels, *Fantasies of Identification: Disability, Gender, Race* (New York: New York University Press, 2014), 2.

41. Robert McRuer, *Crip Theory: Cultural Signs of Queerness and Disability* (New York: New York University Press, 2006), 2.

42. Michal Soffer, Arie Rimmerman, Peter Blanck, and Eve Hill claim that "review of media based research conducted in Israel after the enactment of the 'Equal Rights for Persons with Disabilities Law' shows that the Israeli media lags behind the global currents and progressive definitions, addressing disability primarily via the individualized traditional bio-medical model." Michal Soffer, Arie Rimmerman, Peter Blanck, and Eve Hill, "Media and the Israeli Disability Rights Legislation: Progress or Mixed and Contradictory Images?" *Disability & Society* 25, no. 6 (October 2010): 687. See also Amit Kama, "Images that Injure: Representations of People with Disabilities in the Media" [in Hebrew], in *From Exclusion to Inclusion: Life in the Community for People with Disabilities in Israel*

[Mehadarah lehakhalah], ed. Meir Hovav, Ilana Duvdevany, and Clara Feldman (Jerusalem: Carmel, 2015), 181–213. For the connection between representations of hospitals and disability in Israeli Second Intifada films, see Slava Greenberg, "Embodying Conflict: Representations of Hospitals and Seas in Israeli Cinema after the Second Intifada," *Jewish Film & New Media: An International Journal* 7, no. 2 (2019): 214–35.

43. Tobin Siebers defines and challenges the ideology of ability that leads to a preference for able-bodiedness and defines humanness by bodily measures. Tobin Siebers, "Disability and the Theory of Complex Embodiment: For Identity Politics in a New Register," in *The Disability Studies Reader*, ed. Lennard J. Davis, 5th ed. (New York: Routledge, 2017), 313–30. For more about Siebers's "ideologies of ability," see Tobin Siebers, *Disability Theory* (Ann Arbor: University of Michigan Press, 2008), especially the introduction, pp. 1–33.

44. Heterotopias (literally meaning "other places"), according to Michel Foucault, are spaces that are "something like counter-sites, a kind of effectively enacted utopia in which the real sites . . . are simultaneously represented, contested, and inverted." Michel Foucault, "Of Other Spaces," *Diacritics* 16 (1986): 24.

45. Russell West-Pavlov, *Space in Theory: Kristeva, Foucault, Deleuze* (Amsterdam: Rodopi, 2009), 155.

46. Robert Murphy explores the ambiguous social position of people with disabilities: "The long-term physically impaired are neither sick nor well, neither dead nor fully alive, neither out of society nor wholly in it. They are human beings but their bodies are warped or malfunctioning, leaving their full humanity in doubt. They are not ill, for illness is transitional to either death or recovery. Indeed, illness is a fine example of a nonreligious, nonceremonial liminal condition. The sick person lives in a state of social suspension until he or she gets better. The disabled sped a lifetime in a similar suspended state. They are neither fish nor fowl; they exist in partial isolation from society as undefined, ambiguous people"; Murphy, *Body Silent*, 131.

47. Mitchell and Snyder, *Narrative Prosthesis*.

48. Sarah Smith Rainey, *Love, Sex, and Disability: The Pleasures of Care* (Boulder, CO: Lynne Rienner, 2011), 27.

49. Kaniuk, *Himmo, King of Jerusalem*, 35–36.

50. Kaniuk, *Himmo, King of Jerusalem*, 165.

51. Raz Yosef reads this scene as a homoerotic one: "Possessing the phallic power, Hamutal mediates the homoerotic relation between the wounded soldiers and Himmo. She erotically penetrates her finger into Himmo's mouth in a kind of oral suction or anal penetration figuration, while the men look at the specter with desire." Raz Yosef, *Beyond Flesh: Queer Masculinities and Nationalism in Israeli Cinema* (New Brunswick, NJ: Rutgers University Press, 2004), 82. For an interpretation of this gender role reversal in a post-Orientalist context, see Batya Shimony, "The Mizrahi Body in War Literature," *Israel Studies* 23, no. 1 (2018): 138.

52. Adia Mendelson-Maoz, *Literature as a Moral Laboratory: Reading Selected Twentieth-Century Hebrew Prose* [Hasifrut kemaabada musarit] (Ramat Gan, Israel: Bar Ilan University Press, 2009), 135.

53. Mendelson-Maoz, *Literature as a Moral Laboratory*, 55.

54. The people of Sodom refrained from hospitality and are accused of homosexual relations and sexual violence, as can be seen in the well-known story about Lot and his guests: "And they [the people of Sodom] called unto Lot, and said unto him, Where are the men which came in to thee this night? Bring them out unto us, that we may know them" (Genesis 19:5). In order to expand on the evil of the people of Sodom, the Talmud tells that they had a bed on which guests were laid. If the person was too short for the bed, the people of Sodom stretched him until he attained the correct length. If the person was too long, they would cut his feet short to fit. This story is presented in the Babylonian Talmud, Sanhedrin 109b. A concept similar to the bed of Sodom is found in Greek mythology in the story "The Bed of Procrustes."

55. Kaniuk, *Himmo, King of Jerusalem*, 110.

56. Kaniuk, *Himmo, King of Jerusalem*, 178.

57. Ahuva Ashman, *The Story of Eve: Daughters, Mothers, and Strange Women in Bible* [Toldot Ḥayah: Banot, imahot, ve-nashim nokhriyot ba-Miḳra] (Tel Aviv: Miskal, 2008), 193–216.

58. It should be noted that Hamutal's actions might also be interpreted as a desperate attempt to revive Himmo, to awaken him and to remind his dying body what he can do and how he can feel. In this sense, it is her rebellion against the war and against death. She begins to sleep on his mattress as the hospital staff moves it outside of the room, that is, when Himmo is on his way out of the world. Her body thus supposedly stops death from abducting Himmo.

59. Kaniuk, *Himmo, King of Jerusalem*, 115–16.

60. Scholars often refer to Himmo as dead. Mordechai Avishai, for example, describes Himmo as "a corpse still breathing in a miracle, the living dead," and Adia Mendelson-Maoz refers to Himmo as "doubtedly human." Mordechai Avishai, "About One Change in the Israeli Novel," *Moznayim* 26, no. 189/190 (1968): 433; Mendelson-Maoz, *Literature as a Moral Laboratory*, 129.

61. Raz Yosef understands the film *Himmo, King of Jerusalem* as manifesting a radical and critical position of the (hetero)sexual and nationalistic norms of Israeli society. In this context, according to Yosef, "the homoerotic discourse in the film subverts the national myth of the 'living-dead' that Himmo, the zombie, the Jewish Golem, literalizes. His 'living-dead' body does not represent a transcendental national ideal, but rather individual sexual homoerotic desire." Yosef, *Beyond Flesh*, 83.

62. Meira Weiss, *The Chosen Body: The Politics of the Body in Israeli Society* (Redwood City, CA: Stanford University Press, 2002).

63. Himmo comes from a Sepharadi Jewish family who has been living in Jerusalem for generations. Batya Shimony examines the tension between the "Mizrahiness" and "Westernness" in the novel further in her article "The Mizrahi Body in War Literature," 129–51.

64. Adia Mendelson-Maoz claims that the wounded soldiers in the novel are portrayed as a distorted image of the Zionist project. Because they reveal a potential for weakness, they are the made into others that the Zionist movement wishes to repress. Mendelson-Maoz, *Literature as a Moral Laboratory*, 133.

65. The ableist use of wounded soldiers to make a claim about abled-bodied soldiers is, of course, not unique to Hebrew literature. For a similar claim about American literature on the Vietnam War, see Thomas Jordan, "Disability, Vietnam, and the Discourse of American Exceptionalism," in *Emerging Perspectives on Disability Studies*, ed. M. Wappett and K. Arndt (New York: Palgrave Macmillan, 2013), 47.

66. Kaniuk, *Himmo, King of Jerusalem*, 67.

67. Kaniuk, *Himmo, King of Jerusalem*, 66–67.

68. Christine Kelly, "Building Bridges with Accessible Care: Disability Studies, Feminist Care Scholarship, and Beyond," *Hypatia* 28, no. 4 (Fall 2013): 792.

69. Rachel Adams, "Choosing Disability, Visualizing Care," *Kennedy Institute of Ethics Journal* 27, no. 2 (June 2017): 303.

70. Eva Feder Kittay, *Love's Labor: Essays on Women, Equality, and Dependency* (London: Routledge, 1999), 2. See also Adams, "Choosing Disability, Visualizing Care," 301–21.

71. Jackie Leach Scully, *Disability Bioethics: Moral Bodies, Moral Difference* (New York: Rowman & Littlefield, 2008), 164. See also Adams, "Choosing Disability, Visualizing Care," 304.

72. Gershon Shaked, *Hebrew Narrative Fiction, 1880–1980: On Many Small Windows at Side Entrances* [Be-harbeh ashnavim be-knisot tsdadiyot] (Tel Aviv: Hakibutz Hameuhad-Keter, 1998), 192.

73. Mordechai Avishai, "About One Change," 433.

74. Anne Finger, "Forbidden Fruit," *New Internationalist* 233 (1992): 8–10.

75. Tepper, "Sexuality and Disability."

76. Kaniuk, *Himmo, King of Jerusalem*, 57.

77. Kaniuk, *Himmo, King of Jerusalem*, 58.

78. Tepper, "Sexuality and Disability," 283.

79. Amos Guttman, dir., *Himmo, King of Jerusalem* [Himmo, melech Yeruashalayim] (Beverly Hills: Bleiberg Entertainment, 1987).

80. Shmuel Imberman, dir., *I Don't Give a Damn* [Lo sam zain] (Karachi, Pakistan: Roll Film Studios, 1987).

81. The names of the prostitutes in the film *I Don't Give a Damn* are Ruthie and Mali. The choice of the name Ruthie for a prostitute may not be coincidental.

Ruthie is also the name of the prostitute in the film *The Highway Queen* [Malkat hakvish], directed by Menahem Golan (London: Noah Films Productions, 1971), and in Keren Yedaya's film *My Treasure* [Or] (Paris: Bizibi Studios, 2004).

82. Incidentally, all of these films chose to cast able-bodied actors in the roles of disabled characters.

83. While addressing the juxtaposition of ableism, sexuality, and sexualized violence, it is important to mention that Dan Ben-Amotz, the author of *I Don't Give a Damn*, was convicted in 1984 of indecent assault on a twelve-year-old girl.

84. Preston, *Fantasy of Disability*, 9.

85. Haelyon, *Doll's Leg*, 215.

86. Haelyon, *Doll's Leg*, 210.

87. Haya Milo addresses the cultural (increasing) tendency of IDF soldiers to harass female soldiers and sing sexual folksongs in various military contexts. Inspired by Kate Milt, she claims that those pornographic songs express hostility toward women. They serve not only as a means of creating a sense of male pride and solidarity or as a way to vent aggressive feelings towards the military system but also function as a means of controlling and oppressing women in the Israeli military, which should formally give women equal and nondiscriminatory treatment. Since the pornographic folksongs present men's coercive control over women as a stimulating and exciting situation, rather than as a discriminatory and negative social situation, the patriarchal reality is legitimized and even structured as an integral part of the military experiance. Performing sexual folksongs in military environment thus violates the right of women serving in the IDF to equality and perpetuates their discrimination. Haya Milo, *Talking Songs: Folksongs of Israeli Soldiers* [Shirim bakaneh] (Ra'anana, Israel: The Open University Press, 2016), 302.

88. Haelyon, *Doll's Leg*, 73.

89. Haelyon, *Doll's Leg*, 204.

90. Though my work centralizes disability and gender-based violence in an Israeli cultural context, sexual harassment is part of a larger picture of overall abuse—both verbal and physical, such as assault, stalking, and bullying—in health care settings all over the world. See Roxanne Nelson, "Sexual Harassment in Nursing: A Long-Standing but Rarely Studied Problem," *American Journal of Nursing* 118, no. 5 (2018): 19–20.

91. Haelyon, *Doll's Leg*, 66.

92. Haelyon, *Doll's Leg*, 120.

93. Haelyon, *Doll's Leg*, 120. Certainly, as Robert McRuer reminds us—perhaps with a certain incautious optimism—"abled-bodied heterosexuality's hegemony is always in danger of collapse" (McRuer, *Crip Theory*, 31). Indeed, after Nurse Lisette was harassed by Haelyon, "for a moment [she] froze." She froze in the 1973 novel as a victim, but symbolically became mobile and reactionary in 2008, when the Tel Aviv District Court convicted Yaakov Haelyon of having sexual relations with a fourteen-year-old minor, as well as committing indecent acts against the girl's twenty-one-year-old sister.

94. Haelyon, *Doll's Leg*, 178.

95. Haelyon, *Doll's Leg*, 218.

96. Haelyon, *Doll's Leg*, 217–18. One of the main ways to appropriate disability and incorporate it into the national discourse is through the discussion of heroism. While Hebrew literature does not tend to address this often, the genre of war albums and veterans' stories often invokes injuries in the context of the soldiers' heroism. Thus, for example, the book *The Wounded Did Not Cry: Stories of Men Who Had Not Lost Their Composure When They Were Wounded under Enemy Fire* [Haptuim lo zaaku], which combines stories of soldiers from the Six-Day War, opens with the following statement: "It was a wonderful spirit of heroism that swept past the IDF wounded soldiers, leaving them firm in their spirit even when their bodies groaned with the force of their pain. This is the greatness of the fighters." D. Azaria and A. Alon, eds., *The Wounded Did Not Cry: Stories of Men Who Had Not Lost Their Composure When They Were Wounded under Enemy Fire* [Haptuim lo zaaku] (Tel Aviv: Otiyot Argaman, 1967), 1. In this context, injury and the willingness to bear the pain of injury in stoic silence is upheld as a sort of badge of honor and as a constant reminder of the willingness to sacrifice the soldier's life in war. For more about cinematic images of disability that frames injury as a kind of ornament of heroism, see Kim Wolfson and Martin Norden, "Film Images of People with Disabilities," in *Handbook of Communication and People with Disabilities: Research and Application*, ed. Dawn O. Braithwaite and Teresa L. Thompson (Mahwah, NJ: Lawrence Erlbaum Associates, 2000), 289–305.

97. Mitchell and Snyder, *Narrative Prosthesis*, 56.

98. Haelyon, *Doll's Leg*, 65.

99. For a discussion on the stereotypes of the supercrip and the pitiful disabled in Israeli media, see Amit Kama, "Supercrips versus the Pitiful Handicapped: Reception of Disabling Images by Disabled Audience Members," *Communication* 29, no. 4 (2004): 447–66.

100. Shalom Babayoff, *The Seventh Glory: A Fighter's Story* [Hazohar hashevii: Sipuro shel lohem] (Jerusalem: Iris, 1968).

101. For a profound analysis of sexual harassment situated in situations with extreme power dynamics present in the relationship between harasser and victim, see Orit Kamir, "Sexual Harassment Law in Israel," *International Journal of Discrimination and the Law* 7, no. 1–4 (2005): 315–36.

102. Rainey, *Love, Sex, and Disability*, 31.

103. See Kamir, "Sexual Harassment Law in Israel."

104. Babayoff, *Seventh Glory*, 90.

105. Babayoff, *Seventh Glory*, 84–85.

106. For further discussion of the challenges faced by people who were injured during their military service, see Ela Koren, Yoav S. Bergman, and Michael Katz, "Disability during Military Service in Israel: Raising Awareness of Gender Differences," *Journal of Gender Studies* 24, no. 1 (2015): 117–28.

107. Babayoff, *Seventh Glory*, 89.

108. Sandy Sufian, "Mental Hygiene and Disability in the Zionist Project," *Disability Studies Quarterly* 27, no. 4 (2007): 1. See also Sandra Sufian, *Healing the Land and the Nation: Malaria and the Zionist Project in Palestine, 1920–1947* (Chicago, IL: University of Chicago Press, 2007), especially chapter 1, "Archetypical Landscape: Healing the Land and the People in the Zionist Imagination." It should be emphasized that, as Sandy Sufian mentions, unlike other colonial contexts that tried to sanitize and heal the "natives," the Zionist community aspired to heal its own people. For the relationship between illness (especially Malaria and Tubercular) and the Zionist movement at the beginning of the twentieth century, see Eric Zakim, *To Build and Be Built: Landscape, Literature, and the Construction of Zionist Identity* (Philadelphia: University of Pennsylvania Press, 2006); and Sunny S. Yudkoff, *Tubercular Capital: Illness and the Conditions of Modern Jewish Writing* (Redwood City, CA: Stanford University Press, 2018).

109. Sufian, "Mental Hygiene," 2.

110. Ben-Amotz, *I Don't Give a Damn*, 194.

111. Ben-Amotz, *I Don't Give a Damn*, 275.

112. Rosemarie Garland-Thomson, *Staring: How We Look* (Oxford: Oxford University Press, 2009), 9.

113. Garland-Thomson, *Staring*, 9.

114. Ben-Amotz, *I Don't Give a Damn*, 195.

115. Ben-Amotz, *I Don't Give a Damn*, 196.

116. Judd Neʾeman, *The Wound: Gift of War, Battlefield of Israeli Cinema* [Hapetza matnat hamilhama] (Tel Aviv: Am Oved, 2018), 175–76.

117. McRuer, *Crip Theory*, 30.

118. Babayoff, *Seventh Glory*, 93.

119. Babayoff, *Seventh Glory*, 93.

120. Babayoff, *Seventh Glory*, 99.

121. Ann Karpf explores recurring themes—or "crippling images"—in media representations, and analyzes the invisibility of people with disabilities on television. Ann Karpf, "Crippling Images," in *Framed: Interrogating Disability in the Media*, ed. Ann Pointon and Chris Davies (London: British Film Institute, 1997), 79–83. See also the report of the Ruderman foundation on the underrepresentation of people with disabilities on American television: Danny Woodburn and Kristina Kopić, *The Ruderman White Paper on Employment of Actors with Disabilities in Television*, July 2016. http://www.rudermanfoundation.org/wp-content/uploads/2016/07/TV-White-Paper_final.final_.pdf.

122. Michael Oliver, *The Politics of Disablement* (London: Macmillan, 1990). See also Paul Longmore, "Screening Stereotypes: Images of Disabled People in Television and Motion Pictures," in *Images of the Disabled, Disabling Images*, ed. Alan Gartner and Tom Joe (New York: Praeger, 1987), 65–78.

123. Different scholars refer to injury on the battlefield as an event that arouses fear of feminization in the warrior. Kaja Silverman, for example, claims

that the injury stimulates castration anxiety, and Ne'eman argues that the injury in war movies is represented as a giving birth event. Kaja Silverman, *Male Subjectivity at the Margins* (New York: Routledge, 1992), 62–63; Ne'eman, *Wound*, 152–79.

124. Vic Finkelstein, "Disabled People and Our Culture Development," *Disability Arts in London Magazine*, 8 (June 1987): 1–4; Nili R Broyer, "Stigma and Unconsciousness" (master's thesis, Hebrew University of Jerusalem, 2008), 31.

125. Yoram Avi-Tamar, *Injury* [Ptsia] (Tel Aviv: Am Oved, 1975).

126. Avi-Tamar, *Injury*, 176.

127. Moshe Admon, *Diary of a Soldier* [Yomano shel ḥayal] (Tel Aviv: Otpaz, 1968), 158.

128. McRuer, *Crip Theory*, 15.

Notes to Chapter Four

1. Dorit Avramovitch, *The Naked King: Incest from a Feminist Perspective* [Hamelech eirom] (Tel Aviv: Babel, 2004), 60.

2. Ofra Offer Oren, *Shira and Hiroshima* [Shira vehiroshima] (Tel Aviv: Yedioth Ahronoth, 2003).

3. Ofra Offer Oren. *I Feel Good, I Feel Good—A Letter to Mother: The Memories of the Survivor of Incest* [Yofi li, yofi lLi] (Tel Aviv: Yedioth Ahronoth, 2006).

4. Brenda Daly argues that in the 1970s, women's writings about sexual violence were considered political acts, but by the '90s, the subject had been deemed more personal. While Daly was referring to English writing, in Israeli autobiographical writing by incest victims, the personal is (still) considered political. Brenda Daly, "When the Daughter Tells Her Story: The Rhetorical Challenges of Disclosing Father-Daughter Incest," in *Survivor Rhetoric: Negotiations and Narrativity in Abused Women's Language*, ed. Christine Shearer-Cremean and Carol L. Winkelmann (Toronto: University of Toronto Press, 2004), 139–65.

5. Although the memoirs are written from the perspective of adult women who are aware of the sexualized trauma they have experienced as children, they situate the victims in a variety of circumstances—including different ages and levels of awareness of their abuse and trauma. For example, the texts *Captive: Chronicle of Professional Incest: An Autobiographical Story* and *The Naked King: Incest from a Feminist Perspective* are written from an adult's perspective, while the protagonist in Shez's novel *Away from His Absence* is thirty-four in the text's present time but is referred to as being over the age of sixty at various times. *When Time Stood Still: Incest—from Harm to Growth* is told from the perspective of an adult, but it also represents the voice of the child who was abused.

Maya Reed, *Captive: Chronicle of Professional Incest: An Autobiographical Story* [Shvuya] (Tel Aviv: Tammuz Publishers, 2002); Avramovitch, *Naked King*; Shez, *Away from His Absence* [Harchek meheadro] (Tel Aviv: Am Oved, 2010);

Ziv Koren and Rachel Lev-Wiesel, *When Time Stood Still: Incest—from Harm to Growth* [Keshe hazman amad milechet: Giluy arayot—mepgiah letzmicha] (Kfar Bialik, Israel: Ach Books, 2013).

6. On the absence of photographs of raped women in the media, see Ariella Azoulay, "Has Anyone Ever Seen a Photograph of Rape?" in *The Civil Contract of Photography* (New York: Zone Books, 2008), 217–88.

7. Testimonies of Israeli children who were sexually abused by family members are rare, but do exist, such as in *Shirley's Diary: From the World of a Child Survivor* [Miyomana shel Shirley], edited by Miriam Gilat and Yitzhak Kadman, and in diary segments published in Tamar Cohen's anthology *Living in the Shadow of the Secret: Personal Stories of Incest*. See Tamar Cohen, *Living in the Shadow of the Secret: Personal Stories of Incest* [Liḥyot beṣel hasod: Giluyi arayot: sipurim ishim], Tel Aviv: Modan Publishers, 1991.

8. For a discussion of male sexual trauma, see Effi Ziv, "Masculinity Under Attack: A New Look on Men's Sexual Trauma" [in Hebrew], *Sihot: Journal of Psychotherapy* 27 (2012): 23–33.

9. Shoshan Rotem's memoir *As Though Nothing Happened* [Klum lo kara . . .] is discussed in the current chapter as an exception because it describes sexual abuse perpetrated by both parents. Shoshan Rotem, *As Though Nothing Happened* [Klum lo kara . . .] (Herzliya, Israel: Mendele Electronic Books, 2015).

10. The book *"In Prison I Rest": Women Prisoners beyond the Walls* presents eight interviews with female inmates from Neve Tirza Prison, the only women's prison in Israel. Some of the interviews reveal histories that involve childhood sexual abuse. See Mimi Ajzenstadt, Michal Soffer, and Odeda Steinberg, *"In Prison I Rest": Women Prisoners beyond the Walls* [Bakele ani nacha] (Tel Aviv: Hakibbutz Hameuchad, 2010). For more about sexual abuse among inmates of Neve Tirza Prison, see Michal Latte, "Development of Women Offenders in Israel: An Analysis of Personal Narratives" [in Hebrew] (master's thesis, School of Social Work at Bar-Ilan University, 2000).

11. Diane Russell's study shows "a strong connection between childhood incest and later experiences of sexual abuse." Diana E. H. Russell, *The Secret Trauma: Incest in the Lives of Girls and Women,* rev. ed. (New York: Basic Books, 1987), 158.

12. Zvia Zeligman and Solomon Zahava, trans., *The Secret and Its Breaking: Issues in Incest* [Hasod veshivro] (Tel Aviv: Hakibbutz Hameuchad, 2004), 7.

13. Ziv Koren and Rachel Lev-Wiesel, *When Time Stood Still* (London: Clink Street, 2014), 4. All subsequent citations are from this edition unless otherwise noted.

14. On trauma as an undeliverable experience by definition, see Shoshana Felman and Dori Laub, *Testimony: Crises of Witnessing in Literature, Psychoanalysis, and History* (New York: Routledge, 1992). Felman and Laub deal with the connection between the survivor who gives testimony and the listener. They argue

that the act of listening is crucial to the narration of the trauma, but still, the listener is also experiencing a crisis, and he or she may feel that his/her boundaries, function, and even sanity are in danger.

15. Koren and Lev-Wiesel, *When Time Stood Still*, 73.

16. Koren and Lev-Wiesel, *When Time Stood Still*, 75.

17. Koren and Lev-Wiesel, *When Time Stood Still*, 7.

18. Koren and Lev-Wiesel, *When Time Stood Still*, 14–15.

19. Koren and Lev-Wiesel, *When Time Stood Still* [Keshe hazman amad milechet], 18. This footnote was omitted from the English translation; the translation included is original.

20. My reading of the memoirs as rhizomatic texts is inspired by Effi Ziv's suggestion to place insidious trauma in a rhizomatic model. For more on this subject, see Effi Ziv, "Insidious Trauma" [in Hebrew], *Mafteakh: Lexical Review of Political Thought* 5 (2012): 55–73.

21. Gilles Deleuze and Félix Guattari, *A Thousand Plateaus: Capitalism and Schizophrenia*, trans. Brian Massumi (Minneapolis: University of Minnesota Press, 1987).

22. In an interview following the publication of Ofra Offer Oren's aforementioned novel *I Feel Good, I Feel Good*, the author was asked which other author's line she wished she had written herself. Her answer was, "[Yehuda] Amichai's 'Not like a cypress, / not all at once, not all of me, / but like the grass, in thousands of cautious green exits.' In this manner to live, in this fashion to write: over time, with a stubborn and constant expansion, gently." Thus she preferred the metaphor of grass, which is a growing network of no specific root and no obvious beginning from which all else stems, to the metaphor of the cypress, which is monolithic and has a definite bold thrust of "the one." Ofra Offer Oren, "To Be Precise, and to Give to the World" [in Hebrew], *Haaretz*, January 16, 2006. http://www.haaretz.co.il/literature/1.1075485. Amichai's translation is taken from Yehuda Amichai, *The Selected Poetry of Yehuda Amichai*, ed. and trans. Chana Bloch and Stephen Mitchel (Berkeley: University of California Press, 1996), 12.

23. Shez, *Away from His Absence*, 79–80.

24. Shoshan Rotem, *As Though Nothing Happened*, trans. Yael Shalev (Scott's Valley, CA: CreateSpace, 2015), 245. All subsequent citations are from this edition unless otherwise noted.

25. See Judith Lewis Herman, *Trauma and Recovery: The Aftermath of Violence—from Domestic Abuse to Political Terror* (New York: Basic Books, 1992); Anat Gur, *Foreign Bodies: Eating Disorders and Childhood Sexual Abuse* [Guf zar] (Tel Aviv: Hakibbutz Hameuchad, 2015); Christine A. Courtois, "Healing the Incest Wound: A Treatment Update with Attention to Recovered-Memory Issues," *American Journal of Psychotherapy* 51 (1997): 464–96; Effi Ziv, "From an Object to a Subject—Feminist Therapy for Female Victims of Sexual Abuse in the Family" [in Hebrew], in Zeligman and Zahava, *Secret and Its Breaking*, 257–77.

26. The asymmetry is also evident in the power relations between the writers and the therapy industry, as well as between the writers and the book publishing and marketing industry. Both industries are looking for stories that will supposedly give voice to that which has been silenced, thus making readers feel a sense of comfort, as if listening to these stories made them better people.

27. Rotem, *As Though Nothing Happened*, 234.

28. Rotem, *As Though Nothing Happened*, 245.

29. Rotem, *As Though Nothing Happened*, 258.

30. Rotem, *As Though Nothing Happened* [Klum lo kara . . .], 233.

31. Koren and Lev-Wiesel, *When Time Stood Still*, 52.

32. Laurie Anne Pearlman and Karen W. Saakvitne argue that treating trauma patients generates profound changes in the therapist—an assertion that might be inspiring and disturbing at the same time. See Laurie Anne Pearlman and Karen W. Saakvitne, *Trauma and the Therapist: Countertransference and Vicarious Traumatization in Psychotherapy with Incest Survivors* (New York: W. W. Norton, 1995).

33. Koren and Lev-Wiesel, *When Time Stood Still*, 74.

34. Koren and Lev-Wiesel, *When Time Stood Still*, 29–30; ellipses in brackets mine.

35. Reed, *Captive*, 67. Maya Reed is the pen name of Ruth Gavish.

36. Koren and Lev-Wiesel, *When Time Stood Still*, 48–50; ellipses in brackets mine.

37. Shez, *Away from His Absence*, 154.

38. The abuser is also obviously a witness to the trauma itself. Inspired by Dori Laub and Cathy Caruth's famous argument about the inability to testify about traumatic events, Zvia Zeligman offers to see incest as an experience that has no witnesses. The inability to comprise the harm, as well as the victim's dissociative mechanisms, and her family's denial, all prevent the victim herself from witnessing the incest, thereby forcing it to remain an unformulated experience.

Zeligman also claims that the abuser does not witness the harm as well, because he cannot really see the victim and acknowledge his own crime. Zvia Zeligman, "The Process of Testimony in Treating Trauma of Incest," in Zeligman and Zahava, *Secret and Its Breaking*, 240–56.

39. Koren and Lev-Wiesel, *When Time Stood Still*, 51–52.

40. Lior Gal-Cohen, *Dad's Gift* [Hamatana shekibalti meaba] (Tel Aviv: Hamama Sifrutit, 2012), 231.

41. Gal-Cohen, *Dad's Gift*, 231–32.

42. Gal-Cohen, *Dad's Gift*, 201–2.

43. Perhaps one of the most radical things that the memoirs expose is related to the cultural perception of love. Gadi Taub argues that the author Kathryn Harrison, whose book *The Kiss* addresses incestuous "relationship" between two adults, uncovers a difficult truth that as a society we try to deny:

that people hurt each other so much because they yearn for love. It is easy for us to view people as craving power, but we do not think enough on how much human beings long for love. We try to keep love pure and innocent. We do not confront the desperation to assimilate within others. We do not like to think that this aggressive element is no stranger to love. Gadi Taub, "Daddy's Girls: Incest, Self, Culture, and Comfort" [in Hebrew], *Against Solitude* [Neged bdidut] (Tel Aviv: Miskal-Yediot Ahronoth Books, 2016).

44. Ruti Shalev, *Belly* [Beten] (Jerusalem: Carmel, 2000), 24–25.

45. Herman, *Trauma and Recovery*, 73.

46. Koren and Lev-Wiesel, *When Time Stood Still*, 51.

47. Ziv, "Object to Subject," 257.

48. Anat Gur, "Thoughts on Experts' Legal Opinions in Sexual Traumas Trials" [in Hebrew], *Anat Gur* (blog), March 28, 2009. https://anatgur.wordpress.com/2009/03/28.

49. Koren and Lev-Wiesel, *When Time Stood Still*, 53.

50. Leora Somer, "The Inner World of Incest Victims," in Zeligman and Zahava, *Secret and Its Breaking*, 104.

51. Koren and Lev-Wiesel, *When Time Stood Still*, 53.

52. Shalev, *Belly*, 24–25.

53. Elaine Scarry, *The Body in Pain: The Making and Unmaking of the World* (Oxford: Oxford University Press, 1985), 4.

54. Elaine Scarry joins a long tradition of examining the relationship between pain and language. Alphonse Daudet's nineteenth-century book *In The Land of Pain* addresses the patient's failing search for language to match his suffering: "Are words actually any use to describe what pain (or passion, for that matter) really feels like? Words only come when everything is over, when things have calmed down. They refer only to memory, and are either powerless or untruthful." Alphonse Daudet, *In the Land of Pain*, trans. Julian Barnes (New York: Knopf Doubleday, 2016), 15. In *On Being Ill*, Virginia Woolf describes "the poverty of the language" when it comes to illness and pain, writing that "English, which can express the thoughts of Hamlet and the tragedy of Lear, has no words for the shiver and the headache." Virginia Woolf, *On Being Ill* (Ashfield, MA: Paris Press, 2012), 6. By referring to his own experience of torture, Jean Amery also questions the sufficiency of language to express experiences of pain, and argues that some aspects and qualities of pain remain indescribable and incommensurable: "The pain was what it was. Beyond that there is nothing to say. Qualities of feeling are as incomprehensible as they are indescribable. They mark the limit of the capacity of language to communicate." Jean Amery, *At the Mind's Limits: Contemplations by a Survivor on Auschwitz and Its Realities*, trans. Sidney Rosenfeld and Stella P. Rosenfeld (Bloomington: Indiana University Press, 2009), 33.

55. Shlomith Rimmon-Kenan, "Pain and Language in Illness Narratives: Liasons Dangereuses" [in Hebrew], in *Pain in Flesh and Blood: Essays on Malady,*

Suffering, and Indulgence of the Body [Keev basar vadam], ed. Oreet Meital and Shira Stav (Or Yehuda, Israel: Kineret Zmora Bitan, 2013), 51.

56. Rimmon-Kenan, "Pain and Languages," 57.

57. Teresa de Lauretis, *Alice Doesn't: Feminism, Semiotics, Cinema* (Bloomington: Indiana University Press, 1984) 7.

58. Avramovitch, *Naked King*, 9.

59. Avramovitch, for example, refers to a meeting she had with her father years after his abuse, which helped her to establish her "non-trivial gender identity": "And I, whom the erotic of control has been inscribed on my body before I even got to the stage where I could formulate myself, unknowingly looked for unwitting ways to make it a dismantling and rebellion tool against the omnipotent ruler" (Avramovitch, *Naked King*, 20). The search for control and its dissolution brought her to produce a feminine, playful, egalitarian sexuality that plays with power and allows her to be in contact with her pain, but also to enjoy sexuality, trust, and confidence: "Because if I cannot, like everyone else, exclude myself outside of what my imagination does not know, I can at least make these rules into a mixture of languages, behaviors, and actions that shape gender rules as game tools, a parody limited in time, in which each woman is active, present, wishing, for a moment penetrated and then penetrates her [female] lover" (*Naked King*, 24). Dorit Avramovitch perfectly understands the mechanisms of rape and its "language," and consciously dismantles it, ridicules it, and creates an alternative and carnival sexual-emotional reality out of it.

60. Koren and Lev-Wiesel, *When Time Stood Still*, 52–53.

61. Gur, *Foreign Bodies*, 262. Shoshan Rotem describes her sense of discovery and relief when she understood the psychotraumatic context of some of her symptoms. She describes it as a meaningful moment in which the symptoms cease to be "a shameful phenomenon" (Rotem, *As Though Nothing Happened* [Klum lo kara . . .], 196).

62. Maya Reed, "Dissociative Identity and Its Representation in Contemporary Media" [in Hebrew], *Hebrew Psychology*, 2012, accessed November 23, 2020, http://www.hebpsy.net/articles.asp?t=0&id=2869.

63. Etzel Cardeña, "The Domain of Dissociation," in *Dissociation: Clinical and Theoretical Perspectives*, ed. S. J. Lynn & J. W. Rhue (New York: Guilford Press, 1994), 20.

64. Frank Putnam, *Diagnosis and Treatment of Multiple Personality Disorder* (New York: Guilford Press, 1989).

65. Tzlil Avraham, "Only When You Scream 'Incest' People Understand" [in Hebrew], *Mako*, August 25, 2014. http://www.mako.co.il/culture-books-and-theatre/articles/Article-83f9445eedc0841006.htm. Changing the name as an important and significant act appears in many of the memoirs. Shoshan Rotem writes, "I have always hated my name. I hated Shoshana, Shoshi, and even more so my family name 'Roth.' I found no reason to keep carrying my father's [the abuser] family

name. Leaving the Rehabilitation Center and going out to a new life made me decide to change my name from Shoshi Roth to 'Shoshan Rotem.'" Rotem, *As Though Nothing Happened*, 173; emphasis in source.

66. Ilan Sheinfeld, "Tide: On *Away from His Absence*" [in Hebrew], in *Maariv*, November 24, 2010, http://www.nrg.co.il/online/47/ART2/181/731.html.

67. Shez, *Away from His Absence*, 94–95.

68. Shez, *Away from His Absence*, 95–96.

69. Reed, "Dissociative Identity," 2012.

70. Koren and Lev-Wiesel, *When Time Stood Still*, 52–53.

71. Sheri Oz, epilogue to Reed, *Captive*, 108. See also Sheri Oz and Sarah-Jane Ogiers, *Overcoming Childhood Sexual Trauma: A Guide to Breaking through the Wall of Fear for Practitioners and Survivors* (Abingdon, UK: Routledge, 2014).

72. In this context, Rotem's explanation becomes particularly relevant, as she writes, "Dissociation has different levels. I never lost the sense of time or was disconnected from reality. It has always been clear that the dissociation identities are part of me, that they are my different layers." Rotem, *As Though Nothing Happened*, 244.

73. Koren and Lev-Wiesel, *When Time Stood Still* [Keshe hazman amad milechet], 26; my translation.

74. See, for example, Somer, "Inner World of Incest Victims," 104–24. Also, Rachel Lev-Wiesel in her article "Child Sexual Abuse: A Critical Review of Intervention and Treatment Modalities," takes quite a hierarchical position when addressing the relationship between reason and emotion, as well as between verbal and visual languages arguing, "Creative art (e.g., drawing, clay, or music) may offer something diametrically opposed to the verbal dialogue [. . .]. Being nonverbal in nature, these symbols and images are often difficult to express clearly in verbal form and therefore, lend themselves well to the art medium." Rachel Lev-Wiesel, "Child Sexual Abuse: A Critical Review of Intervention and Treatment Modalities," *Children and Youth Services Review* 30, no. 6 (June 2008): 670.

75. It is interesting in this context to mention the way Ziv Koren defines the relationship between her paintings and working through her trauma, as she writes, "I am undergoing a very complicated process through my paintings. All my life, I was not able to grieve for anything. In therapy, I began to grieve, but I was missing a tombstone and the paintings are a kind of tombstone. It sounds horrible, but it is a form of release to know that my losses have, and I have a place to go to and mourn them . . . the tombstone spent a lifetime inside me and finally I am able to copy it out of me." Koren and Lev-Wiesel, *When Time Stood Still*, 70.

76. Koren and Lev-Wiesel, *When Time Stood Still*, 25.

77. Koren and Lev-Wiesel, *When Time Stood Still*, 32–33.

78. Gal-Cohen, *Dad's Gift*, 172.

79. Nana Ariel, "You Can't Live with Them and You Can't Live Without Them: On Clichés," master's project, Tel Aviv University, 2010, 10.

80. Ariel, "You Can't Live with Them," 12.

81. Roland Barthes, *Mythologies*, trans. Annette Lavers (New York: Farrar, Straus and Giroux, 1972), 89–90. See also Ariel, "You Can't Live with Them," 21.

82. Shearer-Cremean and Winkelmann mention that the healing process of victims of sexual exploitation is perceived as the victim's sole responsibility, and as such, it is actually lacks crucial elements of social responsibility and complicity. Christine Shearer-Cremean and Carol L. Winkelmann, *Survivor Rhetoric: Negotiations and Narrativity in Abused Women's Language*. Toronto: University of Toronto Press, 2007), 7.

83. Irit Rogoff, "Academy as Potentiality," *A.C.A.D.E.M.Y.* (Frankfurt, Germany: Revolver, 2006), 8.

84. Ariel, "You Can't Live with Them," 23.

85. Ruth Amossy and Terese Lyons, "The Cliché in the Reading Process," *SubStance* 11, no. 2 (1982): 37.

86. Ariel, "You Can't Live with Them," 29.

87. Miriam Gilat and Yitzhak Kadman, *Shirley's Diary: From the World of Child Survivor* [Miyomana shel Shirley] (Jerusalem: National Council for the Child, 1999, 2015), 46.

88. Gilat and Kadman, *Shirley's Diary*, 39.

89. Avramovitch, *Naked King*, 12.

Notes to Chapter Five

1. Tsvia Litevsky, *Everything Is Full of Gods: Self and World in Myth* [Hakol male elim: Ha'atzmi veha'olam bemitos] (Tel Aviv: Resling, 2013), 35.

2. Tsvia Litevsky, "From the Album" [Min haalbom], in *One Wall I Called Home* [Lekir ehad kar'ati bayit] (Jerusalem: Carmel, 2007), 31.

3. Maya Bejerano, "The Rivers and the Sun in Their Everyday Reflections" [in Hebrew], *Ha'aretz Book Supplement*, no. 321 (April 20, 1999): 11; Rafi Weichert, "An Entity Etched Out of the Dark" [in Hebrew], *Ma'ariv—Saturday Supplement: Literature and Books* (March 12, 1999, 29); Efrat Mishori, "The Groping Phallus" [in Hebrew], *Yedioth Ahronoth—Weekend Supplement: Culture, Literature, Art* (April 9, 1999): 27–28.

4. Litevsky, *Everything Is Full of Gods*, 59.

5. Tsvia Litevsky, "Calling It by Name" [Likro lazeh bashem], *'Al hakav* 7 (Summer 2004): 37.

6. Litevsky, "Calling It by Name," 43.

7. Tsvia Litevsky, *In Grace of Darkness* [Bahoshekh hameitiv] (Tel Aviv: Hakibbutz Hameuchad, 1998), 79n7.

8. Tsvia Litevsky, "In the House" [Babayit], in Litevsky, *In Grace of Darkness*, 75.

9. For the video interview on the Sofrim Kor'im (Writers Read) web page, see "Sofrim Kor'im—Tsvia Litevsky," YouTube, August 1, 2012, https://www.youtube.com/watch?v=oHBGdSoFsj8. Eight years earlier, Litevsky had written of this formative moment in her essay "Calling It by Name" (2004): "I looked at the clouded sky and swore to keep faith with what I called 'perfection' " (p. 42). The difference in the wording in the earlier and later contexts is fascinating. Where perfection in the later formulation is recognized as an entity encountered in the present, in the earlier one it was a linguistic entity ("What I called perfection"). In the later formulation, moreover, perfection is expressed by the sun breaking through on a wintry day, while in the early one it is expressed by the cloudy sky itself.

10. Tsvia Litevsky, "Actaeon," in Litevsky, *In Grace of Darkness*, 52.

11. The editor and scholar Deborah Greniman pointed out to me that the speaker's identification with Actaeon makes a lot of "poetic sense," given that the writer's name is Tsvia—literally a "female antelope"—and that the abuse victim, like Actaeon, is snared into seeing what she should not have seen.

12. For an artistic treatment of mythological rape stories, see Netalie Braun's film *Metamorphosis* (2006). Brown, who intertwined contemporary rape testimonies with stories from Ovid's *Metamorphoses*, wrote, "The choice of metamorphosis as a metaphor for rape is quite precise; it well conveys the woman's experience of an irrevocable transformation of body and soul, of total upheaval, of becoming absent, foreign to herself." From the film's description on the website of the New Fund for Cinema and TV, accessed June 22, 2015, https://nfct.org.il/blog/movies/%D7%9E%D7%AA%D7%9E%D7%95%D7%A8%D7%A4%D7%95%D7%96%D7%94/. For an analysis of Braun's *Metamorphosis*, see Régine-Mihal Friedman, "Invisible Metamorphoses," *Studies in Documentary Film* 6, no. 3 (2012): 273–90. For an analysis of rape stories in mythology, see Susan Deacy and Karen F. Pierce, eds., *Rape in Antiquity: Sexual Violence in the Greek and Roman Worlds* (London: Bristol Classical Press, 2002); for a feminist analysis of the same stories, see Lev Kenaan, *Pandora's Senses: The Feminine Character of the Ancient Text* (Madison: University of Wisconsin Press, 2008), 150–60.

13. Litevsky, "Calling It by Name."

14. Litevsky, *Everything Is Full of Gods*, 59.

15. Eli Somer, "Trauma in Childhood, Memory Loss and Delayed Exposure" [in Hebrew], position paper for the Council for the Protection of Children, May 1994, accessed August 7, 2015, http://www.somer.co.il; John Briere, *Therapy for Adults Molested as Children: Beyond Survival* (New York: Springer, 1996).

16. Litevsky, "Calling It by Name," 39.

17. Litevsky, *In Grace of Darkness*, 11.

18. Tsvia Litevsky, *The Green towards the Green* [Hayarok bedarko el hayarok], with drawings by Tamra Rickman (Jerusalem: Carmel, 2006), 68.

19. Tsvia Litevsky, "They Left Me Lying There" [Hish'iru oti shokhevet], in *Don't Point Your Finger at Me* [Al tatsbia alai] (Tel Aviv: Helicon, 2003), 10–12;

Tsvia Litevsky, "The Circle Line" [Kav hama'agal], in Litevsky, *Don't Point at Me*, 13–14.

20. Tsvia Litevsky, "Calling by Name" [Likro bashem], in *Liturgy* [Liturgiya] (Tel Aviv: Hakibbutz Hameuchad, 2010), 11.

21. Elaine Scarry, *The Body in Pain: The Making and Unmaking of the World* (London: Oxford University Press, 1985).

22. Patricia Yaeger and Beth Kowaleski-Wallace, eds., *Refiguring the Father: New Feminist Readings of Patriarchy* (Carbondale: Southern Illinois University Press, 1989), xiv.

23. Shira Stav, "Fathers and Daughters: The Entrapment of Incest" [in Hebrew], *Teorya u-vikoret* 37 (Fall 2010): 84.

24. Jane Gallop, *The Daughter's Seduction: Feminism and Psychoanalysis* (Ithaca, NY: Cornell University Press, 1982); Nancy K. Miller, "My Father's Penis," in *Refiguring the Father: New Feminist Readings of Patriarchy*, ed. Patricia Yaeger and Beth Kowaleski-Wallace (Carbondale: Southern Illinois University Press, 1989), 312–16.

25. Stav, "Fathers and Daughters," 85–87.

26. This process is represented in its utmost complexity in the poem "To My Death" [Lemoti], which speaks of death as "my single father / who from my start, before my birth, stowed away just for me / anti-world." Litevsky, *Liturgy*, 57.

27. Litevsky, "They Left Me Lying There," 10–12.

28. Litevsky, *I Shall Die as Born* [Amut kenoledet] (Tel Aviv: Iton 77, 2013), 13.

29. Tsvia Litevsky, "Burner" [Kirah], in Litevsky, *Don't Point at Me*, 33.

30. Litevsky, *Liturgy*, 63. The violence in "The Gully of Zin" is not confined to the father himself but is an essential element of fatherhood, inhering in "all your fathers' fathers." In this sense the poem reinforces Stav's claim that "incest is no mere personal inclination nor even a cultural pathology. Incest lies at the very heart of cultural and social normativity, structured deep in the foundation of the patriarchal relations between fathers and daughters and between men and women, in society and in the family." Stav, "Fathers and Daughters," 71.

31. Anna Freud, *The Ego and the Mechanisms of Defence* (1936) (New York: Routledge, 2018).

32. Sándor Ferenczi, "Confusion of Tongues between Adults and the Child," in *Final Contributions to the Problems and Methods of Psycho-Analysis*, ed. Michael Balint, trans. Eric Mosbacher (1933; London: Hogarth Press, 1955).

33. Litevsky, "Circle Line," 13.

34. Slavoj Žižek, *Sublime Object of Ideology* (London: Verso, 1989), 105. Using psychoanalytic language, Žižek explains that the type of identification in which the subject aspires to resemble the object of his identification is imaginary, while that in which the subject seeks to be worthy of the other's gaze is symbolic; Žižek, *Sublime Object*, 105–7. See also Amos Goldberg, *Trauma in the First Person:*

Diary Writing in the Holocaust Period [Trauma beguf rishon: Ketivat yomanim bitekufat hasho'ah] (Beer Sheva, Israel: Devir–Heksherim, 2012), 308–9 and note 40.

35. Tsvia Litevsky, "Objects" [Ḥafatzim], in Litevsky, *I Shall Die as Born*, 57.

36. "If Being Your Daughter" [Lu heyoti bitekha], in Litevsky, *Don't Point at Me*, 15. In her discussion of Dionysus, Litevsky speaks of the complex connection between the father's abuse, his gaze, and the wounded son's need for recognition: "The unbridled pleasure of the father [Zeus] engenders the existential vulnerability of the son [Dionysus]. For Dionysus, the metamorphosis embodies his continual flight from his father's gaze, ever returning in post-traumatic flashbacks in the various stories about him, and as well in his continual effort to gain his father's recognition." Litevsky, *Everything Is Full of Gods*, 25.

37. Litevsky, "Circle Line," 13.

38. Litevsky, "Bedtime Story" [Sipur lifnei hasheinah], in Litevsky, *Don't Point at Me*, 22.

39. Litevsky, "Worm" (Tola'at), in Litevsky, *Don't Point at Me*, 53.

40. On the male gaze and principally on its (sometimes unstable) tie with the oedipal model, see Laura Mulvey, "Visual Pleasure and Narrative Cinema," *Screen* 16, no. 3 (1975): 6–18; and Diana Fuss, "Fashion and the Homospectatorial Look," *Critical Theory* 18, no. 4 (1992): 728–30.

41. Litevsky, *Don't Point at Me*, 36–37. I am grateful to Professor Adriana X. Jacobs for helping me with this translation.

42. Litevsky, *Liturgy*, 15.

43. Leah Goldberg, *What the Does Do* [Ma osot haayalot] (Tel Aviv: Sifriat Poalim, 1957), 5–7.

44. Leah Goldberg, *Poems* [Shirim], vol. 3, ed. Tuvia Rivner (Tel Aviv: Sifriat Poalim, 1973), 283–84.

45. Litevsky's poem also alludes to Yona Wallach's "Poem," which opens with the lines: "In a hidden crevice in the cliffs / a gazelle is drinking water / what has she got to do with me"; Yona Wallach, *Subconscious: Opening Like a Fan* [Tat hakarah niftaḥat kemenifah] (Tel Aviv: Hakibbutz Hameuchad, 1992), 151. No less interesting, however, I believe, is its connection with Litevsky's own early poem "Gazelle," which describes the love of the leopard for the gazelle, which, after "his teeth sink / into the taste of her blood . . . turns slowly into his own blood and flesh" (*Don't Point at Me*, 61). The metaphoric expression "blood and flesh," ordinarily representing kinship, is restored here to its literal sense, to which is added the element of the father's physical and sexual violence toward his daughter.

46. "The gaze in itself not only terminates the movement, it freezes it." Jacques Lacan, *the Four Fundamental Concepts of Psychoanalysis*, ed. Jacques-Alain Miller, trans. Alan Sheridan (New York: W. W. Norton, 1998), 117.

47. Lacan, *Four Fundamental Concepts*, 117. See also Hanjo Berressem, "The 'Evil Eye' of Painting: Jacques Lacan and Witold Gombrowicz on the Gaze," in *Reading Seminar XI: Lacan's Four Fundamental Concepts of Psychoanalysis*, ed.

Richard Feldstein, Bruce Fink, and Maire Jaanus (Albany: State University of New York Press, 1995), 175–82.

48. Tsvia Litevsky, "An Antelope in the Field" [Tzevi basadeh], in Litevsky, *Liturgy*, 16.

49. Tsvia Litevsky, "Aphrodite," in *In Grace of Darkness*, 11.

50. Litevsky, *Liturgy*, 74.

51. Litevsky, *I Shall Die as Born*, 24.

52. Litevsky, "Aphrodite," 11.

53. Tsvia Litevsky, "Until the Stem Becomes Transparent," *Iton 77*, 349 (August–September 2010), 28.

54. Litevsky, "To My Death," in Litevsky, *Liturgy*, 57.

55. Litevsky, "Chorus" [Zimrah], in Litevsky, *Liturgy*, 77.

56. Litevsky, *One Wall I Called Home*, 15.

57. Litevsky, "Calling It by Name," 41.

58. Litevsky, *Everything Is Full of Gods*, 214.

59. Litevsky attests to her profound affinity with the figure of Dionysus: "Thus does Dionysus, for me, embody my deepest life experience: the self escaping my grasp, and its multiple embodiments [. . .]. He is the answer to the question that has exercised me all my life: 'Who am I?'—and at the same time the evasion of any answer to this question." Litevsky, *Everything Is Full of Gods*, 34–35.

60. Litevsky, *Everything Is Full of Gods*, 35; note the feminine second-person singular form of the imperative.

61. Litevsky, *One Wall I Called Home*, 5–23.

62. Litevsky, *One Wall I Called Home*, 10.

63. Dahlia Ravikovitch, "The Dress," in *Hovering at a Low Altitude: The Collected Poetry of Dahlia Ravikovitch*, trans. Chana Bloch and Chana Kronfeld (New York: W. W. Norton, 2009), 115–16.

64. Litevsky, *One Wall I Called Home*, 15.

65. Litevsky, *One Wall I Called Home*, 15.

66. Sigmund Freud, "Beyond the Pleasure Principle" (1920), in *The Standard Edition of the Complete Psychological Works of Sigmund Freud*, ed. James Strachey, in collaboration with Anna Freud, assisted by Alix Strachey and Alan Tyson, vol. 18 (London: Hogarth Press, 1953).

67. Litevsky, *One Wall I Called Home*, 6.

68. Litevsky, *One Wall I Called Home*, 16.

69. Adrienne Rich, *Of Woman Born: Motherhood as Experience and Institution* (New York: W. W. Norton, 1976), 225. Rich discusses various types of maternal abandonment, claiming that it leaves women (daughters) who have been so abandoned in a weakened position, which, however, can sometimes be transformed into a position of power: "When we can confront and unravel this paradox, this contradiction, face to the utmost in ourselves the groping passion of that little girl lost, we can begin to transmute it, and the blind anger and bitterness that

have repetitiously erupted among women trying to build a movement together can be alchemized. Before sisterhood, there was the knowledge—transitory, fragmented, perhaps, but original and crucial—of mother-and-daughterhood." Rich, *Of Woman Born*, 225.

70. S. Y. Agnon, "In the Prime of Her Life," in S. Y. Agnon, *At the Handles of the Lock* [Al kapot hamanul: Sipure ahavim] (Berlin: Jüdischer Verlag, 1922), 5–54. The quotes in English are translations by Gabriel Levin in S. Y. Agnon, *Eight Great Hebrew Short Novels*, ed. Alan Lelchuk and Gershon Shaked (New Milford, CT: Toby Press, 1983), 165–216.

71. Agnon, "In the Prime of Her Life," in Agnon, *Eight Great Hebrew Short Novels*, 189.

72. Agnon, "In the Prime of Her Life," 189.

73. Agnon, "In the Prime of Her Life," 190.

74. Agnon, "In the Prime of Her Life," 189.

75. The words chosen by Tirtza to describe her nights in the company of her father attest to a similar emotional process: "At ten o'clock my father would rise, stroke my hair, and say, 'And now go to sleep, Tirtza.' How I loved his use of the conjunction 'and.' I always grew happy in its presence: it was as though all that my father told me was but the continuation of his innermost thoughts. That is, first he spoke to me from within his heart and then out loud" (Agnon, "In the Prime of Her Life," 215). In this scene, too, Tirtza must imagine herself as a presence in her father's emotional sphere precisely because she senses her absence from it.

76. This is movingly fleshed out in the scene in which the mother burns Akavia Mazal's writings, of which Tirtza relates, "The door opened twice, three times, but she did not ask who was there, and when I spoke to her she did not answer" (Agnon, "In the Prime of Her Life," 191).

77. This process illuminates the difficulty of establishing a female voice, not only because women are constituted as objects of desire but also because of their being a lack, an absent presence—not only not subjects but in effect not even objects of desire.

78. Many interpretations of "In the Prime of Her Life" take the view that Tirtza blots out her mother and then identifies with her for the purpose of entering into her place and rectifying the ruin of her relations with Akavia Mazal. According to Adi Zemach, for example, Tirtza wants to "make of her own life a kind of second, improved version of her mother's, by marrying the man (Akavia Mazal) whom her mother had not dared to wed"; Adi Zemach, "In a Double Image: On S. Y. Agnon's 'In the Prime of Her Life'" [in Hebrew], *Moznayim* 62, no. 7–8 (1989): 43, and see 45. Efrat Golan argues, "[Tirtza's] free choice of Mazal does not stem from true freedom, but is, rather, an unconscious reinforcement of her identification with her mother"; Efrat Golan, "A Feminist Reading of [Agnon's] 'In the Prime of Her Life'" [in Hebrew], *'Alei siaḥ* 27–28 (1990): 82, and see 87.

Shlomo Herzig, in his paraphrase of the story's plot, writes that Tirtza "sets out on a 'romantic' mission whose goal is to rectify the deformity in her mother's love life"; Shlomo Herzig, "An Idol in the Temple: On Intersexuality and Its Significance in S. Y. Agnon's 'Bidemi Yemeiha' " [in Hebrew], *Alei siah* 46 (2001): 69. Michal Arbel, too, though she suggests reading Tirtza's passion for Akavia Mazal as a creative act, sees it as intended to "reflect and reconstruct the past, reverse the direction of time and in so doing right its wrongs"; Michal Arbel, *Written on the Dog's Hide: On S. Y. Agnon's Conception of Artistic Creativity* [Katuv 'al 'oro shel hakelev: 'Al tefisat hayetzirah etzel S. Y. 'Agnon] (Jerusalem: Keter–Heksherim, 2006), 42. Even Ruth Golan, who offers a psychoanalytic interpretation of the character of Tirtza, argues, "Tirtza, the product of her parents' lack of love, tries to please both her father and her beloved—Mazal—and so to gain for herself the love of both and their acknowledgement of her existence"; Ruth Golan, "Agnon's 'Bidemi Yemeiha'—From Divided Object to Split Subject" [in Hebrew], *Alei siah* 29–30 (1991): 84. Beyond this, I believe, it can be argued that Tirtza "wants to *be*" Akavia Mazal—the object of her mother's desire. Her wedding to Mazal, her pregnancy and what she sees as its "purpose," and the flow of writing that ensues from the creation of a quiet space for Mazal's work—all these attest to her self-effacement and total assimilation of Mazal's needs. According to this interpretation, Tirtza's bond with Akavia Mazal should be understood not as an attempt to right a wrong in the relations between Leah and Mazal but as a rectification—fake and perverted—of the relations between Leah and Tirtza. Tirtza, the abandoned daughter who grew up in the shade of her mother's beloved, tries to become that beloved and so, in effect, to win her mother's love.

79. Litevsky, *One Wall I Called Home*, 7.

80. Dina Vardi speaks of the second generation of Holocaust survivors, who became a kind of living memorial to the victims, as "memorial candles"; see Dina Vardi, *Marked for Life: Dialogue with the Second Generation of Holocaust Survivors* [Nos'ei hahotam: Di'alog 'im benei hador hasheni lesho'ah] (Jerusalem: Keter, 1990).

81. Yona Wallach, "Cassius," in *Let the Words: Selected Poems of Yona Wallach*, trans. Linda Zisquit (Riverdale-on-Hudson, NY: Sheep Meadow Press, 2006), 5.

82. The throng of crows in Litevsky's poem is not the flock of crows from Natan Yonatan's "Lament for the Death of our Brothers" ("desolation and wind, a tear and a song, / singing and weeping / a flock of crows"), nor does it allude to the crow that told Apollo of his lover Coronis's betrayal, or to the arrogant old raven in the poem by Edgar Allen Poe. It does, however, seem close in spirit to the crows in Van Gogh's *Wheat Field with Crows* (1890), which turned out to be his last painting; to the ominous crows of Hitchcock's *The Birds* (1963); and to the crows in Ahuva Lubartowska's paintings, messengers of evil and heralds of death and loss; Ahuva Lubartowska, "Crows: Exhibition of the Paintings of Ahuva Lubartowska" (Mazkeret Batya, Israel: Eran Shamir Village Museum, 2005). Translator's note: The Hebrew word *'orev* denotes both crows and ravens.

83. Babylonian Talmud, Ketubot 49b.

84. Pirkei deRabbi Eliezer, chap. 21, Sefaria, accessed December 18, 2020, https://www.sefaria.org/Pirkei_DeRabbi_Eliezer.21?lang=bi.

85. Babylonian Talmud, Eiruvin 22a.

86. Litevsky, *One Wall I Called Home*, 7.

87. In the essay "Calling It by Name," Litevsky attests to her identification with Jesus: "What enabled me to survive was lifting myself to the level of a symbol of human suffering in the world. I sanctified suffering; I made it an altar for religious devotion. The sense of the intensity of my suffering defined my existence for me. I (without making a public declaration of it, of course) was a new manifestation of Jesus, an incarnation of Raskolnikov, a mirror image of Descartes, agonized by doubt. I was a symbol fleshed out in a human body." Litevsky, "Calling It by Name," 42.

88. Litevsky, *One Wall I Called Home*, 12.

89. Litevsky, *One Wall I Called Home*, 13.

90. Jacques Lacan, *Ecrits: A Selection*, trans. Alan Sheridan (New York: W. W. Norton, 1977).

91. Therese of Lisieux, *Story of a Soul: The Autobiography of St. Therese of Lisieux,* trans. John Beevers (New York: Doubleday, 2001), 88.

92. Litevsky and Dahlia Ravikovitch represent almost opposite trajectories. While Ravikovitch wants to be swallowed up into the other in order to reach the sublime, Litevsky is assimilated into her mother but wants to extract herself. Perhaps this disparity is associated with the difference between being orphaned as a child (Ravikovitch) and losing one's mother as an adult (Litevsky), and also with the gender gap between losing a mother (Litevsky) and losing a father (Ravikovitch). For a detailed discussion of this issue in Ravikovitch's works, see Ilana Szobel, *A Poetics of Trauma: The Work of Dahlia Ravikovitch* (Waltham, MA: Brandeis University Press, 2013).

93. On the motif of Veronica's veil in Hebrew literature, see Ruth Karton-Blum, *The Veil of Veronica: Israeli Literature Reads the New Testament* [Hamitpachat shel veronica: Hasifrut haisraelit vehbrit hachadasha] (Tel Aviv: Hakibutz Hameuhad, 2019).

94. Luce Irigaray, "And the One Doesn't Stir Without the Other," trans. Helene Vivienne Wenzel, *Signs* 7, no. 1 (1981): 60–67.

95. Translator's note: the Hebrew phrase *shem veshamayim* plays on the resemblance between the Hebrew words for "name" (*shem*) and "heaven" (*shamayim,* which could even be read as "double name"), and also on the expression *shem shamayim,* the Name of Heaven, an epithet for God. Needless to say, both words occur in Genesis 2.

96. Litevsky, "Calling by Name," 11.

97. Sandra Gilbert and Susan Gubar discuss the phallic aspect of writing and male ownership of the pen and the voice in their book *The Madwoman in*

the Attic: The Woman Writer and the Nineteenth-Century Literary Imagination (New Haven, CT: Yale University Press, 1979).

98. Litevsky, *One Wall I Called Home*, 10.

99. In "Calling by Name," identification with the mother is also evident in the speaker's "in between" position, which parallels the liminal position occupied by the mother in "Embalmed, I Lie" (Litevsky, *One Wall I Called Home*, 12). The speaker in "Calling by Name" sets herself in the "in between" position (both "in" and "between"): for her as a poet, giving a name is an act of mediation and designation, but mediation is simultaneously the self-image of the incest survivor, all of whose boundaries have been breached, as well as being an expression of her infinite need to please.

100. Litevsky, *One Wall I Called Home*, 14.

Notes to the Conclusion

1. Amalia Kahana-Carmon, "The Whirling Sword" [Hacherev ham-ithapechet], *Masa* supplement in *Lamerhav*, June 29, 1956.

2. *La'Isha* 3595 (March 7, 2016) [in Hebrew]. This cover was inspired by the cover of the July 27 issue of *New York* magazine (photographed by Amanda Demme), which featured thirty-five women who accused Bill Cosby of sexual assault.

3. The Tel Aviv Sexual Assault Crisis Center was founded in 1978 and was the first such entity in Israel. Following it, eight more Sexual Assault Crisis Centers were established: in Haifa in 1979, in Jerusalem in 1981 (by the Woman to Woman organization), in the Sharon region in 1984, in the Negev in 1988, in Nazareth (for Arab women) in 1992, in Jerusalem (for religious women) in 1993, in Kiryat Shmona in 1994, and in the Shefela area in 1998. All centers provide emotional support and guidance to the victims, and they all operate emergency hot lines staffed by volunteers twenty-four hours a day. In 1990, the Association of Rape Crisis Centers in Israel was established, and it serves as an umbrella organization that operates at the national level, promotes legislative initiatives, and works to strengthen awareness. Tal Dekel, *Gendered: Art and Feminist Theory* [Memugdarot] (Tel Aviv: Hakibutz Hameuhad, 2011): 190–91.

4. Irit Negbi analyzes Supreme Court rulings about rape cases in Israel. She reveals hidden gendered assumptions in the legal documents and claims that the perceptions regarding normative femininity and masculinity shape the way criminal cases are perceived in court. She thus argues that gender perceptions determine the fate of the legal case no less, and perhaps even more than, the language of the law. Irit Negbi, *Rape Stories in the Court: Narrative Analysis of Supreme Court Judgments* [Sipurey ones bebeit hamishpat] (Tel Aviv: Resling, 2009).

5. There is irony inherent within the very title of the "Heroines" (Giborot) project, as the Hebrew term *heroism* (*gvura*) and the word *man* (*gever*) share the same root.

6. Linda Alcoff and Laura Gray, "Survivor Discourse: Transgression or Recuperation?" *Signs* 18, no. 2 (Winter 1993): 281.

7. Alcoff and Gray, "Survivor Discourse," 267. See also Susan Brownmiller, *Against Our Will: Men, Women, and Rape* (New York: Simon & Schuster, 1975); and Leigh Gilmore, *Tainted Witness: Why We Doubt What Women Say about Their Lives* (New York: Columbia University Press, 2017).

8. In her article "Homefront as a Battlefield: Gender, Military Occupation and Violence against Women," Simona Sharoni explores the connection between military occupation and gender-based violence within the specific sociopolitical context of the third decade of Israeli occupation of the West Bank and Gaza. Simona Sharoni, "Homefront as Battlefield: Gender, Military Occupation and Violence against Women," in *Women and the Israeli Occupation: The Politics of Change*, ed. Tamar Mayer (London: Routledge, 1994), 107–22.

9. Susan J. Brison, *Aftermath: Violence and the Remaking of a Self* (Princeton, NJ: Princeton University Press, 2002), 30–33.

10. Michal Zamir, *A Ship of Girls* [Sfinat hababot] (Tel Aviv: Xargol Books, 2005).

11. The 1986 rock opera *Mami* (a colloquialism meaning "sweetie"), written by Hillel Mittelpunkt, deals directly with the Israeli occupation and draws a connection between Palestinian national oppression and women's oppression. Interestingly, the musical presents the rape of an Israeli Jewish woman by Palestinians. As a result, it unintentionally exposes the limitations of Israeli discourse and bias, even in intellectual places that are politically radical. Hillel Mittelpunkt, *Mami* (Tel Aviv: Tzavta Theatre 1986).

12. Even Tal Nitzan's study "Controlled Occupation: The Rarity of Military Rape in the Israeli-Palestinian Conflict" (master's thesis, Hebrew University of Jerusalem, 2006) deals with the connection between the Israeli occupation and rape, but effactully ends up contributing to the continued suppression of the link between sexual violence and the Israeli-Palestinian conflict. The study focuses on the lack of IDF rapes of Palestinian women. It argues that because of the vagueness of the spatial borders in the Israeli-Palestinian conflict, the ethnic boundaries are engraved on the soldiers' bodies and the crossing of borders is physically rejected as a self-explanatory mechanism that accompanies them wherever they are. In other words, the rarity of reported military rape expresses and reinforces the intensity of the ethnic boundaries and distinctions between Israeli soldiers and Palestinian women.

13. There is no official data on sexual violence in the Palestinian occupied territories, but Muhammad Mansour, a psychologist and volunteer at Physicians

for Human Rights, reports that more than a third of the children (ages five to thirteen) he met in Jabalya reported that they had been sexually abused by adults or by other children. Ayelett *Shani*, "Gaza Kids Live in Hell: A Psychologist Tells of Rampant Sexual Abuse, Drugs and Despair," *Haaretz*, November 11, 2017, https://www.haaretz.com/middle-east-news/palestinians/MAGAZINE-gaza-kids-live-in-hell-a-psychologist-tells-of-sex-abuse-drugs-and-despair-1.5464038. For an analysis of initial data about sexual abuse of Palestinian Israeli girls, see Nadera Shalhoub-Kevorkian, "Disclosure of Child Abuse in Conflict Areas," *Violence Against Women* 11, no. 10 (2005): 1263–91.

14. Lily Rattok, *Amalia Kahana-Carmon: Monograph* [Monographia: Amalia Kahana-Carmon] (Tel Aviv: Sifriat Poalim, 1986), 19–20. For more on the development and rewriting of both versions, see Yael Levi Hazan, *What Do You Know about It: Women's Writing on War in Hebrew Literature* [Ma at mevinah: Nashim kotvot al milhamah basifrut haivrit] (Beer Sheva: The Ben-Gurion Institute for the Study of Israel and Zionism at Ben-Gurion University of the Negev, 2019), especially 20–40. Kahana-Carmon, "Whirling Sword" 1–2. Amalia Kahana-Carmon, "Beer Sheva, the Capital of the Negev" [Beer Sheva birat hanegev], in *Under One Roof* [Bikhefifah ahat] (Tel Aviv: Hakibbutz Hameuchad, 1966), 52–59.

15. The Palmach was the enlisted brigade of the Haganah, which constituted the military defense force of the Jewish Yishuv and Zionist movement prior to the establishment of the state of Israel.

16. Kahana-Carmon, *Under One Roof*, 54.

17. Yair Mazor, "The Place Where Fiction Launches Poetry" [in Hebrew], *Moznayim* 6 (1983): 46–51.

18. Hanna Herzig and Nurith Gertz, *Israeli Fiction in the 1960s* [Hasiporet haIsraelit bishnot hashishim] (Tel Aviv: Open University, 1982), 4.

19. Lily Rattok, "Women in the War of Independence: Myth and Memory" [in Hebrew], in *Sadan: Studies in Hebrew Literature*, vol. 5, ed. Hannah Naveh and Oded Menda-Levy (Tel Aviv: Tel Aviv University, 2002), 293.

20. Yael Levi Hazan, "Rewriting the War? Rewrites, Editing and Versions in Women's Fiction about the 1948 War," *BGU Review* (2017): 15.

21. The connection between the bird of prey and impurity in Jewish tradition is evident, for example, in Mishnah Chullin 3:6: "The signs of cattle and a wild animal are stated from the Torah, but the signs of a bird are not stated. But the Sages said, 'Any bird which attacks [prey] is prohibited (*tamei*, literally meaning "impure").'"

22. Kahana-Carmon, *Under One Roof*, 55.

23. Kahana-Carmon, *Under One Roof*, 55.

24. Kahana-Carmon, *Under One Roof*, 66. Translated by Levi Hazan, "Rewriting the War?," 16.

25. Herzig and Gertz, *Israeli Fiction in the 1960s*, 8.

26. Kahana-Carmon, "The Whirling Sword," 105. Translated by Yael Levi Hazan, "Rewriting the War?," 14.

27. Kahana-Carmon, "Whirling Sword," 105.

28. Herzig and Gertz, *Israeli Fiction in the 1960s*, 14. In contrast to Hannah Herzig, Tal Nitzan argues that the story depicts the inability to experience feminine sexuality in a Zionist environment that demands the individual blend in with the collective (and violent) experience. Tal Nitzan, "Zionism and Eros in 'Beer Sheva, the Capital of the Negev' by Amalia Kahana-Carmon," [in Hebrew], *Amirot*, August 2013, http://amirot.blogspot.com/2013/08/blog-post_12.html.

29. Rattok, *Amalia Kahana-Carmon*, 20–21.

30. Levi Hazan, "Rewriting the War?," 14. For more about the criticism against the war in Amalia Kahana-Carmon's "Beer Sheva, the Capital of the Negev," see Rattok, "Women in the War," and Hazan, *What Do You Know about It*.

31. Kahana-Carmon, "Whirling Sword," 107.

32. Kahana-Carmon, *Under One Roof*, 53.

33. Kahana-Carmon, *Under One Roof*, 58.

34. In this context, it is important to note that in the later version—namely, in "Beer Sheva, the Capital of the Negev"—Kahana-Carmon omitted the expression "the State of Israel" and its positive description that appear in the original version of the story on page 107 (omitted from Kahana-Carmon, *Under One Roof*, 58).

35. Amalia Kahana-Carmon, *"Whirling Sword,"* 52.

36. Amalia Kahana-Carmon, "Here Is the Book," *Moznaim* 5/6 (1984): 14.

37. Rivka Feldhay claims that the story expresses the repression of various Others, such as women, Arabs, and Mizrahi Jews from Israeli culture. Rivka Feldhay, "A Feminine Midrash" [in Hebrew], *Teorya u-vikoret* 2 (1992): 85–86.

38. Shimrit Peled, *The Israeli Sovereign: The Novel and the Discourse, 1967–1973* [Haribon haisraeli] (Jerusalem: The Hebrew University Magna Press, 2014), 94.

39. This tendency of exploring the connection between national violence and sexual violence expands in Hebrew literature from the 1970s on. For example, in 1976, Dahlia Ravikovitch published the story "A Short Delay" (Ichur katan), which deals explicitly and directly with sexual harassment in the IDF. Also, in 1969, Raquel Chalfi published the poem "A German Boot," which portrays the connection between the Israeli occupation and sexual exploitation. Both Ravikovitch's story and Chalfi's poem, although written by canonical writers, have been almost entirely ignored in the research. See Dahlia Ravikovitch, *Death in the Family* [Mavet bamishpahah] (Tel Aviv: Am Oved, 1976), 26–33; Raquel Chalfi, "A German Boot" [in Hebrew], in *Love of the Dragon* [Ahavat ha-drakon] (Tel Aviv: Hakibbutz Hameuchad, 1995), 45. For a detailed analysis of Chalfi's "A German Boot," see Ilana Szobel, "'God of Fury' and His Victims: The Binding of Isaac (*Akedah*) in Hebrew Women's Poetry, 1930–1970" [in Hebrew], *Jerusalem Studies*

in Hebrew Literature 22 (2008): 87–91. For a discussion about Ravikovitch's "A Short Delay," see Szobel, *Poetics of Trauma*, 48–51.

40. Kahana-Carmon, "At Knife Point," 2.

41. Rivka Feldhay describes the language of the stories in *Under One Roof* (Bikhefifah ahat) as a distinguished language characterized by an abundance of archaic layers, a restless wandering through the textual space of the Hebrew literary tradition, complex images, and breaking of syntactic conventions (Feldhay "Feminine Midrash," 69).

42. Leora Bilsky, "The Violence of Silence: Searching for the Woman's Voice on Trial" [in Hebrew], in *The Voice and the Gaze* [Hakol vehamabat], ed. Vered Lev-Cnaan and Michal Gruber-Friedlander (Tel Aviv: Resling, 2002), 59–80.

43. Gilmore, *Tainted Witness*.

44. Kahana-Carmon, *Under One Roof*, 58.

45. Since the term *dispersions* (*pzurot*) is taken from Jeremiah 50:17 ("Israel are scattered [*pzurot*] sheep, harried by lions"), the sentence might be interpreted in the context of national and religious exile—as rhetoric of national mystical longing expressed in the story as a personal and feminine longing.

46. Esther Fuchs, *Israeli Women's Studies: A Reader* (New Brunswick, NJ: Rutgers University Press, 2005), 284.

47. Herzig and Gertz, *Israeli Fiction in the 1960s*, 7.

48. Kahana-Carmon, *Under One Roof*, 59.

Bibliography

Abramson, Glenda. *Hebrew Writing of the First World War*. London: Vallentine Mitchell, 2008.

Adams, Rachel. "Choosing Disability, Visualizing Care." *Kennedy Institute of Ethics Journal* 27, no. 2 (June 2017): 301–21.

Admon, Moshe. *Diary of a Soldier* [Yomano Shel Ḥayal]. Tel Aviv: Otpaz, 1968.

Agnon, Shmuel Yosef. *At the Handles of the Lock* [Al kapot hamanul: Sipure ahavim]. Berlin: Jüdischer Verlag, 1922.

———. "In the Prime of Her Life." In *Eight Great Hebrew Short Novels*, edited by Alan Lelchuk and Gershon Shaked, 187–245. Translated from the Hebrew by Gabriel Levin. New Milford, CT: Toby Press, 1983.

Ajzenstadt, Mimi, Michal Soffer, and Odeda Steinberg. *"In Prison I Rest": Women Prisoners beyond the Walls* [Bakele ani nacha]. Tel Aviv: Hakibbutz Hameuchad, 2010.

Alcoff, Linda, and Laura Gray. "Survivor Discourse: Transgression or Recuperation?" *Signs* 18, no. 2 (Winter 1993): 260–90.

Alexander, M. Jacqui. "Not Just (Any) Body Can Be a Citizen: The Politics of Law, Sexuality and Postcoloniality in Trinidad and Tobago and the Bahamas." *Feminist Review* 48 (1994): 5–23.

Alexander, M. Jacqui, and Chandra Talpade Mohanty, eds. *Feminist Genealogies, Colonial Legacies, Democratic Futures*. New York: Routledge, 1996.

Almog, Shulamit. *Prostitution: Cultural and Legal Aspects* [Nashim mufkarot]. Tel Aviv: Ministry of Defense–Modan, 2008.

Alon, Ketzia. "Shoshanah Shababo: About Fracturing and Collapse, Disappearance and Evading" [in Hebrew]. *Hakivun Mizrach* 19 (2009): 13–20.

Alper, Rivka. "Mistake" [Shgaga]. Unpublished story. Gnazim Archive of the Hebrew Writers Association in Israel, GI 472/68508. N.d.

Amery, Jean. *At the Mind's Limits: Contemplations by a Survivor on Auschwitz and Its Realities*. Translated by Sidney Rosenfeld and Stella P. Rosenfeld. Bloomington: Indiana University Press, 2009.

Amichai, Yehuda. *The Selected Poetry of Yehuda Amichai*. Translated and edited by Chana Bloch and Stephen Mitchel. Berkeley: University of California Press, 1996.

Amossy, Ruth, and Terese Lyons. "The Cliché in the Reading Process." *SubStance* 11, no. 2, issue 35 (1982): 34–45.

Anthias, Floya, and Nira Yuval-Davis. "Contextualizing Feminism: Gender, Ethnic and Class Divisions." *Feminist Review* 15 (1983): 62–75.

Appadurai, Arjun. *The Future as Cultural Fact: Essays on the Global Condition*. New York: Verso Books, 2013.

Arbel, Michal. *Written on the Dog's Hide: On S. Y. Agnon's Conception of Artistic Creativity* [Katuv 'al 'oro shel hakelev: 'Al tefisat hayetzirah etzel S. Y. 'Agnon]. Jerusalem: Keter–Heksherim, 2006.

Ariel, Nana. "You Can't Live with Them and You Can't Live Without Them: On Clichés" [in Hebrew]. Master's thesis, Tel Aviv University, 2010.

Arieli, L. A. *Collected Works* [Kitvei L. A. Arieli: Sipurim, mahazot, hagadot, ma'amarim, igrot]. Edited by Michael Arfa. New York: Israel Metz Foundation–Dvir, 1999.

Armstrong, Louise. *Rocking the Cradle of Sexual Politics: What Happened When Women Said Incest*. Boston, MA: Addison-Wesley, 1994.

Artman-Partock, Tali. "Erua sifruti vesiper histori: Ben hazal le'avot haknesiah" [Literary event and historical narrative: Between Rabbinic and Patristic literature]. *Mekharei Yerushalaim besifrut 'Ivrit* 24 (2011): 23–54.

———. "Haznut: Ben Yahadut Lenatsrut" [Prostitution: Between Judaism and Christianity]. *Adken* 56 (2012): 24–29.

Ashman, Ahuva. *The Story of Eve: Daughters, Mothers, and Strange Women in Bible* [Toldot Ḥavah: Banot, imahot, ve-nashim nokhriyot ba-Miḳra]. Tel Aviv: Miskal, 2008.

Avishai, Mordechai. "About One Change in the Israeli Novel." *Moznayim* 26, no. 189/190 (1968): 431–34.

Avi-Tamar, Yoram. *Injury* [Ptsia]. Tel Aviv: Am Oved, 1975.

Avraham, Tzlil. "Only When You Scream 'Incest' People Understand" [in Hebrew]. *Mako*, August 25, 2014. http://www.mako.co.il/culture-books-and-theatre/articles/Article-83f9445eedc0841006.htm.

Avramovitch, Dorit. *The Naked King: Incest from a Feminist Perspective* [Hamelech eirom]. Tel Aviv: Babel, 2004.

Azaria, D., and A. Alon. *The Wounded Did Not Cry: Stories of Men Who Had Not Lost Their Composure When They Were Wounded Under Enemy Fire* [Haptuim lo zaaku]. Tel Aviv: Otiyot Argaman, 1967.

Azoulay, Ariella. "Has Anyone Ever Seen a Photograph of Rape?" In *The Civil Contract of Photography*, 217–28. New York: Zone Books, 2008.

Babayoff, Shalom. *The Seventh Glory: A Fighter's Story* [Hazohar hashevii: Sipuro shel lohem]. Jerusalem: Iris, 1968.

Bachi Kolodny, Ruth. "Like a Beast Devouring Her Blouse" [in Hebrew]. *Haaretz*, May 22, 2007. https://www.haaretz.co.il/.premium-1.2291395.

Bal, Mieke. *Death and Dissymmetry: The Politics of Coherence in the Book of Judges*. Chicago, IL: University of Chicago Press, 1998.

Bar-Yosef, Hamutal. "Sanctity of the Holy Land: Reflections on Three Poems of the Third Aliyah." In *The Land of Israel in 20th Century Jewish Thought* [Eretz Israel bahagut hayehudit], edited by Aviezer Ravitsky, 388–98. Jerusalem: Yad Izhak Ven-Zvi, 2004.

Barry, Kathleen L. *Female Sexual Slavery*. New York: New York University Press, 1984.

Bartana, Ortsion. *Fantasy in Israeli Literature in the Last Thirty Years, 1960–1989* [Hafantasya besiporet dor hamedina]. Tel Aviv: Hakibbutz Hameuchad, 1989.

Barthes, Roland. *Mythologies*. Translated by Annette Lavers. New York: Farrar, Straus and Giroux, 1972.

Behar, Moshe. "The Centennial of 'Flora Saporto': Thoughts on the Possibility of a Mizrahi-Feminist Alliance" [in Hebrew]. *Pe'amim: Studies in Oriental Jewry* 139–40 (2014): 9–54.

Bejerano, Maya. "The Rivers and the Sun in Their Everyday Reflections" [in Hebrew]. *Ha'aretz*, book supplement, no. 321, April 20, 1999, p. 11.

Ben-Amotz, Dan. *I Don't Give a Damn* [Lo sam zain]. Tel Aviv: Bitan, 1973.

Ben-Ari, Nitsa. *Suppression of the Erotic in Modern Hebrew Literature*. Ottawa: University of Ottawa Press, 2006.

Benjamin, Jessica. *The Bonds of Love: Psychoanalysis, Feminism, and the Problem of Domination*. New York: Pantheon Books, 1988.

Benjamin, Walter. *Charles Baudelaire: A Lyric Poet in the Era of High Capitalism*. London: New Left Books, 1973.

Berlovitz, Yaffah. "Prose Writing in the Yishuv: 1882–1948." In *Jewish Women: A Comprehensive Historical Encyclopedia*. Jewish Women's Archive. Last modified March 1, 2009. http://jwa.org/encyclopedia/article/prose-writing-in-yishuv-1882-1948.

———. "A Study of Nechama Pohatchevsky's Work." In *A Window into the Lives of Women in Jewish Societies* [Eshnav lehayehen shel nashim behevrot yehudiyot], edited by Yael Azmon, 325–36. Jerusalem: Merkaz Zalman Shazar, 1995.

———, ed. *Tender Rib: Stories by Women Writers in Pre-State Israel* [Sheani adamah veadam]. Jerusalem: Hakibutz Hameuhad, 2003.

Berressem, Hanjo. "The 'Evil Eye' of Painting: Jacques Lacan and Witold Gombrowicz on the Gaze." In *Reading Seminar XI: Lacan's Four Fundamental Concepts of Psychoanalysis*, edited by Richard Feldstein, Bruce Fink, and Maire Jaanus, 175–82. Albany: State University of New York Press, 1995.

Bezalel, Yitzhak. "The Stories, the Roots, the Fate: Interview with Yoram Kaniuk" [in Hebrew]. *Masa*, January 13, 1967.

Bialik, H. N. *The Complete Works of H. N. Bialik* [Kol shirei H. N. Bialik]. Edited by Yitshak Fiksler. Tel Aviv: Dvir, 1973.

Bilsky, Leora. "The Violence of Silence: Searching for the Woman's Voice on Trial." In *The Voice and the Gaze* [Hakol vehamabat], edited by Vered Lev-Cnaan and Michal Gruber-Friedlander, 59–80. Tel Aviv: *Resling*, 2002.

Bloch, Chana, and Chana Kronfeld, *Hovering at a Low Altitude: The Collected Poetry of Dahlia Ravikovitch*. New York: W. W. Norton, 2009.

Bourke, Joanna. "Sexual Violence, Bodily Pain, and Trauma: A History." *Theory, Culture & Society* 29, no. 3 (May 2012): 25–31.

Boyarin, Daniel. *Unheroic Conduct: The Rise of Heterosexuality and the Invention of the Jewish Man*. Berkeley: University of California Press, 1977.

Bracken, Patrick. "Hidden Agendas: Deconstructing Post Traumatic Stress Disorder." In *Rethinking the Trauma of War*, edited by P. Bracken and C. Petty. London: Free Association Books, 1998.

Braun, Netalie, dir. *Metamorphosis*. Israel: Claudius films. 2006.

Brenner, Yosef Haim. *Collected Works* [Ktavim]. 4 vols. Tel Aviv: Hakibbutz Hameuchad, 1977.

———. *Collected Writings* [in Hebrew]. 8 vols. New York: Shtibl Press, 1937.

———. "The Eretz Israel Genre and Its Artifacts (1911)." In *The Collected Works of Y. H. Brenner* [Kol Kitvei Y. H. Brenner], 569–78. Tel Aviv: Hakibbutz Hameuchad, 1985.

Briere, John. *Therapy for Adults Molested as Children: Beyond Survival*. New York: Springer, 1996.

Brison, Susan J. *Aftermath: Violence and the Remaking of a Self*. Princeton, NJ: Princeton University Press, 2002.

Bristow, Edward J. *Prostitution and Prejudice: The Jewish Fight against White Slavery, 1870–1939*. Oxford: Clarendon Press, 1982.

Brown, Wendy. *States of Injury: Power and Freedom in Late Modernity*. Princeton, NJ: Princeton University Press, 1995.

Brownmiller, Susan. *Against Our Will: Men, Women, and Rape*. New York: Simon & Schuster, 1975.

Broyer, Nili R. "Stigma and Unconsciousness" [in Hebrew]. Master's thesis, The Hebrew University of Jerusalem, 2008.

Burla, Yehuda. *His Hated Wife: Luna* [Ishto hasenuah: Luna]. Tel Aviv: Am Oved, 1959.

———. "Marya" [in Hebrew]. *Moznayim* 4, no. 8 (1932): 11–12.

Butler, Judith. *Frames of War: When Is Life Grievable?* New York: Verso Books, 2009.

———. *Gender Trouble: Feminism and the Subversion of Identity*. New York: Routledge, 1990.

Cardeña, Etzel. "The Domain of Dissociation." In *Dissociation: Clinical and Theoretical Perspectives*, edited by S. J. Lynn and J. W. Rhue, 15–31. New York: Guilford Press, 1994.

Chalfi, Raquel. *Love of the Dragon* [Ahavat ha-drakon]. Tel Aviv: Hakibbutz Hameuchad, 1995.

Cixous, Helene, and Catherine Clement. *Newly Born Woman*. Translated by Betsy Wing. Minneapolis: University of Minnesota Press, 1986.

Cohen, Tamar. *Living in the Shadow of the Secret: Personal Stories of Incest* [Liḥyot beṣel hasod: Giluyi arayot: Sipurim ishim]. Tel Aviv: Modan, 1991.

Cohen, Uri S. *Security Style and the Hebrew Culture of War* [Hanosach habitchoni]. Jerusalem: The Bialik Institute, 2017.

Courtois, Christine A. "Healing the Incest Wound: A Treatment Update with Attention to Recovered-Memory Issues." *American Journal of Psychotherapy* 51 (1997): 464–96.

Cover, Robert. "The Folktales of Justice: Tales of Jurisdiction." In *Narrative, Violence, and the Law: The Essays of Robert Cover*, edited by Martha Minow, Michael Ryan, and Austin Sarat, 173–202. Ann Arbor: University of Michigan Press, 1993.

Crenshaw, Kimberlé. "Demarginalizing the Intersection of Race and Sex: A Black Feminist Critique of Antidiscrimination Doctrine, Feminist Theory, and Antiracist Politics." *University of Chicago Legal Forum* 140 (1989): 139–67.

———. "Mapping the Margins: Intersectionality, Identity Politics, and Violence against Women of Color." *Stanford Law Review* 43, no. 6 (1991): 1241–99.

Daly, Brenda. "When the Daughter Tells Her Story: The Rhetorical Challenges of Disclosing Father-Daughter Incest." In *Survivor Rhetoric: Negotiations and Narrativity in Abused Women's Language*, edited by Christine Shearer-Cremean and Carol L. Winkelmann, 139–65. Toronto: University of Toronto Press, 2004.

Daudet, Alphonse. *In the Land of Pain*. Translated by Julian Barnes. New York: Knopf Doubleday, 2016.

Davis, Angela Y. "Rape, Racism and the Capitalist Setting." *Black Scholar* 12, no. 6 (1981): 39–45.

Deacy, Susan, and Karen F. Pierce, eds. *Rape in Antiquity: Sexual Violence in the Greek and Roman Worlds*. London: Bristol Classical Press, 2002.

De Vries, David, and Talia Pfeffermann. "The Ordeal of Henya Pekelman, a Female Construction Worker." In *Struggle and Survival in Palestine/Israel*. Berkeley: University of California Press, 2019.

de Certeau, Michel. *The Practice of Everyday Life*. Berkeley: University of California Press, 1984.

DeFrancisco, Victoria Pruin, Catherine Helen Palczewski, and Danielle D. McGeough. *Gender in Communication: A Critical Introduction*. New York: SAGE Publications, 2013.

de Lauretis, Teresa. *Alice Doesn't: Feminism, Semiotics, Cinema*. Bloomington: Indiana University Press, 1984.

———. "On the Subject of Fantasy." In *Feminisms in the Cinema*, edited by Laura Pietropaolo and Ada Testaferri, 63–85. Bloomington: Indiana University Press, 1995.

———. *Technologies of Gender: Essays on Theory, Film, and Fiction*. Bloomington: Indiana University Press, 1987.

Dean, Carolyn J. *The Fragility of Empathy after the Holocaust*. Ithaca, NY: Cornell University Press, 2004.

Deer, Sarah. *The Beginning and End of Rape: Confronting Sexual Violence in Native America*. Minneapolis: University of Minnesota Press, 2015.

Dekel, Mikhal. "From Where Have I Eaten My Poetry? On Bialik and the Maternal." *Shofar: An Interdisciplinary Journal of Jewish Studies* 31, no. 1 (Fall 2012): 93–111.

———. " 'From the Mouth of the Raped Woman Rivka Schiff,' Kishinev, 1903." *Women's Studies Quarterly* 36, no. 1/2 (2008): 199–207.

———. *The Universal Jew: Masculinity, Modernity, and the Zionist Moment*. Evanson, IL: Northwestern University Press, 2010.

Dekel, Tal. *Gendered: Art and Feminist Theory* [Memugdarot]. Tel Aviv: Hakibutz Hameuhad, 2011.

Deleuze, Gilles, and Félix Guattari. *A Thousand Plateaus: Capitalism and Schizophrenia*. Translated by Brian Massumi. Minneapolis: University of Minnesota Press, 1987.

Dickman, Aminadav. "Tirgumim Basifrut Ha'ivrit Bitkufat Hatehiah" [Translation in Hebrew Literature during the Revival Period]. In *New Jewish Time: Jewish Culture in a Secular Age* [Zman yehudi hadash: Tarbut yehudit be'idan hiloni], edited by Dan Miron and Hannan Hever, 3:94–98. Tel Aviv: Lamda, 2007.

Doezema, Jo. "Loose Women or Lost Women." *Gender Issues* 18 (Winter 2000): 23–50.

Downing, Lisa, and Robert Gillett. "Georges Bataille at the Avant-garde of Queer Theory? Transgression, Perversion and Death Drive." *Nottingham French Studies* 50, no. 3 (September 2011): 88–102.

Dworkin, Andrea. *Intercourse*. New York: Free Press Paperbacks, 1987.

———. *Life and Death: Unapologetic Writings on the Continuing War against Women*. New York: Free Press, 1997.

Dwyer, Daisy, H. *Images and Self-Images: Males and Female in Morocco*. New York: Columbia University Press, 1978.

Eagleton, Terry. *The Rape of Clarisse: Writing, Sexuality, and Class Struggle in Samuel Richardson*. Oxford: Basil Blackwell, 1982.

Eilon, Gilad. "Gilgulah Shel Milah-'Rishrush': Me'eifo Hegi'a La'ivrit Hatslil Hamatok Shel Hakesef?" [The incarnation of the word "rustling": Where did the sweet sound of money come to the Hebrew?]. *Haaretz*, February 22, 2013. https://www.haaretz.co.il/magazine/the-edge/mehasafa/1.1934286.

Farley, Melissa. *Prostitution, Trafficking, and Traumatic Stress.* New York: Psychology Press, 2003.

Feldhay, Rivka. "A Feminine Midrash" [in Hebrew]. *Teorya u-vikoret* 2 (1992): 69–88.

Felman, Shoshana, and Dori Laub. *Testimony: Crises of Witnessing in Literature, Psychoanalysis, and History.* New York: Routledge, 1992.

Ferenczi, Sándor. "Confusion of Tongues between Adults and the Child." In *Final Contributions to the Problems and Methods of Psycho-Analysis*, edited by Michael Balint, translated by Eric Mosbacher, 156–67. 1933. London: Hogarth Press, 1955.

Fine, Michelle. Foreword to *All about the Girl: Culture, Power, and Identity*, edited by Michelle Fine and Anita Harris. New York: Routledge, 2004.

———. "Sexuality, Schooling, and Adolescent Females: The Missing Discourse of Desire." *Harvard Educational Review* 58 (1988): 29–53.

Fineman, Martha Albertson. *The Autonomy Myth: A Theory of Dependency.* New York: The New Press, 2005.

Finger, Anne. "Forbidden Fruit." *New Internationalist* 233 (1992): 8–10.

Finkelstein, Vic. "Disabled People and Our Culture Development." *Disability Arts in London Magazine*, June 8, 1987. http://www.independentliving.org/docs3/finkelstein87a.pdf.

Foucault, Michel. "Of Other Spaces." *Diacritics* 16 (1986): 22–27.

Frawley-O'Dea, Mary Gail. *Perversion of Power: Sexual Abuse in the Catholic Church.* Nashville, TN: Vanderbilt University Press, 2007.

Freud, Anna. *The Ego and the Mechanisms of Defence.* 1936. New York: Routledge, 2018.

Freud, Sigmund. "Beyond the Pleasure Principle." 1920. In *The Standard Edition of the Complete Psychological Works of Sigmund Freud*, edited by James Strachey, in collaboration with Anna Freud, assisted by Alix Strachey and Alan Tyson, 7–64. Vol. 18. London: Hogarth Press, 1953.

———. "Fetishism." 1927. In Strachey, *Complete Psychological Works*, 21:149–57.

———. "The Question of Lay Analysis." 1926. In Strachey, *Complete Psychological Works*, 20:183–250.

———. "Three Essays on the Theory of Sexuality." 1905. In Strachey, *Complete Psychological Works*, 7:125–244.

Friedman, Régine-Mihal. "Invisible Metamorphoses." *Studies in Documentary Film* 6, no. 3 (2012): 273–90.

Fuchs, Esther. *Israeli Women's Studies: A Reader.* New Brunswick, NJ: Rutgers University Press, 2005.

Fuss, Diana. "Fashion and the Homospectatorial Look." *Critical Inquiry* 18, no. 4 (1992): 728–30.

Gabrovec, Branko, and Ivan Eržen. "Prevalence of Violence towards Nursing Staff in Slovenian Nursing Homes." *Zdravstveno Varstvo* 55, no. 3 (May 2016): 212–17.

Gal-Cohen, Lior. *Dad's Gift* [Hamatana shekibalti meaba]. Tel Aviv: Hamama Sifrutit, 2012.

Gallagher, Catherine. "George Eliot and Daniel Deronda: The Prostitute and the Jewish Question." In *Sex, Politics, and Science in the Nineteenth-Century Novel*, edited by Ruth Bernard Yeazell, 39–62. Baltimore, MD: Johns Hopkins University Press, 1985.

Gallop, Jane. *The Daughter's Seduction: Feminism and Psychoanalysis*. Ithaca, NY: Cornell University Press, 1982.

Garland-Thomson, Rosemarie. "Misfits: A Feminist Materialist Disability Concept." *Hypatia* 26, no. 3 (2011): 591–609.

———. *Staring: How We Look*. Oxford: Oxford University Press, 2009.

Gates, D. M., E. Fitzwater, and U. Meyer. "Violence against Caregivers in Nursing Homes: Expected, Tolerated, and Accepted." *J Gorontol Nurs.* 25, no. 4 (1999): 12–22.

Gavriely-Nuri, Dalia, and Tiki Balas. "'Annihilating Framing': How Israeli Television Framed Wounded Soldiers during the Second Lebanon War (2006)." *Journalism* 11, no. 4 (2010): 409–23.

Gez, Ronit. *Women's and Men's Fiction in the Yishuv Period: Negotiations over the National Narrative* [in Hebrew]. Unpublished doctoral dissertation. Beer Sheva, Israel: Ben Ben-Gurion University of the Negev, 2011.

Gilat, Miriam, and Yitzhak Kadman. *Shirley's Diary: From the World of Child Survivor* [Miyomana shel Shirley]. Jerusalem: National Council for the Child, 1999.

Gilbert, Sandra M., and Susan Gubar. *The Madwoman in the Attic: The Woman Writer and the Nineteenth-Century Literary Imagination*. New Haven, CT: Yale University Press, 1979.

Gilfoyle, Timothy J. "Prostitutes in History: From Parables of Pornography to Metaphors of Modernity." *American Historical Review* 104, no. 1 (1999): 117–41.

Gilmore, David D. *Misogyny: The Male Malady*. Philadelphia: University of Pennsylvania Press, 2001.

Gilmore, Leigh. *Tainted Witness: Why We Doubt What Women Say about Their Lives*. New York: Columbia University Press, 2017.

Gluzman, Michael. *The Zionist Body: Nationalism, Gender, and Sexuality in Modern Israeli Literature* [Haguf hatzioni: Le'umiut, migdar uminiut basifrut ha'israelit hachadasha]. Tel Aviv: Hakibbutz hameuchad, 2007.

Gluzman, Michael, Hannan Hever, and Dan Miron. *In the City of Slaughter: A Late Visit upon the Hundredth Anniversary of Bialik's Poem* [Be'ir haharegah: Bikur me'uhar bemel'at me'ah shanah lapoemah shel Bialik]. Tel Aviv: Resling, 2005.

Golan, Menahem, dir. *The Highway Queen* [Malkat hakvish]. London: Noah Films Productions, 1971.

Golan, Efrat. "A Feminist Reading of [Agnon's] 'In the Prime of Her Life'" [in Hebrew]. *'Alei siah* 27–28 (1990): 81–92.

Golan, Ruth. "Agnon's 'Bidemi Yemeiha': From Divided Object to Split Subject" [in Hebrew]. *'Alei siah* 29–30 (1991): 83–88.

Goldberg, Amos. *Trauma in the First Person: Diary Writing in the Holocaust Period* [Trauma beguf rishon: Ketivat yomanim bitekufat hasho'ah]. Beer Sheva, Israel: Devir–Heksherim, 2012.

Goldberg, Leah. *Poems* [*Shirim*]. Vol. 3. Edited by Tuvia Rivner. Tel Aviv: Sifriat Poalim, 1973.

———. *What the Does Do* [Ma osot haayalot]. Tel Aviv: Sifriat Poalim, 1957.

Gormezano Goren, Yitzhak. "My Journey with the Rose: An Encounter with Shoshanah Shababo's Work" [in Hebrew]. *Hakivun Mizrach* 19 (2009): 8–12.

Gormezano-Gorfinkel, and Bat-Shachar, eds. *Hakivun Mizrach* [Eastward: Culture and literary journal] 19 (2009).

Govrin, Nurit. *Brenner: "Nonplussed" and Mentor* [Brenner: Oved 'etsot u-moreh derekh]. Tel Aviv: Misrad ha-biṭaḥon, 1991.

———. "In Praise of the 'Genre': Brenner as the Supporter of the 'Palestinian Genre'" [in Hebrew]. *Dappim: Research in Literature* 3 (1986): 97–116.

———. "Mavo: Mahalakhah shel habikoret al sipurei G. Shofman." In *G. Shofman: A Selection of Critical Essays on His Literary Prose* [G. Shofman: Mivḥar ma'amarei bikoret al yetsirato], edited by Nurit Govrin, 7–42. Tel Aviv: Am Oved, 1978.

———. *Reading the Generations: Contextual Studies in Hebrew Literature* [Keri'at hadorot: Sifrut 'ivrit bema'agaleha]. Vols. 1–2. Tel Aviv: Gevanim, 2002. Vols. 3–4. Jerusalem: Carmel, 2008.

Govrin, Nurith, and Avner Holtzman. *Devorah Baron: The First Half* [Devorah Baron: Hamaḥatsit harishonah, hayehah viyetsiratah]. Jerusalem: Mosad Byaliḳ, 1988.

Graetz, Naomi, and Julie Cwikel. "Trafficking and Prostitution: Lessons from Jewish Sources." *Australian Journal of Jewish Studies* 20 (2006): 25–58.

Greenberg, Jay R., and Stephen A. Mitchell. *Object Relations in Psychoanalytic Theory*. Cambridge, MA: Harvard University Press, 1983.

Greenberg, Slava. "Embodying Conflict: Representations of Hospitals and Seas in Israeli Cinema after the Second Intifada." *Jewish Film and New Media: An International Journal* 7, no. 2 (2019): 214–35.

Griffin, Susan. *Pornography and Silence: Culture's Revenge against Nature*. New York: HarperCollins, 1981.

Grosz, Elizabeth. *Jacques Lacan: A Feminist Introduction*. London: Routledge, 1990.

Gur, Anat. *Foreign Bodies: Eating Disorders and Childhood Sexual Abuse* [Guf zar]. Tel Aviv: Hakibbutz Hameuchad, 2015.

———. "Thoughts on Experts' Legal Opinions in Sexual Traumas Trials" [in Hebrew]. *Anat Gur* (blog). March 28, 2009. https://anatgur.wordpress.com/2009/03/28.

Guttman, Amos, dir. *Himmo, King of Jerusalem* [Himmo, melech Yerushalayim]. Beverly Hills, CA: Bleiberg Entertainment, 1987.

Haelyon, Yaacov. *A Doll's Leg: A Story of a War Injury*. Translated by Louis Williams. Cape Town: John Malherbe, 1974.

Halevi, Yossef. *A Modern Daughter of the Orient: On the Work of Shoshana Shababo* [Bat hamizrach hahadash]. Ramat Gan, Israel: Bar-Ilan University Press, 1996.

Halpern, Roni. *Body and Its Discontents: Israeli Women's Literature from 1985 to 2005* [Guf belo nahat]. Tel Aviv: Hakibbutz Hameuchad, 2012.

Hameiri, Israel. *Wildness* [Praut]. Tel Aviv: Hakibbutz Hameuchad, 1972.

Handley-Cousins, Sarah. "'Wrestling at the Gates of Death': Joshua Lawrence Chamberlain and Nonvisible Disability in the Post–Civil War North." *Journal of the Civil War Era* 6, no. 2 (2016): 220–42.

Hatuka, Shoshi. "Women's Day 2016: 'Heroes and Brave Despite the Bleeding Wound'" [in Hebrew]. *Mako*, July 3, 2016. https://www.mako.co.il/news-israel/local-q1_2016/Article-8478cd53fc15351004.htm.

Heise, Thomas. *Urban Underworlds: A Geography of Twentieth-Century American Literature and Culture*. New Brunswick, NJ: Rutgers University Press, 2011.

Herman, Judith Lewis. *Father-Daughter Incest*. Cambridge, MA: Harvard University Press, 2000.

———. *Trauma and Recovery: The Aftermath of Violence—from Domestic Abuse to Political Terror*. New York: Basic Books, 1992.

Herzig, Hanna, and Nurith Gertz. *Israeli Fiction in the 1960s, Units 9–11* [Hasiporet haIsraelit bishnot hashishim]. Tel Aviv: The Open University, 1982.

Herzig, Shlomo. "An Idol in the Temple: On Intersexuality and Its Significance in S. Y. Agnon's 'Bidemi Yemeiha'" [in Hebrew]. *'Alei siah* 46 (2001): 69–79.

Hess, Tamar S. "Henya Pekelman: An Injured Witness of Socialist Zionist Settlement in Mandatory Palestine." *WSQ: Women's Studies Quarterly* 36, nos. 1 & 2 (Spring/Summer 2008): 208–13.

———. "Henya Pekelman's Memories." In Henya Pekelman, *The Life of a Worker in Her Homeland* [Hayey po'elet ba-aretz], 219–35. Beer Sheva, Israel: Kinneret, Zmora-Bitan, Dvir, 2007.

Hever, Hannan. *From the Beginning: Three Essays on Nativist Hebrew Poetry* [Mereshit: Shalosh masot al shira ivrit yeldit]. Tel Aviv: Keshev, 2008.

———. *The Narrative and the Nation: Critical Readings in the Canon of Hebrew Fiction* [Hasipur vehale'um: Kri'ot bikortiyot bakanon hasiporet ha'ivrit]. Tel Aviv: Resling, 2007.

———. "Yitzhak Shami: Ethnicity as an Unresolved Conflict." *Shofar: An Interdisciplinary Journal of Jewish Studies* 24, no. 2 (2006): 124–39.

Higgins, Lynn A., and Brenda R. Silver, eds. *Rape and Representation*. New York: Columbia University Press, 1991.

Hirsch, Marianne. *The Mother/Daughter Plot: Narrative, Psychoanalysis, Feminism*. Bloomington: Indiana University Press, 1989.

Hite, Shere. *The Hite Report*. New York: Macmillan, 1976.

Hochberg, Gil Z. *In Spite of Partition: Jews, Arabs, and the Limits of Separatist Imagination*. Princeton, NJ: Princeton University Press, 2010.

Holtzman, Avner. "The Mark of Fire: Forty Years of Writing about the Yom Kippur War" [in Hebrew]. *OT: A Journal of Literary Criticism and Theory* 4 (2014): 43–74.

hooks, bell. *Yearning: Race, Gender, and Cultural Politics*. Boston, MA: South End Press, 1990.

Horowitz, Sara R. "The Rhetoric of Embodied Memory in 'In the City of Slaughter.'" *Prooftexts* 25 (Winter/Spring 2005): 73–85.

Hurwich, Baruch. *"The Fifth Front:" The Israeli Solider Military Medicine in Israel: The War of Independence, 1947–1949* [Kol hayal hazit]. Jerusalem: Misrad habitahon, 2000.

Ilkkaracan, Ipek, and Gulsah Seral. "Sexual Pleasure as a Woman's Human Right: Experiences from a Grassroots Training Program in Turkey." In *Women and Sexuality in Muslim Societies*, edited by Pinar Ilkkaracan, 187–98. Istanbul: Women for Women's Human Rights, New Ways, 2000.

Imberman, Shmuel, dir. *I Don't Give a Damn* [Lo sam zain]. Karachi, Pakistan: Roll Film Studios, 1987.

Irigaray, Luce. "And the One Doesn't Stir without the Other." Translated into English by Helene Vivienne Wenzel. *Signs* 7, no. 1 (1981): 60–67.

———. *This Sex Which Is Not One*. Translated by Catherine Porter, with Carolyn Burke. Ithaca, NY: Cornell University Press, 1985.

Izak, Rotem. "Nano Shabtai Thought She Was Writing about Love" [in Hebrew]. *At Magazine*, March 31, 2016.

Jacobs, A. C. *Collected Poems and Selected Translations*. London: Menard Press, 1996.

Jacobs, Steven L., trans. *Shirot Bialik: A New and Annotated Translation of Chaim Nachman Bialik's Epic Poems*. Columbus, OH: Alpha, 1987.

Jordan, Thomas. "Disability, Vietnam, and the Discourse of American Exceptionalism." In *Emerging Perspectives on Disability Studies*, edited by M. Wappett and K. Arndt, 41–65. New York: Palgrave Macmillan, 2013.

Kahana-Carmon, Amalia. "Here Is the Book" [in Hebrew]. *Moznaim* 5/6 (1984): 12–18.

———. *Under One Roof* [Bikhefifah ahat]. Tel Aviv: Hakibbutz Hameuchad, 1966.

———. "The Whirling Sword" [Hacherev hamithapechet]. *Masa* supplement in *Lamerhav*, June 29, 1956.

Kama, Amit. "Images that Injure: Representations of People with Disabilities in the Media." In *From Exclusion to Inclusion: Life in the Community for People with Disabilities in Israel* [Mehadarah Lehakhalah], edited by Meir Hovav, Ilana Duvdevany, and Clara Feldman, 181–213. Jerusalem: Carmel, 2015.

———. "Supercrips versus the Pitiful Handicapped: Reception of Disabling Images by Disabled Audience Members." *Communication* 29, no. 4 (2004): 447–66.

Kamir, Orit. "Sexual Harassment Law in Israel." *International Journal of Discrimination and the Law* 7, no. 1–4 (2005): 315–36.

Kaniuk, Yoram. *Himmo, King of Jerusalem.* Translated by Yosef Shachter. New York: Atheneum, 1969.

———. *Vultures and Villainy* [Etim unevelot]. Tel Aviv: Yediot Aharonot, 2006.

Karamcheti, Indira. "The Geographics of Marginality: Place and Textuality in Simone Schwarz-Bart and Anita Desai." In *Reconfigured Spheres: Feminist Explorations of Literary Space,* edited by Margaret R. Higonnet and Joan Templeton, 125–46. Amherst: University of Massachusetts Press, 1994.

Karpf, Ann. "Crippling Images." In *Framed: Interrogating Disability in the Media,* edited by Ann Pointon and Chris Davies, 79–83. London: British Film Institute, 1997.

Karton-Blum, Ruth. *The Veil of Veronica: Israeli Literature Reads the New Testament* [Hamitpachat shel veronica: Hasifrut haisraelit vehbrit hachadasha]. Tel Aviv: Hakibutz Hameuhad, 2019.

Kayir, Arsalus. "Women and Their Sexual Problems in Turkey." In *Women and Sexuality in Muslim Societies,* edited by Pinar Ilkkaracan, 253–68. Istanbul: Women for Women's Human Rights, New Ways, 2000.

Kelly, Christine. "Building Bridges with Accessible Care: Disability Studies, Feminist Care Scholarship, and Beyond." *Hypatia* 28, no. 4 (Fall 2013): 784–800.

Keren, Nitza. *Like a Sheet in the Hand of the Embroideress: Women Writers and the Hegemonic Text* [Kayeria beyad harokemet]. Ramat Gan, Israel: Bar-Ilan University Press: 2010.

Keshet, Yeshurun. "Nefesh Hador o Nefesh Hayahid?" [The generation's soul or the individual's soul?]. In *G. Shofman: A Selection of Critical Essays on His Literary Prose* [G. Shofman: Mivhar ma'amarei bikoret al yetsirato], edited by Nurit Govrin, 93–96. Tel Aviv: Am Oved, 1978.

Kittay, Eva Feder. *Love's Labor: Essays on Women, Equality, and Dependency.* London: Routledge, 1999.

Klausner, Joseph. "G. Shofman." In *G. Shofman: A Selection of Critical Essays on His Literary Prose* [G. Shofman: Mivhar ma'amarei bikoret al yetsirato], edited by Nurit Govrin, 67–80. Tel Aviv: Am Oved, 1978.

Klein, Melanie. *Envy and Gratitude and Other Works, 1946–1963.* London: Hogarth Press / Institute of Psycho-Analysis, 1975.

Kleinman, Arthur. *Writing at the Margin: Discourse between Anthropology and Medicine.* Berkeley: University of California Press, 1997.

Koren, Ela, Yoav S. Bergman, and Michael Katz. "Disability during Military Service in Israel: Raising Awareness of Gender Differences." *Journal of Gender Studies* 24, no. 1 (2015): 117–28.

Koren, Ziv, and Rachel Lev-Wiesel. *When Time Stood Still.* London: Clink Street, 2014.

———. *When Time Stood Still: Incest—from Harm to Growth* [Keshe hazman amad milechet: Giluy arayot—mepgiah letzmicha]. Kfar Bialik, Israel: Ach Books, 2013.

Kraemer, Shalom. "Darko Be'omanut Hasipur" [His way in the art of storytelling]. In *G. Shofman: A Selection of Critical Essays on His Literary Prose* [G. Shofman: Mivḥar ma'amarei bikoret al yetsirato], edited by Nurit Govrin, 136–50. Tel Aviv: Am Oved, 1978.

Kristeva, Julia. *Desire in Language: A Semiotic Approach to Literature and Art.* Translated by Thomas Gora, Alice Jardine, and Leon S. Roudiez. New York: Columbia University Press, 1980.

Lacan, Jacques. *Ecrits: A Selection.* Translated by Alan Sheridan. New York: W. W. Norton, 1977.

———. *The Four Fundamental Concepts of Psychoanalysis. Edited by* Jacques-Alain Miller. Translated by Alan Sheridan. New York: W. W. Norton, 1998.

LaCapra, Dominick. *History in Transit: Experience, Identity, Critical Theory.* Ithaca, NY: Cornell University Press, 2004.

Lachman, Lilach. "The Reader as Witness: 'City of the Killings' and Bialik's Romantic Historiography." In *The Jews and British Romanticism: Politics, Religion, Culture,* edited by Sheila A. Spector, 211–32. Basingstoke, UK: Palgrave Macmillan, 2005.

Laplanch, Jean, and Jean-Bertrand Pontalis. "Fantasy and the Origins of Sexuality." In *Formations of Fantasy,* edited by Victor Burgin, James Donald, and Cora Kaplan, 5–28. London: Methuen, 1986.

Latte, Michal. "Development of Women Offenders in Israel: An Analysis of Personal Narratives" [in Hebrew]. Master's thesis, School of Social Work of Bar-Illan University, 2000.

Lavie, Smadar. *Mizrahi Wrapped in the Flag of Israel: Mizrahi Single Mothers and Bureaucratic Torture.* Oxford: Berghahn Books, 2014.

Lavie, Smadar, and Ted Swedenburg, eds. *Displacement, Diaspora, and Geographies of Identity.* Durham, NC: Duke University Press Books, 1996.

Layoun, Mary. "The Female Body and 'Transnational' Reproduction; or, Rape by Any Other Name?" In *Scattered Hegemonies: Postmodernity and Transnational Feminist Practices,* edited by Inderpal Grewal and Caren Kaplan, 63–75. Minneapolis: University of Minnesota Press, 1994.

Lev Kenaan, Vered. *Pandora's Senses: The Feminine Character of the Ancient Text.* Madison: University of Wisconsin Press, 2008.

Levi Hazan, Yael. "Rewriting the War? Rewrites, Editing and Versions in Women's Fiction about the 1948 War." *BGU Review* (2017): 1–29.

———. *What Do You Know about It: Women's Writing on War in Hebrew Literature* [Ma at mevinah: Nashim kotvot al milhamah basifrut haivrit]. Beer Sheva, Israel: The Ben-Gurion Institute for the Study of Israel and Zionism at Ben-Gurion University of the Negev, 2019.

Lev-Wiesel, Rachel. "Child Sexual Abuse: A Critical Review of Intervention and Treatment Modalities." *Children and Youth Services Review* 30, no. 6 (2008): 665–73.

Liggins, Emma. "Prostitution and Social Purity in the 1880s and 1890s." *Critical Survey* 15 (2003): 39–55.

Lindholm, Charles. *The Islamic Middle East: An Historical Anthropology*. Cambridge, MA: Blackwell, 1996.

Lindisfarne, Nancy. "Variant Masculinities, Variant Virginities: Rethinking 'Honor and Shame.'" In *Dislocating Masculinity: Comparative Ethnographies*, edited by Andrea Cornwall and Nancy Lindisfarne, 82–96. New York: Routledge, 1994.

Litevsky, Tsvia. *Ascending to Light* [Migufo shel olam]. Jerusalem: Carmel, 2019.

———. "Calling It by Name" [Likro lazeh bashem]. *'Al hakav* 7 (Summer 2004): 37–45.

———. *Don't Point Your Finger at Me* [Al tatsbia alai]. Tel Aviv: Helicon, 2003.

———. *Everything Is Full of Gods: Self and World in Myth* [Hakol male elim: Ha'atzmi veha'olam bemitos]. Tel Aviv: Resling, 2013.

———. *Fields of Infinite* [Arugot haeinsof]. Tel Aviv: Hakibbutz Hameuchad, 2016.

———. *The Green towards the Green* [Hayarok bedarko el hayarok]. With drawings by Tamra Rickman. Jerusalem: Carmel, 2006.

———. *In Grace of Darkness* [Baḥoshekh hameitiv]. Tel Aviv: Hakibbutz Hameuchad, 1998.

———. *I Shall Die as Born* [Amut kenoledet]. Tel Aviv: Iton 77, 2013.

———. *Liturgy* [Liturgiya]. Tel Aviv: Hakibbutz Hameuchad, 2010.

———. *One Wall I Called Home* [Lekir eḥad kar'ati bayit]. Jerusalem: Carmel, 2007.

———. "Until the Stem Becomes Transparent." *Iton 77* 349 (August–September 2010): 28–29.

Longmore, Paul. "Screening Stereotypes: Images of Disabled People in Television and Motion Pictures." In *Images of the Disabled, Disabling Images*, edited by Alan Gartner and Tom Joe, 65–78. New York: Praeger, 1987.

Loshitzky, Yosefa. "The Bride of the Dead: Phallocentrism and War in 'Himmo, King of Jerusalem.'" *Literature/Film Quarterly* 21, no. 3 (1993): 218–29.

Lubartowska, Ahuva. "Crows: Exhibition of the Paintings of Ahuva Lubartowska." Mazkeret Batya, Israel: Eran Shamir Village Museum, 2005.

Lubin, Orly. "From Territory to Site: The Oriental Woman in the Film *Jacky*" [in Hebrew]. *Bikoret veparshanut* 34 (2000): 177–93.

MacKinnon, Catharine. "Rape: On Coercion and Consent." In *Writing on the Body: Female Embodiment and Feminist Theory*, edited by Katie Conboy,

Nadia Medina, and Sarah Stanbury, 42–58. New York: Columbia University Press, 1997.

———. *Toward a Feminist Theory of the State*. Cambridge, MA: Harvard University Press, 1989.

Malkki, Liisa H. "Speechless Emissaries: Refugees, Humanitarianism, and Dehistoricization." *Cultural Anthropology* 11, no 3 (August 1996): 377–404.

Matalon, Ronit. "My Father at Age Seventy-Nine." Translated by Mikhal Dekel. *Callaloo* 32, no. 4 (2009): 1182–88.

Mazor, Yair. "The Place Where Fiction Launches Poetry" [in Hebrew]. *Moznayim* 6 (1983): 46–51.

McNaron, Tori A. H., and Yarrow Morgan, eds. *Voices in the Night: Women Speaking about Incest*. Minneapolis, MN: Cleis Press, 1982.

McRuer, Robert. *Crip Theory: Cultural Signs of Queerness and Disability*. New York: New York University Press, 2006.

Mendelson-Maoz, Adia. *Literature as a Moral Laboratory: Reading Selected Twentieth-Century Hebrew Prose* [Hasifrut kemaabada musarit]. Ramat Gan, Israel: Bar Ilan University Press, 2009.

Miller, Nancy K. "My Father's Penis." In *Refiguring the Father: New Feminist Readings of Patriarchy*, edited by Patricia Yaeger and Beth Kowaleski-Wallace, 312–16. Carbondale: Southern Illinois University Press, 1989.

Milo, Haya. *Talking Songs: Folksongs of Israeli Soldiers* [Shirim bakaneh]. Ra'anana, Israel: The Open University Press, 2016.

Mintz, Alan L. *Ḥurban: Responses to Catastrophe in Hebrew Literature*. New York: Columbia University Press, 1984.

———. "The Russian Pogroms in Hebrew Literature and the Subversion of the Martyrological Ideal." *AJS Review* 7/8 (1982/1983): 263–300.

———, ed. "Kishinev in the Twentieth Century." Special issue, *Prooftexts* 25 (Winter/Spring 2005).

Miron, Dan. *The Blind Library: Assorted Prose Pieces, 1980–2005* [Hasifria ha'iveret: Proza me'urevet, 1980–2005]. Tel Aviv: Yediot Aharonot, 2005.

———. *Founding Mothers, Stepsisters: The Emergence of the First Hebrew Poetesses* [Imahot meyasdot, achayot chorgot]. Tel Aviv: Hakibbutz Hameuchad, 1991.

———. *H. N. Bialik and the Prophetic Mode in Modern Hebrew Poetry*. Syracuse, NY: Syracuse University Press, 2000.

Mishori, Efrat. "The Penis Puts Out a Hand." *Yedi'ot Aḥaronot, Weekend Supplement: Culture, Literature, Art*, April 9, 1999, 27–28.

Mitchell, David, and Sharon L. Snyder. *Narrative Prosthesis: Disability and the Dependencies of Discourse*. Ann Arbor: University of Michigan Press, 2000.

Mittelpunkt, Hillel, dir. *Mami*. Tel Aviv: Tzavta Theatre, 1986.

Mohanty, Chandra Talpade. "Under Western Eyes: Feminist Scholarship and Colonial Discourses." In *Third World Women and the Politics of Feminism*, edited by Chandra Talpade Mohanty and Ann Russo, 51–80. Bloomington: Indiana University Press, 1991.

Morag, Raya. "Kol, Dimui, Vezikaron Hateror: Hakolno'a Hayisraeli Ha'alilati Bitkufat Ha'intifadah Hashniyah" [Sound, image, terror, and memory: Israeli narrative cinema in the age of the second intifada]. *Yisrael* 14 (2008): 71–88.

Moran, Jon. *Crime and Corruption in New Democracies: The Politics of (In)Security*. London: Palgrave MacMillan, 2011.

Motzafi-Haller, Pnina. "Reading Arab Feminist Discourses: A Postcolonial Challenge to Israeli Feminism." *Hagar: International Social Studies Review* 1, no. 2 (2000): 63–89.

Mulvey, Laura. "Visual Pleasure and Narrative Cinema." *Screen* 16, no. 3 (1975): 6–18.

Munk, Yael. "Actualization of Political Protest—Between Literature and Film." *Resling* 3 (1997): 42–45.

Murphy, Robert F. *The Body Silent: The Different World of the Disabled*. New York: W. W. Norton, 2001.

Narayan, Uma. "Towards a Feminist Vision of Dignity, Political Participation, and Nationality." In *Reconstructing Political Theory: Feminist Perspectives*, edited by Mary Lyndon Shanley and Uma Narayan, 48–67. University Park: Penn State University Press, 1997.

Naveh, Hannah. "Migdar Vehazon Hagavriyut Ha'ivrit" [Gender and the vision of Hebrew masculinity]. In *New Jewish Time: Jewish Culture in a Secular Age* [Zman yehudi hadash: Tarbut yehudit be'idan hiloni], edited by Dan Miron and Hannan Hever, 3:117–23. Tel Aviv: Lamda, 2007.

———. "A Group Portrait *Agav Orha*: Was It Or Was It Not? More of Y. H. Brenner." In *Literature and Society—Studies in Contemporary Hebrew Culture, Papers in Honor of Gershon Shaked* [Sifrut ve-hevra ba-tarbut ha-ivrit ha-hadasha], edited by Yehudit Bar-El, Yigal Schwartz, and Tamar Hess, 82–100. Tel Aviv: Hakibbutz Hameuchad and Keter, 2001.

Ne'eman, Judd. *The Wound: Gift of War, Battlefield of Israeli Cinema* [Hapetza matnat hamilhama]. Tel Aviv: Am Oved, 2018.

Negbi, Irit. *Rape Stories in the Court: Narrative Analysis of Supreme Court Judgments* [Sipurey ones bebeit hamishpat]. Tel Aviv: *Resling, 2009.*

Neumann, Boaz. *Land and Desire in Early Zionism*. Waltham, MA: Brandeis University Press, 2011.

Nitzan, Tal. "Controlled Occupation: The Rarity of Military Rape in the Israeli-Palestinian Conflict." Master's thesis, Hebrew University of Jerusalem, 2006.

———. "Zionism and Eros in 'Beer Sheva, The Capital of the Negev' by Amalia Kahana-Carmon" [in Hebrew]. *Amirot*. August 2013, http://amirot.blogspot.com/2013/08/blog-post_12.html.

Nord, Deborah Epstein. *Walking the Victorian Streets: Women, Representation, and the City*. Ithaca, NY: Cornell University Press, 1995.

Ofek, Uriel. *From the War: Fiction and Poetry* [Min hamilchamah: Siporet veshirah]. Tel Aviv: The Ministry of Defense, 1969.

Offer Oren, Ofra. *I Feel Good, I Feel Good—A Letter to Mother: The Memories of a Survivor of Incest* [Yofi li, yofi li]. Tel Aviv: Yedioth Ahronoth, 2006.

———. *Shira and Hiroshima* [Shira vehiroshima]. Tel Aviv: Yedioth Ahronoth, 2003.

———. "To Be Precise, and to Give to the World" [in Hebrew]. *Haaretz*. January 16, 2006. http://www.haaretz.co.il/literature/1.1075485.

Oliver, Michael. *The Politics of Disablement*. London: Macmillan, 1990.

Oppenheimer, Yochai. *Barriers: The Representation of the Arab in Hebrew and Israeli Fiction, 1906–2005* [Meever lagader: Yitsug ha'aravim basiporet haivrit vehayisraelit, 1906–2005]. Tel Aviv: Am Oved, 2008.

Orpaz Averbuch, Yitzhak. *Daniel's Trials* [Masa Daniel]. Tel Aviv: Am Oved, 1969.

Oz, Sheri. Epilogue to *Captive: Chronicle of Professional Incest: An Autobiographical Story* [Shvuya], by Maya Reed, 107–13. Tel Aviv: Tammuz, 2002.

Oz, Sheri, and Sarah-Jane Ogiers. *Overcoming Childhood Sexual Trauma: A Guide to Breaking through the Wall of Fear for Practitioners and Survivors*. Abingdon, UK: Routledge, 2014.

Pagis, Dan. "Kavim Lebiografiah" [An outline for biography]. In *Collected Poems* [Kol shirei David Vogel], edited by Dan Pagis, 11–70. Tel Aviv: Agudat Sofrim, 1966).

Pearlman, Laurie Anne, and Karen W. Saakvitne. *Trauma and the Therapist: Countertransference and Vicarious Traumatization in Psychotherapy with Incest Survivors*. New York: W. W. Norton, 1995.

Pekelman, Henya. *The Life of a Worker in Her Homeland* [Hayey po'elet ba-aretz]. Beer Sheva, Israel: Kinneret, Zmora-Bitan, Dvir, 2007.

Pelak C. F. "Negotiating Gender/Race/Class Constraints in the New South Africa." *International Review for the Sociology of Sport* 40, no. 1 (2005): 53–70.

Peled, Shimrit. *The Israeli Sovereign: The Novel and the Discourse, 1967–1973* [Haribon haisraeli]. Jerusalem: The Hebrew University Magna Press, 2014.

Peleg, Yaron. *Homoeroticism in Modern Hebrew Literature, 1880–2000* [Derech Gever]. n.p: Shufra Publication, 2003.

Peri, Menahem. "A Comment on the Book's Style" [He'ara al nosah hasefer]. In *Married Life* [hayei nisu'im], by David Vogel, 331–33. Tel Aviv: Hakibbutz Hameuchad, 2000.

Peristiany, Jean George, ed. *Honor and Shame: The Values of Mediterranean Society*. Chicago, IL: Chicago University Press, 1966.

Presner, Todd Samuel. *Muscular Judaism: The Jewish Body and the Politics of Regeneration*. New York: Routledge, 2007.

Preston, Jeffrey. *Fantasy of Disability: Images of Loss in Popular Culture*. London: Routledge Press, 2018.

Putnam, Frank W. *Diagnosis and Treatment of Multiple Personality Disorder*. New York: Guilford Press, 1989.

Rainey, Sarah Smith. *Love, Sex, and Disability: The Pleasures of Care*. Boulder, CO: Lynne Rienner, 2011.

Ramras-Rauch, Gilah. *The Arab in Israeli Literature*. Bloomington: Indiana University Press, 1989.

Rattok, Lily. *Amalia Kahana-Carmon: Monograph* [Monographia: Amalia Kahana-Carmon]. Tel Aviv: Sifriat Poalim, 1986.

———. "Women in the War of Independence: Myth and Memory" [in Hebrew]. In *Sadan: Studies in Hebrew Literature*, vol. 5, edited by Hannah Naveh and Oded Menda-Levy 203–87. Tel Aviv: Tel Aviv University, 2002.

Ravikovitch, Dahlia. *Death in the Family* [Mavet bamishpahah]. Tel Aviv: Am Oved, 1976.

———. *Hovering at a Low Altitude: The Collected Poetry of Dahlia Ravikovitch*, 115–16. Translated by Chana Bloch and Chana Kronfeld. New York: W. W. Norton, 2009.

Raz-Krakotzkin, Amnon. "Galut Betokh Ribonut: Lebikoret 'Shelilat Hagalut' Batarbut Hayisraelit" [*Exile* within sovereignty: Critique of "The Negation of *Exile*" in Israeli culture]. *Teorya u-vikoret* 4 (1993): 23–55 and 5 (1994): 113–23.

Reed, Maya. *Captive: Chronicle of Professional Incest: An Autobiographical Story* [Shvuya]. Tel Aviv: Tammuz, 2002.

———. "Dissociative Identity and Its Representation in Contemporary Media" [in Hebrew]. *Hebrew Psychology*, November 21, 2012. http://www.hebpsy.net/articles.asp?t=0&id=2869.

Ribot, Théodule-Armand. *Diseases of Memory: An Essay in the Positive Psychology*. Translated by William Huntington Smith. New York: Appleton, 1887.

Rich, Adrienne. *Of Woman Born: Motherhood as Experience and Institution*. New York: W. W. Norton, 1976.

Rimmon-Kenan, Shlomith. "Pain and Language in Illness Narratives: Liasons Dangereuses" [in Hebrew]. In *Pain in Flesh and Blood: Essays on Malady, Suffering, and Indulgence of the Body* [Keev basar vadam], edited by Oreet Meital and Shira Stav, 51–61. Or Yehuda, Israel: Kineret Zmora Bitan, 2013.

Rogoff, Irit. "Academy as Potentiality." In *A.C.A.D.E.M.Y.*, edited by Angelika Nollert and Irit Rogoff, n.p. Frankfurt, Germany: Revolver, 2006.

Root, Maria P. P. "Women of Color and Traumatic Stress in 'Domestic Captivity': Gender and Race as Disempowering Statuses." In *Ethnocultural Aspects of Posttraumatic Stress Disorder: Issues, Research, and Clinical Applications*, edited by Anthony J. Marsella, Matthew J. Friedman, Ellen T. Gerrity, and Raymond M. Scurfield. Washington, DC: American Psychological Association, 1996.

Roskies, David. *Against the Apocalypse: Responses to Catastrophe in Modern Jewish Culture*. Syracuse, NY: Syracuse University Press, 1999.

Rotem, Shoshan. *As Though Nothing Happened*. Translated by Yael Shalev. Scotts Valley, CA: CreateSpace, 2015.

———. *As Though Nothing Happened* [Klum lo kara . . .]. Herzliya, Israel: Mendele Electronic Books, 2015.

Roxanne, Nelson. "Sexual Harassment in Nursing: A Long-Standing but Rarely Studied Problem." *AJN: American Journal of Nursing* 118, no. 5 (2018): 19–20.

Russell, Diana E. H. *The Secret Trauma: Incest in the Lives of Girls and Women*. Rev. ed. New York: Basic Books, 1987.

Sabbah, Fatna A. *Woman in the Muslim Unconscious*. New York: Pergamon Press, 1984.

Samuels, Ellen Jean. *Fantasies of Identification: Disability, Gender, Race*. New York: New York University Press, 2014.

Saxton, Libby. "Anamnésis: Godard/Lanzmann." *Trafic* 47 (Autumn 2003): 48–66.

Scarry, Elaine. *The Body in Pain: The Making and Unmaking of the World*. London: Oxford University Press, 1985.

Schiller, Nina Glick, and Georges E. Fouron. "Terrains of Blood and Nation: Haitian Transnational Social Fields." *Ethnic and Racial Studies* 22, no. 2 (1999): 340–66.

Scholem, Gershom. "Reflections on S. Y. Agnon." *Commentary*, December 1967. Accessed July 1, 2020. https://www.commentarymagazine.com/articles/gershom-scholem/reflections-on-s-y-agnon/?utm_source=copy&utm_medium=website&utm_campaign=SocialSnap.

Scully, Jackie Leach. *Disability Bioethics: Moral Bodies, Moral Difference*. New York: Rowman & Littlefield, 2008.

Segev, Tom. "A Story of Love and Death" [in Hebrew]. *Haaretz*, April 16, 2008. https://www.haaretz.co.il/misc/1.1319327.

Seidman, Naomi. " 'It Is You I Speak from within Me': David Fogel's Poetics of the Feminine Voice." *Prooftexts* 13, no. 1 (January 1993): 87–102.

Shababo, Shoshana. "Authors and Poets: Shoshana Shababo, 1932" [in Hebrew]. *Do'ar Yisrael* [IsraelPost.co.il)]. Accessed June 25, 2020. http://www.israelpost.co.il/unforget.nsf/lettersbycategory/5857FA97C3CE396E42256C1A00345771?opendocument.

———. *Love in the Town of Safed* [Ahava bitzfat]. 1942. Tel Aviv: Bimat Kedem Lesifrut, 2000.

———. *Maria: A Novel Concerning the Lives of Nuns in the Holyland* [Marya: Roman mehayey hanezirot baaretz]. Edited by Orna Levin. 1932. Tel Aviv: Bimat Kedem Lesifrut, 2002.

Shabtai, Nano. *The Book of Men* [Sefer hagvarim]. Jerusalem: Keter, 2015.

Shaked, Gershon. *Dead End: Studies in J. H. Brenner, M. J. Berdichevsky, G. Shoffman, and U. N. Gnessin* [Lelo motsa: Al Y. H. Brenner, M. Y. Berdichevsky, G. Shofman, ve U. N. Gnessin]. Tel Aviv: Hakibbutz Hameuchad, 1973.

————. *Hebrew Narrative Fiction, 1880–1980: In the Land of Israel and the Diaspora* [Hasiporet haivrit, 1880–1980]. Tel Aviv: Hakibutz hameuhad-Keter, 1983.

————. *Hebrew Narrative Fiction, 1880–1980: On Many Small Windows at Side Entrances* [Be-harbeh ashnavim be-knisot tsdadiyot, 1880–1980]. Tel Aviv: Hakibutz Hameuhad-Keter, 1998.

Shalev, Ruti. *Belly* [Beten]. Jerusalem: Carmel, 2000.

Shalhoub-Kevorkian, Nadera. "Disclosure of Child Abuse in Conflict Areas." *Violence Against Women* 11, no. 10 (2005): 1263–91.

Shamir, Ziva. *No Story, No History: Bialik's Stories from Texture to Context* [Be'ein 'alilah: Sipurei Bialik bema'agaloteihem]. Tel Aviv: Hakibbutz Hameuchad, 1998.

Shani, Ayelett. "Gaza Kids Live in Hell: A Psychologist Tells of Rampant Sexual Abuse, Drugs and Despair." *Haaretz*, November 11, 2017. https://www.haaretz.com/middle-east-news/palestinians/MAGAZINE-gaza-kids-live-in-hell-a-psychologist-tells-of-sex-abuse-drugs-and-despair-1.5464038.

Shapira, Anita. *Futile Struggle: Jewish Labor, 1929–1939* [Hama'avak hanikhzav: Avoda ivrit, 1929–1939], Tel Aviv: Hakibutz Hameuhad and Tel Aviv University, 1977.

————. *Land and Power: The Zionist Resort to Force, 1881–1948*. Oxford: Oxford University Press, 1992.

Sharoni, Simona. "Homefront as Battlefield: Gender, Military Occupation and Violence against Women." In *Women and the Israeli Occupation: The Politics of Change*, edited by Tamar Mayer, 107–22. London: Routledge, 1994.

Shearer-Cremean, Christine, and Carol L. Winkelmann. *Survivor Rhetoric: Negotiations and Narrativity in Abused Women's Language*. Toronto: University of Toronto Press, 2007.

Sheinfeld, Ilan. "Tide: On *Away from His Absence*" [in Hebrew]. *Maariv*, November 24, 2010. http://www.nrg.co.il/online/47/ART2/181/731.html.

Shenfeld, Ruth. *Metamorphosis of a Story: The Formation of Bialik's Stories* [Gilgulo shel sipur: Al darkei hahithavut shel sipurei Bialik]. Tel Aviv: Katz Institute, Tel Aviv University, 1988.

Shez. *Away from His Absence* [Harchek meheadro]. Tel Aviv: Am Oved, 2010.

Shilo, Margalit. *Girls of Liberty: The Struggle for Suffrage in Mandatory Palestine*. Waltham, MA: Brandeis University Press, 2016.

Shimony, Batya. "Identity under Trial: Yehuda Burla's Fiction between Sepharadi Manners and Zionist Existence" [in Hebrew]. *El Perizente* 1 (2007): 45–60.

————. "The Mizrahi Body in War Literature." *Israel Studies* 23, no. 1 (2018): 129–51.

Shofman, Gershon. *Collected Works of G. Shofman* [Kol kitvei G. Shofman]. Tel Aviv: Am Oved, 1945.

Shohat, Ella. "Rupture and Return: Zionist Discourse and the Study of Arab Jews." *Social Text* 75, vol. 21, no. 2 (2003): 49–74.

Shuttleworth, Russell, Nikki Wedgwood, and Nathan J. Wilson. "The Dilemma of Disabled Masculinity." *Men and Masculinities* 15, no. 2 (2012): 174–94.

Siebers, Tobin. "Disability and the Theory of Complex Embodiment: For Identity Politics in a New Register." In *The Disability Studies Reader,* edited by Lennard J. Davis, 313–30. 5th ed. New York: Routledge, 2017.

———. *Disability Theory.* Ann Arbor: University of Michigan Press, 2008.

Siegel, Andrea. "Rape and the 'Arab Question' in L. A. Arieli's *Allah Karim!* and Aharon Reuveni's *Devastation.*" *Nashim* 23 (2012): 110–28.

———. "Women, Violence and the Arab Question in Early Zionist Literature." PhD diss., Columbia University, 2011.

Silverman, Kaja. *Male Subjectivity at the Margins.* New York: Routledge Press, 1992.

Simmons, Erica B. *Hadassah and the Zionist Project,* London: Rowman & Littlefield, 2006.

Soffer, Michal, Arie Rimmerman, Peter Blanck, and Eve Hill. "Media and the Israeli Disability Rights Legislation: Progress or Mixed and Contradictory Images?" *Disability & Society,* 25, no. 6 (October 2010): 687–99.

Somer, Leora. "The Inner World of Incest Victims." In *The Secret and Its Breaking: Issues in Incest* [Hasod veshivro], edited by Zvia Zeligman and Solomon Zahava, 104–24. Tel Aviv: Hakibbutz Hameuchad, 2004.

Sommer, Eli. "The Devastating Consequences of Engaging in Prostitution" [Hatotsa'ot hanafshiyot shel ha'isuk bezanut]. Lecture given at the conference "Sakhar Benashim, Zanut Uma Shebeineihem" [Trafficking in women, prostitution, and everything in between], Tel Aviv, September 22, 2000.

———. "Trauma in Childhood, Memory Loss and Delayed Exposure" [in Hebrew]. Position paper for the Council for the Protection of Children, May 1994. Accessed August 7, 2015. http://www.somer.co.il.

Stanislawski, Michael. *For Whom Do I Toil? Judah Leib Gordon and the Crisis of Russian Jewry.* New York: Oxford University Press, 1988.

Stav, Shira. "Fathers and Daughters: The Entrapment of Incest" [in Hebrew]. *Teorya u-vikoret* 37 (Fall 2010): 69–95.

Sufian, Sandra M. *Healing the Land and the Nation: Malaria and the Zionist Project in Palestine, 1920–1947.* Chicago, IL: University of Chicago Press, 2007.

———. "Mental Hygiene and Disability in the Zionist Project." *Disability Studies Quarterly* 27, no. 4 (2007): n.p.

Suleiman, Susan Rubin. "Transgression and the Avant-Garde: Bataille's *Histoire de L'oeil.*" In *On Bataille: Critical Essays,* edited by Leslie Anne Boldt-Irons, 313–33. Albany: State University of New York Press, 1995.

Szobel, Ilana. "Choreographing the Disabled Body: Performing Vulnerability and Political Change in the Work of Tamar Borer." *Journal of Jewish Identities* 12, no. 1 (2019): 55–74.

———. *A Poetics of Trauma: The Work of Dahlia Ravikovitch.* Waltham, MA: Brandeis University Press, 2013.

———. " 'God of Fury' and His Victims: The Binding of Isaac (*Akedah*) in Hebrew Women's Poetry, 1930–1970" [in Hebrew]. *Jerusalem Studies in Hebrew Literature* 22 (2008): 65–92.

Taub, Gadi. "Daddy's Girls: Incest, Self, Culture, and Comfort" [in Hebrew]. In *Against Solitude* [Neged bdidut]. Tel Aviv: Miskal-Yediot Ahrounoth Books, 2016.

Tepper, Mitchell S. "Sexuality and Disability: The Missing Discourse of Pleasure." *Sexuality and Disability* 18, no. 4 (2000): 283–90.

Therese of Lisieux. *The Story of a Soul: The Autobiography of St. Therese of Lisieux*. Translated by John Beevers. New York: Doubleday, 2001.

Tsamir, Hamutal. *In the Name of the Land: Nationalism, Subjectivity, and Gender in the Israeli Poetry of the Statehood Generation* [Beshem hanof: Le'umiyut migdar vesobyektiviyut bashirah hayisraelit bishnot hahamishim vehash-ishim]. Jerusalem: Keter Books / Beer Sheva, Israel: Heksherim Center, 2006.

———. "Lilit, hava Vehagever Hamit'apek: Hakalkalah Halibidinalit shel Bialik Ubnei Doro" [Lilith, Eve, and the self-restraining man: The libidinal economy of Bialik and his contemporaries]. *Mehkarei Yerushalaim besfrut 'ivrit* 23 (2009): 151–63.

———. "Love of the Homeland and a Deaf Dialogue: A Poem by Esther Raab and Its Masculine Critical Reception" [in Hebrew]. *Teorya u-vikoret* 7 (1995): 124–45.

Vardi, Dina. *Marked for Life: Dialogue with the Second Generation of Holocaust Survivors* [Nos'ei hahotam: Di'alog 'im benei hador hasheni lesho'ah]. Jerusalem: Keter, 1990.

Vogel, David. *Collected Poems* [Kol hashirim]. Edited by Aharon Komem. Tel Aviv: Hakibbutz Hameuchad, 1998.

———. *Married Life* [hayei nisu'im]. Translated by Dalya Bilu. New Milford, CN: Toby Press, 2007.

———. *Viennese Romance* [Roman vina'i]. Tel Aviv: Am Oved, 2012.

Wallach, Yona. *Let the Words: Selected Poems of Yona Wallach*. Translated by Linda Zisquit. Riverdale-on-Hudson, NY: Sheep Meadow Press, 2006.

———. *Subconscious Opening Like a Fan* [Tat hakarah niftahat kemenifah]. Tel Aviv: Hakibbutz Hameuchad, 1992.

Walseth, K. "Young Muslim Women and Sport: The Impact of Identity Work." *Leisure Studies* 25, no. 1 (2006): 75–94.

Weichert, Rafi. "En Entity Etching Itself Out of the Darkness" [in Hebrew]. "Literature and Books," weekend supplement, *Ma'ariv*, March 12, 1999, 29.

Weiss, Meira. *The Chosen Body: The Politics of the Body in Israeli Society*. Redwood City, CA: Stanford University Press, 2002.

West-Pavlov, Russell. *Space in Theory: Kristeva, Foucault, Deleuze*. Amsterdam: Rodopi, 2009.

Wolfson, Kim, and Martin Norden. "Film Images of People with Disabilities." In *Handbook of Communication and People with Disabilities: Research and Application*, edited by Dawn O. Braithwaite and Teresa L. Thompson, 289–305. Mahwah, NJ: Lawrence Erlbaum Associates, 2000.

Woodburn, Danny, and Kristina Kopić. *The Ruderman White Paper on Employment of Actors with Disabilities in Television*, July 2016. http://www.rudermanfoundation.org/wp-content/uploads/2016/07/TV-White-Paper_final.final_.pdf.

Woolf, Virginia. *On Being Ill*. Ashfield, MA: Paris Press, 2012.

Yaeger, Patricia, and Beth Kowaleski-Wallace, eds. *Refiguring the Father: New Feminist Readings of Patriarchy*. Carbondale: Southern Illinois University Press, 1989.

Yaffe, Avraham Benjamin. *Written in 1918: A Collection of Stories and Poems Written during the War of Independence* [Nikhtav betashah]. Tel Aviv: Reshafim, 1989.

Yedaya, Keren, dir. *My Treasure* [Or]. Paris: Bizibi Studios, 2004.

Yosef, Raz. *Beyond Flesh: Queer Masculinities and Nationalism in Israeli Cinema*. New Brunswick, NJ: Rutgers University Press, 2004.

Yudkoff, Sunny S. *Tubercular Capital: Illness and the Conditions of Modern Jewish Writing*. Redwood City, CA: Stanford University Press, 2018.

Zakai, Orian. "A Uniform of a Writer: Literature, Ideology and Sexual Violence in the Writing of Rivka Alper." *Prooftexts* 34, no. 2 (Spring 2014): 232–70.

Zakim, Eric. "Between Fragment and Authority in David Fogel's (Re)Presentation of Subjectivity." *Prooftexts* 13, no. 1 (January 1993): 103–24.

———. *To Build and Be Built: Landscape, Literature, and the Construction of Zionist Identity*. Philadelphia: University of Pennsylvania Press, 2006.

Zamir, Michal. *A Ship of Girls* [Sfinat hababot]. Tel Aviv: Xargol Books, 2005.

Zeligman, Zvia. "The Process of Testimony in Treating Trauma of Incest." In *The Secret and Its Breaking: Issues in Incest* [Hasod veshivro], edited by Zvia Zeligman and Solomon Zahava, 240–56. Tel Aviv: Hakibbutz Hameuchad, 2004.

Zeligman, Zvia, and Solomon Zahava. *The Secret and Its Breaking: Issues in Incest* [Hasod veshivro]. Tel Aviv: Hakibbutz Hameuchad, 2004.

Zemach, Adi. "In a Double Image: On S. Y. Agnon's 'In the Prime of Her Life'" [in Hebrew]. *Moznayim* 62, no. 7–8 (1989): 43–49.

Ziv, Amalia. "Ben Sehorot Miniyot Lesovyektim Miniyim: Hamakhloket Hafeministit al Pornografiya" [Between sexual goods and sexual subjects: The feminist controversy over pornography]. *Teorya u-vikoret* 25 (Fall 2004): 163–94.

Ziv, Effi. "From an Object to a Subject—Feminist Therapy for Female Victims of Sexual Abuse in the Family" [in Hebrew]. In *The Secret and Its Breaking: Issues in Incest* [Hasod veshivro], edited by Zvia Zeligman and Solomon Zahava, 257–77. Tel Aviv: Hakibbutz Hameuchad, 2004.

———. "Insidious Trauma" [in Hebrew]. *Mafteakh: Lexical Review of Political Thought* 5 (2012): 55–73.

————. "Masculinity Under Attack: A New Look on Men's Sexual Trauma" [in Hebrew]. *Sihot: Journal of Psychotherapy* 27, no. 1 (2012): 23–33.

Žižek, Slavoj. *The Sublime Object of Ideology*. London: Verso, 1989.

Zohar, Marva. "From Marginalized Notes on Silence/Suicide/Violence." *Ilanot Review*, December 8, 2020. http://www.ilanotreview.com/theft/from-marginalized-notes-on-silence-suicide-violence/.

Index

able-bodiedness: and heterosexuality, 13, 78, 203n43; in Israeli society, 78, 98; preference for, 203n43; resistance to, 95; Zionism and, 97

Abramovich, S. Y., 21

Abramson, Glenda, 24

Adams, Rachel, 85

Admon, Moshe, 98

agency: and choice in prostitution, 19–20, 179n18; desires of the child for, 36–37; in survivorship, 161

Agnon, Shmuel Yosef, 188n98, 191n32; "In the Prime of Her Life," 149–50, 221nn75–78; "Ovadia the Cripple," 77; "The Lady and the Peddler," 182n40

Ajzenstadt, Mimi, "In Prison I Rest," 210n10

Alcoff, Linda, 161

Alon, A., 207n96

Alon, Ketzia, 189n14

Alper, Rivka, 8, 166; "Mistake," 7, 8; Quivers of Revolution, 193n51, 198n111

Alterman, Nathan, 56–57; "The Silver Platter," 83

Amery, Jean, 213n54

Amichai, Yehuda, 211n22

Amossy, Ruth, 125

Andersen, Hans Christian, 91

antimemory, 38

Arachne, literary legacy of mythological figure of, 41–44, 188n1

Arbel, Michal, 222n78

Ariel, Nana, 124

Arieli, Levi Arieh, 16; "Adventures in Love," 27

Artman-Partock, Tali, 18

art therapy, 114–15, 122, 215nn74–75. See also When Time Stood Still

Ashman, Ahuva, 54, 82

Association of Rape Crisis Centers (Israel), 159

As Though Nothing Happened (Rotem), 108, 115, 210n9

Avishai, Mordechai, 86

Avi-Tamar, Yoram, Injury, 97–98

Avramovitch, Dorit, 99, 115, 127, 214n59

Away from His Absence (Shez), 106–107, 112, 119–20, 209n5

axe, literary symbolism of, 28–29, 183n55

Azaria, D., 207n96

Babayoff, Shalom, disability of, 79.
  See also *The Seventh Glory*
Bal, Mieke, 194n60
Balas, Tiki, 199n8
Barash, Asher, 45
Baron, Devorah, 195n68; "Leizer-
  Yessel," 77
Bartana, Ortsion, 73
Barthes, Roland, 124, 125, 185n71
Bar-Yosef, Hamutal, 56
Baudelaire, Charles, 16–17
Bausch, Pina, *1980* (dance work), 2
"Beer Sheva, the Capital of the
  Negev" (Kahana-Carmon):
  ambiguity about sexual violence
  in, 171; analysis of sexual scene
  in, 167–68, 227n28; national
  violence and sexual violence in,
  169–70, 227n34, 227n37; poetics
  of dispersions in, 172, 228n45;
  women's experiences and Zionism
  in, 170–71
Behar, Moshe, 195n67
Beit HaNassi, significance of event at,
  1, 3
Ben-Amotz, Dan, 13, 70, 206n83. See
  also *I Don't Give a Damn*
Ben-Ari, Nitsa, 195n83
Benjamin, Jessica, 36–37
Benjamin, Walter, 17
Ben-Yehuda, Hemda, 195n68
Berdichevsky, Micah Joseph, 47
Bialik, Hayim Nahman: compared to
  Shofman, 29; empowerment in, 36;
  juxtapositions in work of, 12; "On
  the Slaughter," 22, 23, 28, 180n28;
  other writers' dialogue with, 17; on
  Shofman's "Trifles," 183n53; theme
  of power in, 186n88; victimhood,
  weakness, and femininity in, 28,

37–38, 188n94. *See also* "In the
  City of Slaughter"
biblical references: Jacob and Esau,
  152; Jacob and Naphtali, 143; Jesus's
  command in Matthew 19:14, 153;
  Jonah, 170; prophecy of doom,
  23; Samson, 53–54; Sodom and
  Gemorrah, 82, 204n54
Bilsky, Leora, 172
Blanck, Peter, 202n42
Bourke, Joanna, 176n11
Boyarin, Daniel, 37, 54
Bracken, Patrick J., 175n6
Braun, Netalie, *Metamorphosis* (film),
  217n12
Brenner, Yosef Haim, 16, 18, 45,
  190n25, 191n32
Brenner, Yosef Haim, works by:
  Around the Point, 29–30, 184nn58–
  59; *Breakdown and Bereavement*,
  38; "The Eretz Yisrael Genre and
  Its Artifacts," 46; "He Sent Me a
  Long Letter," 183n55; *Nerves*, 38;
  Only Yesterday, 38
Briere, John, 135
Brison, Susan, 164
Brown, Wendy, *States of Injury*, 74
Burla, Yehuda: change in writings of,
  191n28; influence of, 196n78; irony
  in repression of Shababo's work, 47;
  "Luna," 59–60, 62, 190n19; Mizrahi
  women in work of, 195n79; need
  for approval, 45, 190n21; review
  of Shababo's *Maria*, 44–45, 46,
  189n14, 190n18; Shababo's writing
  compared to, 48, 59–60, 62; as
  Zionist writer, 45–46, 190n24
Butler, Judith, 74–75

Cardeña, Etzel, 118
Carstani, David, 189n14
Caruth, Cathy, 212n38

Certeau, Michel de, 58
Chalfi, Raquel, "A German Boot,"
    227n39
childhood survivors of sexual abuse,
    117. *See also* incest survivors,
    memoirs of; *Shirley's Diary* (ed.
    Gilat and Kadman)
Christianity: love for Jesus's face in,
    154–55; Shababo's writing about,
    189n14 (see also *Maria*); veil of
    Veronica, 155–56; views of women
    and prostitution, 18
Cixous, Hélène, 62
clichés as rhetorical devices, 124, 125
Cohen, Uri S., *Security Style and the
    Hebrew Culture of War*, 199n5
colonialism, rape culture in, 193n51
confessions in survivorship, 161–62
Cover, Robert, 186n85
Crenshaw, Kimberlé, 50;
    "Demarginalizing the Intersection
    of Race and Sex," 177n26
critical race theory, 67
crows, symbolism of, 152–53, 222n82

Dad's Gift (Gal-Cohen), 113, 123
Daly, Brenda, 209n4
Daudet, Alphonse, *In the Land of
    Pain*, 213n54
Deer, Sarah, 193n51
Dekel, Mikhal, 181n28, 181n34
Deleuze, Gilles, *A Thousand Plateaus*,
    105
depressive anxiety, 35, 38
disability: and dependency, 72, 76,
    84–85; fantasy of disability, 78, 88;
    literature and ideological positions
    related to, 5; as lived experience
    in Israeli society, 80; narrative
    prosthesis, 79–80, 201n24; and
    the price of war, 73, 74; quotes on
    soldiers and, 69; transformation

and adaptation to social norms, 97.
    See also *A Doll's Leg*; *Himmo, King
    of Jerusalem*; *I Don't Give a Damn*;
    The Seventh Glory
disabled populations: dependency
    and helplessness of, 76–77;
    effeminization and asexualization
    of, 77, 81, 82, 208n123; hospitals
    as settings for stories about, 79;
    overcoming disability, 79, 84, 91,
    95, 98; sexuality and, 86–88; social
    position and humanity of, 203n46;
    viewed through lens of male sexual
    potency, 77–78
dissociation: behaviors in, 135; cliché
    as variant of, 124; depathologization
    of, 118; healing from
    understanding, 214n61; as literary
    device, 119–20; as protection for
    trauma survivors, 117
dissociative identity disorder (DID),
    117–19, 120–21
A Doll's Leg (Haelyon): affirmation
    of the national project in, 91;
    disability and the costs of war,
    73–74; gender-based violence
    and disability in, 79; in Hebrew
    literature, 70; male agency
    through sexual harassment, 90–91;
    neutralization of disability in,
    91, 98; origin of title of, 201n21;
    quotes from, 69, 75; as story of
    rehabilitation, 89, 91–92
Dworkin, Andrea, 62–63

Eagleton, Terry, 44
Elisha, Rotem, 160, 165
Eretz, Israel, writings about, 190n14,
    190n25. See also Rabb, Esther
ethnicity: in Brennan's universalism,
    46; and Eurocentricity of Zionism,
    47; literature and ideological

ethnicity *(continued)*
positions related to, 5; sexual
assault in social construction of,
12. *See also* Jewish masculinity;
Oriental women; Sepharadi women;
Shababo, Shoshana
Etzioni, Amitai, 70
European literature, prostitution in,
16–17

fantasy, theory of, 25–26
fathers and the father's body, power
of, 137, 138
Feldhay, Rivka, 227n37, 228n41
Felman, Shoshana, 210n14
female sexuality: bell hooks on racism
and, 198n94; girls' education
about, 197n87; and the literary
canon, 189n14; personal control
of, 214n59; prostitution and, 32; in
Shababo's *Maria*, 57–63; and the
striptease, 185n71; women's control
over, 198n95
femininization in Jewish literature,
22, 24
feminists and feminism: analysis of
rape by, 64; calls for social change,
6; culture and female identity,
182n47; and education about
female sexuality, 197n87; influence
on approaches to sexual violence,
160; intercourse for women and,
62–63; paradox for, 116; and
recovery after incest, 122–23; and
survivor speech, 162; and visibility
of sexual violence, 9–10; and white
feminism, 66–67. *See also* Alper,
Rivka
Ferenczi, Sándor, 138, 139, 186n76
Fine, Michelle, 197n87
Fineman, Martha Albertson, 72
Finger, Anne, 86
Finkelstein, Vic, 97

Foucault, Michel, 178n5, 203n44
Frawley-O'Dea, Mary Gail, 63–64
Freud, Anna, 138, 139
Freud, Sigmund: on client fantasies
from interaction with prostitutes,
184n59; *fort/da* of, 26, 147;
hysteria and sexual violence,
185–86n76; killing one's father, 141;
Nachträglichkeit, 37–38; threat of
femininity, 32
Fuchs, Esther, 172

Gal-Cohen, Lior, 113, 123
Gallop, Jane, 137
Garland-Thomson, Rosemarie, 72,
94–95
Gavriely-Nuri, Dalia, 199n8
gender and gendered power
dynamics: in "Beer Sheva," 169;
biases in legal cases, 224n4; in
biblical stories, 54, 194nn60–61;
challenges to dichotomies in, 30;
in the disabled's sexuality, 89;
in *Himmo*, 81–82; literature and
ideological positions related to,
5; in prostitution, 27; racialized
discourse on, 66–67; reinforcement
of stereotypes, 23; in *The Seventh
Glory*, 92; sexual assault in gender
construction, 12; Shababo's
exposure of oppression of, 67; in
Shababo's "Honeymoon," 51–52;
Shofman's concept of victimhood
and, 28
Gez, Ronit, 193n52
Gilady, Nitzan, *Wedding Doll* (film),
88, 206n82
Gilfoyle, Timothy J., 178n5
"Give Me a Face" (Litevsky): about,
145–46; centrality of mother to
daughter's identity, 146, 152–53;
daughter's self-annihilation in,
147, 152, 153, 155; fantasy of

separation from mother, 146–48; identifications with Jesus in, 153–55; maternal abandonment in, 145, 149, 150; pain and name giving in, 157–58; symbolism of veil of Veronica in, 155–56

Gluzman, Michael, 180n28; *Revisiting "In the City of Slaughter"* (with Hever and Miron), 21, 22, 36

Golan, Menahem, *The Highway Queen* (film), 206n81

Golan, Ruth, 222n78

Goldberg, Amos, 180n19

Goldberg, Leah, 142–43; "Returning," 143

Gorfein, Rivka, 19

Gormezano Goren, Yitzhak, 189n14

Govrin, Nurit, 46, 190n25

Gray, Laura, 161

Greek mythology: Achilles, 152; as narrative of sexual victimization, 135–36; rape and metamorphosis in, 135, 217n12; Theseus and the minotaur, 141–42

Greniman, Deborah, 217n11

Griffin, Susan, 185n70

Guattari, Pierre-Félix, *A Thousand Plateaus*, 105

Gur, Anat, 114, 118

Guttman, Amos, 75, 87

Haelyon, Yaacov: ableism and sexual aggression in work of, 13; conviction of, 206n93; disability of, 73, 79; on feeling helpless, 76; "That's How I Was Injured," 70; on wounded soldiers, 72. See also *A Doll's Leg*; *Himmo, King of Jerusalem*; *The Seventh Glory*

Hakivun mizrach, special issue on Shababo, 44

Halevi, Yossef, 195n68; *A Modern Daughter of the Orient*, 43

Hameiri, Israel, "Beer Sheva Is Close," 77

Harrison, Kathryn, *The Kiss*, 212n43

Hasfari, Shmuel, *Shchur* (film), 88, 206n82

Hazan, Yael Levi, 168

healthcare workers, 71–72, 206n90. See also *A Doll's Leg*; *Himmo, King of Jerusalem*

Hebrew literature: Arachne as icon in, 41–44; diversity of emotional responses to violence in, 163; the erotic in, 189n14, 195n83; focus on survivors, 164; gender-based sexual violence in, 3, 4, 6–7, 8–12, 160–61, 166; glorification of war in, 71; intersectionality in, 48; literary aesthetics of, 45, 46; Mizrahi writers in, 59; national and sexual violence in, 227n39; nation building, morality, and, 44; sexual violence as literary device, 5; stylistic tradition of writing about sexual violence in, 172–73; untold narratives of sexual violence in, 163–64; women's empowerment in, 160–61; women writers of, 41; wounded soldiers ignored in, 70, 71, 78, 199n5, 200n12; writers' self-image as whore, 184n63. See also Alper, Rivka; *Away from His Absence*; Babayoff, Shalom; Ben-Amotz, Dan; Bialik, Hayim Nahman; Brenner, Yosef Haim; Burla, Yehuda; disability; Haelyon, Yaacov; Halevi, Yossef; Hendel, Yehudit; incest survivors, memoirs of; Israeli war literature; Kahana-Carmon, Amalia; Kaniuk, Yoram; Litevsky, Tsvia; Oren, Ofra Offer; Pekelman, Henya; prostitution; Ravikovitch, Dahlia; revival literature (telushim); Shababo,

Hebrew literature *(continued)*
  Shoshana; Shofman, Gershon;
  Vogel, David; wounded soldiers;
  writing; Zionism
Heise, Thomas, 18
Hendel, Yehudit: "His Memory Was
  Damaged," 70; *Street of Steps*, 70;
  "The Sons' Grave," 71
Herman, Judith Lewis, 1, 6, 114
"Heroines" project, 159–60, 161,
  225n5
Herzig, Hannah, 167, 168
Herzig, Shlomo, 222n78
heterosexuality and able-bodiedness,
  89
heterosexuality and with able-
  bodiedness, 206n93. See also
  A Doll's Leg; *Himmo, King of
  Jerusalem*; *The Seventh Glory*
heterotopias, 203n44. See also
  hospitals
Hever, Hannan, 46, 56–57, 187n88;
  Revisiting "In the City of Slaughter"
  (with Gluzman and Miron), 21
Higgins, Lynn, 42, 198n106
Hill, Eve, 202n42
Himmo, King of Jerusalem (Kaniuk):
  cinematic adaptation of, 87,
  204n61; disability and the national
  project in, 73, 83–85, 205n64;
  ethnic tension in, 205n63; in
  Hebrew literature, 70; inspiration
  for character of Himmo, 201n30;
  interpretation of Himmo as dead
  in, 204nn60–61; neutralization of
  disability in, 98; nurse's exploitation
  of Himmo, 80–83, 203n51, 204n58;
  sexuality and disability in, 86–88;
  synopsis of, 75; value of injured
  soldier's life in, 75–76
Holtzman, Avner, 200n9
homosexuality, 82

hooks, bell, 198n94
Horowitz, Sara R., 23–24, 181n33
hospitals as heterotopian spaces, 75,
  79–80, 92

identification: with the abuser, 139;
  compared to empathy, 183n54;
  fantasy and dimensions of, 26,
  202n40; penis envy, 36; with the
  prostitute, 30; with woundedness
  and metamorphosis, 134–35
identity: disability and able-bodied
  identity, 98; GendeRace approach
  to, 66; injury's politicization of,
  66; mother-daughter relationships
  and, 146; national, 5, 12, 46 (*see
  also* national project; Zionism);
  reclamation of, 159–60. See also
  subjectivity
I Don't Give a Damn (Ben-Amotz):
  cinematic adaptation, 87–88;
  disability and sexuality in, 87; as
  major representative of wounded
  soldiers, 70; names of prostitutes
  in, 205n81; photographing injured
  bodies in, 94–95; questions about
  national project in, 95; quote from,
  69
Imberman, Shmuel, 87
incarcerated women, 210n10
incest: in the church, 64; father-
  daughter relationships and, 137,
  218n30; overcoming trauma of, 103;
  and patriarchal norms, 176n14;
  silence and silencing around, 114;
  taboos against, 176n13; witnesses
  to, 212n38
incest survivors: and complexity
  of responses to abuse, 100; and
  continuing violence, 101, 210n11;
  desire to tell their stories, 108–109,
  116; relationships with their

abusers, 100–101, 109–13, 138; silenced voices among, 101, 210n21; worthiness and invisibility of, 139, 218n34

incest survivors, memoirs of: cliché quality in, 123–27; as creative spaces, 13; dissociative structures in, 119; explaining the unexplainable, 114–15, 116; hybridity in, 115–17; importance of, 100, 101; intertwining of love and humiliation in, 113; multidimensional descriptions of experience in, 126–27; nature of genre, 10; perspectives used in, 209n5; as political speech, 123, 209n4; revelation and concealment in, 124; as rhizomatic texts, 105–108, 211n20; similarities and privilege among authors of, 101–102

insidious trauma: as cumulative load of small injuries, 2; incidents and experiences comprising, 3–4. *See also* incest; prostitution; rhizomatic texts; Sepharadi women; wounded soldiers

intercourse, political and personal meanings in, 62–63

intersectionality: coinage of term, 177n26; in identity construction, 67; power of experience of, 50; related to sexual violence, 13

"In the City of Slaughter" (Bialik): compared to "On the Slaughter," 180n28, 181n33; Dekel on, 181n34; ethnicity and gender-based violence in, 28; Horowitz on, 181n33; literary responses to, 23, 24; and power in the Jewish world, 21, 23, 25; rage against victims in, 22

Irigaray, Luce, 62

Israeli cinema, 87–88, 205–6nn81–82, 217n12

Israeli Defense Force's (IDF), 72, 165, 207n96, 225n12, 227n39

Israeli media, 5, 199n8, 202n42, 208n121

Israeli media and the traumatized, 1

Israeli occupation, 93–94, 165, 193n51, 225n8, 225nn11–13, 227n39

Israeli-Palestinian conflict, 166, 225nn11–12

Israeli society: attitudes toward sexual violence, 9–10, 11; the chosen body in, 84; coping with trauma in, 162; effects of the occupation on, 165; heroism in, 73; independence in, 84–85; integration of the disabled in, 79, 97–98; political violence and sexual brutality, 165; sexual assault legislation and rulings in, 160, 224n4; use of clichés and membership in, 126–27; view of wounded soldiers in, 70–71; vulnerability and victimhood in, 72, 164

Israeli war literature: heroism in, 71, 78, 207n96; scarcity of IDF soldiers in, 72; sexual harassment of nurses in, 72; topics in, 69; wounded soldiers in, 71

Jewish Europe marginalization of sexual violence in, 11

Jewish masculinity: ableism in, 97, 98; adoption of macho ethos into, 54; based on model of mythical tragedy, 181n34; male agency through sexual harassment, 206n87; the new Jewish man, 30, 35–36, 37, 53, 54, 187n88, 194n62; prostitution and, 12; provocation of activism in,

Jewish masculinity *(continued)*
23; rapes in Bialik's poetry and, 28;
sexual savagery and, 52; violence
in, 193n51, 194n54; Zionist view of,
192n41
Jewish nationalism: as context for
Hebrew literature, 21–25; and
empowerment in Jewish masculine
subjectivity, 37; in Shababo's
writing, 48; terror underlying,
186n85. *See also* Zionism

Kahana-Carmon, Amalia: approach
to the representation of sexual
violence, 166; deliberate poetics
of, 170, 171–72, 228n41; difference
with literary tradition, 173; struggle
with issues in sexual assault, 161.
See also "Beer Sheva, the Capital of
the Negev"
Kaniuk, Yoram: ableism and sexual
aggression in work of, 13; disability
of, 79; *Vultures and Villainy*, 200n9;
as wounded soldier, 201n30. See
also *Himmo, King of Jerusalem*
Karamcheti, Indira, 48–49
Karpf, Ann, 208n121
Katsav, Moshe, 2
Keren, Nitza, *Like a Sheet in the Hand
of the Embroideress*, 41–42, 188n1
Keshet, Yeshurun, 19
Klausner, Joseph, 19
Klein, Melanie, 34–35, 36, 38
Koren, Ziv: about, 102–103; on
complicated relationship with her
abuser, 111–12; on her dissociation,
121; on memoir's intelligibility,
114; on painting in trauma therapy,
215n75; on photograph in memoir,
109–10; on society in relation to
sexual abuse, 114. See also *When
Time Stood Still*

Korman, Asaf, *Next to Her* (film), 88,
206n82
Kovner, Abba, 55
Kowaleski-Wallace, Beth, 137, 182n47
Kraemer, Shalom, 19
Kristeva, Julia, 38

Lacan, Jacques, 137, 143, 154,
219n46
La'Isha, story on women survivors
of sexual assault, 159, 224n2
Laplanch, Jean, 25, 26
Laub, Dori, 210n14, 212n38
Lauretis, Teresa de, 26, 44; *Alice
Doesn't,* 116
Layoun, Mary, 55
Lev-Wiesel, Rachel, 102–103, 105;
"Child Sexual Abuse," 215n74. *See
also* Koren, Ziv; *When Time Stood
Still*
Liggins, Emma, 178n2
Litevsky, Tsvia: allusions to the
Holocaust in, 147–48; the concrete
and symbolic father in, 137–38,
218n26; crows in, 151; Dionysus
in, 129, 132, 145, 219n36, 220n59;
grasping the elusive in, 143–44;
on her mother's love, 144–45;
identification with Jesus, 153–55,
223n87; metamorphosis as
psychopoetic tool of, 133–36; and
multifacetedness of father-daughter
relationships, 138–40, 221n75;
overview of poetic oeuvre of,
130–31; on pain, 8; poetic murders
of fathers in, 140–42; privation
and the mother figure in, 144–53;
relationship of distress and creative
writing in work of, 13; worthiness
of the daughter in, 139–40; writing
and naming in, 156–58. *See also*
"Give Me a Face"

Litevsky, Tsvia, works by: "Actaeon,"
133–34, 217n11; "Aphrodite," 135–
36; "Calling by Name," 136, 156–57,
224n99; "Calling It by Name," 135,
136, 217n9, 223n87; "Chorus,"
144; "The Circle Line," 136, 139;
"Conversation with Borges," 143–44;
"Dionysus: Chapters of a Biography,"
132; "From the Album," 129–30;
"Gazelles," 142–43, 219n45; "The
Gully of Zin," 137–38, 218n30; "If
being your daughter," 139; "The
Minotaur's Daughter," 140–41;
"Tammuz," 136; "They Left Me
Lying There," 136; "To My Death,"
218n26; untitled poems, 151–52, 154
Loshitzky, Yosefa, 202n35
love, 92–93, 212n43
Lubin, Orly, 196n77
Lyons, Terese, 125

MacKinnon, Catharine, 64, 65,
198n95
male gaze, notion of, 61–62
Mansour, Muhammad, 225n13
marginalization, 17–18, 162
Maria (Shababo): Burla's review of,
44–45; duality of female body
and subjectivity in, 59, 196n77;
ethnogeographic setting of, 47–48;
marriage to God in, 58, 61, 62,
196n85; masturbation in, 60–62,
63, 64; original title of, 189n6;
overview of, 57–59; publication of,
43; recognition for, 43–44; sexual
encounters with priests in, 63–64
Married Life (Vogel): attempted
rape in, 185n76; feelings of fear
and revulsion in, 15–16, 31–32,
35; Jewish national meaning in,
182n40; masculine weakness in, 33,
34, 36; prostitution's relationship

with notions of manhood, 16,
33–34, 35; violence in, 32–33, 34;
Zakim on, 186n79
masculinity, 5, 8, 38, 185n70, 202n35.
See also gender and gendered
power dynamics; Jewish masculinity
Matalon, Ronit, 191n34
Mazor, Yair, 167
McNaron, Tori A. H., Voices in the
Night, 176n13
McRuer, Robert, 78, 206n93
Meatyard, Ralph Eugene, 130
Mendelson-Maoz, Adia, 81, 205n64
metamorphosis: of Actaeon, 133–34;
Litevsky quote on, 131; as poetic
dissociation, 135; and rebirth, 144
Miller, Nancy K., 137, 188n1
Milo, Haya, 206n87
Milt, Kate, 206n87
Miron, Dan, 56, 181n36, 182n40,
185n65; Revisiting "In the City
of Slaughter" (with Gluzman and
Hever), 21
Mitchell, David T., 79, 91, 201n24
Mittelpunkt, Hillel, Mami (rock
opera), 225n11
Mizrahi femininity, sexual violence
and construction of, 5, 50
Morag, Raya, 38
Morgan, Yarrow, Voices in the Night,
176n13
Moyal, Esther Azhari, 195n67
multiple personality disorder. See
dissociation
Mulvey, Laura, 61
Munk, Yael, 73
Murphy, Robert, 76, 203n46
mythology, perfection and
imperfection in, 132–33

The Naked King (Avramovitch), 115,
117, 209n5

narrative prosthesis, 79–80, 201n24
national project: exploitation in, 54; from victim to survivorship in, 165; the wounded and the costs of war, 73, 74
nativeness, Zionist ideal of, 56–57
Naveh, Hannah, "Aryeh the Muscleman," 186n88
Ne'eman, Judd, 95
Negbi, Irit, 224n4
Neumann, Boaz, 52
Nitzan, Tal, 227n28; "Controlled Occupation," 225n12
Nord, Deborah, 17
nurses, sexual exploitation of, 71–72, 77. See also *A Doll's Leg*; "Beer Sheva, the Capital of the Negev"; *Himmo, King of Jerusalem;* hospitals as heterotopian spaces; *The Seventh Glory*

Ofek, Uriel, *From the War*, 69, 199n5
Oliver, Michael, 96
Oppenheimer, Yochai, 191n28
oppression: as condition of insidious trauma, 4; in the demand to articulate trauma, 162; ethnic-gender oppression, 46; intersectionality in, 11, 65; survivors' responses to, 12
Oren, Ofra Offer, 211n22; *I Feel Good, I Feel Good—A Letter to Mother*, 99–100; *Shira and Hiroshima*, 99–100
Oriental women: and female sexuality, 61–63; femininity of, 196n77; racialized and gendered subjectivity of, 50, 65, 67
Ovid, *Metamorphoses*, 133
Oz, Amos, *My Michael*, 2
Oz, Sheri, 108, 121

Pagis, Dan, 39

Palestine, marginalization of sexual violence in, 11
paranoid anxiety, 34–35
parental abuse and abandonment, 131, 136, 145–46, 149, 220n69. *See also* "Give Me a Face"; incest; Litevsky, Tsvia
patriarchy and patriarchal societies, 6, 140. See also *Maria* (Shababo)
Pearlman, Laurie Anne, 212n32
Pekelman, Henya, 166; *The Life of a Woman Worker in the Homeland*, 9–10, 177n24
Peled, Shimrit, 169–70
Peri, Menahem, 185n76
phallicism and women's breasts, 62
poetry: nature of the poetic act, 131; processing of trauma through, 5
Pontalis, Jean-Bertrand, 25, 26
Preston, Jeffrey, 78
prostitution: as gender-based violence, 51; Hebrew writers and, 17–19; insidious character of trauma in, 38; marginalization in, 30; and men's fear of women, 32; and social determinism, 19–20; trope of, 25–29. *See also* Arieli, Levi Arieh; Brenner, Yosef Haim; Reuveni, Aharon; Shofman, Gershon; Vogel, David
Puhachevsky, Nehama, 195n68
punctuation: as expressive of the unspoken, 104; as literary device, 9, 177n24
Putnam, Frank W., 119

Quincey, Thomas de, *Confessions of an English Opium Eater*, 16–17

Rabb, Esther, Shababo's work compared to, 55–57
rabbinic literature: the raven in, 153; views of women, men, and

prostitution in, 18, 178n9. *See also* biblical references
Rainey, Sarah, 80, 92–93
Ramras-Rauch, Gilah, 196n78
rape: Jewish literature's avoidance of detail about, 66; link with the occupation, 193n51, 225nn12–13; psychological trauma of, 176n11; in scholarly work about Hebrew literature, identity, and Zionism, 42; silencing of victims of, 135; as a social and political story, 55; and unheard voices, 64, 198n106. *See also* Alper, Rivka
rape crisis centers, 122, 159, 160, 224n3
Rattok, Lily, 167, 168
Ravikovitch, Dahlia, 161, 223n92; "A Short Delay," 227n39; "The Dress," 147
readers: clichés as communicative devices with, 124; publishers' goal with survivor stories, 212n26; writers' alliances with, 107–109, 117
Reed, Maya: *Captive*, 110–11, 115, 209n5; "Dissociative Identity and Its Representation in Contemporary Media," 118–19
Reuveni, Aharon, 16
revival literature (telushim), 17–18, 30, 36, 37, 178n2, 188n94
rhizomatic texts: clichés in, 126; contradictory experiences in, 111, 113; as disruptive, 109; enabling communication through, 108; experiencing an encounter through, 107; incest survivors' memoirs as, 104; interconnected nature of, 105; metaphor of grass and, 211n22; multidimensionality of, 106–107
rhizome, concept of, 105
Ribot, Théodule-Armand, 38
Rich, Adrienne, 149, 220n69

Rimmerman, Arie, 202n42
Rimmon-Kenan, Shlomith, 116
Rivlin, Nechama, 1–3, 5
Rogoff, Irit, 124–25
Root, Maria P. P., 4
Rotem, Shoshan, 108–109, 214n61, 214n65, 215n72
Russel, Diane, 210n11

Saakvitne, Karen W., 212n32
"Samson at the Harvest Season" (Shababo): as conquest story, 52, 53; ethnicity as dimension in, 65; exploitation of female bodies in, 55; exposure of Zionist project in, 52; Gez on, 193n52
Samuels, Ellen, 202n40
Scarry, Elaine, 116, 137, 213n54
The Secret and Its Breaking (Zeligman and Zahava, trans.), 102
Segev, Tom, 201n30
Seidman, Naomi, 181n36
Sela, Rachel Bluwstein, 56–57
Sephuradi Jews, 189n4, 196n78
Sephuradi women: multidimensionality of, 49; racialized and gendered subjectivity of, 67; sexual violence against, 42–43, 65, 66; and Zionism as invasive, 57
The Seventh Glory (Babayoff): gender-based violence and disability in, 79, 92–96; gendered power dynamics of romance in, 76, 92; in Hebrew literature, 70; love in, 92–93, 95–96; neutralization of disability in, 98; wounded soldiers and expansion of Israel in, 93–94
sexual misconduct, medical definition of, 71–72
sexual violence and trauma: cultural mediation of, 5; in female experience, 50; incest survivors'

sexual violence and trauma *(continued)*
openness about, 100; insidious
nature of, 3; intersectionality of, 6,
12; Israeli representations of, 11;
randomness of, 164, 165; Rivlin's
speech on, 2–3; roles of tropes of,
5; social and political responsibility
for, 124, 216n82; social context
of, 4, 175n6; and the status quo,
6–7; writing about, 171, 209n4.
See also incest; parental abuse
and abandonment; prostitution;
rape; Sephardi women; wounded
soldiers

Shababo, Shoshana: absence from
the literary canon, 43–44, 189n14;
complexity of female sexuality in
stories of, 10; depictions of sexual
violence in, 12–13, 49, 66; ethnicity
and intersectionality in work of,
46–49, 65, 191–92n34; firsts as
Hebrew writer, 55–56, 195–96n67;
focus on "daughters of the East,"
65; Gez on, 193n52; letter to Burla,
45; struggle with issues in sexual
assault, 161; subjugation and sexual
violence in literature of, 42–43;
as unfamiliar model of a Jewish
woman, 57; "view from elsewhere"
in, 44; work compared to Esther
Rabb, 55–57; Zionism in work of,
48, 166, 191–92n34

Shababo, Shoshana, works by:
"Honeymoon," 51, 67; *Love in the
Town of Safed*, 43, 59, 65–66, 67.
See also *Maria*; "Samson at the
Harvest Season"

Shabtai, Nano, *The Book of Men*, 2–3,
9

Shahaf, Alicia, 159

Shaked, Gershon, 47, 86, 190n19

Shalev, Ruti, 115; *Belly*, 115

Shami, Yitzhak, 48, 59, 196n78

Shamir, Moshe, *He Walked Through
the Fields*, 71

Sharoni, Simona, "Homefront as a
Battlefield," 225n8

Sheinfeld, Ilan, 119–20

Shez. See *Away from His Absence*
(Shez)

Shimony, Batya, 190n19, 190n24,
195n79

Shirley's Diary (ed. Gilat and Kadman),
126–27, 210n7

Shlonsky, Avraham, 56–57

Shofman, Gershon: compassion in
stories of prostitution, 10, 16, 22;
ethnicity and gender-based violence
in, 29; image of the axe in, 28–29;
juxtapositions in work of, 12; mise-
en-scène of desire in prostitution
stories of, 26; and rabbinic
conceptions of prostitution, 18;
representations of prostitution by,
17, 19–20; struggle with issues
in sexual assault, 161; universal
themes in stories of, 20–21;
victimhood, strength, and weakness
in, 37, 38, 39

Shofman, Gershon, stories by: "The
Axe," 183n55; "Between Night
and Day," 19; "The City's Edge,"
19; "Henia," 19, 20–21, 23, 28–29;
"Lights in the Darkness," 19;
"A Sanatorium for Soldiers," 70;
"Trifles," 19, 27, 183n50, 183n53

Shohat, Ella, 47

Showalter, Elaine, 188n1

Shuttleworth, Russell, 202n35

Siebers, Tobin, 203n43

Siegel, Andrea, 52–53, 66

silence and silencing: challenges
against assumptions of, 9–10;
clichés as mediators of, 125; and

expressing the inexpressible, 171;
literary representation of, 177n24;
project to break, 159–60; women
writers' exposure of, 170. *See also*
metamorphosis
Silver, Brenda, 42, 198n106
Silverman, Kaja, 208n123
Six-Day War, 73, 201n20
Snyder, Sharon L., 79, 91, 201n24
social determinism, prostitution and,
19–20
Soffer, Michal, 202n42; *"In Prison I
Rest,"* 210n10
Somer, Eli, 135
Somer, Leora, 114–15
Stav, Shira, 7, 137, 176nn13–14,
218n30
Steinberg, Odeda, *"In Prison I Rest,"*
210n10
strength/weakness duality, 35, 37
subjectivity: clichés and membership
in society, 125–26; gendered
notions of trauma and, 38; sexual
violence and ethno-gendered
subjectivity, 43, 49–52, 64–65
Sufian, Sandy, 94, 208n108
survivors of sexual assault: compared
to victims, 161; inclusion of
multiple voices from, 162; negative
feelings in rehabilitation of, 163;
traumatic speech of, 172. *See also*
incest survivors; rape

Taub, Gadi, 212n43
Tchernichovsky, Shaul, "Parashat
Dinah," 2
Tepper, Mitchell S., 77, 86
therapy and therapists: asymmetry
with survivors, 103–104, 212n26;
changes from treating trauma
patients, 212n32; collaboration with
patients, 107–108

Thérèse de Lisieux, 154–55
tikkun olam (repairing the world), 2,
41
Torch Lighting Ceremony (2016), 160,
165
trauma: insidious trauma, 2, 3–4;
medical concept of, 3; need for
listeners about, 210n14; pain in,
116; posttraumatic stress disorder
(PTSD), 175n6, 200n9; testifying
about, 212n38
Tsamir, Hamutal, 25, 36, 37, 56, 57,
58, 186n88, 188n94

universalism: ethnicity and, 46,
65; Shababo's, 49–50; and white
feminism, 66–67

victims and victimhood: Bialik's
indifference to, 21; and changing
power dynamics, 31, 138,
221n69; disabled populations in
Hebrew literature, 96–97; and
empowerment, 10; and feelings of
annihilation, 21 (*see also* Litevsky,
Tsvia); multidimensionality of,
26–28; prostitutes as victims,
19–20; and re-victimization, 114;
and rhetoric of superiority, 74; and
support systems, 100; survivorship
compared to, 161
Victorian literature, 17, 178n2
Vigolik, Amnon, 201n30
Vogel, David: embrace of weakness
in, 36, 39; empathy for prostitutes'
marginal status in work of, 16;
empowerment and vulnerability in,
37; gendered oscillations of power
in, 30–31; juxtapositions in work
of, 12; masculinity and femininity
in work of, 181n36; and rabbinic
conceptions of prostitution, 18;

Vogel, David *(continued)*
representations of prostitution by,
17; and upstanding citizens, 187n89
Vogel, David, works by: "I Said to
the Men," 184n65; "I've Butchered
My Wife," 23–24, 25; *Viennese
Romance*, 29, 30–31. See also
Married Life
vulnerability: and invulnerability
through violence, 74–75; as threat
to society, 72. *See also* strength/
weakness duality; wounded soldiers

Wallach, Yona: "Cassius," 152; "Poem,"
219n45
Wedgwood, Nikki, 202n35
Weiss, Meira, 84
West-Pavlov, Russell, 79
When Time Stood Still (Koren and
Lev-Wiesel): genres included in,
115; hybridity and identity splitting
in, 121–22; Koren's resistance and
frustration in, 104; perspective
used in, 209n5; as rhizomatic text,
105–107; therapy and the voice of
the therapist in, 102–104
Wilson, Nathan J., 202n35
women: ownership of their own
bodies, 8; trauma as private for, 1.
See also female sexuality; gender
and gendered power dynamics
women's literature, 44, 45
Woolf, Virginia: "A Room of One's
Own," 8; *On Being Ill*, 213n54
The Wounded Did Not Cry (Azaria
and Alon), 207n96
wounded soldiers: and able-bodied
identity, 96, 98; cultural attitudes
toward, 70–71; as the *dead-living*,
73, 83–84, 85; dependency of,
85; and euthanasia, 75, 76; as

heroes in expansion of Israel,
93; in Israeli society, 200n12;
literary representations of, 96;
readers' invulnerability through
representations of, 74–75; rhetoric
of vitality about, 74; viewed
through lens of male sexual
potency, 77–78. *See also* Babayoff,
Shalom, disability of; Ben-Amotz,
Dan; Haelyon, Yaacov; Kaniuk,
Yoram
writing: about pain, 213n54; with
multidimensionality, 127; poetics of,
8; therapeutic effects of, 5, 157–58;
and transformation of trauma,
136; verbalizing sexual abuse,
142–43

Yaeger, Patricia, 137, 182n47
Yedaya, Keren, *My Treasure* (film),
206n81
Yizhar, S., *Days of Ziklag*, 71
Yosef, Raz, 203n51, 204n61

Zakai, Orian, 7–8, 177n18, 193n51,
193n54, 198n111
Zakim, Eric, 186n79
Zamir, Michal, *A Ship of Girls*, 165
Zeligman, Zvia, 212n38
Zionism: in Bialik's writing, 25, 37;
the chosen body in, 84; context
for Shofman's "Henia," 21; and
Eurocentric views of Jewish history,
47; and failure to meet expectations
of, 38–39; healing its members,
208n108; ideal of nativeness in,
56–57; Matalon on, 191–92n34; and
nation building, 93–94, 192n41;
sexual aggression and violence in,
7–8, 52–55, 166, 168–69, 225n8,
225n11; shadow side of, 42; view

of women under, 194n62; wounded
soldiers and, 72, 205n64. *See
also* Alper, Rivka; Bialik, Hayim
Nahman; Brenner, Yosef Haim;
Burla, Yehuda; Jewish masculinity;
Pekelman, Henya

Zionist literature: Burla and Shababo's
views of, 45–46; non-urban focus
of, 56; soldiers in, 71; unifying
elements in, 49

Ziv, Effi, 114, 211n20

Žižek, Slavoj, 139, 218n34

www.ingramcontent.com/pod-product-compliance
Lightning Source LLC
Chambersburg PA
CBHW030349270326
41926CB00009B/1023